KV-019-415

THE AMERICAN MERCHANT EXPERIENCE IN NINETEENTH-CENTURY JAPAN

Kevin C. Murphy

University of Nottingham
Hallward Library

 RoutledgeCurzon
Taylor & Francis Group
LONDON AND NEW YORK

First published 2003 by RoutledgeCurzon
2 Park Square, Milton Park, Abingdon, Oxon OX14 4RN (UK)

Simultaneously published in the USA and Canada
by RoutledgeCurzon
711 Third Avenue, New York, NY 10017 (US)

First issued in paperback 2013

Routledge is an imprint of the Taylor & Francis Group, an informa business

© 2003 Kevin C. Murphy

Typeset in Times by GreenGate Publishing Services, Tonbridge, Kent

All rights reserved. No part of this book may be reprinted or reproduced
or utilised in any form or by any electronic, mechanical, or other means,
now known or hereafter invented, including photocopying and recording,
or in any information storage or retrieval system, without permission in
writing from the publishers.

British Library Cataloguing in Publication Data
A catalogue record for this book is available from the British Library

Library of Congress Cataloging in Publication Data
Murphy, Kevin C.
The American merchant experience in nineteenth-century Japan / Kevin C. Murphy.
p. cm
Includes bibliographical references and index.
1.United States--Commerce--Japan--History--19th century. 2.
Japan--Commerce--United States--History--19th century. 3. Merchants--United States. 4.
Merchants--Japan. 5. Americans--Japan--History--19th century. 6. Corporations,
American--Japan--History--19th century. I. Title.

HF3127 .M87 2002
382'.0973052--dc21

2002068006

ISBN 0-415-29683-8

ISBN 978-0-415-86832-7 (Paperback)

1007567888

For my daughters
Rinnie, Nicki, Maggie and Jill

Everyone carries his own inch-rule of taste, and amuses himself by applying it, triumphantly, wherever he travels.

Henry Adams

10 0756788 8 09

UNIVERSITY ... NOTTINGHAM

WITHDRAWN FROM THE LIBRARY

THE AMERICAN MERCHANT EXPERIENCE IN NINETEENTH-CENTURY JAPAN

UNIVERSITY LIBRARY

30 JUN 2016

HALL 66

The story ... Japan in the nineteenth century is that of the ge... telegraph and technological expansion which character... nineteenth century. Politically, the ...ation to which A... merchants ... was one of classic imperialism, where stronger Western ... forced ... ... to ...ure mercantile a... ...rights to Western nations.

Amer... merchants established trading firms in the ports of Yokohama, Kobe and Nag... which ...ed from 1855-56 until the repeal of the unequal treaties. The merchants who worked in these firms were members of a privileged, semi-col... society who enjoyed a flourishing club life in near total isolation from the greater milieu of Japanese life. This book explores commercial interaction in the treaty ports by looking seriously at the question of how successful American businessmen were in turning their ... personal imperial advantages into actual business hegemony, personal and cultural.

Kevin C. Murphy argues that American merchants in Japan were products of a Victorian culture ambiguously but deeply concerned with order and opportunity, restraint and dominance, conservation and progress. In seeking to impose the culturally familiar upon the unknown and foreboding landscape of Japan, they defined the limitations of American business in Japan.

Kevin C. Murphy is Chair of the Department of History at Millikin University, Decatur, Illinois.

NEW YORK
FROM THE LIBRARY

CONTENTS

ILLUSTRATIONS

Figures

Tables

ABBREVIATIONS

AHC   Augustine Heard Collection, Baker Library, Harvard University

ARP   Applications and Recommendations for Public Office, RG 59, National Archives

JWM   *Japan Weekly Mail*

KD   Kanagawa Despatches, M135, RG 59, National Archives

MD   Despatches from U.S. Ministers in Japan, M133, RG 59, National Archives

ND   Nagasaki Despatches, M131, RG 59, National Archives

NMC   Nagasaki Miscellaneous Correspondence (Letters Received) RG 84, National Archives

OHD   Osaka-Hiogo Despatches, M460, RG 59, National Archives

OHMC   Osaka Hiogo Miscellaneous Correspondence (Letters Received) RG 84, National Archives

PREFACE

Jacob Burckhardt once wrote that history is "what one age finds worthy of note in another". The history of American merchants living in their insular little foreign communities in the treaty ports of nineteenth-century Japan is, in many ways, what I find worthy of note in my own experience. After more than three years in Japan, I naturally wondered how this earlier group reacted to things Japanese. Now, after even longer in the company of American merchants of the last century, I offer this work as an interpretation of those merchants' experience that I hope combines sympathy with criticism, awareness of their circumstances with the need to judge their actions and attitudes.

In the U.S. my thanks go out to Marlene Mayo at the University of Maryland, College Park (who suggested this topic), to Frank Joseph Shulman for the loan of his formidable bibliographic skills; to Harold Otness for sharing sources from his personal collection; to Dane Hartgrove at the National Archives for his help locating and pulling records never before used; to Wayne McWilliams for my first exposure to East Asia and for twenty-five years of friendship, help and criticism; and to David Grimsted, whose direction of the original dissertation, patience, and careful criticism I particularly appreciate. My special thanks go to my friend Paul Moreno at Hillsdale College for his willingness to read the entire manuscript, point out errors and offer suggestions for stylistic and structural changes that substantively improved this book.

In Japan, I extend my appreciation to Hisamaro Kanan of Japan Microfilm Service Center Company, Inc., who generously brought me copies of Japanese newspapers unavailable in the U.S.; to Dave Ouchi, who made available early materials concerning the Kobe Athletic and Regatta Club; to Tsunao Ohyama, who helped locate sources; and especially to my mizushobai friend Dave Turri, whose cooperation and good humor locating, copying and mailing me material solved many a research problem. My own Kobe, past and future, is bound to him in ways my merchants would have appreciated.

My thoughts also wander toward John Martin and Jim Vander Schaaf, friends of the mind and heart I will never forget, with whom I celebrated good and bemoaned evil for five precious years. I also think now of my brother-in-law Ed Naylor, whose life was the study in understanding and service in his world that I hope this book constitutes in mine. And my daughters still understand a father who always says that money has only two purposes.

Kevin Murphy
October, 2001
Decatur, Illinois

Figure 1 Location of the three treaty ports in Japan in the 1860s
Source: James L. McClain, *Japan: A Modern History*. NY: WW Norton, 2002: 139

INTRODUCTION

I

The story of the Western intrusion into East Asia in the nineteenth century is that of the general economic, political, religious and technological expansion that characterized the mid and late nineteenth century. The treaty port system, established earlier on the China coast, was based on the assumption that trade with "backward" countries would benefit the more industrialized West by creating markets for finished industrial products and a cheap supply of desired primary exports. The treaty port system was intended to work economically to the advantage of Western traders, with the benefits of "civilization" transferred to Asia through the trade it generated.[1] Politically, the situation to which American merchants came in Japan was one of "classic" imperialism: stronger Western powers forced Japan to accept "unequal" treaties intended to insure mercantile advantages to Euro–American nations.

Few Westerners knew anything of the political, social or economic realities of Japan before they encountered that exotic land. The Tokugawa shogunate, once a powerful central governing entity, had been severely weakened by the economic transformation that had accompanied more than 250 years of peace and stability. "Urbanization, the commercialization of agriculture, the growing wealth of city and rural merchants engaged in protoindustrial production, flourishing domestic trade, increasing access to education – all these indicated the degree to which Japan was moving away from an agrarian-based feudal society". The shogunate, "ideologically and economically" unable to adjust to such profound changes, found itself in an increasingly precarious position.[2]

Samurai warriors had transformed themselves into bureaucratic administrators during the more than two centuries when Westerners (save a few Dutch traders on a tiny island in Nagasaki harbor) had been excluded from the land. During those years, Japan fell far behind the West's technological development, leaving the nation unprepared for any serious challenge to its isolation from Western powers. Commodore Matthew Perry, who arrived in Japan in 1853 demanding the "opening" of the country, exacerbated problems long unaddressed by the shogunate, and created a crisis of grave proportions. Though the social and political order of the

Tokugawa years was weakened by the time Perry arrived in 1853, and considerable debate about continued isolation had been under way since about 1800, the Japanese tradition of seclusion – in place since the seventeenth century – still profoundly informed government policy and popular opinion.

Though the problem was pressing, no consensus emerged. Some Japanese argued that the obvious course was to acknowledge the superior technology that Perry's "black ships" represented and enter into commercial and diplomatic relations with the West. Others ranged themselves against the foreign intrusion and demanded that the shogunate preserve Japan's integrity by "revering the emperor and expelling the barbarians" (*sonno-joi*). Recognizing its own weakness, the "Bakufu", or shogun's government, agreed in 1858 to a commercial treaty negotiated by U.S. representative Townsend Harris under duress in order to avoid the catastrophe that would result from any application of superior Western force. Looming in the background to the negotiations with Harris was the threat of intervention in Japan by the British fleet – then prosecuting the Arrow War against China – whose aggressive intentions in East Asia were first manifest clearly against China in the opium war of 1839–42.[3] In the early years of the foreign presence, the Bakufu – though too weak militarily to oppose the treaty powers – was nevertheless sensitive to the deep-rooted opposition to any foreign treaty which opened the country to foreign trade.[4] While respecting the letter of the treaty requirements, Japanese activities reflected a strong desire to isolate and control the foreign settlements.

The Harris commercial treaty set the basic framework for Japanese relations with the West for the next four decades, and served as a model for the treaties of Great Britain, France, Germany and other nations, all of which contained the "most favored nation" clause, guaranteeing that the concessions granted any one power automatically accrued to all powers.[5] Thus cooperative action among the treaty powers ensured Japan's continued formal subordinate status. The treaty of 1858 set the tariff rates for all articles. Export duties were 5 percent, and import duties were generally 20 percent, both calculated on an *ad valorem* basis. Though providing commercial advantage in some ways, the treaties restricted Western merchants to the treaty ports, legally barring travel more than ten *ri* (about twenty-five miles) in any direction. The treaties guaranteed foreigners the right to lease land, buy buildings and erect dwellings and warehouses, and provided for Americans' free exercise of their religion.[6]

The key features of the Harris treaty – the creation of treaty ports, extraterritoriality and foreign control of Japanese import and export tariffs – ensured that foreign merchants in Japan were subject to their own law and assured favorable tariffs.[7] Extraterritoriality and the treaty port system persisted in Japan until 1899. During the four decades of its existence, the foreign merchant community in the three main treaty ports of Yokohama (Kanagawa), Hyogo (Kobe) and Nagasaki grew substantially, with Americans the second most numerous nationality.

Because of Japanese inexperience in trade with the West and lack of credit, American companies such as Augustine Heard and Company, Walsh, Hall and Company and Smith, Baker and Company, and British companies such as Jardine,

Matheson and Company took up residence in the treaty ports and dominated Japan's overseas trade.[8] The merchants who worked in these firms faced the business landscape of Japan from inside a highly insular, semi-colonial society. Such men realized that their privileged status rested on the tariff structure and the continuation of extraterritoriality that were central to the unequal treaties.

Civil war in Japan in the 1860s ultimately led to the defeat of the Bakufu, and the new Meiji leadership, after its victory in 1868, inherited the problem of the unequal treaties and the unwelcome merchants living and trading in the treaty ports. Well aware of the indignities the treaty port system had inflicted on China, the Meiji leadership was steadily determined to escape the worst effects of the unequal treaties which deprived them of the right to set tariffs and gave foreigners the right to live on their soil without being subject to Japanese law, and they employed various means to control the foreign communities. Initially rebuffed by the Western powers in their attempts to revise the treaties, Japan recognized that ridding the nation of the embarrassment of extraterritoriality and foreign mercantile enclaves would involve offering the quid pro quo of opening the Japanese interior to foreign residence and commerce. Until treaty revision could be secured, Americans and other Westerners would remain in the treaty ports, where they could be controlled and their influence could be confined:

> Meiji Japanese feared that the Western merchants would expand their activities to control the domestic economy directly by replacing the Japanese trading companies and producers. The experience of Asian and Near Eastern peoples under Western dominance clearly illustrated that Japan was in danger of becoming a plantation of the Western powers, a source of materials they wanted and a captive market for their goods .... Above all, a Japan dependent on foreign intermediaries would never be able to exercise normal control over its own domestic economy, promote immediately unprofitable but potentially lucrative products competitive with Western industries, or acquire first-hand familiarity with Western markets and merchandising and with foreign trade.[9]

Such anxiety was understandable but, in the event, not justified by Western merchant attitudes. Far from demanding further penetration of the Japanese market, American merchants were content to remain in the ports as a relatively salutary and manageable presence. Above all, the Western trading presence during the treaty port years provided Japan with a way of handling international trade until Japan could handle it herself. Americans' tractability, born of cultural insularity, made them serve Japanese interests admirably well.

These interests are summed up in the slogan *fukoku-kyohei* ("Enrich the country, strengthen the army"), emphasizing the need to adopt Western methods to strengthen Japan against the West and to remove the embarrassment of a foreign presence on Japanese soil. Okubo Toshimichi, one of the Meiji oligarchs, advocated taking "steps quickly to stimulate domestic production and increase our exports, so as to repair our weakness by attaining national wealth and strength".[10] An important part of this process was the control of foreign trade.

Although the treaties were unequal, the peculiar circumstances of their application made them less unequal than legalities would indicate. Limitations on Western power to enforce the unequal treaties, and Japanese desire and ability to control the foreigners in the ports, placed real limits on how deeply foreigners of any nationality could penetrate the Japanese market. Japan steadily protested the treaties, but was in fact able to use them in slowly gaining the strength that was to bring them to an end at the turn of the century. Hence the Japanese gradually strengthened their *de facto* control until they could escape their *de jure* subordination.

Aided to some extent by Great Britain's sea power in East Asia, the small merchant colonies in the ports benefited from the treaties by clinging to their formal advantages and implicitly accepting the limitations on their power, even over their own businesses. If imperialism is defined as a more powerful nation advancing its own interests – economic, strategic or political – at the expense of a weaker nation, that definition applied most imperfectly to the Japanese treaty ports. Foreign diplomatic officials, acting in the economic interests of their nationals in the ports, could not threaten to apply military force without running the risk of graphically illustrating their weakness to the Japanese. To a large extent, Western merchants were left in the treaty ports to fend for themselves – or at least to depend on purely political intervention that in fact understood the limits of Western power. In this context, their cultural attitudes became important determining factors in their success or failure as businessmen.

Euro-Americans in the treaty ports, then, were not simply privileged beneficiaries of treaties rendering them immune to Japanese law and favoring their commercial interests. They functioned in an alien environment without real support other than that of their consular service and the flimsy text of the treaties. For these reasons the potential for success of American merchants related primarily to their own attitudes and initiative, and the degree to which the Japanese government found it advisable to aid them.

One historical study places merchants' experience in the context of Japanese resistance to Western imperialism, and suggests that Western merchants' success was largely dependent on Japan's response to the Western intrusion. Shinya Sugiyama has argued that because Western merchants were limited to the treaty ports and denied access to Japan's interior markets, the treaty port system

> in effect hindered attempts by Western capital and trade to enter, infiltrate, or expand into domestic distribution. Externally, not only did the agency house system by which Western merchants operated prove inefficient, but the Western powers did not have the military capability to force Japan to observe the requirements of "free trade" … the treaty port system as a whole functioned as a non-tariff barrier in Japan's favor.[11]

Since the treaties provided the formal context for Western mercantile interests, Japan resorted to "indirect ways of restricting imports".[12] In essence, Sugiyama suggests that Western merchants, herded together in the treaty ports and cut off from interior markets, were vulnerable to Japanese control.

Basic to Sugiyama's approach is the assumption that Western merchants' success or failure depended largely on the degree of Japanese resistance. Indeed, the treaties provided the Japanese, paradoxically, with the means by which to control the Western merchants while building their capacity to take over control of their own international commerce. Sugiyama's theory of Japanese resistance, however, assigns no importance to the actions and cultural assumptions that Euro–American merchants brought with them, and leaves unexamined the crucial question of the ability of Western merchants to exploit the political context of the unequal treaties. The situation was two-sided, and Japanese resistance interacted with Western merchant practices in promoting Sugiyama's result of largely aiding Japanese development.

II

How, I initially wondered, did Americans of the last half of the nineteenth century work upon Japan and how did Japan work upon them? Others have gone before me in this venture, and some scholarship on Americans abroad in Meiji Japan suggests the intersection of Americans with Japan in textured and meaningful ways. F.G. Notehelfer, in his examination of L.L. Janes as an influential religious leader in Meiji Japan, suggests that Janes was charged with reformist zeal and the "religious conviction that the millennium could be achieved in this world".[13] Janes' Japan was exceptionally eager to hear his message in the 1870s, and he fulfilled the most optimistic expectations of his Japanese hosts, as he "opened their eyes to the importance of the West, but at the same time broadened their belief in the value and significance of their own cultural tradition". Janes, Notehelfer suggests, had a lasting influence as "a carrier of American culture".[14] Notehelfer's analysis does not suggest that Janes adapted to Japan, Indeed, it was his essence as a Westerner that constituted his appeal to his hosts – had he been less Western, his appeal would have diminished in proportion. Janes was a Westerner whom the Japanese wanted as a Westerner, a man whose occidental personality gave him historical force and agency.

Sandra C. Taylor's volume on Sidney Gulick, a missionary and "Japan expert" who served from 1887 to 1913 on the American Board of Commissioners for Foreign Missions, deals thoughtfully with his evangelical experience in several locations in Japan. Taylor emphasizes the significance of his broader career as a champion of the Japanese in the U.S. and argues that he "represented the best strains of Christian internationalism". Though Gulick's causes failed, Taylor correctly sees his career as significant.[15]

Books on the foreign employees hired by the Meiji government also give clues to the nature of cultural contact between Japan and the United States. In the spirit of the Charter Oath of 1868, which declared that knowledge was to be sought throughout the world, the Meiji government recruited these men, and Hazel Jones' work on foreigners hired by the Meiji government contains two excellent chapters, "The Yatoi Self-Image" and "The Japanese Image of Yatoi", that shed some light on the cultural encounter between Japan and the U.S., but her work deals with foreigners from a variety of Western nations – more than two dozen in all.[16] Ardath Burks' edited work is a second useful volume on foreigners hired by the Meiji government to advise the Japanese in public works, education and other areas the Meiji leaders considered to be essential for national self-strengthening. It contains several essays dealing directly with the *oyatoi* (government foreign employee), more than 200 of whom were American. While these essays are helpful in understanding the basic demography of these foreign hires and contain much useful statistical information, there is little that addresses the nature of the cultural encounter between Americans and Japanese.[17]

Robert Rosenstone has offered an analysis of three Americans in Meiji Japan (William Elliot Griffis, Samuel Edward S. Morse and Lafcadio Hearn), and sets out to show "not How We changed Them by bringing the benefits of technology and republican institutions, but how They taught Us in ways much less easy to specify". Rosenstone argues that the three men's lives were "altered greatly" by their experience in Japan.[18] He sees all three men in complex intersection with Japan, with their own cultures and with him as the author, and his approach illuminates the cultural encounter in significant ways.

Lawrence Chisolm describes another American, Ernest Fenollosa, a student of Japanese art who concluded that in their pursuit of Western ideas, "the Japanese were denying an artistic heritage which they should honor and which the West could no longer overlook". His zeal to restore and preserve traditional Japanese art forms met with considerable success. One of Fenollosa's students, Okakura Kazuko, helped found the Tokyo School of Art, where the renaissance Fenollosa promoted continued to flourish.[19]

Donald Roden has contributed a piece on the confrontation between American and Japanese baseball teams at the end of the treaty port era whose result was less clear. Roden suggests that the nature of the cultural encounter was essentially ambivalent – Americans wanted to spread their values abroad through baseball (and thereby make Japan less "inscrutable"), but balked at the idea of "little brown people" actually winning the games. Japanese attached equally ambivalent meanings to their victories, on the one hand arguing that their triumph represented redress for the injustices of the unequal treaties, on the other that baseball was a way of forging "harmonious relations" between the U.S. and Japan.[20]

One study that deals directly with the American experience in the treaty ports is F.G. Notehelfer's edited version of the journal of Francis Hall, an American businessman who lived and worked in Yokohama from 1859 to 1866. Hall was a "leading business pioneer in Japan, correspondent for Horace Greeley's *New York Tribune*, world traveler, opinion maker" whose detailed journal sheds enormous light on American business endeavors in the early years of the treaty ports. An acute observer with an intense curiosity and a wide range of interests, Hall was genial and adventurous, and his journal is an exceptionally valuable record.[21] Studies that deal with cultural relations provide context, but do not further illuminate the nature of direct encounters between the peoples of Japan and the United States.[22]

All of these scholarly interpretations have constituted some modest advance in our understanding of the nature of cultural contact between visiting Americans and Meiji Japan. But the largest group of Americans in nineteenth-century Japan – the sizeable community of merchants who made their homes in the three treaty ports of Yokohama, Hyogo, Kobe and Nagasaki – have until now remained unexamined, their voices silent. Almost all Western visitors to Japan passed through the ports, commented briefly and perhaps disdainfully on their appearance, and moved on. I have remained in the ports with these heretofore nameless men and their small trading companies to explore their experience critically and, I hope, sympathetically.

III

When Japan received its invitation to attend the Chicago World's Columbian Exposition in 1893, it responded quickly and enthusiastically, eventually spending "more than $630,000", among the most substantial expenditures of any nation invited to exhibit. A Japanese architect designed the Ho-o-den Palace, Japanese workers sent from Japan built it, and members of the Tokyo Art Academy decorated its interior. The Japanese Minister to Washington, Gozo Tateno, "explained that his country was enthusiastic about participating in the exposition because of Japan's interest in furthering commercial ties with America as well as proving 'that Japan is a country worthy of full fellowship in the family of nations.' American officials welcomed the Japanese, apparently with few reservations".[23]

This official response suggested that Japanese fellowship in the family of nations constituted no threat to Americans, and for those who strolled the midway gawking at the strange exhibitions from abroad, perhaps that was true. Yet the Exposition was held just one year before a significant event occurred for American merchants living in Japan. In 1894 Japan finally succeeded in revising the unequal treaties imposed cooperatively by Western powers nearly four decades before. After a five-year waiting period, Japan would again control her tariff structure, be able to try Western lawbreakers in Japan according to Japanese law, and rid herself of the "treaty ports" that embarrassed her sovereignty. American merchants who had been living and trading in the treaty ports of Yokohama, Hyogo and Nagasaki were, at the time of the Exposition, reaching the end of their tenure as privileged residents, and would have viewed Japan's exhibit on the "choicest location on the fairgrounds, the Wooded Isle"[24] with anxiety and even alarm.

Their anxiety was born in an age of rapid change and grew with their rising awareness that change was eroding their known place in the world. In this they were much like Americans in the U.S. The four decades after the American Civil War brought enormous changes to American life. Large scale and rapid industrialization spawned new opportunities and class tensions, urbanization brought Americans together in new and often uncomfortable ways, and population increased dramatically. The frontier could not remain open in the face of relentless westward movement and the completion of a nationwide transportation network. Unprecedented accumulations of wealth and economic power in the hands of a few called up new, vexing questions about the role and function of government. One historian has called it the "age of energy" – expended in great quantities and with great enthusiasm, much of which "flowed in contradictory directions".[25]

The age produced the Brooklyn bridge, innovative production techniques that brought cheaper consumer goods to millions, the transcontinental railroads and an integrated national marketplace, and exciting new ways of spending newly-created leisure time. Its material accomplishments were great; equally it was an age that produced dislocation and anxiety on an unprecedented scale. Americans were being educated, sometimes uncomfortably, to the new imperatives of a collective age, recasting their notions of individualism to fit the demands of collective action and reaction, finding ways to exist in new bureaucratic structures, and dealing with the enervating, even emasculating consequences of industrialization. Some scholars have asserted that the challenge of women in the workforce and fears about the "feminization" of America were but two indications of a general *fin de siècle* malaise brought on by the confluent power of multiple disruptive forces in American life. Much of the tension of the age was expressed in a crescendo of unease, anomie and violence in the 1890s, when a severe economic depression threw the nation's problems into sharp relief. Not long before the century's end, intense labor violence, the Populist challenge in national politics, and a war with Spain expressed unresolved tension on a grand scale.[26]

More traditional Victorian notions of self-restraint, order and control seemed an imperfect response to this new and confusing reality. These events and their cumulative aftermath left Americans, in T.J. Jackson Lears' phrase, with a feeling of "weightlessness". By the turn of the century, "the self seemed neither independent, nor unified, nor fully conscious, but rather interdependent, discontinuous, divided". Over-civilized and "physically enervated", the modern American character was in a kind of cultural and spiritual limbo.[27] Many believed the solution to the problem of "over-civilization" was to be found in the strenuous life or in other ways by which Americans could rediscover their energizing impulses. In this process, men redefined concepts of manhood in terms of combat against both the debilitating effects of industrialization/urbanization, and the sedentary and routine-dominated work environments that undermined their dignity and independence.

One of the most important tensions in Gilded Age American life concerned the issue of immigration. The racially different new immigrants from eastern and southern Europe presented unique challenges to those who would make a place in the American polity, society and economy for these new people – or bar them from any such place. The American experience with foreign peoples after the Civil War through the early-twentieth century was marked by ambivalent attitudes towards them. On the one hand their appearance ratified the comforting ideology of the promise of equality for all under American republican government, defined eloquently by Lincoln as the "last, best hope for men on earth". In economic terms, the influx of immigrant peoples fueled the great engines of American industry.

Yet on the other hand, Americans were unable to decide if immigrants were salutary or debilitating in the fabric of national life, a constructive or destructive presence:

> If Roosevelt and others identified a renewed, "strenuous" barbarism as a salve to the encroachments of modernity, the "barbarism" of national or racial "inferiors" also provided a ready-made rationale for conquest and domination. If the delicate U.S. experiment in democracy required a particularly virtuous polity, then the nation's very destiny as "steward to the backward races of the world" and as "asylum for the world's oppressed" was fraught with peril.[28]

By the time the country came to its uncomfortable rendezvous with the new century, much had occurred to shake many Americans' faith and reason regarding the place of foreign peoples in the republic. Anti-Chinese agitation had begun in earnest in the 1870s, the Haymarket riot in 1886 raised the specter of imported radicalism, and Henry Cabot Lodge and the Immigration Restriction League articulated grave concern that the American polity could not absorb so many different immigrants. America's racial understanding sometimes lagged in proportion to her growth:[29]

> If the exposition in Philadelphia in 1876 represented a grand unveiling of the nation's new wares and its new thinking on the importance of securing a world market, it also hinted at one of the peculiar social dynamics that this global trade would create: in their economic affairs Americans were becoming set on becoming more and more engaged with the world's peoples, but in their social outlook they were not necessarily becoming any less parochial than they had ever been".[30]

Matthew Frye Jacobson provides a compelling insight into the period in a recent work, suggesting that immigration and expansion can be viewed as part of the same equation:

> As modern American nationalism took shape within an international crucible of immigration and empire building, some of its harsher strains derived less from a confidence in American virtues than from a disturbing recognition of the barbarian virtues. American integration into the world economic system in this period of breath-taking industrialization exposed

a rather profound dependence upon foreign peoples as imported workers for American factories and as overseas consumers of American products – including "rat-eyed young men" from the shtetls [Jewish villages] of Eastern Europe ... and the grass-skirted natives as far-flung as the South Pacific. In this respect, immigration and expansion constituted two sides of the same coin.[31]

If immigration and expansion indeed constituted "two sides of the same coin", would the American reaction to foreign peoples be the same abroad as it was at home?

This book describes an episode in the story of the American encounter with those foreign peoples in an intensely exotic nineteenth-century setting, and the ways in which Americans responded to that encounter. How much of the America described above was true, and how much of it came with them to the treaty ports of Japan? This study seeks to shed light on some aspects of American Victorian culture in a unique, microcosmic setting.

IV

I set out to answer some salient questions. Was the American merchant experience in Japan an example of continuity or of discontinuity with the general American experience with foreign peoples about which historians have responsibly generalized? How would the freight of American merchants' Victorian culture – with all its strength and brittleness – equip these men for the challenges of life and work abroad? Would they illustrate adaptive patterns of behavior that set them in creative counterpoint to their home culture? Or would the imperative of replicating their familiar home culture as closely as possible define their activity? What results would attach to either response? Would their interaction with the Japanese and other groups verify broad generalizations about Victorian racism? How successful were American businessmen in turning their formal, political imperial advantages into actual business hegemony, personal and national?

As I attempted to answer this first set of questions, a second set emerged. What was the nature of Japanese–American trade over the last forty years of the nineteenth century? Who held power in the treaty ports, and for whose benefit was it used? What were the pressures for and against change over time, and from where did they come? Who benefited politically and economically from the "unequal treaties" and why? Here was a forty-year window of opportunity (1859–99, the length of time that Americans lived in the ports under protected status) during which to take some measure of the Victorian American mind abroad.

What is distinctive about these merchants and their story? Obviously, they came to Japan and functioned there in a cooperative, cohesive group that defined its common interests with considerable precision. This feature of the merchant experience alone sets it significantly apart from other American interaction with

Meiji Japan. Merchants functioned, not largely in isolation from each other as did other visitors, but together in constant, close professional and social association with each other and other Westerners, primarily the British. A second feature of the merchant experience sets it apart – unlike Janes and the foreign experts who came at the behest of the Japanese government, American merchants came to Japan as unwelcome guests and were viewed with considerable ambivalence by a national leadership carefully charting a course toward national strength and international respectability.

As my research unfolded, two centrally-defining features of the American merchant experience in Japan became increasingly clear. First, this little community considered itself dependent – on its consuls to resolve matters of dispute, on its servants for basic needs, on Japanese and Chinese employees to negotiate the shoals of the marketplace, on the British for the lead in providing a stable social structure, on the Japanese government to enforce what American consuls could not and, ultimately, on the unequal treaties that temporarily gave them favorable conditions under which to live and trade. American merchants' sense of individual and collective agency was severely limited and they responded, perhaps understandably, by closing ranks and seeking security in the ways available to them.

The second, equally important defining feature of the community was its insularity. Because it was so insular, the temptation to explain its behavior (considering its Asian setting) largely in terms of Victorian imperialism and racism is strong. But while a virulent strain of racism was certainly manifest in treaty port merchants' attitudes and behavior, it formed only a part of the cultural baggage these men took across the Pacific. Rather than viewing these Americans solely or even largely as haughty, racist imperialists, this study seeks to understand them as products of a Victorian culture ambiguously but deeply concerned with order and opportunity, restraint and dominance, conservatism and progress.

A most striking parallel exists between the American community in the ports and what Robert Wiebe describes as the isolated communities of the 1870s in the U.S. that, collectively, formed an American "distended society" without a core. Wiebe might have been describing Yokohama or Hyogo when he stated that "beneath that flat surface" of such small communities, each

> was divided by innumerable, fine gradations. Distinctions that would have eluded an outsider – the precise location of a house, the amount of hired help, the quality of a buggy or a dress – held great import in an otherwise undifferentiated society … . At the top stood the few who not only had greater wealth than their neighbors but controlled access to it as well … . Variations in religion, accent, and skin coloring distinguished individuals, groups and even entire communities from one another. Except in rare circumstances, custodians of a genteel but explicit Protestantism with Anglo-Saxon names enjoyed a powerful advantage over all competitors.[32]

These "island communities" formed the basic social reference point for Americans, and "as men ranged farther and farther from their communities, they tried desperately to understand the larger world in terms of their small familiar environment. They tried, in other words, to impose the known upon the unknown".[33] This essentially conservative and parochial effort quite accurately describes the American experience in the treaty ports.

This book is essentially a work of American social and cultural history set in the treaty ports of Japan, and its central argument, then, is that American merchants living in that setting responded to the unknown by struggling to recreate the known with enormous exactitude. These men consistently sought to order their lives along familiar cultural lines. The fate of those attempting to impose the known upon the unknown in the U.S. was to fail, "usually without recognizing why";[34] their American compatriots across the ocean fared no better in their Japanese island communities. The nature of American merchants' behavior dictated that this study be arranged thematically instead of chronologically. It quickly became apparent that after the uncertainties and speculations of the very first years, merchants' business operations changed little through their forty-year tenure in the ports; attitudes and business practices, once in place, hardened into almost a canon of accepted practices with the inevitable corollary of higher levels of anxiety when change intruded upon stasis.

V

One problem in researching the merchant experience is a dearth of manuscript sources. The records of only one American firm in Japan, Augustine Heard and Company – which ceased its Japan operations in the 1870s – have survived. Another limitation is that merchants left few accounts of their sojourns in Japan, unlike missionaries, who wrote voluminously of their experiences. Because of these gaps, this study relies heavily on three kinds of sources. The English language press in the treaty ports, particularly the *Japan Weekly Mail* – a paper published throughout most of the treaty port years – provides a running commentary on merchants' concerns. While it was usually sympathetic to the merchant's position, the paper printed enough letters from correspondents to provide a reasonable cross-section of opinion. Other newspapers, such as the *Hiogo News*, the *Tokio Times* and the *Japan Gazette*, supplement the *Mail*, and frequently provide competing views.[35]

A second major source is the internal consular archive of Hyogo/Kobe, a treasure-trove which has never been tapped before.[36] Here merchants' concerns appear in their daily correspondence with their consuls, which to a large extent compensates for the paucity of company records. The great Kanto earthquake and fire of 1923 destroyed the internal archive of the Kanagawa consulate, but since there was little difference between the society and business culture of the three main ports, to a large extent this study assumes that what was true of Hyogo/Kobe was generally true of Yokohama. I have concentrated on the Kobe/Hyogo archive because Nagasaki had ceased to be important as a trading center by the early 1870s and for that reason is less significant. Closely linked if sometimes competitive, Yokohama and Hyogo/Kobe defined, to a large extent, the foreign mercantile presence in Japan. To a lesser degree, I have relied on the consular and minister's dispatches from Japan, collections that reflect merchant concerns through the filter of those officials who interacted with them on a daily basis, and sometimes provide information on the composition of the merchant community.[37] The *Chronicle and Directory for China, Japan and the Philippines* provides information concerning the numbers of companies and their employees. Because Kobe and Hyogo are used interchangeably in most of the sources, I have used them interchangeably in this study.

The third major source is the considerable number of visitors' accounts, almost all of whom commented on treaty port society, however briefly, before moving on to the interior or other Pacific destinations. These accounts often corroborate and sometimes clarify data from other sources, and help form a more complete picture of treaty port life.

This study sees the merchants "from the American side" and also relies upon a number of relevant works dealing with masculinity, race, immigration, nativism, and U.S. business history. Where I believe they illuminate the cultural assumptions and behaviors of these merchants in the context of the broader American Victorian society, I have applied their many insights. The available sources prevent any generalization about these merchants' cities or regions of origin in the U.S. Encountering nothing during my research to suggest that these men came largely from any one geographic area, I have proceeded on the assumption that their places of origin were various.

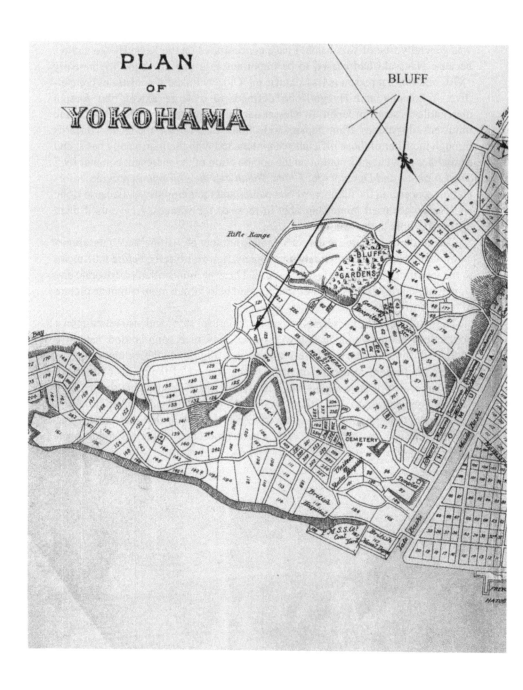

Figure 2 Plan of Yokohama, c. 1899
Source: OHMC, National Archives, RG 84, 8-1-99

BANKS.

Chartered of I., A., & C.	78
Comptoir N. d'Escompte	2
Hongkong & Shanghai	2

CHURCHES.

Christ Church	105
Roman Catholic	80
Union Church	167

CONSULATES

Austro-Hungarian	Bluff 215
Belgian	Bluff 118B
British	172
Chinese	135
Danish	209
French	84
German	81
Italian	Bluff 211
Netherlands	93
Peruvian	70
Portuguese	Bluff 90
Russian	171
Spanish	Bluff 32
Swedish and Norwegian	92
Swiss	169
United States	224

HOTELS.

Club Hotel	5
Grand Hotel	18, 19-20
Haefker's Hotel Main St.	57

MERCHANTS, &c.

Ahrens & Co., H.	29
Bavier & Co.	209
Bing & Co., S.	75
Bayes & Co.	143
Browne & Co.	72
Butterfield & Swire	7
China & Japan Trad'g Co.	89c
Cornes & Co.	50
Dell'Oro & Co.	91
Dodwell, Carlill & Co.	54
Findlay, Richardson & Co.	6
Fraser, Farley, & Varnum [143, 216-218	
Frazar & Co.	200
Grosser & Co.	180
Hellyer & Co.	210
Hunt & Co.	211
Illies & Co.	54
Jardine, Matheson & Co.	1
Kelly & Walsh, Ld.	61
Lane, Crawford & Co.	59
Mollison & Co.	48
Morf & Co., H. C.	176
Mourilyan Heimann & Co.	35
Oppenheimer Frères	13
Pila & Co., Ulysse	2
Raspe & Co., M.	199
Reimers & Co., Otto	198
Robison & Co.	3
Rohde & Co., C.	70
Samuel Samuel & Co.	27
Siber, Brennwald & Co.	90
Smith, Baker & Co.	178
Simon, Evers & Co.	25
Strachan & Co., W. M.	71
Walsh, Hall & Co.	2

NEWSPAPERS.

Daily Advertiser	26
Japan Gazette	70
Japan Herald	28
Japan Mail	51

S. S. COMPANIES.

Austro-Hung'n Lloyd's	214
Canadian Pacific	200
Indo-China S. N. Co.	1
Messageries Maritimes	9
Nippon Yusen, Kaigan-dori	
Northern Pacific R. Co.	59
Occidental & Oriental	4A
Pacific Mail S. S. Co.	4A
Peninsular & Oriental	15

MISCELLANEOUS.

Chamber of Commerce	61
Club Germania	235-237
Masonic Hall	50
Police Station	203
Public Hall	Bluff 257
Yokohama Fire Brigade	238
Yokohama United Club	5

BUND

ENGLISH HATOBA

1

FROM FRENZY TO INSECURITY

The contours of trade

The West has not ... made any pretense of adapting itself to the East.[1]

American merchants were drawn to Japan by the lure of profits. Over the forty years during which Western merchants enjoyed favored commercial status in the treaty ports, they developed a system of doing business that enthusiastically accepted isolation from the Japanese marketplace under the protection of the political structure of the unequal treaties. The liabilities associated with this fixed way of doing business did not, however, become apparent until changes in the Japanese economy and growing Japanese control of its own trade began to render the treaty ports superfluous. The history of treaty port business progressively highlighted Western merchants' vulnerability to growing Japanese competition.

I

What was the overall nineteenth-century context in which American trade developed? During the mercantilist era the states of Europe substantially restricted trade and "attempted to reserve certain trades and manufactures to privileged groups of their own nationals". They accomplished this through state action or through "some form of regulated corporation. Long-distance trade in particular was subject to these methods because of the important function it was believed to play in assuring the strength of the state". One example of this was in Buenos Aires, where Spanish mercantilism was replaced by an "extremely cosmopolitan mercantile culture, well integrated with the local landed and government élites"; another example was the gradual replacement of the British East India Company by a new generation of private traders.[2]

By the early nineteenth century, these mercantilist empires had ceased to function, and simultaneously, important changes in "location, techniques and cost of manufacture, but also in the geographical pattern and composition of international trade" occurred. These developments destroyed the old eighteenth-century mercantile élite, but soon "new and innovative intermediaries developed: wholesale warehouses to serve the export trade, and a new kind of international firm, the commission agency, comprising partners of limited capital but extensive resourcefulness". This in turn spawned an international trading community – merchants traveling the world in search of export products, settling in various foreign ports, where

> English was widely used as a common language … it was a dispersed community, spread out across the trading cities of the world, in any one of which a man of middling origins might make his way among acquaintances and friends of friends on the basis of little more than a letter of introduction and a clean record, and perhaps not even that. Finally, while it was substantially, though by no means entirely, a Protestant world, its most fundamental legitimising ideology was a secular one – economic liberalism: a profound faith in the collective virtue of aggregated individual self-interest and the moral validity of market sanctions.[3]

By the middle of the century, the markets and products of foreign countries became available just at the time when exceptional growth in the American domestic economy created more foreign trade. Economic expansion, unlike territorial expansion, did not require population shifts or annexation of land, only products to buy and sell, and the cooperation of foreign governments.

American merchants were positioned to become part of this international trading community – when colonial American commerce began with Europe and the Caribbean, "other Americans made it their business to represent them abroad in buying and selling transactions, and American settlements appeared all over the world. These were permanent establishments with trading facilities and, even more important, knowledge of local tastes, currencies and officials at the disposal of any businessman, American or foreign, for a fee".[4] American merchants had a presence in Mexico, Central and Latin America, the Caribbean, China, West Africa and East Asia, where they handled and sometimes promoted trade under a wide variety of fluctuating local circumstances.[5]

The U.S. government's attitude toward international trade vacillated throughout the century, but especially after the Civil War. Before the 1960s, historians of U.S. foreign relations tended to treat the post-Civil War years as episodes in isolation or in loose association with each other.[6] Many subsequent interpretations have conceptually resembled the work of William Appleman Williams, whose *The Tragedy of American Diplomacy* argues that American expansion was a deliberate and coherent process.[7] Neither approach is entirely satisfactory. Perhaps the best description of post-Civil War economic expansion calls it a "tentative, experimental process".[8] It was a time of "uncertainty, improvisation and frequent arguments over foreign affairs", but American uncertainty notwithstanding, "America's expanding foreign commerce … benefited enormously from the internationalization of trade, capital, and labor then taking place under European, especially British, leadership".[9]

Enormous domestic economic growth in the last three decades of the century hinted at much more extensive American integration into the world's economy, and proponents of expansion justified their arguments by advancing the theory of overproduction and, to a lesser extent, the idea that American economic expansion would promote the "spiritual or ideological influence of American liberal democracy abroad".[10] Political disagreement over these issues, and fundamentally over the purpose of the tariff, however, continued to divide the American government and cripple the expansionist impulse.

Developments on the far side of the Pacific made American expansion there possible, however. The appearance of the China treaty ports after the opium war in 1842 marked the acceleration of Western expansion into East Asia. When the Suez canal opened in 1869 the distance between western Europe and East Asia was reduced by nearly half.[11] British firms such as the Peninsular and Oriental Steam Navigation Company and Alfred Holt and Company established the shipping patterns that supported East Asian commercial contact with the West. Later firms, such as the Pacific Mail Steamship Company, expanded established trade routes by inaugurating the first scheduled service across the Pacific in 1867 and then instituting a bi-monthly run between San Francisco and Shanghai in 1874. The competition among shippers led to reductions in rates, providing a basic prerequisite for an expanding trade.[12] After 1871, Japan was connected telegraphically to Europe and the U.S., greatly improving communication: immediate access to market information was available and telegraphic transfers were possible.[13]

As Western commercial contact with China began to expand in the 1830s, and particularly after the opium war of 1839–42, when the China coast became more accessible to Western merchants, the mercantile firms seeking a foothold in that country faced many problems, not the least of which was the absence of a stable, unified currency and the financial and commercial apparatus necessary to support complex mercantile operations. As a consequence, Western merchants in China expanded their operations, promoting insurance companies and undertaking banking and foreign exchange businesses as well as entering into transport. Such subsidiary enterprises, once established, formed a base from which Western business in Asia could expand.[14]

Foreign merchants starting companies in Japan could rely on the network of insurance and banking firms already established on the China coast, mainly in Shanghai and Hong Kong. Entering a geographic region for which the tools to conduct foreign trade had already been established, they did not need to diversify as had earlier arrivals such as the British firms of Jardine, Matheson and Company, and Dent and Company. Two American firms, the China and Japan Trading Company, and Augustine Heard and Company, had substantial ties to the China trade, but most American companies concentrated on Japanese trade alone.[15]

Certainly American merchants faced problems moving into Japan, as the mortality rate of firms in the early years suggests. Even during the years of increased political stability after the Meiji Restoration, Japan's imperfect credit system, high interest rates and the lack of "uniformity in the quality" of its manufactures militated against foreign confidence. But Americans in the Japanese treaty ports were not faced with building the apparatus of trade: the cumulative effect of the Suez canal opening and the establishment of trade routes and commercial banks enabled firms without huge capital reserves to compete with older and richer companies.[16]

In this context, individual Americans sought to enrich themselves by seeking greener economic pastures. What motivated Americans to come to the treaty ports? The virtual absence of merchant diaries or personal letters necessitates speculation based on much less direct sources. Richard Peterson's study of fifty western U.S. mining entrepreneurs offers an assessment of their motivations that may, at least in some ways, parallel the motivations of American merchants. His book is an analysis of the social origins and business behavior of these mining entrepreneurs in the years 1870–1900. The "aspiring bonanza kings" moved west in search of new lives, some trying to escape the drudgery of work on family farms, "as clerks in banks or general merchandising houses". Others went west "driven by economic dislocation" while a few "sought to escape illness or family problems". Other attractions included "a love of nature and the freedom of movement provided by the wilderness". Peterson concludes that the most important motivation was "the quest for wealth".[17]

Peterson states that about one third of those who made their fortunes after 1870 had migrated west much earlier, attracted by the gold rushes in California and Colorado in the 1840s and 1850s. Nathaniel P. Hill was one such seeker of wealth. In 1857 he wrote of the west of the U.S. as the best place in the country for fortune seeking. In 1863 Hill was teaching chemistry at Brown University when a group of manufacturers asked him to investigate "mineral potential" in Colorado. He seized the chance and wrote his wife, "This presents one of the finest opportunities to make not only some money, but also some fame that has ever presented itself to me. If it turns out that the tract is rich in precious metals, I want no better fortune". Easterners desirous of such fortune undertook passages to their land of opportunity that were at least as arduous as the journey to Japan, coming west "by wagon along the Oregon Trail, by steamer via the Isthmus of Panama, or by sailing ship around Cape Horn".[18] Peterson concludes that "preoccupation with quick wealth left little time or inclination to build a permanent, stable material or spiritual life on the frontier". When such men came to understand the "unpredictable" nature of mining, their attitudes "became more realistic. Those who overcame their initial disillusionment either eventually decided to stay or were forced to remain for financial reasons".[19]

Peterson offers some useful statistical data on the fifty successful entrepreneurs for the period 1870–1900. More than half of these men came from the New England or Mid-Atlantic states, 17 percent came from the east north central region, and 23 percent came from the south. Forty-one percent of their fathers were businessmen, 39 percent farmers. In family class or status, 20 percent came from upper class backgrounds, 44 percent from the middle class, and 36 percent from the lower class. These data seem to confirm that many of these men saw themselves as upwardly mobile, and were willing travel long distances to improve their economic prospects.[20] This composite profile probably describes the men attracted to Japan's treaty ports in the early years. Few must have come across the Pacific to indulge a love of nature or of the wilderness, so we are left primarily with the economic motivation.

II

By 1869, in accordance with the treaties, a total of seven foreign settlements were open. Of the seven, only Yokohama, Kobe and Nagasaki thrived; the others failed for various reasons. The decline of Hakodate, opened initially to serve the needs of the whaling ships, reflected the decreasing importance of that industry in the years after 1860. It was too far north to be of service on the trade routes and soon the port had no purpose. Russia, which had earlier maintained a naval establishment there, gradually abandoned it by the 1870s.[21]

Niigata, opened to foreigners in 1868, was – from the American point of view – a complete failure. In part because of its unpleasant climate, but mainly because a sandbar blocked the entrance to the river on whose opening the town stood, Niigata was never an important port for foreign trade. By 1871 only four foreigners resided there and the only functioning consulate closed; by 1884 six missionaries remained.

Tokyo and Osaka were unique in that they were not "open ports" but rather "open cities". Though the two cities were the administrative and commercial capitals of Japan, import and export trade did not thrive in either location because the status of "open city" did not include the right to conduct a direct import–export trade. The right to reside, divorced from the right to trade, was of limited value to any foreign merchant. In September 1868, a new agreement went into effect allowing direct trade, but by then the merchant community in Kobe – begun in January 1868 – had already established itself and merchants were reluctant to set up duplicate facilities in Osaka.[22] Western residents in Osaka and Tokyo blended with the dominant societies of Kobe and Yokohama.

The Western intrusion presented the Japanese with two alternatives: driving out technologically superior foreigners, a course fraught with obvious danger, or granting the concessions demanded and carefully isolating foreign merchants within the treaty ports to buy the time necessary to strengthen the nation sufficiently to meet the Western threat. Expediency and weakness dictated the latter course, and the resultant ideology of *fukoku-kyohei* was to define a generation of Japanese leadership. The pressures generated by the Western intrusion generally stimulated a shift in Japanese political institutions away from older Chinese to recent Western models. The motivation was obvious and two-fold. First, presenting an appearance of Western modernity would facilitate revision of (and escape from) the unequal treaties. Second, it was "logical that the administration of a tax system, armed forces, and industrial structure on Western lines – the elements of wealth and strength – should be entrusted to a Western-style government".[23] Foreigners who settled in the ports were nevertheless unwelcome; they had come against the wishes of the majority of the "daimyo" (feudal lords), and their activities took place in the context of a society and economy placed under enormous stress, not only by the intrusion of the West, but by changes taking place within it.

The Japan to which Commodore Matthew Perry came in 1853 had been largely isolated from outside contact since the seventeenth century. Japan had rebuffed earlier attempts in the nineteenth century to open the country in order to expand contact with foreigners. One Japanese response to the opening of the country was intimately bound up in the domestic political situation: the social system of Japan, set in place in the seventeenth century and gradually eroding since, still provided the underpinning that kept the élite samurai in positions of power. The debate that followed the Perry expedition in 1853 clearly showed samurai distrust of the commoners who, they feared, would collaborate with foreign powers out of ignorance and undermine existing power relations. Soon after Perry arrived, one Japanese official stated:

> Regarding the arrival of foreign vessels in the past few years, recently members of the baser classes have been suffering particular hardships and their mental outlook has been poor … . It is said that some are bitter about the existing state of affairs. Now, the foreigners are *especially adept at attracting the ignorant people to their side*. If the foreigners were to take advantage of this situation in which *there is bitterness about the times and existing conditions* and to shower the common people with favors, serious difficulties would ensue.

Moreover, the Japanese military aristocracy regarded foreign merchants with the same animus as their native Japanese counterparts. One memorial to the Bakufu stated, "All merchants are led astray by profits. Many knowingly break the law and undergo severe punishments. But it is not likely that they will change their ways. In a crisis, we cannot predict what they might not do in league with the enemy".[24]

Another response to Perry's visit and Harris' treaty in 1858 was an intensification of the *sonno-joi* movement ("revere the emperor and repel the barbarian"). *Sonno-joi* had immediate consequences for the newly-forming merchant community at Yokohama in the late 1850s and early 1860s. The "shishi", often referred to as "men of high purpose", were mainly lower samurai, and political extremists, many of whom argued for immediately driving out the foreigners. To accomplish this, some shishi undertook to assassinate members of the foreign community.

Their purpose was associated with the "preservation of the 'sacred land' from the impurity of foreign occupation".[25]

Beginning with the murder of two Russian sailors in the summer of 1859, proponents of *sonno-joi* struck with sufficient regularity to cause the foreign residents of Yokohama to fear for their lives.[26] In March, 1860, Ii Naosuke, the Japanese regent who had favored the treaties with the West, was assassinated, and the dangers of residence in Japan were brought home to Americans when Henry Heuskin, the Dutch interpreter for Townsend Harris, was cut down in January, 1861. At least one Chinese servant of a foreigner was killed, and a Japanese named Dankichi, who flaunted his Western dress and manner, was murdered a year earlier. He was helping some boys fly their kites in a street when "suddenly a man, with a great broad straw hat down over his face came behind him, plunged a cruelly-sharp dirk into Dan's back, twisted it round in the wound ... and ran off like a deer".

Three months later, another assassination rocked Yokohama. The victims were Dutch, the captains of a barque and brig then in port. The pair was walking along the main street in the native town when the assassin attacked them from behind with a sword: one of the two "left his hat and an arm about two blocks away from his body". The most notable killing was that of Charles Richardson, an English merchant from Shanghai, who refused to give way on a public thoroughfare to a Satsuma daimyo procession and was hacked to death by members of the daimyo's retinue in September, 1862. Though such attacks diminished in frequency – they had nearly ceased by the early 1870s – their frequency in the early years was enough to create an atmosphere of tension and foreboding in the foreign settlement. In the wake of these incidents, the foreign community organized a Committee of Safety, and the Japanese authorities increased security.[27] But murderous attacks were not limited to zealous Japanese. In 1868 Paul Mosco, a drunken sailor from an American ship, stabbed to death a Japanese named Awaki Hajima, an officer of the Japanese police. Mosco's motives, if any, were never determined.[28] The shishi, like Mosco, acted without official sanction, and the Bakufu took more constructive measures to control the foreign community whose presence was sanctioned by the treaties. The Japanese officials conducted all the initial arrangements for foreign residence, as the local population had been warned to have no direct contact with foreigners.[29]

The purpose of the unequal treaties, of course, was to provide favorable conditions under which foreign trade could flourish. Fully recognizing that the Japanese agreed to the treaties under duress and that they could hardly expect enthusiastic cooperation, the Western powers' officials sought to avoid a replication of the situation that had obtained in Nagasaki for over two centuries.

The port of Nagasaki had a long history of contact with the Western world. When the Tokugawa shoguns closed Japan to Western contact in the seventeenth century, the window of Nagasaki was left open, and the Dutch maintained, under the most humiliating of circumstances, a tiny trading post on the artificially constructed island of Deshima in Nagasaki harbor. Dr Engelbert Kaempfer, a

German physician attached to the Dutch East India Company's factory there, left a remarkable record in the 1690s of this small Western outpost in feudal Japan. Kaempfer described the complete isolation of Deshima, noting that the island was surrounded by "thirteen posts standing at proper distances, with small wooden tablets at the top, upon which is written in large Japanese characters an order from the governors, strictly forbidding all boats or vessels under severe penalties to come within these posts or to approach the island".

To maintain trading rights, the director of the Dutch factory was required to travel to Yedo, the Shogun's capital, first annually and later every two to four years. Strictly supervised by as many as 150 Japanese, the Dutch delegation made its way to Yedo "in a manner like prisoners, deprived of all liberty, except that of looking about the country from [their] horses. Nay, they watch us to that degree that they will not leave us alone, even for the most necessary reasons".[30]

Townsend Harris was no doubt cognizant of the Dutch experience at Deshima when negotiating his treaty with the Japanese in 1858. Article III clearly stated that "No wall, fence or gate shall be erected by the Japanese around the place of residence of the Americans, or anything done which may prevent a free egress or ingress to the same". The Harris treaty provided for the opening of Kanagawa on July 4, 1859, but made no mention of Yokohama.[31] The latter town, the name signifying "opposite shore", a sleepy fishing village three miles away and accessible to Kanagawa only by an elevated causeway, seemed to Harris a spot where the Japanese authorities could quarantine the new American settlement, if not as formally as at Nagasaki with the Dutch, then as effectively.

The reference to Deshima was a common one. George Smith, a visitor to Yokohama, noted that:

> The Japanese officials seem bent on the determination to form a second Deshima at this port, and to cut off Yokuhama [sic] from the adjoining country by a line of newly dug canals drawn as a cordon around the town and intended to separate and confine the European inhabitants in the enclosed quarter.[32]

In fact, a map of the early Yokohama settlement (see Figure 2, pages 14–15) clearly shows the reality, even if not the actual Japanese intention, of isolating foreigners precisely as Smith observed.[33] Though some Japanese, no doubt, would have justified Harris' worst fears with regard to a "second Deshima", there was a more practical reason for locating the new settlement at Yokohama. Harris' treaty had intensified the national debate concerning opening Japan to foreigners, and neither the foreign ministers nor the merchants themselves anticipated the repercussions. Since 1635, daimyo and their large retinues had been plying the *tokaido* (eastern sea road) in Japan, and its proximity to Kanagawa would be an irritant to those daimyo opposed to the opening of the country and a distinct physical danger to foreigners. Ii Naosuke, the *tairo*, or regent, refused to accept the political risks of foreigners living at Kanagawa, and instead prepared Yokohama, "in the belief that the merchants would recognize the desirability of the site".[34]

In the summer of 1859 the American Consul Eben Dorr said to Townsend Harris, "I observe that they are erecting houses on the flat opposite to Kanagawa. I suppose the Japanese Government intend this for a second Deshima, but of course we cannot accept that sort of thing". Harris replied, "Certainly not, but that will be a battle you will have to fight since you are the consul of the port".[35] Dorr, considering his other capacity as agent for Augustine Heard and Company, must have smiled inwardly at this. Indeed, merchants cared little about any Japanese intent to isolate them, and in fact accepted, even sought, isolation at Yokohama, heedless of the worries of diplomatic officials, whose concerns extended beyond the purely mercantile. Foreign merchants did not hesitate to put their mercantile concerns ahead of the considerations of their ministers, even if Yokohama appeared in 1859 to be a second Deshima; they willingly paid for the deeper harbor with isolation at Yokohama. Japanese officials, then, wished to replicate as closely as possible the isolation of foreigners that had characterized Deshima and, in the event, Western merchants were happy to comply – even though in so doing they contravened their consuls' wishes.

Though Harris and Rutherford Alcock remained in Kanagawa as a matter of principle, merchants accepted Yokohama as the site of the settlement. The village had the natural advantage of frontage on deep water and a good harbor, and its isolation mattered little to merchants. In fact, it was the American firm of Hall and Company that "immediately backed the merchants' view" and "leased a plot of land on the Yokohama side", which became known as No. 2 Bund. Immediately afterward, the British firms of Jardine, Matheson and Company and Dent and Company, leased land in Yokohama, while Kanagawa remained the residence only of the consuls and a few missionaries.[36] A British resident of Yokohama summed up the dichotomy nicely by saying that "the ministers look to national and permanent interests, the merchants to what was individual and temporary".[37] The Japanese built guard-huts at the end of each bridge leading to the settlement and enclosed the roadways with "sturdy gates which were shut at sunset", but the merchants "cared little whether they were isolated from the natives or not".[38] A broader pattern than even Harris feared was being set, though it was to be of preferred, as much as enforced, Western merchant segregation.

III

In spite of the dangers that Japan held for foreigners, some Americans were attracted there by a "gold rush" every bit as exciting as the one that drew the forty-niners west to California. A decade later, on July 4, 1859, the first Americans landed on shore at Yokohama, took up residence and "formally opened the port to trade". The U.S. Minister to Japan, Townsend Harris, and officers of the U.S.S. *Mississippi* ran the stars and stripes up at precisely noon. Joseph Heco, a participant in a prescient ceremony, related that "we opened champagne, sang the Star Spangled Banner, and drank 'To our prosperity, Long may the Stars and Stripes wave'". The following year, American flags floated over every American residence in Yokohama.[39]

The prosperity to which they drank came to some in the form of the initial product traded in the treaty ports – money. Because of the treaty provision requiring weight-for-weight currency exchange, Japan proved for a lucky few to be the dreamed-of El Dorado. As the Tokugawa period wore on, the Bakufu, with a monopoly on silver coinage, increasingly found it to its advantage to increase the value of silver compared to gold. By the time Townsend Harris negotiated the treaty allowing Americans to reside in Yokohama, the value of silver in Japan stood at 1:5 relative to gold, while in the outside world its value was 1:15. To facilitate foreign trade, the Japanese coined silver ichibus, and foreign merchants soon realized that four ichibus bought one whole cobang of gold, which they could then export and sell outside, immediately trebling their investment. Soon "merchants ceased to bother about such cumbersome items as teas and silk and bought as much gold as they could lay their hands on and exported it as fast as they could find a ship to take it away". For a few "glittering months" in the autumn of 1859, something like a frenzy obtained in Yokohama, with merchants of all nationalities cashing in until the Japanese government realized that its artificially high silver valuation relative to that of the world market was draining the country of gold.[40]

Any foreign merchant bringing in his own currency of Mexican dollars faced the problem of getting it changed into the Japanese ichibu, with which he could then purchase gold cobangs. The treaties stated that the merchants' currency would be exchangeable weight for weight into Japanese silver ichibu, and this meant that $100 Mexican bought 311 ichibu. Merchants then exchanged the ichibu into cobangs, shipped them abroad – usually to the China market – and realized enormous profits. The agency controlling such exchanges was the Japanese customshouse, which merchants felt was slow in responding to their frenzied requests for silver ichibu. Merchants applied to the customshouse officials for "as large a quantity of ichibus as they had the audacity to ask for, sometimes supplementing their applications with additional ones in fictitious names, often ribald and in bad taste".[41]

Francis Hall described the place in the customshouse where the exchanges occurred as "a long room one half of which is occupied by a platform raised a couple of feet from the dirt floor of the remaining half", where a

> half dozen officials are squatted on the mats. Beside them is a block for counting money upon, a pair of scales for weighing, ink box and pens, and a few boxes of coin .... Standing in a group on the earth floor and confronting them are the merchants and merchant clerks, princes and officers on leave from the men of war, sea-captains and adventurers like myself waiting their turn for receiving ichibus for dollars weight for weight.

Because of the incredible demand for exchange, the Japanese authorities "adopted the rule that a *pro rata* distribution should be made on the amount applied for". Hall related that the applicants made a mockery of this system by applying for outlandish amounts, some as large as "millions and tens of millions". Hall stated that there was "a general strife among the applicants to see who should claim the greatest amount" and that "millions, quatrillions and sextillions were small figures". One ship captain, "procuring a roll of Japanese paper at least fifty feet long, inscribed it with a row of figures from one end to the other"; one observer noted that foreigners' "claims were expressed in a long line of figures ... and pressed upon the Japanese in terms bordering at least on menace and insult".[42] Such ludicrous demands led to the establishment of a rule limiting each applicant to requesting $5,000 per day.[43]

This gold rush complicated all business dealings in the early treaty port days. Joseph Heco, an American of Japanese birth, recalled that to begin business with his partner, he needed first to exchange their currency into Japanese money in order to buy goods to fill their empty ship. Heco observed that "The native dealers would not accept foreign dollars at the government rate, and the government mint at Yedo was totally unable to coin sufficient[ly] for foreign exchange. To get our $10,000 changed into Japanese money at the Custom-house would take about two months, as there was a limitation to the daily amount that might be exchanged there". Eager to employ their idle ship, Heco and his partner advertised for freight for Hong Kong while engaging in the tedious task of exchanging their dollars each day up to the amount permitted. The limit on exchange – by this time no more than ten dollars per day – had the inevitable effect of causing traders to make application under false names.[44]

Indeed, Japanese customshouse employees on the jetty at Yokohama were literally "bribed and besieged by clamoring merchants" and at least two American naval officers, en route to San Francisco, "resigned their commissions on the spot, chartered ships and started export firms". In this way, "a few wily early birds among the foreign merchants had time to make their fortunes without so much as filling a warehouse".[45] Those daring to circumvent the customshouse altogether and share their enormous profits found eager accomplices among local Japanese dealers, who "came to the foreign quarters with stores of koban [cobang] concealed in the folds of their garments".[46]

Such practices led Sir Rutherford Alcock, the British Minister to Japan, to refer to Yokohama merchants as "the scum of Europe", while one source stated that "reputable foreign merchants" felt "great indignation" at the activities of the "carpetbagger types" who stooped to such measures.[47] Such moral segregation in the gold trade never occurred. Small companies, such as the one formed on the spot by the two American naval officers, probably made substantial profits in currency exchange in late 1859. Larger profits were available to companies with greater reserves of capital, such as Augustine Heard and Walsh, Hall. Considerable evidence suggests that reputable foreign – including American firms – also attended the savory, if brief, barbecue. In October 1859, at the height of the exchange frenzy, Franklin Field of Augustine Heard and Company wrote to the company's offices in China to relate that:

> The *Carthage* is in … Kobangs plenty! I am itching to get up there [to Yokohama] and have a finger in the pie. Suppose I make you a proposition … charter in Shanghai a really good vessel … put on board Mexican dollars, 50,000 or 75,000 or 100,000 even, send her over here to me, and I will step on board and proceed in her to Kanagawa. With the aid of the Captain, officers and crew, we will manage to get the money changed and then invest in Kobangs, copper and silk. I will take, for my valuable services, one fourth part of the profits. You might send over someone to relieve me and to remain permanently – I should expect to make a small fortune, and there would be no necessity of returning here. What do you say? Pray, if you do anything, do it chop-chop and secretly, dollars are the thing – no goods.

Later, Field apologized for his cupidity. "Excuse my proposition on the first page", he wrote, "I get excited when a chance to make money shows itself".[48] By January, 1860, Field reported to Shanghai with disappointment that the "prospect for business here is not so favorable as we had hoped to find it … the Cobang branch of trade is officially stopped, government having called in the coin at prices that prevent their sale for export … they can only be obtained in small quantities from the custom house – 10,000 are daily divided amongst the foreign community".[49]

There is no doubt that Heard and Company was involved in the type of currency speculation Field proposed. Moreover, Heard took full advantage of the position of Eben M. Dorr – its agent in Yokohama – as U.S. consul.[50] Consuls, as official representatives of their country's governments, could use their influence to get larger amounts of currency exchanged. Dorr noted that his "office capacity gives me plenty of Credit … in time I shall be able to do much". Earlier, Dorr had written a private and confidential letter to Albert Heard at Shanghai in which he described the nature of an agreement he had made with Heard and some of the problems he encountered:

> My agreement with your brother was that your house shall furnish funds as required. I have control and investment here and you in China and to divide profits and all based upon my knowledge and experience here, and who was the first civilian in this port. Our agreement went so far as to preclude my doing anything with or for anyone else …. I know my dear friend you would go almost crazy if you had half to contend with that I do in this place – new port as it is and slow and troublesome as the government and officials are and annoyed as I am by constant growls by Americans who cannot at one fell swoop swallow all Japan and make the Japanese gov't give them all they want and not allow them to smuggle.

Dorr concluded by pleading with Heard, "Don't keep me here short of funds – what is 10 or 20 or 50,000 dollars to your house with such margins as I can and do show here?"[51]

Later, Dorr took pains to remind Heard of the advantages drawn from his official position in Kanagawa. "If I was not consul", he wrote, "I could not get this $20,000 changed into itzubu [ichibus] ... in 25 days, say nothing about purchasing cargo. It takes 2 or 3 hours to get $1,000 exchanged and when others [merchants without official connections] are now getting $50 per day per man I am getting $1,000 ... every day, ship or no ship, you see, I could get ahead and buy kobans [cobangs] or anything else", this in spite of being "quite knocked up with the bite of a centipede on [his] ankle" that had kept him in bed for six days.[52] Throughout late 1859, Dorr constantly asked Heard and Company for money in advance to exchange, but he sometimes failed to pay back entirely such unsecured advances.[53]

Perhaps one reason Heard and Company was somewhat reluctant to give Dorr all of the advances he requested was that the company itself was almost certainly engaged in eliminating one third of the exchange procedure and the difficulty with the customshouse by making its own ichibus. Franklin Field, the Heard representative in Nagasaki, collected examples of every coin minted in Japan, and wrote that "the Itsebus [ichibus] are very rough and I think could be made without difficulty", and T.H. King, captain of a Heard ship in the same port, noted that "the Japanese merchants of this place have large amounts of Mexican dollars which they will readily exchange".[54] This counterfeiting operation, in conjunction with the agreement with Eben Dorr, suggests a vision of business in Japan that was informed by short-range opportunism uncurbed by legal scruple. And all of this was practised best by the most reputable of firms.

Like the American officers who resigned from the navy to take advantage of a profitable opportunity when they saw it, some in the carrying trade to and from Japan sought to cash in on the favorable exchange rate before the Japanese government took corrective action. A Mr Dexter of Appleman and Company, a shipping firm that transported goods from Asian ports to the U.S., wrote from Yokohama in November that "there has been a splendid chance for money making in the past two months – whether I am too late or not is not yet certain ... we have great difficulty getting money changed by [the] government". Disappointed that he had missed the earlier bonanza, he wrote in December that the "present price of gold gives about a 20% profit" but that "the cream of this business is over and I shall continue investing my money while a fair profit remains".

Dexter referred to several Yokohama companies that had made money on the export of gold, especially the British firm of Dent and Company, whose profits "are purported to have been at 3 to 400,000" Mexican dollars. Dexter stated that Dent and Company were large buyers of gold in the halcyon month of October, with one departing steamer containing "30,000 cobangs for them". He mentioned that Jardine, Matheson and Company, another British firm, and the American Walsh, Hall and Company also made money: "I fancy Walsh and Co. the most" among the smaller firms in the port.[55]

Dexter's assumption about Walsh and Company was correct. Though Francis Hall was acquainted with Eben Dorr, it seems unlikely that Dorr, as agent for Heard and Company, would have used his influence with the Japanese customshouse to exchange currency on Hall's behalf. Nevertheless, Hall refers several times to making applications for exchange through regular channels. On November 8, 1859, for example, Hall reported that the customshouse was giving out $50 on each $5,000", and on the 24th, he concluded to "write home for [his] funds". The next day, Hall visited Yokohama again to exchange ichibus, and met there a German Jew who furnished him with an unspecified amount of gold cobangs, and on January 10, 1860, Hall referred again to exchanging currency.[56] One foreign newspaper, looking back more than twenty years later, observed that "The largest and most lucrative part of the business done by foreigners was in the purchase of gold coin; and probably more than one million dollars worth of those coins was exported during that year".[57]

The gold rush frenzy, though brief, attracted numerous opportunists seeking short-term profits. Into the frontier of the treaty ports came all manner of drifter, opportunist and aspiring entrepreneur, "the disorderly elements of Californian adventurers, Portugese [sic] desperadoes, and the moral refuse of European nations".[58] Trade on the China coast had become competitive by the 1850s, and some whose acquisitiveness had not been fully sated there thought of Japan as a destination where profits would be easy. Adventurers from Nagasaki, Shanghai and Hong Kong quickly moved into "every rickety hut, every flimsy godown [warehouse] and every yard of swamp they could afford".[59]

Yokohama by the early 1860s resembled a Wild West boom town, "populated largely by Jacks-of-all-trades, rootless, incurably optimistic men who liked to make up laws to fit their own particular needs as they bowled along from one adventure to the next". Some of these men flocked in from China, others from elsewhere; temporary men who came down the gangplank of "some slow, smutty little cargo boat" hoping for prosperity initially occupied the temporary town. Such aspiring merchants had only to "rent a piece of swampy land, stake a fence round it, build a shack on it and he was equipped for trade".[60]

By 1860, there were 100 foreign merchants of all classes at Yokohama, and one visitor noted that "Foreign residents, whether Europeans or Americans, who come to these eastern lands, are not ordinarily more reckless, overbearing, or oppressive than persons of the same class in their native country", but that Englishmen in Japan would do well to abandon their "East Indian pride of conquest and arrogant assumption of superiority of race" while in Japan.[61] Two years later, another visitor recalled that Yokohama

> is the most curious motley imaginable. English, French, Dutch, German, Italian, Americans, Greeks, Chinese, niggers all live together, the most incongruous elements that ever made up a "happy family". They are a rather rough lot in some cases, but good fellows enough in their way, and men who have traveled so much generally besides knowing how to take

care of themselves, are helpful and kind to others in a way quite unknown in Europe.

By 1867, however, his attitude had changed drastically, writing that "I thoroughly detest Yokohama ... You never were brought into contact with such a set of snobs and ruffians as the majority ... who infest these Eastern trading places, and they give themselves the airs of Princes of the blood".[62]

The experience of Joseph Heco illustrates early business arrangements. In September 1859, a certain "Mr K" approached Heco and advised him to leave the employ of the American consulate to enter into business with him. "K", hoping to capitalize on Heco's knowledge of Japanese, promised to furnish the capital for the business, and all the fittings for the house and office. He claimed to know "many wealthy men in San Francisco" who would support the business, and asked Heco only for his services in order to share the profits with him equally. "K" went to San Francisco and returned to Yokohama in March 1860 with a ship and $10,000 in "treasure", both to be consigned to the new firm. He also brought the furniture and fittings for the house and office. But Heco complained that "beyond this there was nothing, and inasmuch as the $10,000 had to be invested in merchandise to be sent back on the barque, there was no great abundance of the wherewithal to conduct our operations". When "K" landed, "he had not a dollar to his name", and Heco "had to advance the sum necessary for preparing the office, for rent, and generally for carrying on the business".[63]

Some businessmen attracted to the ports were ne'er-do-wells who saw the Far East as a new frontier, or perhaps simply a place beyond the reach of Western law. One such man, Charles Sloos, lived in Kobe and was successful enough in business to accumulate $5,000 Mexican by 1873. In January 1874, Sloos assaulted Lawrence Cook, a British subject, over a business dispute. In September of the same year, Sloos assaulted two women, one of them the wife of a Japanese named Hirabayashi, "without any reason whatsoever", and Sloos was found guilty and given a $125 fine. At about the same time, Sloos was accused of involvement in the mysterious abortion of a Japanese child. He denied any complicity and stated that the woman had procured her own abortion by taking "medicine called shitakki mixed in saki and other medicine".[64]

Early the following year, an American citizen named Baldwin entrusted a sum of money to Sloos to carry back to the U.S. for Baldwin's brother, but Sloos failed to deliver the money, prompting Baldwin to call him a "bare-faced and impudent swindler" and bring Sloos again before the U.S. consular court. Sloos continued in business in Kobe, but was unable to avoid further clashes with the law. In 1876, Japanese police – one of whom he struck and "kicked in the head" – apprehended Sloos in Osaka, where, while extremely drunk, he was "chasing Japanese". Though he was "ashamed" of what he had done, U.S. authorities transported Sloos back to Kobe in handcuffs, imprisoned him for ninety days and fined him fifty dollars, which by then he could not pay. After serving his time, he was released and, one assumes, moved out of the ports or faded into oblivion.[65]

Another such man was George Lake of Massachusetts. Lake established a general trading business in Nagasaki soon after the Harris treaty opened Japan to foreign residence. In 1865, Lake was fined for pulling a gun on a Japanese policeman who tried to remove a Japanese servant from his home. Lake, "obviously possessed of a volatile temper", continued his lawless ways, causing the Japanese government to deport him in 1871. His younger brother Edward continued the family business uninterrupted until 1893, when Lake returned to Nagasaki to try to take control of the business, attacked his brother and "was charged with assault". Unable to secure protection from the U.S. consulate, Lake was once again deported. He then moved to Korea, where he was murdered in 1898.[66]

In spite of the easy opportunities associated with the gold rush, the early years were hard on Western entrepreneurs seeking a toehold in Asian treaty ports. In China, only fifty-five of 111 firms listed in 1865 in Hong Kong and forty-eight of ninety in Shanghai survived until 1870. Mortality was even higher in Yokohama, where only nineteen of fifty-one firms survived during the same period.[67] Doubtless many of the firms that did not survive were sole proprietorships or partnerships which were undercapitalized and unprepared to weather the vicissitudes of the early business environment in Japan.

IV

Soon after Yokohama opened, George Smith observed that relations between the Japanese and the rest of the world would improve when

> the true representatives of the Christian civilization of Britain and the United States shall have flocked to this land in greater number, and when the disorderly elements of the California adventurers, Portuguese desperadoes, runaway sailors, piratical outlaws and the moral refuse of European nations who hasten as first settlers to any new region and infest with their lawlessness and violence the aboriginal races of the East shall be swept away by the strong arm of the law.[68]

If the gold rush and the treaty ports' Wild West flavor attracted "adventurers and desperadoes" such as "K", Sloos and Lake, other, more substantial businessmen settled in the ports, men who for forty years made up the core of the Western mercantile community in Japan.

After the "gold rush" Westerners interested in longer-term operations set about making more permanent arrangements for their businesses. Although the foreign settlements in Japan began at different times, certain general features were common to all. The Japanese government was responsible for the expense and preparation of the settlement sites; no Japanese could occupy land inside the settlements; the administration of the settlements was separate from native Japanese municipalities; all land rented in perpetuity by foreigners was subject only to a fixed ground rent per tsubo (about 6 feet square) which did not change, even when the land was improved; and the Japanese government eventually bought all the land in the foreign concessions, though some was initially owned by individual Japanese.

The Yokohama Land Regulations of 1860 specified that bona fide residents wishing to lease land simply apply to their consul, who would then grant requests on a first-come-first-served basis. Leasers were then required to erect buildings on their property valued at $150 Mexican per 100 *tsubo* if water lots, fifty dollars if on rear lots. Notwithstanding these stipulations, some renters engaged in land speculation, and some lots increased from no value to four or five thousand dollars by 1864.[69] When the original land was auctioned off in Yokohama, the selling price was fixed not with reference to the costs incurred by the Japanese government in preparing it, but with regard to the selling value of the land in the neighborhood. The Japanese expected the competition for lots to be high, and expected to recover all or most of their costs. But the foreigners combined beforehand and agreed on who would buy what lots at what price, and got them very cheaply. They demanded exemption from municipal expenses at that time.[70]

When that portion of Yokohama available to Japanese was first opened, the government at Yedo made land available tax-free for three years.[71] Though some public services were to be provided by the Japanese, Article IX of the regulations stated that the consuls would somehow tax foreign residents to pay for the lighting and maintenance of the streets and a police force to ensure order, especially over unruly Western sailors. By 1864, squabbles over municipal responsibilities led the foreign community to take over maintenance of the settlement without help from the Japanese, and all agreed that 20 percent of their land rent be paid into a municipal fund to be used for public services. For three years Yokohama administered its own affairs, but the Municipal Council, pinched for revenue, was forced to levy additional taxes on foreign residents to provide basic services.

Some residents refused to pay and complained before the consuls, who decided that the council had no such power. Without adequate finances, the foreign community turned municipal control over to the Japanese again in December 1867. At least the appearance of foreign participation continued briefly in the form of a Municipal Office, whose director acted as a liaison between the foreign community and the Japanese. Later, Japanese officials administered the foreign settlement directly. On the other hand, Kobe residents voluntarily submitted to more taxation so as to keep control of their own municipal concerns. The monies collected were administered by foreign consuls and a standing committee of the foreign community in tandem with local Japanese authorities, resulting in relatively harmonious relations until 1899.[72]

Representatives of the foreign business community in all three ports quickly banded together in chambers of commerce, which usually met twice a year. Multi-national in character, the chambers promoted the business interests of the foreign community, dealt with the business minutiae of treaty port life, and published trade statistics, market reports. Sub-committees gathered economic data and dealt with questions such as the rates Western merchants were charged for storage in Japanese godowns,[73] the inconvenience of working around Japanese holidays, the availability and expense of Japanese boatmen and coolie labor, the condition of the native currency, and proposals to the consuls to facilitate trade.[74]

How many foreigners lived in the treaty ports? A primary characteristic of the early foreign settlements was transience, and any examination of the consular correspondence, the "arrival and departures" sections of any of the treaty port newspapers or perusal of the conflicting figures found in primary and secondary sources quickly reveals the difficulties of ascertaining with any precision how many foreigners lived in the ports at any given time. The first problem concerns the definition of the term "foreigner". Sometimes the substantial Chinese community was included; more often – particularly in sources emanating from the Western port residents – it was not.

A second problem concerned the geographical definition of the treaty ports. A glance at the maps of the foreign concessions themselves shows them to be clearly defined areas, neatly divided into small plots of land. Here were the signature edifices of the treaty ports: the bund, the consulates, the customs house, the godowns, hotels and saloons. Some businessmen lived in the foreign concession in the same houses with their offices. More frequently, businessmen lived outside the foreign concession itself, in more attractive adjacent areas such as the Bluff in Yokohama or Kitano-cho in Kobe beyond the foreign concession area. Moreover, as years passed, and more and more foreigners moved away from the ports themselves under one pretext or another, it became difficult for an increasingly undermanned and harried American consular staff to count its nationals in a given consular district. In Kobe, for example, the consulate was responsible for a wide area including not only the foreign settlements at Hyogo and Osaka, but all the way inland to Kyoto. Through this large area passed hundreds of Americans: seamen, storekeepers, shopowners, merchants, employees of the Japanese government, missionaries and travelers. Some stayed for long periods of time, others only briefly.

A third problem concerns the British and French garrisons stationed at Yokohama. Foreign troops first came to Yokohama in 1864, and the number was largest until 1869, when there were never fewer than 500 soldiers at any one time, but some remained until all were withdrawn in 1875. These soldiers were never included in contemporary estimates of the foreign population. Neither is it possible to calculate the number of sailors of all nationalities who made the ports their temporary homes. Some 10,000 sailors passed through Yokohama on British ships alone each year, while Kobe and Nagasaki hosted between 4,000 and 6,000 each. Sir Harry Parkes, the British Minister to Japan, estimated that, by 1879, 15,000 seamen per year passed throgh Yokohama.[75] Shinya Sugiyama, relying on the British consular reports, arrived at one set of figures detailing the foreign population throughout the treaty port years (see Table 1).[76]

As on the China coast, the majority of Western residents was British. At Yokohama in 1861 there were fifty-five British residents out of 126; Nagasaki

Table 1 Foreign population throughout the treaty port years (after Shinya Sugiyama)

Year	U.S.	British	French	German	Other	European (total)	Chinese	Grand total
1870	229	782	158	164	253	1,586	n.a.	–
1875	353	1,282	254	279	415	2,583	n.a.	–
1880	407	1,057	184	309	402	2,359	3,584	5,943
1885	447	1,065	201	269	316	2,298	3,876	6,174
1890	495	1,236	236	333	507	2,807	4,373	7,180
1895	584	1,424	252	347	603	3,227	3,373	6,598

in 1870 had eighty out of 208; Kobe in 1886 had 228 out of 390. Yokohama's foreign population in 1893 comprised 869 British, 369 Americans, with French and Germans only slightly more than American total. In the same year Tokyo residents totaled 761, of whom 224 were British and 196 American, some of them missionaries. All contemporary estimates of the numbers of foreigners in Japan agree that Americans were the second most numerous group, with the French and Germans third and fourth.[77] According to Sugiyama's figures, in 1870 Americans accounted for 14.4 percent of the Western population, a percentage that rose to 18.1 percent in 1895.

Yokohama was the largest of the three foreign settlements throughout the treaty port period. Its foreign population gradually increased from about 1,200 in 1870 to around 5,000 by the 1890s, Western residents numbering about 2,400. The port at Kobe, the next largest, grew from 150 in September 1868 to about 1,000 by 1885 to almost 2,000 by the mid-1890s, with the Chinese and Western segments roughly equal until the exodus of Chinese resulting from the Sino-Japanese war in 1895. Nagasaki was poorly located for trade across the Pacific, and its foreign population peaked in about 1880 between 800 and 1,000, only about 300 of whom were Westerners.[78]

Establishing any specific occupational breakdown of the American population presents great difficulties. State Department regulations required American consuls to send a copy of a register of American citizens residing in their districts to the Department of State at the end of each year, and the reports from Kobe listed the individual's name, occupation, place and date of birth, and the date of arrival in the consular district. Though not available for every year, these returns are valuable as one of two sources providing systematic lists of any kind. Taking 1890 as a year of Kobe's maturity as a port of foreign residence, we find 203 Americans listed. Eighty-five were adult missionaries with fifty-six children. Of the remaining sixty-two, thirty-three were a varied group: travelers, a physician, a stevedore, electrician, mariner, chaplain, engineer, several teachers and the Americans employed by their consulate in some official capacity. The remaining twenty-nine were engaged in business: twenty-seven as merchants, clerks, tea buyers or tasters, one accountant and one auctioneer. Of the adult population of 147 then, about 20 percent were engaged in trade,[79] a figure clearly impossible considering the actual number of American firms in the ports. Table 2, also taken from British consular reports, illustrates the total number of foreign firms in the treaty ports by nationality.[80]

The definition here of the term "firm" is broad enough to include operations of any description – including trading firms as well as small shops and insurance companies – but it is nevertheless clear that the larger American trading companies, like their British competitors, employed as many as half a dozen men or more. By 1893, The China and Japan Trading Company employed seven men in Yokohama, seven in Kobe and four in Nagasaki; Walsh, Hall and Company employed five in Yokohama and two in Kobe; Smith, Baker and Company employed seven in Yokohama and three in Kobe.[81]

Any totals based on consular returns are seriously misleading for several reasons. It is certainly true that many merchants found advantage in officially registering with their consulates. When the frequent disputes – particularly involving the larger firms – with Japanese and other countries' nationals occurred, consuls required some proof of American citizenship before intervening on their behalf; in some cases consuls declined to intervene in cases where individuals could not prove American citizenship. Common sense dictated registration with the consulate as a basic business precaution. Yet in numerous cases, individuals listed in the *Chronicle and Directory for China, Japan and the Philippines* – a list of business firms and individuals throughout Asia – do not appear on the consular registration lists, suggesting that the legal concern was addressed by the registration of the firm principal or partner alone.[82] Second, by a State Department law enacted in 1873, Americans were not required to register at their consulate while abroad.[83] Third, it is reasonable to assume that those employed by the larger firms in middling positions or shopkeepers selling to ships and the general foreign population would have little reason to register; their transactions with the Japanese were limited and they rarely sued in consular court. Probably many American merchants simply considered their nationality self-evident and their protection secure under corporate or customary procedures so that yearly registering at the consulate was superfluous. Fourth, doubtless the

Table 2 Total number of foreign firms in the treaty ports, by nationality

Year	U.S.	British	French	German	Other	European (total)	Chinese	Grand total
1870	33	101	39	45	38	256	n.a.	–
1875	30	109	42	43	33	257	n.a.	–
1880	40	108	37	41	32	258	102	360
1885	46	91	18	33	22	210	139	349
1890	53	113	30	36	27	259	305	564
1895	73	148	38	57	39	355	33	388

registration lists reflect a larger percentage of missionaries – who often applied for passports for movement inland and needed to be registered with the consulates for that purpose – than merchants, who had little interest in moving beyond the treaty limits.

Because of these difficulties, it is impossible to know with any real precision how many Americans worked in a mercantile capacity at any time in the ports. Some evidence suggests that no one knew precisely how many Americans lived where at any given time. Once, the American consul at Kobe, responding to a request from the Japanese government for the number of U.S. citizens at the port, wrote to the local foreign chamber of commerce asking for a list of Americans residing outside the foreign concession. The chamber wrote back saying it did not know and suggested that the consul check with the Japanese government, which got its figures from repeated requests to the American consulates.[84] The foreign communities in the open cities of Osaka and Tokyo highlighted the problem of counting individuals outside the foreign concessions. In 1881, the American consulate listed 357 Americans as residents of either Yokohama or Tokyo.[85]

The sheer number of American firms in the ports at any given time suggests that the consular registrations grossly underestimate the number of Americans engaged in trade of one kind or another, as well as the total Western population in the ports. Table 3, calculated from the *Chronicle and Directory*, illustrates the numbers of firms and employees clearly identifiable as American.[86] Since by 1895 there were seventy-three American firms in Japan, there remained approximately fifty-nine U.S. firms whose identities cannot be determined. If each of these firms employed three men – a conservative estimate – the minimum number of American merchants was 260 by the mid-1890s.

The first decade of Yokohama's existence saw the sheer adventurer and the inadequately financed weeded out, leaving a substantial corps of firms stable and profitable enough to survive well into the 1890s. A survey of eight of the most prominent American firms in the ports suggests some significant patterns. Six of the companies remained in business for twenty-four years or longer, while the other two operated for at least twelve years. The firms' size remained fairly uniform. In 1870, they employed an average of 5.7 employees; by 1881 6.1, and by 1893 7.2. Smith, Baker and Company retained three key employees for a minimum of twenty-four years, and each of the other five longest-lived firms retained at least one key man for as long. Moreover, all six firms in this group retained an average of slightly more than three employees for at least twelve years, with two

Table 3 Numbers of firms and employees clearly identifiable as American

Year	Number of American firms	Number of employees
1870	11	71
1881	13	62
1893	14	83

companies retaining five. The British firm of Jardine, Matheson and Company employed the largest number, fifteen by 1893.[87]

Frazar and Company provides an example of extreme longevity. Everett Frazar, twenty-one year-old son of a New England sea captain, persuaded two of his cousins to combine resources, bought a 300-ton vessel, loaded it with "Yankee notions" and sailed for China. Upon arrival in Shanghai, Everett sold his ship interests to his cousins, went ashore and founded the firm in 1856. Two years later Frazar joined Perry's expedition to Japan, and returned in 1867 to found Frazar and Company, Yokohama, a concern that operated continuously from then until 1941. Everett returned to the U.S. to live in New York in 1872, and his son, Everett Welles Frazar, inherited the company when his father died in 1901.[88]

Other American firms expired earlier. Warren Tillson and Company operated in Kobe from at least 1873 through the mid-1880s.[89] Augustine Heard and Company, the great trading firm from the China coast, opened its operations in Japan in 1859, but was out of business by the mid-1870s. Some companies, such as J. Bush and Company, J.C. Fraser and Company and Fischer and Company, maintained offices or stores for a decade or less and disappeared without a trace, leaving only scattered communication with their consuls and a short listing in the port directory to confirm their relatively brief existence. The American Trading Company and McGlew and Company are typical of firms appearing in the later 1880s and early 1890s.[90] Death of the proprietor or repatriation to the U.S. partially accounts for the high rate of company mortality. One small merchant of this sort was Henry Bonham, a native of Tennessee, who died intestate in Yokohama on December 27, 1870. His estate, a portion of which was kerosene oil, was appraised at $8,436 Mexican. Apparently his partner, Morris Hoeflict, decided to close the business after Bonham's death; the records contain no further reference to either man.[91]

The largest business firms had been called "hongs" in the Chinese treaty ports, and the name described them in Japan as well, the term applying to all "important foreign business houses in the Far East".[92] Western trading companies comprised several men authorized to conduct business on the company's behalf, an office and storefront, a series of warehouses for storing goods purchased outright or accepted on consignment, occasionally machinery or equipment necessary to do business, and a fluctuating staff of Japanese or Chinese employees who were hired for many of the day-to-day transactions of the firms. These large business establishments built and maintained the most imposing buildings in the foreign quarters. In some cases, the firms had a central office in the U.S. or in Europe to which they reported.

The company compounds were extensive affairs. Schultze, Reis and Company occupied lot number 8 in Kobe on the bund, an area 225 feet by 95 feet. On it was a house measuring 60 feet by 67 feet on the first floor of which was a general office, private office, "tea room", banto's[93] office, dining room, parlor, pantry, and wine and china closets, fronted by a verandah. Upstairs were four bedrooms, each 20 feet by 28 feet, and four bathrooms. To the east of the house was an area with trees and shrubs, and servants' quarters with a brick kitchen attached nearly abutted the house on the north. Sixty-five feet away was a stone godown measuring 90 feet by 42 feet, and across from this structure lay the tea-firing godown, some 33 feet by 90 feet. Inside the tea-firing godown was space for 112 pans and a packing room. Augustine Heard and Company's compound on lot 6 was similar.[94]

The amount of land controlled by given companies depended on the nature of their business. One of the largest firms operating in Kobe was the American J.D. Carroll and Company. Carroll controlled leases in the foreign concession extensive enough to permit sub-letting to other concerns – the *Hiogo News* and the Globe Hotel occupied two of its buildings. He also operated a ship chandlery and general store in Hyogo to service merchant and naval vessels, and sold miscellaneous merchandise at a general store in addition to importing and exporting goods. Walsh, Hall and Company established its office in Hyogo in September 1868, and the partnership admitted Arthur O. Gay to assist its operations in Hyogo. Like many foreign companies doing business in the treaty ports, Walsh's interests were varied. In May 1869, he was admitted as a partner in the *Hiogo News*, an English language newspaper.[95]

Despite their limitations, the citizen registries nevertheless hint at some of the basic demographic features of the American community in the ports. The 1890 Kobe registry – with its sample of twenty-nine merchants – reveals that merchants' average age was forty, and that the average individual had resided in Kobe for 5.7 years. Sixteen of these men lived in Kobe for five years or longer and seven resided there ten years or longer, with J.D. Carroll and J. Walsh having been there twenty-two years, since the opening of the port.[96] Applying the general logic of the Kobe registries to Yokohama, it seems clear that there was a core of "old hands" which provided continuity for the American community.

V

When Yokohama opened to foreign commerce, Japanese merchants appeared there from all over the country eager to do business. "Few were foreign traders in any real sense, however; they merely sold indigenous products – chiefly raw silk – to foreign firms in the open ports, and in turn bought foreign goods for resale either to the government or public".[97] Although considerable internal trade characterized Japan's traditional economy, Japanese merchants had little experience with Western markets at the beginning of the treaty port era, giving more stable Western firms a tremendous advantage: near total monopolization of the import and export trades. Though the techniques of foreign trade and commercial information were not difficult to acquire, most Japanese foreign trade remained in Western hands into the 1890s because Japan lacked "the power to win and hold the confidence of suppliers and customers – a power that a newcomer only gradually acquires". Foreign firms enjoyed "for a long period a goodwill not shared by their Japanese competitors".[98]

Another reason for foreign control of Japanese trade was Japan's lack of shipping. One historian of Japan's economic development observed that:

> In 1880, when Japan conducted only 22% of its foreign trade with Asia, as much as 54.5% was with Europe and 22.8% was with North America. But in the 1880s the outer limit of Japanese shipping capacity was still within Asia. Japanese ships could not go where most of Japan's trade went. This was the main reason why the country's foreign trade, the basis for any overseas shipping, was still mainly in the hands of foreign merchant houses and why the transport of commodities remained in control of the powerful foreign shipping companies with close connections to the trading houses.[99]

With nearly complete control of Japan's direct trading, proprietors of lasting companies settled into patterns of trade that remained relatively unchanged until the 1890s. The coming of the telegraph, the opening of the Suez canal, and the establishment of steam lines permanently changed the business tone of the treaty ports. Faster communications meant more competition from newly-arrived merchants who, if not prepared to move beyond the treaty ports, at least intended to stay longer than many who had been disappointed in the autumn of 1859.

The Bakufu debased its gold coins in early 1860, which largely corrected the scramble for currency, and foreign merchants turned their attention to handling more traditional commodities. Japan's foreign trade grew enormously thereafter. The tonnage of exports and imports increased from 566,000 tons in 1873 to 1,654,000 in 1890 to 3,608,000 tons in 1899, an increase of some 537 percent, but the large number of foreign companies, excluding Chinese, in the ports – 256 in 1870 and 355 in 1895 – competing to handle this trade tended to keep profits down.[100]

The Pacific Mail Steamship Company began scheduled service across the Pacific, from San Francisco to Hong Kong via Japan, in 1867. Four wooden paddle-wheeled steamers supplemented by sails – "the largest oceangoing side-wheelers ever built" – began carrying passengers and freight, though their design was obsolete even as they came new out of the shipyards. More modern designs incorporated the far more efficient screw propeller.[101] A typical cargo bound for eastern ports from America's west coast would have been "agricultural machinery, carriages, furniture, flour, fruits, butter, patent medicines, and Mexican silver".[102] The nature of the East Asian market prevented the export of more industrial goods, and Japan's "predominant exports were tea, silk thread, marine products, rice, coal, copper and miscellaneous handicraft goods such as ceramics". Heading this list in importance was silk, by the early 1890s accounting for more than 40 percent of the total.[103]

Assisted by crop failures in Europe until the 1870s, the Japanese silk industry grew rapidly until by the turn of the century her silk production outstripped that of all of Western Europe combined. Rice exports were significant, but were characterized by violent fluctuations in amounts sent abroad. A broad and somewhat amorphous category of exports was curios, which included Japanese artwork, pottery, porcelain, lacquerware and wood and ivory carvings. Paper exports grew substantially from the 1860s onward. Japan also exported marine products to China, Hong Kong and Korea.[104] Foreign trading firms handled all these products on a commission basis, or sometimes bought products for export on their own behalf.[105]

One commodity which affected life in the treaty ports far beyond its simple export value was tea.[106] The districts of Mie, Aichi and Shizuoka sent their tea to Yokohama for export, and the number of their Japanese agents handling shipments grew until by the mid-1870s they combined to form companies such as Seiru Company and Seikon Company. Tokyo wholesalers also shipped tea to Yokohama's foreign firms from the provinces of Yamashiro, Ise, Omi, Shimosa, Totomi, Suruga and others. By 1885, 109 wholesalers were selling tea to Yokohama firms, and the American firms of Smith, Baker and Company, Fraser, Farley and Company, the China and Japan Trading Company and Walsh, Hall and Company were purchasing a substantial percentage of tea for export from Japan.[107]

Though the best tea remained in Japan, Western merchants were generally happy with the quality of Japanese tea wholesalers made available for export.[108] Unlike Chinese tea, however, which arrived in Chinese treaty ports packed, cured and ready for shipment, the Japanese variety had been fired only once and required refiring to refine it and remove moisture which could damage it during transportation across long distances. Consequently, Western tea exporters built tea-firing establishments in the ports (see Figures 3 and 4, page 42). Already by 1860, two Western firms were operating such establishments, and, after the opening of Kobe in 1868, when Western merchants obtained access to more of the tea-producing regions of central Japan, the number of tea-firing operations in the ports grew dramatically. By 1872, there were eleven in Kobe, six in Nagasaki and fifteen in Yokohama; by the late 1880s, two of the thirteen firms with refiring facilities in Kobe and eleven of twenty-eight in Yokohama were American.[109]

Imports to Japan included kerosene, textile goods, especially wool and cotton, which was spurred by the spread of Western fashion, metal manufactures and foodstuffs. Japan depended on foreign sources of supply for almost all its metal items – bridge and railway construction material as well as locomotives and other kinds of machinery. Petroleum imports were considerable, for heating and lighting as well as for use in crop preservation. Foodstuffs not produced in Japan included sugar, beans, peas and flour, while rice was also heavily imported in bad harvest years.[110] The U.S. trade balance with Japan until the 1890s was unfavorable. The value of U.S.-purchased silk and tea far outweighed the kerosene oil, machinery, leather and clocks purchased by Japan. Raw silk exports to the U.S. increased after the duty was removed in 1865, and exports to the U.S increased from an annual average of just 328 bales in 1873 to an average of 23,251 bales in 1893. Of total exports to the U.S. of ¥13,000,000 in 1884, green tea and raw silk accounted for 90 percent of the total.[111]

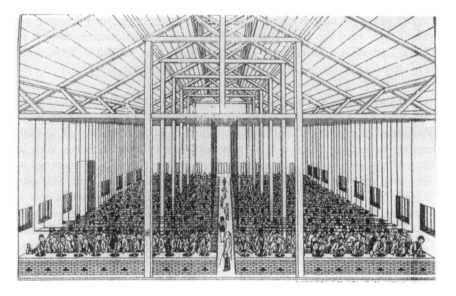

Figure 3 A foreign tea-firing godown, c. 1884
Source: Henry Gribble, "The Preparation of Japan Tea", *Transactions of the Asiatic Society of Japan*, 12 (1883–84).

Figure 4 Roping and finishing, c. 1884
Source: Henry Gribble, "The Preparation of Japan Tea", *Transactions of the Asiatic Society of Japan*, 12 (1883–84).

Temporary interludes of depression punctuated the general trend toward expanding trade. Though some businesses ceased operation because of death or repatriation, others failed or suffered periods of decline because of the vicissitudes of the market. The first decade of trading in the ports was characterized by demand comfortably exceeding supply abroad and a slower business atmosphere before the advent of the telegraph and faster, more efficient transportation. Especially because of the depression of the 1870s, merchants were subject to fluctuations on the world market in the value of their primary items of export. In 1876, the committee managing the temperance hall in Yokohama hesitated to ask the foreign community for money because "trade ha[d] been cruelly unremunerative" after "two or three years of commercial depression and disaster".[112]

Prices of some of the major export commodities handled by foreigners showed a tendency toward decline over time. From the mid-1870s, tea prices fell due to overproduction in Japan, "hurried and careless preparation", and competition in the major U.S. market from Formosan tea. One expert on Japanese tea graphically illustrated the decline in tea prices: the "choice" grade declined from about forty dollars in 1867 to about thirty-two dollars per picul (133 lbs) in 1883, and the price of "good medium" and "common" grades fell proportionately.[113]

Silk exports were not immune to the downward trend in prices. Initially, the appearance of silkworm disease in Europe stimulated Japanese raw silk production. As a consequence, exports from Japan boomed, with silkworm eggs and raw silk comprising about two thirds of exports in 1868. The recovery of the French silk industry led to a decline in Japan by the 1870s, and, though the opening of the Suez canal meant that Japanese silk could compete in the European market, prices tended to fall.[114] One contemporary attributed the silk trade depression to production outstripping consumption, and warned that "the foreign merchant *unless he be very prudent* would secure little from his venture". The Yokohama chamber of commerce reported that the overall value of imports and exports combined dropped more than 4 percent in 1883. Tea exports remained the same in volume but the price declined and there was a worrisome drop in the prime American market; the season was "one of disappointment".[115]

Complaints about temporary periods of decline notwithstanding, Western merchants were more than compensated in the long run by handling ever-increasing amounts of trade. The Yokohama chamber of commerce report for 1887, for example, noted that imports increased by $15,340,000 and exports by $3,143,000 over the previous year.[116] In a revealing statement in 1887, one Western teaman said that while tea exports were not robust, they were "quite sufficient to go round even".[117] Perhaps earlier dreams of Japan as El Dorado had been disappointed, but trade protected by the unequal treaties proved adequate to keep Western trading houses in business and generally prosperous, and supported a society whose structure and insularity addressed the Western need for security.

Indeed trade, until the 1890s, was a gentleman's activity. Given sufficient profits to maintain the pleasing society of the treaty ports, Western merchants were content to limit the rhetoric, volume and variety of their complaints. More complex justifications for their course appeared in their reaction to the most visible manifestation of growing Japanese confidence and power – the proposed treaty revision.

VI

By the 1890s, patterns of trade were changing, and the agency house system came under attack from the twin forces of deep changes in the Japanese economy and aggressive Japanese attempts to gain control of foreign trade. The Japanese economy began to show signs of the shift toward a dual economy, one with a small but significant modern sector, as early as the 1880s. Japanese officials and individual entrepreneurs both realized that until Japan took control of her own foreign trade, American and other foreign merchants could control Japan's foreign commerce. Until the Japanese found a way to do this, "Japanese companies merely accepted orders from resident Westerners, collected export good from local producers, and delivered them to the warehouses of the foreign merchants or received imported products from the Westerners for local distribution".[118] Table 4 demonstrates the magnitude of the growth in Japan's foreign trade in the period 1873–99.[119]

Not only did the volume of Japan's overseas trade increase dramatically, but its character changed. The rapid shift toward an industrial economy is clear in figures representing the value of Japan's export of textile manufactures, which, together with raw silk exports, accounted for over half of its exports by the end of the century (see Table 5).[120] Straw plaits, straw braids, floor matting and camphor exports became significant in the two decades before 1900. Coal exports increased more

Table 4 Growth in Japan's foreign trade, 1873–99

Year	Value (millions of yen)	Tonnage (thousands of tons)
1873	53	566
1880	70	691
1890	149	1,654
1899	434	3,608
Percent increase	719%	537%

Table 5 Value of Japan's export of textile manufactures

Year	Cotton yarn	Silk fabrics	Cotton fabrics
1890	¥2,000	¥3,818,000	¥173,000
1900	¥20,589,000	¥22,000,000	¥5,723,000

than eleven-fold from 1880 to 1900, and copper exports increased ten-fold in the 1880s.[121]

The last decade of the century saw Japan begin gradually to correct its earlier lack of shipping to handle a larger share of the new trade. As Japanese industry grew, trade closer to home increased. By 1910, nearly 45 percent of Japan's trade was with Asia, and only about 30 percent with Europe, while North America's share remained about the same; the "growing proximity of its major trading partners enabled Japan to take a larger role in the transport of its imports and exports".[122]

By the early 1870s, Japan began exporting directly, and on some occasions it bought "stocks of tea and rice" for sale abroad. In 1876, the Japanese company Mitsui Bussan Kaisha was founded and soon began to secure a share of raw silk exports, and the same year Japanese merchants showed products at an international exhibition in Philadelphia. In 1885, thirty Japanese exhibitors attended an international exposition in New Orleans and received first class medals. In the late 1870s, the Japanese government initiated efforts to gain control of the tea trade, sponsoring four reprocessing companies in the period. The Japanese merchants Saka Saburo and Eda Jisuke started a company with ¥360,000 capital and began exporting tea on consignment to Mitsubishi's New York office. Most of these companies failed because of inexperience or poor management, but they reflected a strong Japanese desire to gain control of their trade. Renewed efforts in the mid- and late-1890s brought considerable success.[123]

Silk was of such crucial importance that it received special emphasis. The Japanese government promoted foreign trade as a means by which to obtain foreign exchange for buying Western equipment, and Okuma Shigenobu "used his political influence to encourage Japanese merchants to engage in foreign ventures". Japanese were also quick to follow up on trade begun by Western merchants. Westerners who initially exported silk fabrics, for example, soon found themselves in competition with the Japanese firm of Horikoshi, which began its own export operations to the U.S.[124]

Profoundly important to Japan's economic development, "the raw silk trade financed no less than 40 percent of Japan's entire imports of foreign machinery and raw materials used domestically" between 1870 and 1930. In addition,

> the silk industry was a training school for Japanese industrialization. Silk and other export commodities gave Japanese entrepreneurs important opportunities for profitable investment, and manufacturing for foreign markets imposed a clear need for the standardization of products and more efficient commercial organization.[125]

Diseases affecting silkworms were controlled by "mandatory inspection of silkworm eggs, standardized production, and eventually the licensing of egg producers. ... Constant scientific experimentation led to the development of better silkworm strains and higher yields ..."[126] Beyond this, different kinds of rural cooperatives in the 1870s and 1880s engaged in "weighing, packing and

shipping of silk to Yokohama", and by the early twentieth century, small producers "joined together in kumi, or unions, to obtain financing from Yokohama
wholesalers".[127]

The business ventures of Ryoichiro Arai provide a notable example of
Japanese direct trade in silk. Settling in New York in the early 1870s, Arai began
calling on silk traders. His first visit to one such trader, William Skinner, introduced Arai to the difficulties he would face:

> Taking [Arai] to the back of his office and pointing to a bundle of silk,
> which on examination revealed pieces of metal ... mixed in to increase
> its weight, he shouted angrily, "See here, I don't want this kind of stuff.
> Young man, you get out!" Dishonest Japanese merchants, exporting
> through foreign traders in Yokohama, had won a bad reputation through
> tricks of this sort.[128]

Arai overcame such distrust with aggressive marketing and by establishing a reputation for unquestionable honesty. In his first business deal with an important
New York merchant named Richardson, Arai took a considerable loss of $2,000
on a sizeable silk shipment in order to gain the trust of his American counterpart.
Arai, working alone from 1875 to 1877, overcame other problems, such as New
York banks refusing to issue him bills of exchange to facilitate transmission of
money back to Japan. Such difficulties were not fully overcome until 1879, when
the Yokohama Specie bank was established and provided "modern financial facilities for Japanese trading abroad".[129]

Arai dealt with further problems, among them the difficulty in diversifying
imports to the U.S. In 1878 he formed a partnership with a Japanese who owned a
wholesale and a retail store. In July of that year Arai received a note from Japan,
informing him of the difficulty in finding articles Americans would buy. It stated,
"in Japan there is not much necessary thing we can export, except raw silk ..."[130]
And even in the silk market, he encountered continuing difficulties. As late as 1879,
"Arai was still only receiving piecemeal information about the Yokohama silk market, since Western traders, who still controlled 95 percent of all exports, continued
to withhold information about marketing transactions elsewhere in the world as well
as the trade journals that included news of the worldwide silk trade".[131]

Arai's persistence resulted in increasing profits, and in 1879 was supported by
the timely activities of Japanese Finance Minister Matsukata, who late that year
used official government sponsorship to promote silk production in support of
fukoku-kyohei:

> The outcome of trade is inseparable from the interests of the nation, and
> it is of greater consequence than the bloodshed and disaster which come
> from wars ... in the war of trade, money should serve as our weapons
> and supplies, and national production must be our generals and soldiers.
> If production is low, we must use to our advantage our military supplies,

scattering silver and gold and using them to start silk industries and increase production.

This appeal resulted in the establishment of the Doshin Kaisha, jointly owned by a number of Japanese silk industrialists, and capitalized at ¥300,000. This organization built a warehouse in Yokohama and separated itself from Western handlers of Japanese silk for export. Arai accepted a position with the Doshin Kaisha, and thus was able to participate in another step in the process by which Japan secured control of its own trade.[132] Japanese efforts toward this goal were handsomely rewarded – by 1888 "Japanese firms handled only about 8 per cent of silk exports, but by 1912, this had increased to over 53 per cent".[133]

Western merchants were loathe to surrender obvious elements of their control to Japanese who made their intent to erode that control increasingly clear, and attached great symbolic value to "supervising" business transactions on their home turf. In 1881 a group of Japanese merchants established an association with headquarters outside Yokohama's foreign concession that sought to control all silk transactions handled by foreign houses. The association required that foreign merchants conduct their business – weighing, inspecting and paying for the silk – at the association building before taking delivery. American merchants, whose silk business was a substantial percentage of their overall trade, considered this process "entirely impracticable", because of the additional work it would entail and because of the limited facilities for weighing and inspecting the silk at the association building. In addition, handling the silk had always been done at their own places of business, ensuring that they were not "swindled" by the Japanese merchants.

So repugnant was the prospect of doing business on the association's terms that the foreign silk merchants met three times and unanimously decided to boycott silk purchases from it. The merchants clearly thought that the damage to their own financial interests justified by the principle at stake – they were convinced that the Japanese government had propped up the association with "a million or more of money".[134] Moreover, the observation that repeated visits to the association's building involved increased labor suggests a certain concern with exerting their control over what *could* be controlled. Accustomed to having the Japanese silk dealers come to their own compounds where their own employees – usually Chinese compradors (see Chapter four) – could inspect and weigh the silk, and where they could hover nearby, merchants were unwilling to accommodate the Japanese, even at the considerable cost a boycott in purchases entailed. Merchants insisted that the transactions take place where their control was more obvious.

As evidence that the Japanese were engaged in the heresy of direct trade by circumventing their establishments, the foreign merchants presented figures in 1881 for one shipment showing that three Japanese merchants exported silk to the U.S. valued at more than fourteen times that of a single American merchant. Such direct trade, ran their argument, was both a "bold attempt to ruin foreign trade in Japan" and a "gross violation of the free and untrammeled right of trade between native producers and foreign merchants".[135] For Western merchants, "free and untrammeled" trade was that given to them to enjoy alone by the treaty port system, and they were eager to protest by the time they noticed that Japan was increasingly in control of its own trade. By 1897, the annual report of the Yokohama Chamber of Commerce noted with dismay that the Imperial Diet had passed a bill providing for the payment of a bounty to all Japanese exporters of raw silk.[136] The merchants' complaint, of course, failed to distinguish between Japan's "foreign trade" in general and their own definition of "foreign trade through the foreign agency houses", a distinction extremely important to the Japanese.

Competition between Western and Japanese merchants over control of silk exports led to the founding of the Yokohama Commercial School. Chafing at the on-going foreign control of silk exports, some Japanese merchants established the Yokohama Chamber of Commerce in 1880 and the Federated Raw Silk Warehouse a year later. Ono Mitsukage, a driving force in the Japanese attempt to "win back Japan's commercial rights" opted to "establish a night school to train qualified trading agents". Though the idea was popular, this first attempt at such a school ended in failure after four months.[137]

Undeterred, Ono continued to promote the idea of the school, and by 1881 he had attracted sufficient support to re-open, this time with the even more far-sighted purpose of teaching "trading practices and provid[ing] professional business education to the children of Yokohama businessmen". Misawa Susumu, its principal for forty years, launched the endeavor with five teachers and four students attending day school and fourteen attending at night, and its curriculum comprised business, English and the Chinese classics. Practical education was the guiding principle, and the school's business courses gave students "first-hand experience in different professions. A customshouse, a post office, a telephone exchange, wholesale transportation firms, a bank, a stock exchange, a currency exchange office, a brokerage, and a retail store were actually set up on campus". Realistic interaction with the Kobe and Osaka business community followed, with students trying out various business roles. By August 1883, students' work in the form of book-keeping and English composition were displayed at the World's Fair in New Orleans.[138]

The closing decade of the century saw Japanese houses handle the largest portion yet of their country's foreign trade and, by 1900, Japanese merchants had wrested control over slightly less than two-fifths of the total.[139] Tables 6 and 7 on p.49 illustrate the pattern of increasing Japanese control and diminishing foreign participation.[140]

Such increases were possible in part through increased control of the coastal carrying trade. By 1875, Mitsubishi was in position to challenge foreign companies, and slashed prices on the Yokohama to Shanghai line by one third and on the domestic route between Yokohama and Kobe by even more. In February, the Pacific Mail Steamship Line offered to sell the Shanghai line. J.G. Walsh, the firm's American agent in Yokohama, wrote to Hirai Yoshimasa of the Foreign Ministry, warning that the Pacific Mail "cannot be expected to give up the fruits of their enterprise without

Table 6 Imports by government, Japanese and foreigners, 1877–1900

Year	By government		By Japanese		By foreigners	
	¥000	%	¥000	%	¥000	%
1877	410	(1)	426	(2)	26,995	(97)
1880	665	(2)	1,939	(5)	35,031	(93)
1885	1,258	(4)	2,345	(8)	25,725	(88)
1890	1,174	(1)	19,522	(24)	61,033	(75)
1895	2,000	(2)	38,829	(30)	88,432	(68)
1900	1,091	(0)	112,737	(39)	173,434	(60)

Table 7 Exports by Japanese and by foreigners, 1877–1900

Year	By Japanese		By foreigners	
	¥000	%	¥000	%
1877	842	(4)	21,689	(96)
1880	4,468	(16)	23,020	(84)
1885	3,394	(10)	31,390	(90)
1890	6,124	(11)	48,768	(89)
1895	26,329	(20)	107,188	(80)
1900	73,382	(37)	124,682	(63)

a struggle, even if their opponents have the support of the Japanese government". He also began the letter claiming that the Pacific Mail "can also afford to lose a good deal of money as the government and people of America would probably sympathize with them, and give them some assistance in their efforts".

Walsh's claim was untrue, as he himself knew. In fact, in the second half of his letter, Walsh came to "abandon the hard line and virtually plead with the Japanese government for a settlement". In March the U.S. Congress abrogated the second Pacific Mail contract, reducing the company's million-dollar annual subsidy to $500,000. Congress attacked the company for using Asian crews and for the shady business practices of its president. In September, 1875, Iwasaki Yataro obtained the consent of Okubo Toshimichi and Okuma Shigenobu to borrow $810,000 to buy the Shanghai line. Finally, the two companies reached terms of sale in October, Iwasaki Yataro, founder of Mitsubishi, securing Okuma and Okubo's consent to borrow the required amount from the Japanese government to purchase the line.[141]

The Japanese government followed up this victory by imposing a modest tax on its citizens travelling by foreign steamers between open ports. The foreign community assumed this to be a protective measure to assist the Mitsubishi Company and help create a monopoly in coastal transportation. While it was technically within the treaty requirements, merchants objected strongly to the violation of the "principle" of government non-interference in commerce.[142]

Even favorable decisions in the Japanese courts sometimes failed to stem the rising tide of Japanese control, and proved little more than "moral" victories. In 1895, a British firm sued a Japanese for losses sustained when the Japanese refused to take delivery of some goods ordered. The British firm won the judgment, involving "tens of thousands of dollars", in a Japanese court, a decision the Japanese "neither appealed nor declined to pay". The British firm was discreetly informed, however, that "it might be to their advantage to compromise". If the Western firm decided to press for its money, the Japanese threatened a boycott against it "in all the chief commercial and industrial centers of the empire". In the face of this determined cooperative opposition, "to have enforced payment in full would have meant ruin to the successful but nevertheless unfortunate plaintiff firm". Westerners could do little to counter such extra-legal activity.[143]

The pattern of increasing Japanese control was reflected in other areas as well. In the early 1870s, the Meiji government (continuing an initiative begun by the Bakufu) actively recruited foreign experts in a number of fields to assist the process of modernization and self-strengthening. The influx of *oyatoi* (foreign advisors) occurred simultaneously with the sending of Japanese students (*ryugakusei*) abroad to replace foreign employees upon their return. Though *oyatoi* provided over 9,500 man-hours of service to the central and local Japanese governments, as early as the 1880s the trend toward replacement with native Japanese was well underway. The average overall length of *oyatoi* employment was only five years. From a high of 527 *oyatoi* in 1875, by 1880 the figure dropped to 237.[144] Nippon Yusen Kaisha, for example, reduced the number of foreign officers – and their high salaries – by 30 percent between 1886 and 1893, and by 1913 only sixteen were left.[145] *Oyatoi*, even at their highest levels in the 1870s, made no policies, but were hired to implement Japanese policies and programs.

These developments did not escape the notice of the foreign communities. As early as 1882, the *Japan Weekly Mail* voiced its displeasure at the failure of the Japanese to confer official rank on *oyatoi*; the Japanese explained wryly that extraterritoriality prevented this. Foreign employees, the paper noted, were made to feel as though they are in Japan "on sufferance only, to be dismissed at the earliest opportunity". By 1891, the paper, lamenting the release of another foreign employee, plaintively wrote that the Japanese would sing "We're going to do without 'em. We don't want any more" if it could be set to the *koto* or *samisen* (Japanese stringed musical instruments). Indeed, the spirit of independence had been growing among the Japanese until by the 1890s it was "almost morbid".[146] But it was Western merchants' control of trade that was dying.

The Japanese desire for independence was clearly visible to anyone in the ports. Two Americans owned two repair docks, one of them called the Vulcan Iron Works, in Kobe. The Japanese government bought them out and later sold the facility to Kawasaki Seizo, where it later grew into the Kawasaki shipbuilding company. Two other Americans named Copeland and Wiegand started a beer brewery in Yokohama in 1872, but sold out in 1885 to the Japan Brewery Company.[147] Mitsubishi purchased the Yokohama Engine Works in 1875 to enter the ship repair business through joint investment with the English firm of Boyd and Company. By 1879 the British partner was out, leaving Mitsubishi the sole owner.[148]

Western merchants were also vulnerable to trademark violations on products they imported. As time wore on, the shops of the native towns in the ports increasingly sold Western products, and numerous foreign merchants complained of large-scale counterfeiting by Japanese. Routine violations included Bass and Guinness ale, brandy, wine, condensed milk, preserved beef and, at one restaurant, any drink a customer preferred, where it was only necessary to wait for the barman to affix the appropriate label. One less than skillful attempt to clone a baby nurser bore the words, "Manufactured by the Good Year Rabber Company".[149] An American firm invented a device which turned tea leaves in the tea refiring process mechanically, saving the need for coolie labor, but the lack of patent laws forced the firm to dismantle and lock away the machine every night, for fear that the Japanese would reproduce it.[150]

The Japanese also began encroaching on the retail business in the ports, long dominated by Westerners and Chinese. One observer noted that:

> Well within a period of five-and-twenty years after the institution of the concessions and the establishment of these colonies of foreign traders, the latter, who had in course of first decade begun to calculate how long it would be ere they could get the whole country into their own hands, were brought to understand completely how the astute Japanese had misled them by apparent submission; and to realize that whilst the younger Japanese were serving them in the capacity of clerks, warehousemen and wharfingers, they were but at school learning how the foreigner did things.

By the 1890s, Western retailers who once lived in foreign-owned hotels could no longer afford it, and were forced into native houses, where even the cost of a servant might strain their budgets. Such new domiciles sported less imposing furniture, some of it Japanese, and the Westerners occupying them wore cheaper clothes of Japanese manufacture. Foreigners increasingly found that such everyday items as tooth-powder, tobacco, photographs and English language books were cheaper when purchased from Japanese. Native grocers, fishmongers, butchers, milkmen and physicians served the needs of Westerners, and Japanese beer and wine found a place at their tables.[151]

Such vigorous Japanese competition in the ports damaged some Western trading firms. By the 1890s, some of the larger firms doing business in certain export commodities began to fail. Walsh, Hall and Company, long the pre-eminent American firm in the ports, sold out to Mitsubishi, shortly to reorganize, like Mitsui, as a top holding company with numerous subsidiaries, in 1897.[152] The British firms of Butterfield and Swire and Company and Bernard, Wood and Company either dissolved or withdrew from the tea trade in 1892. Three years later, C.P. Low and Company went bankrupt trading in raw silk, the China and Japan Trading Company discontinued its tea business, and Carter, Macy and Company reduced its Japan operations. Yokohama had more than 100 tea dealers in 1885, but only twenty-nine by 1895; eleven companies exported more than 1,300,000 lbs of tea that year. By the 1890s, one writer suggested that, "even the biggest firms realized that to hold their own would not be easy, even with a couple of generations experience in the European markets". Though many of the larger firms continued to prosper, the "small man" was "doomed" by Japanese competition.[153] Members of the larger firms, however, persisted in the conviction that they were impregnable; the "delusion remained that the great firms of exporters and importers occupied so strong a position, that they were … immune to attack". Believing that "they could for an indefinite period continue to control the whole of the native commerce with Western nations", Westerners disdained Japanese competition, while fearing its effectiveness.[154]

Until they achieved the control they desired, the Japanese were not at all averse to using Western firms to acquire the means to modernize. William Lockwood has noted that the American firm Frazar and Company "introduced a series of products into Japan which reads like a roster of American engineering achievements during the period". In 1887, the firm supplied the Japanese their first electric light plant, for use in the Imperial Palace, and later introduced Tokyo's first streetcars and its first phonograph. Later still the firm "met a rush order for 100 British-type locomotives" for use in Manchuria in the Russo-Japanese War, "completing delivery in the record time of six months".[155]

As the pattern of Japan's foreign commerce changed in the 1890s to reflect its increasing industrialization, the agency house system to which long-term port residents clung showed itself to be increasingly outmoded. By 1900 Japan's three primary exports of raw silk, tea and rice, though still important, were supplemented by manufactured items such as cotton yarn, piece goods and silk fabrics, and Japanese firms "secured a large proportion of the export of these new goods".[156] This shift meant that merchants of countries supplying raw materials, such as Germany, became more important. As early as 1886, Germany subsidized a monthly steamer service between Bremen and China.[157] As German economic activities grew in the Far East, other nationals grew concerned. In 1890 a U.S. consul received an invitation from Korea to inspect its gold, silver and copper mines, and he requested a leave of absence from his post in Japan to introduce American machinery and capital into that country. He was eager for the opportunity to get there before the Germans who, he wrote, were "very active in the East".[158]

As latecomers to Far Eastern markets, the Germans came unimpeded by the agency house mentality and "did not sit and wait in Yokohama or Kobe until the Japanese came to them. They were expected to learn Japanese and go to seek business", if necessary with the active aid of their diplomatic officials. Other Western merchants, wedded to the treaty port system, somewhat indignantly attributed German success to "unfair advantage" rather than reassessing their own practices. The percentage of Japan's total imports from Germany increased from four to ten percent from 1880 to 1900.[159]

VII

Scott Miyakawa summed up the changing trade reality well, and suggested something of the essential conservatism of the Western firms, a conservatism increasingly incompatible with Japanese priorities:

> The foreign merchants had been extremely helpful when Japan had to establish contacts with the outside world for the first time in the modern era, but as a whole they had acquired a vested interest in maintaining monopolies and strengthening their own economic positions and were not concerned with advancing the Japanese economy. They had no reason to defer their own gains to enhance the long-term benefits of Japanese producers or to train Japanese to take over their businesses.[160]

By the 1890s, foreign merchants watched while the Japanese "usurped" the trade they considered rightfully theirs. The dramatic increase in Japan's foreign trade created profits that allowed most of the established American firms to remain in business and produced new business opportunities for foreign firms. But the changing Japanese economy and increasing Japanese intervention exposed the weaknesses of the treaty port system of doing business, even as the numbers of Western firms grew.

The largest jump occurred in the 1890s, at precisely the time when shifts in the Japanese economy and increasing Japanese control demonstrated their vulnerability. Though increasing competition with the Japanese and among Western firms created pressures that put some flagship companies out of business and forced others toward specialization in certain products, Western firms derived clear advantages from the overall growth in Japanese trade. On the one hand, the trade foreigners handled grew enormously in the 1890s, imports by some 280 percent and exports by more than 250 percent. But on the other, their control of Japan's overall trade decreased substantially, down to 60 percent of imports and 63 percent of exports by 1900.

In some small measure, the increase in firms over the treaty port years lies in the distinction between Western firms engaging in importing and exporting and those who were primarily retailers in the ports. The overall increased volume of trade and shipping gave rise to numerous small foreign firms engaged solely in the myriad port services required by this increased traffic. Though Sugiyama cites British consular reports' claim that the total number of U.S. firms rose from thirty-three in 1870 to seventy-three in 1895, a close examination of the *Chronicle and Directory*, the only source that systematically lists Western business firms by name in the ports, reveals that the number of larger firms – identifiable as

American – engaged in the import and export business grew from eleven in 1870 to fourteen in 1893. Individual American firms remained in business for relatively long periods of time, and the pattern of business expansion and growth from which all foreign firms benefited was unmistakable.[161]

Equally unmistakable by the 1890s was the trend toward ultimate Japanese control. Though Westerners enjoyed the benefits of their privileged position in the ports more than ever in the last decade of the century, approaching treaty revision threatened the underpinnings of the treaty port system of trade. Though distasteful because of its explicit recognition of Japanese equality, it became increasingly clear that repeal of the unequal treaties – with its promise of interior trade – was an alternative to existing practices, but one that held little interest for merchants.

After the Meiji Restoration in 1868, Japan continued its battle for treaty revision and equal status on the political front. Western powers rebuffed the initial Japanese efforts at treaty revision in 1872 and 1873, but at a conference in Tokyo in 1882, the Japanese government offered to enlarge foreigners' "rights of residence and land tenure within the Treaty Ports" and to grant them permission to travel, "though not to reside, or hold land, in the interior". At a second conference in 1886, in return for gradual abolition of extraterritoriality, Japan offered to open the interior entirely to foreign trade and residence. After the abolition of extraterritoriality, foreigners would be allowed to own real estate outside the treaty ports.[162] Thus one of the keys to treaty revision became Japan's ability and willingness to offer the quid pro quo of expanded foreign rights in Japan. That the foreign merchant community generally opposed treaty revision suggested how treaty port isolation had constricted its economic vision, and also underscored the effective efforts of the Japanese to create more comfortable (and therefore more easily controlled) merchant intruders.

The isolation that merchants readily accepted became a permanent condition of Western business in Japan. From Yokohama's modest beginning grew a sizeable Western business community whose population was to engage in business practices that allowed its hosts, deeply concerned with Westerners' disruptive potential, to control and manipulate them effectively. Japanese official and Western merchant alike agreed on the initial isolation of the foreign community that remained a salient feature of the treaty ports for their forty-year history. Westerners' acceptance of the Japanese selection of Yokohama over Kanagawa for commercial purposes dovetailed perfectly with the Bakufu's priority of protecting foreigners from shishi while isolating them at Yokohama. The result, codified by treaty, changed little until the turn of the century.

Confronted with the approaching reality of formal Japanese control, Western merchants responded not with flexibility or accommodation, but (as subsequent chapters will show) with arguments whose purpose was to delay treaty revision in order to sustain their society and their security. The changed business environment of the 1890s would graphically expose the brittle attitudes that informed the defense of a system whose primary function was not to develop cooperative or profitable relations with the Japanese, but to maintain cultural distance, a pleasant society and a business status quo. Spurning the Japanese offer to open interior markets, merchants clung to the features of the unequal treaties that they believed sustained them – foreign tariff control and extraterritoriality – even while substantive power relations were changing permanently. Ironically, Westerners' real insecurity in the treaty ports was never more pronounced than when, in their sunset years, some enjoyed their benefits most completely.

2

LIFE ON THE EDGE

Treaty port society

The Bluffers live on the Bluff, and the Flats live on the flat.[1]

When we're rich, we ride in "rickshaws" But when we're poor they call us chickshaws.[2]

Western merchants found themselves far from the comfortable, day-to-day affirmations of identity readily available to those living in their own culture. Encountering the unfamiliar spatial, social and business world of Japan, Americans tried to order that world as best they could. In their attempts to do so, they closely replicated general patterns of Victorian masculine behavior and demonstrated many of the values upon which that behavior rested. Insecure in their new environment, American merchants of the treaty ports sought security, affirmation of their identities as men, as businessmen and as Westerners bound by a common heritage to other Westerners.

Americans revealed the depth of their commitment to the central values of their home culture, clung to them tenaciously, and found that they were not, in some respects, markedly different from those of the British with whom they shared their home in the ports. In their efforts to order their world and in their response to those who criticized the world they made, American merchants' behavior offers a glimpse of Victorian men working out the meaning and consequences of masculinity and community abroad in a highly insular, highly stratified and overwhelmingly male world.

In the post-Civil War United States, traditional notions of manhood were being reconfigured under pressure from a variety of destabilizing forces, and men sought to express both old and new forms of their masculinity in the saloon, the club and in sports. American merchants in Japan were threatened no less severely, and responded to those pressures with intensely focused efforts to create a stable world of cultural solidarity to insulate them from the various and diverse attacks to which they believed themselves vulnerable. The social tone of the ports was predominantly British and semi-colonial, and the classic criticism of the Englishman abroad – that his insularity made him intolerant of the unfamiliar[3] – applied equally to Americans, who were largely occupied with the enormous task of finding their own forms of social and psychic security. For almost all, this quest left no time to interact significantly with Japan at any level, and they remained isolated from things Japanese.

I

Already on the other side of the world, struggling with business imperatives they never fully understood, Americans sought to insulate themselves from the unknown and from the disruptive alike. The treaty ports proper – effectively cut off from the Japanese hinterland – would seem to have been an adequate haven for merchants seeking solidarity and security among others of the same race, language and general cultural heritage. But the concession areas of the ports themselves rapidly became a confused and confusing welter of transient social outcasts, marginal hangers-on, and Chinese and Japanese associated with retail or trading business in one way or another. In this world Americans saw disorder, instability and insecurity.

To accommodate the newcomers, the Japanese constructed buildings for businesses along the sea frontages, and set aside areas for shopkeepers in the back streets. In June 1859, when the foreign representatives arrived, "they found a new port ready for trade, with residences for the consuls and merchants, shops, a custom-house, a governor's office, and two 'really imposing and beautifully constructed landing-places, with flights of well-laid granite steps of great extent'".[4]

From the first, the settlements took on a Western appearance. The Yokohama foreign concession was rectangular and about one square mile. The plan of the settlement was "very liberal in the matter of the roadway and streets, some of them being twice as wide as th[o]se of the usual Japanese town". One early visitor observed that the thoroughfares were "wide and cross each other generally at right angles, containing on either side merchants' godowns and offices, or the warehouses and shops in which the Japanese expose their wares for sale".[5]

In the early years at Yokohama, there was "a sense of negligence and discomfort throughout the whole place, and everything was in a state of transition towards something which it was hoped would be improvement".[6] The Japanese carpenters had erected crude, multi-purpose buildings with "barn-like" interiors, some of which the merchants used as business compounds, dividing offices from storage space by installing partitions. Merchants used others as godowns, while publicans "transformed some into saloons". The temporary nature of the dwellings is clear from one description:

> A few folding screens in the corners, flowered Japanese paper on the walls, essential furniture such as beds, dining tables and long easy chairs – on which the master could drift off into sleep after the midday meal – some odd pieces of lacquered furniture, a pair of paper lanterns hanging from the ceiling, and two or three fans tacked on the walls, transformed a portion of the building into a place of residence.[7]

Sanitary measures were practically non-existent, and the swampy area behind settlement, "ditched with broad shallow tidal channels, filled with the concentrated essence of life and drainage, which the sea did its humble best twice a day, at the fall of the tide, to carry away". Two reeking cattle-yards, a necessary corollary to the foreign preference for beef, exacerbated the problem. Five hotels sprang up almost immediately, and over twenty grog shops in a seedy area of the concession known as "Bloodtown", where cheap boarding-houses and gambling dens attracted the crews of whalers and sealers and where the "hair-raising knife fights" that gave the area its name occurred. Japanese of the common class, forbidden to ride horses, were particularly offended by the riding habits of foreigners, including Chinese servants, who often charged down the streets at break-neck speeds, endangering pedestrians. The port no doubt deserved its reputation for heavy drinking; the settlement's foreign police were constantly busy chasing "drunken sailors and beachcombers" out of the settlement.[8]

As if to purge the port of its temporary character, the great fire of November 26, 1866, consumed a large portion of the original foreign settlement of Yokohama and much of the native town. The rebuilt port, if not picturesque, at least had the virtue of greater permanence. The swamp behind the concession was filled in, improving sanitary conditions, and a ground for recreation set aside. The main road dividing the foreign and native settlements was lined with shrubbery for its length, and the streets of the settlement generally improved. Many of the old wooden godowns were replaced with newer ones made of stone or mud.[9] By 1880, the new Yokohama had taken shape. Though it continued to grow slowly thereafter, the foreign population stabilized at about 1,600, and foreigners occupied practically all the land of the settlements and the surrounding areas.

The first sight to greet visitors to the ports were the bunds: wide, paved avenues running along the waterfront. Along the Yokohama bund were the largest and most prestigious hongs (Western business firms), the Yokohama United Club, the Grand and Windsor hotels, from which residents and visitors could enjoy the harbor view. It was here that merchants strolled in the late afternoon for pleasure, passing the English and French "hatobas" (piers) jutting into the harbor and the "jinrikisha" (rickshaw) men waiting for fares. Behind the bund lay the business district with its solid brick and stone buildings, the banks and the business compounds of the hongs, with their offices, godowns and bustle.

Some visitors commented favorably on the appearance of the rebuilt town. One American visitor noted that "the houses are built of a light framework of wood, neatly joined by ridges of white mortar; the roofs are covered with tile, thus giving to the town a sort of checkered appearance that from a distance is very neat. Since the fire ... quite a number of houses have been erected of a light green stone, almost equal to marble in texture".[10]

But many more visitors saw and commented on another, less attractive reality. Isabella Bird observed in 1878 that "Yokohama does not improve on further acquaintance. It has a dead-alive look. It has irregularity without picturesqueness, and the grey sky, grey sea, grey houses and grey roofs, look harmoniously dull".[11]

Eleven years later, Rudyard Kipling described the foreign section of Kobe as "a raw American town" with

> wide, naked streets between houses of sham stucco, with Corinthian pillars of wood, wooden verandas and piazzas, all stony grey beneath stony grey skies, and keeping guard over raw green saplings miscalled shade trees. In truth, Kobe is hideously American in externals. Even I, who have only seen pictures of America, recognized at once that it was Portland, Maine.

The same view reminded another English visitor of a "Welsh seaside resort not one hundred miles from Liverpool".[12] The Bund and the business district could not conceal the other Yokohama, a "dreary, monotonous, shabby-genteel, down-hearted place"[13] that lurked behind the bright chatter of the well-to-do merchants, naval officers and globetrotters in the Grand Hotel.

Beyond and apart from the foreign quarter in Yokohama was the "native town", in which every self-respecting globetrotter purchased keepsakes. The main thoroughfare, Honcho-dori, was a shopper's mecca for Japanese goods including silk, lacquerware and bronze, with the entire fronts of the cheaper shops open to view from the street. The next street over was Benten-dori, loaded with imported goods of all kinds for home use and several bathhouses. Shopping on either street – where spirited bargaining was an acquired art – could be hazardous for the uninitiated.[14] Outside the shopping district, the "native town" of Yokohama was (according to visitors and Western residents of the ports) quite seedy. One could visit a "cheap theatre street" crowded in the evenings with lower sorts of the East and West and, if so inclined, view some of the tawdrier shows: cheap circus and magic tricks, a crippled girl making drawings or wrestling matches. For the scientific-minded there were demonstrations of electric lights and phonographs. Large numbers of what one visitor called "perambulating restauranteurs" and outdoor entertainers wound their way among second-hand clothes bazaars, merry-go-rounds, and toy and curio shops.[15]

The Chinese vigorously segregated themselves. Chinatown, where visitors always noted a sign that read "Cock Eye, tailor", was filled with "vermilion paper, baggy clothes, pigtails, harsh voices, and vile odors", josshouses, gambling and opium dens; everything about it seemed to proclaim its separateness from Japanese and Westerner alike. Chinese New Year brought festivals and a "carnival of lanterns, firecrackers, incense, paper flowers, varnished pigs and cakes". Weddings, too, were accompanied by fireworks and drums, and the inevitable complaints of the Western foreign community followed such celebrations.[16] Beyond all this sprawled the dark mass of the actual city of Yokohama, where some 60,000 lived by 1890, on which merchants never commented and, presumably, rarely saw.

One feature of foreign trade contributed to the foreign quarter's urban problems. The tea-firing establishments, such as the one operated in Yokohama by Smith,

Baker and Company were large, one-storey godowns from which the smell of tea was noticeable from blocks away. The larger facilities employed hundreds of Japanese women and girls who worked, one embarrassed visitor noted, "with bare arms and bosoms", and did not cover up at the sight of a foreign guest. The Japanese mixed a chemical powder with the leaves, then bent over kettles each holding 5 lbs of tea, which they stirred with their hands for about ten minutes. The women replaced the tea in 5-lb increments and repeated the process. It was intensely hot inside with fires under each kettle, but the visitor was certain that the

> Japanese are salamanders; heat has no terror for them. These women and girls look healthy and contented, though they work ten hours a day, they receive only ten or fifteen cents for it all. They used to get 25 cents a day; but the price of tea fell, and the wages were reduced. The employers told me they never had any trouble with these women, some of whom have stirred tea leaves in the same hot kettle for ten years.

The Japanese coolies sweated in the godowns from May through August, and the large number of willing workers near the ports ensured a cheap labor supply; there were no strikes.[17]

One visitor decried the tea-firing industry which crammed the godowns with "dirty and perspiring women of the lowest class", and defiled the streets of Yokohama with "their wretched children ... morning and evening, as they tramp to and from their squalid villages", often as far as five or six miles from the godowns.[18] A resident described the scene with equal distaste, complaining of "the troops of tea-firing men, women and children who clatter past our windows at an unearthly hour in the morning, and who make day hideous with their noise, singing and crying". Inside the women stirred the tea leaves while singing, "interrupted by the occasional shouts of the overlookers or by the motherly attentions required by the children slung on their backs or tugging at their skirts".[19] The tunes of the women caused foreigners puzzlement and Japanese passers-by amusement, since the "lascivious jokes in the songs ... often lampooned the 'hairy foreign barbarians'".[20]

Some contemporaries understood other liabilities associated with foreigners and Japanese in close proximity. In 1871, on behalf of the Hyogo chamber of commerce, the American merchant Albert O. Gay reminded the American consulate that "Japanese of the lowest class" were building houses of the "poorest description" along the Ikuta road just north of the foreign concession in Kobe. Gay argued for their removal because of the fire and sanitary hazard that the cheap wooden structures presented. Gay understood that the people living inside the houses – servants, coolies or workers in tea-firing godowns drawn to the employment opportunities of the ports – would have to be removed along with the dwellings, and would be unable to conform to foreign regulations concerning the class of houses, width of streets, drainage and the other sanitary requirements Gay proposed.[21]

The presence of Japanese in the foreign concessions was unpleasant for merchants in other ways as well. According to the treaty provisions, foreigners were forbidden to purchase real estate outside the concessions, and Japanese forbidden to rent or own inside. Both restrictions were broken by Japanese and foreigner alike with relative impunity. Since the illegal leases in both cases were held informally in the names of legitimate lessees, foreigners buying property outside the settlement were forced to hold their property in cooperation with Japanese of the "lower orders", over whom they had no control. Merchants regarded Japanese living or doing business inside the foreign settlement of the "smallest respectability". One press item complained that even house servants were no longer polite, the *pidjin* they were forced to use to communicate with Westerners having caused them to abandon their manners and become surly. The barriers set up by the treaties isolated foreigners from the more desirable types of Japanese, causing "mutual ostracism" to "prevail in the settlements". A correspondent calling himself "Old Resident" echoed these sentiments, arguing for abolition of the settlements that would give foreigners access to the "better sort" of Japanese and that would facilitate solution of the complicated jurisdictional problems common in the settlements.[22]

Merchants fled more than the Japanese of a "lower order". For every young "merchant prince" who disdained the noise and chaotic reality of the foreign concession or took his ease in one of the hotels along the bund, there were those of his own race living in the foreign concession who were less fortunate and prosperous. These were men who did not catch on with any of the foreign firms trading in the ports, usually seamen who managed a hand-to-mouth existence. Robert Coy, for example, arrived in Yokohama in 1882. When he died of cholera in August 1888, he was "wholly destitute of means" and his funeral expenses were raised by contribution to the consulate.[23] Such men, usually single former sailors, rented cheap flats or rooms in the settlement and made up the clientele of the seedier bars and roadhouses in "Bloodtown" – the section of Yokohama that caught the drifter and down-and-out. Thomas Van Buren summarized the way the respectable pictured these groups:

> Since we came to Yokohama we have discovered that all the vile luxuries which many sailors delight in are to be had here at the lowest rates. Jack can have any amount of sprees here and plenty of the vilest liquor to drink at the lowest prices. When he arrives in port he is lured by the representations of those land-sharks who endeavor to persuade him that this is a perfect paradise .... Coming on shore he finds friends like the spider to the fly, who will take him in till all his money is expended, and when he is destitute, turn him into the street to find his way into prison if not successful in getting another ship.[24]

The gap between the upper and lower strata of treaty port society was wide. Joseph Portell, a ne'er-do-well who appeared in Yokohama in 1887, was a "notorious thief" who had served time in Hong Kong and Singapore jails. He had just finished serving a two-year sentence for larceny in Kobe, but was arrested a day after arriving in Yokohama for another theft and sentenced to two more years. He escaped from the Yokohama jail and immediately stole again. The U.S. consul, who mused that Porter was apparently "imbued with a desire to obtain notoriety by getting his name in the newspaper", observed that precautions to keep him from escaping cost more than the government allowance for maintaining prisoners, and asked that he be transferred to San Quentin in California. He added plaintively that "there is no way by which I can have him taught a trade here".[25] Indeed, in broad terms, no "trades" existed for Westerners in the treaty ports, and the "middling" class of those few pursuing any such activities – mainly a collection of individuals with special skills of use in certain aspects of the treaty port economy – was completely excluded from the respectable social life of the ports. A yawning chasm of status separated merchants from those below them.

Certainly many law-abiding Westerners lived on the fringes of Yokohama's economic life, and completely outside of its respectable social life. One such man, Sam Heath, was born in Gardiner, Maine, and moved to New York City when he was twelve years old. He served in the U.S. Navy during the Mexican war and found his way to Yokohama about 1870, where he lived for sixteen years, mostly employed by the Pacific Mail Steamship Company, toward the end of his life as a private watchman at its warehouses. He owned no real property, had no interest in any business operation and claimed to have no relations in Japan or elsewhere. Heath was "very reticent as to his life and family". When cholera visited the port in the summer of 1886, he contracted the disease and died at the approximate age of sixty-three.

Heath left no will and, as no one stepped forward as a friend, the U.S. consul appointed Richard McCance and Joseph Gorham – good, solid citizens to whom Japan had been kinder – to make an inventory of, and appraise, his meager estate. They went to his room and found that Sam Heath made do with three pairs of pants, a coat and vest, ten flannel shirts, four pairs of drawers and assorted hats, shoes and handkerchiefs. His furniture included a sturdy iron bedstead, two tables and four chairs, a sideboard, chest of drawers and a washstand. Nine plates and four wine glasses suggested the occasional visitor. His personal effects were spartan – a clock, looking glass and a revolver. McCance and Gorham dutifully assigned a value to each item, and decided that all of Heath's worldly goods – not counting a lottery ticket at whose value they did not guess – amounted to $36.13 Mexican, though they did find $16.36 in cash and a bank receipt for $900. The two men collected their two-dollar fee and turned their list in to the consul, who saw that Heath's personal belongings were sold at public auction. Sam Heath was buried at the Yokohama foreign cemetery, apparently unmourned.[26]

Americans did feel some sense of responsibility toward such men, and did take a few faltering steps toward ameliorating the social problems of Yokohama. Among the most glaring of port problems was that accompanying the hordes of sailors passing through the port. As the foreign settlements took on a more permanent character, residents were increasingly embarrassed by the drunkenness and occasional depredations of sailors on liberty.[27] The manager of the Yokohama temperance hall tried to dissuade merchant sailors from taking their discharge in the port, but, if they insisted on doing so, urged them to take up residence in the temperance hall, which had an operating budget of some $9,700 per year. Yokohama residents contributed books to the hall's library and sometimes gave cash or held benefits such as musical entertainments and tea-meetings to raise money.[28]

Merchant *noblesse oblige* took other forms. Charles Arthur, a resident of Yokohama, apparently went insane, threatened to kill a man, and created a disturbance in a local hotel in 1896, and the U.S. Consul raised his return fare to the United States by soliciting contributions from "public spirited Americans" in the port. John Holden was typical of scores of indigent and destitute sailors in Yokohama – he led an "idle and vagrant life", died of chronic alcoholism at the age of twenty-seven, and was buried with the charitable assistance of American residents.[29]

Respectable merchants sympathized, but wanted little to do with such men. When the Japanese Imperial Household held a reception in 1890 which, apparently, some members of the *hoi polloi* attended, the editors of the *Japan Weekly Mail* argued for greater exclusivity. "Wide and genial hospitality", they wrote, while admirable, when abused "loses more than half its grace .... it is not given for every man to go to Corinth".[30] Merchants defined their social problems not just in terms of race – both Japanese and Western undesirables accounted for the disorder of the concessions.

II

How did Americans respond to the world of the treaty ports as they encountered it, and what were the benefits they derived from that response? Gay had proposed an unrealistic solution to the problem of treaty port urban blight, and if Japanese and Westerners of the "low social orders" and outright riff-raff could not be held at bay, the solution was obvious enough. Westerners solved creeping urban problems by moving out of the concessions. American merchants with sufficient means created a much more manageable and orderly world – a world away from the unsightly, multi-racial, disturbing and sometimes violent concessions. One brief visitor to Yokohama might have spoken for the merchants when he called the town "the finest place in all the world to get away from".[31] The flight from this place was a search for stability and order that took the form of a process of "suburbanization", and this spatial separation of merchants from the lower orders had a twin effect. It further insulated merchants from their host country, reducing ever further any genuine possibility of meaningful connection to or interaction with Japan. But this liability, if any merchants even perceived it as such, was more than offset by the rewards that attached to their new physical environment – one that supported merchants' central need to affirm their identities in a community of the like-minded.

Though isolated and sporadic attacks against foreigners continued into the 1870s, the *sonno-joi* movement had abated by the late 1860s, and owners and operatives of the larger companies moved outside the foreign concession areas. After the fire, many foreign merchants who once occupied cramped quarters above their businesses in the small foreign concession now began taking up residence on the Bluff overlooking Yokohama Bay, while those in Kobe moved beyond the settlement to Kitano-cho. The senior members of trading firms rented the more prestigious homes, while junior members, until their salaries justified it, sometimes "lived in official 'messes,' somewhat like small clubs or fraternities".[32] Houses on the Bluff were large, freestanding affairs outside the foreign settlement, which was, of course, outside Japan. Now the well-to-do merchants looked down from picturesque hillsides on their warehouses, tea-firing godowns and offices as well as on the chaos and squalor of Yokohama. Foreign staffs of trading companies, then, came down from the Bluff and from Kitano-cho to work; Japanese employees came either from the native town or from outside of Yokohama. The road from the Bluff in Yokohama to the Bund was filled with a "clattering succession of burnished carriages crowding jinrikishas to the gutter".[33]

If Yokohama itself looked to many visitors like a hybrid and sometimes squalid offspring of East and West, the Bluff and Kitano-cho more closely resembled an English or American country setting. The higher vantage point improved the view of the harbor, increased residents' privacy and lent a certain cachet and refinement to life in the ports. The villas and bungalows of the Bluff varied in size and architectural detail – most were made of wood and plaster with heavy tile roofs – but a verandah and garden were common to all. Shrubbery surrounded many, and the occasional banana or palm tree punctuated the landscape; the wealthiest enjoyed extensive gardens and lawn tennis courts. The servants' quarters and kitchens were always in separate buildings, and high fences protected privacy. The Bluff sported a ladies tennis club with five well-maintained courts. Little wonder that Bluff residents considered themselves "of a slightly higher social order than the inhabitants of the plain". The houses were numbered as built, so no particular order prevailed, but the residents themselves, as well as coolies, servants and jinrikisha men, knew precisely to whom "Number four Gentleman" or "Number five Lady" referred. Smaller houses rented for about thirty-five yen, or about seventeen dollars, per month, larger ones for around twice that.[34]

Landholders on the Bluff were concerned about more than maintaining distance from the urban decay of the ports proper. In 1876, a number of Bluff residents held a meeting to inquire into the reasons lots were depreciating in value. They complained that ground rents were out of proportion to the value of their land, and one attender suggested that this was because the Japanese had "pushed fresh land upon the market before the old allotments had been disposed of". The meeting adjourned with a resolution to inquire into the matter further.[35] Such concerns suggest that merchants expected to benefit economically as well as socially from their ownership of Bluff leases.

Situated in their elevated ghettos, merchants on the Bluff and on Kitano-cho enthusiastically set about the task of replicating their home culture as closely as possible, and the urge to recreate the familiar is sharply illustrated by the career of James Dennis Carroll, owner of Hyogo's Carroll and Company. Carroll was born in Wexford, Ireland, in 1828 and naturalized in New York in 1853. He came to Japan in 1863 in command of the American barque Oriental which was wrecked near Yokohama. Salvaging his fortunes, he shortly afterward commenced in business in Yokohama, then moved to Hyogo, where his various ventures – a ship chandlery and general store in Hyogo to service merchant and naval vessels, selling miscellaneous merchandise at a general store and importing and exporting goods as a merchant – were extremely successful. Carroll died at the age of sixty-four in January 1892, and left his money and property to an adopted child in England and to relatives in Ireland. The consulate in Hyogo appraised his estate at a very sizeable $147,510, including more than $83,000 deposited at interest in the Hong Kong and Shanghai Bank. He had no relatives in Japan, and apparently little connection to his adopted homeland.

A detailed inventory of Carroll's possessions revealed that he was a man of some refinement as well as of wealth. His home contained a conservatory with flowers and pictures, a sitting room with a piano and expensive sundries along with almost 300 books, a bedroom with mahogany furniture, another bedroom he used as a wardrobe, a dining room replete with expensive flatware and assorted high-quality glassware, and fifty-one bottles of whiskey and wine. Outside on the verandah the assessors found that Carroll owned two jinrikishas, sixty-three potted plants and one American cow, a "splendid milker". Among the 282 lots into which the assessors organized all of this material splendor, only three suggest any cultural connection to the source of Carroll's wealth: a large album with Japanese photos, two books on the history of Japan and, outside on the verandah, one old bronze figure of Daikoku, the god of wealth.[36]

Carroll doubtless bought Daikoku in one of the curio shops in the native portion of the settlement. From such places came the eastern decorative touches that graced many merchant homes. One visitor to the home of a young "merchant prince" of Kobe wrote that his establishment combined "oriental luxuriance and American taste, barbaric pomp and cozy comfort",[37] and most foreign residents owned at least a hanging scroll or some Japanese lacquer ware. But Western furnishings were the standard interior decor of foreigners' homes. Often foreigners acquired their furniture at the numerous auctions held to dispose of the belongings of the deceased, the bankrupt and the outward bound. In such transient communities, it was not uncommon during visits for guests to notice – and remark on, if ill-mannered enough – furniture they remembered from the residences of recently departed foreigners.[38] One globe-trotter recalled the auction of the goods of a nine-year resident of Yokohama and recommended that inexperienced travelers attend such affairs, where they could obtain "articles which have cost the original owners years of curio-hunting to collect".[39] These "floating goods", though supplemented by items of Japanese

manufacture, suggest a bourgeois concern with material trappings, but also perhaps, comfort with the familiar – even if recycled.

More subtly, Americans expressed their need for an orderly and predictable
world by their enthusiastic embrace of the rigid class distinctions that defined the
ports' social world. Indeed, if the gulf between Western treaty port society and
greater Japan was evident, divisions within that society were equally apparent. The
common contemporary critique of the ports focused on their class consciousness.
The distinction between a merchant and a mere shopkeeper, for example, was quite
an important one. The American William Elliot Griffis noted that a

> great gulf is fixed, socially and commercially, between the two castes,
> and the difference is mountainous. With us, a shopkeeper is a man and a
> brother; in Yokohama, in the eye of the clubs, and with the elect of
> wealth, fashions and the professions, he is but a heathen and a publican.

Advertising by means of sign boards was a sure indicator of lower social standing,
and "consign[ed] the offender to the outer darkness, far away from the happy club
men and select visitors". Griffis believed Englishmen – whom he deemed enthusiastic participants in the social ranking so prevalent in the ports – lacked "social
pressure from above", without which they became "most radical and finical concerning every idea, custom, ceremony or social despotism of any kind supposed
to be English". It was this type that formed "the army of hard-heads and civilized
boors in Japan, to which our own country furnishes recruits". These foreigners, he
claimed, never hesitated to apply the "fist, cane or boot" to their servants.[40] Treaty
port isolation and insecurity bred desire to cling to such odd proofs of status,
democratic Americans being quite enthusiastic about emulating the British as
self-made autocrats.

Albert Farley, the manager of the Yokohama branch of Augustine Heard and
company, described Harry Livingstone, one of his employees, as "a valuable man,
he is honest, steady and hard-working – socially, he don't amount to much but we
want men for work".[41] If Livingstone amounted to little socially, perhaps he was
particularly awkward or that rare individual who cared little for the society of the
ports. Years later, Lafcadio Hearn, a man who rejected the parochial values of the
treaty port resident, wrote that the populations of the ports were "afflicted with
bourgeoisme" because they were made up "almost exclusively of the mercantile
middle classes, who are made by conventions and … the conventions themselves,
transplanted to exotic soil, must there obtain a savage vigor unknown in the mother
country". The ports, according to Hearn, were regulated by "codes, contracts, and
opinions dry and tough as Mexican jerked beef".[42] Not surprisingly, some
Japanese thought foreign treaty port society pretentiously hierarchical as well,
claiming it comprised "young clerks" and unsuccessful businessmen who came to
Japan hoping to get rich. Lacking social position in their homelands, they sought to
create an ersatz society they could dominate through their "Lilliputian races and
regattas, imitative Chambers of Commerce and their pot-house clubs".[43]

Indeed, visitors to the ports were often struck by the clinging to Euro-American customs. One globetrotter called Yokohama "a sort of half-way house to Japan", a place where a person could avoid Japan indefinitely.[44] Foreigners in Japan recreated "in miniature form" the home life they thought appropriate. Because of the geographical compression of the ports everyone was on display, and newspapers, whose reporters attended virtually every event in the ports, acted as a magnifier of daily life. The frequency of social events – amateur theatre, clubs, tennis, dinners, and their attendant gossip, lent them a "super-intensified realism", with a "consciousness of seriousness and of superiority in them common to all amateurish human knowledge".[45] Another visitor noted that "Something was always going on, and pleasant society was not wanting, whenever one felt the need of it. Evening parties and entertainments were frequent among the foreign residents, and the elegance and style seen on such occasions reminded one more of fashionable life at home than of residence in a pagan city".[46]

The predominating influence in the treaty ports was, like the population, English, and there is little question that Americans gravitated without any real reluctance toward English social and cultural norms. There is no evidence that Americans sought to create a separate society as the French and Germans did.[47] While it is true that some American residents and visitors occasionally commented negatively on British behavior, nothing suggests that Americans considered or conducted themselves as a community apart from the British. Though some Englishmen disdained the "frivolity of dum crambo and charades" at American gatherings, the two nationalities mixed together socially; indeed one resident suggested that Americans were "more English" in matters of etiquette and society than the English themselves.[48] No American club graced the Bund; no American athletic clubs existed. There were, of course, both economic and social tensions between Americans and the British, but the two groups melded together naturally in the context of the ports. Americans were more numerous than either the French or the Germans, and had been in the ports the same amount of time, but felt no compulsion to distance themselves from the British by creating especially American institutions.[49]

The American need to meld with the British social world was sometimes manifest in public debate. The Yokohama Racing Association was founded in 1862 and, four years later, a club comprising British residents took control of it and restricted the use of the Yokohama race course to its own members. By the mid-1870s some members of the community came to believe that the "English clique" was too exclusive and was not using the course for the maximum public benefit. The controversy stemmed from the application of a man of unknown nationality whom the screening committee rejected by a narrow margin. Though the club committee was quick to point out that this was the only instance in nine years that any applicant had been refused, Thomas Van Buren, the American consul, made a speech in which he argued that all members of the community should be allowed access to the club and the races to improve the overall quality of the sport. Supporters of the applicant drew up a memorial to the effect that the club was "usurping the rights of the community" and obtained 130 signatures.[50] The motive of the Americans in this case was to support egalitarian measures if the results assured them equal access – to an exclusive social world. The evidence suggests that here in British-style social stratification Americans found a ready-made template, a linguistic and social zone of safety into which they were welcomed.

III

Just as the settlement itself had matured physically and geographically by the 1880s, so too had residents' attitudes. The bases of Victorian racism are clear enough as general background to merchant attitudes. In the treaty ports, however, racist attitudes toward the Japanese in the ports were but one expression of merchants' need for solidarity and security. Different expressions involved enthusiastic exclusion of others (short-term visitors, women, Japanese and missionaries) symbolically and concretely from the well-defined groups that gave them a sense of connected comfort.

This over-riding feature of American merchant behavior showed itself in many ways. Some visitors commented on what seemed the inordinately pronounced anti-Japanese feeling pervading the settlements, particularly in Yokohama. One Yokohama race meeting posted a sign stating that "NO NATIVES" will be admitted within the enclosure", and a sign reading "Japanese May Not Enter" decorated the Yokohama Athletic Club grounds. As late as 1890 foreign banks in Yokohama refused to honor drafts presented by Japanese.[51] In 1876 a member of the Yokohama Chamber of Commerce proposed a Japanese for membership, and, while there was nothing in the rules to prevent his election, the feeling was that "as the chamber has been formed to promote the interests of foreign trade, it would be undesirable for Japanese to be admitted to its membership", and the sponsor promptly withdrew the application.[52] One foreign employee of the Japanese government left the country at the end of his employment term, saying that "next time he would go to a country where the monkeys had tails".[53]

Merchants saw themselves as besieged (as later chapters will make clear) on a number of fronts: short-term visitors misapprehended the nature of their world, missionaries unfairly criticized their behavior, consuls inadequately protected their interests, Japanese and Chinese employees of their trading firms directed essential aspects of their businesses, and rapacious Japanese merchants violated all rules of business. Merchants' response was, increasingly, to close ranks and define themselves significantly by whom they were not. Those who demonstrated any deviation from agreed upon notions constituting "Western-ness" were censured.

The chasm Americans created between themselves and the Japanese was never more obvious than when either group took on characteristics of the other. Convinced that Japanese were profoundly alien, and simultaneously believing themselves to be aliens in Japan, American merchants refused to take them seriously when Japanese were perceived to be in the half-world between East and West. For example, natives on the street dressed in odd combinations of Japanese and Western garb often drew negative comment. At the ceremony honoring the war dead after the Satsuma Rebellion, one foreign observer disdained the appearance of photographers and officers in Western dress at a Shinto ceremony; better, he thought, to honor the dead in a "genuine" Shinto service rather than in the "irresistibly ludicrous" blending of old and new.[54]

This attitude was apparent in the U.S. as well. Americans, encountering Japanese at the Philadelphia Centennial Exhibition in 1876, "longed for the quaint and the different and were invariably disappointed at half-measures" and William Dean Howells "recorded his disappointment on seeing only one Japanese man in national costume ... there is a lamentable lack of foreignness in the dress at the Centennial". Gilded Age Americans "expected foreigners to behave like foreigners; imitation seemed like a form of cultural dilution".[55]

Westerners who broke racial or cultural ranks were subjected to especial opprobrium, suggesting something of the brittle quality of the ports' social arrangements. One of the most notable instances was the 1872 trial in U.S. consular court of E. Peshine Smith, formerly employed by the U.S. Department of State, for failing to register as a U.S. citizen. Smith was employed by the Japanese foreign office in an advisory capacity and was noted for his virulent anti-merchant feeling. He claimed that, during the period of shishi attacks, not more than "one [Westerner] in ten in Japan was murdered that ought to have been murdered", called the foreigners living in Japan "unprincipled, rapacious thieves", and made no secret of his belief that the unequal treaties were morally wrong. Perhaps to draw attention to the issues of extraterritoriality and consular jurisdiction, Smith refused to register with his consulate as an American citizen, and in fact appeared in public in Japanese samurai attire, replete with two swords. At his trial for non-registration, Smith made a mockery of the proceedings, claiming to be a "only a weak, ignorant, heathen Japanese" and challenging the court to produce evidence that he was American.[56]

The response was predictable and overwhelming. "God help us all!" ejaculated the editors of the *Japan Weekly Mail*; "What business has Mr Peshine Smith or any other man to be bringing such ridicule on this country and his own? Does he think that like a scurvy politician he can cover all this shameful drivel here by his appeal to 'bunkum' ...?" The Japanese, claimed the Mail, did not distinguish among foreigners of different types, and the foolish behavior of one brought shame upon all.[57] The paper crowed when Smith retired and returned to the United States, its parting salvos accusing him of inflicting "grievous discredit" on the U.S. government and the American community in Japan. The editors noted that Smith had certain abilities, but only "during such lucid intervals as confirmed habits of inebriety permitted him to enjoy".[58]

The *Mail*'s response illustrates the foreign community's expectation that all Westerners should close ranks to protect common interests, and that any attempt to bridge the gap between Japanese and Westerner was perforce inappropriate or even ridiculous. When the *Mail* stated that the Japanese did not distinguish among foreigners, it spoke directly to merchants' discomfort with any type of foreigner who violated the solidarity of their community.

Merchants' attitudes are more clearly understood in relation to the issue of the servants they at once depended upon and disdained. Though Sam Heath illustrates that it was possible to drift off a merchant or navy ship and eke out a marginal existence in the ports, not even such men did manual labor as servants. An important underpinning of treaty port society was the presence of large numbers of Asian servants. As growing centers of business, the ports attracted many unemployed Japanese, to whom were open employment opportunities as house servants, jinrikisha men, coolies, bettos and bantos,[59] and Americans who would have toiled away in anonymity as owners or clerks in shops in New York or Philadelphia were served by platoons of servants. The sheer number of Japanese and Chinese servants in foreign employ in the ports was staggering: by 1897, the 2,500 Western foreigners in Yokohama alone employed some 6,000 servants;[60] they were so cheap that the "servant question [was] practically eliminated from the small talk" of the settlement. A six or eight-room bungalow including servants' rooms on the Bluff rented for about twenty-five dollars per month in 1894, and servants furnished their own quarters, except for the tatami mats, which were supplied by the lessee.

Servants provided a layer of insulation between foreign residents and much of the unpleasantness and the mundaneity of day-to-day life in the ports. The boy, "first in dignity in every household", was generally over thirty and had his own Japanese family. For wages of about eight dollars per month he acted as chambermaid and butler, answered the door and served meals, and frequently went with his *danna-san*, or master, when dining out. The boy also acted as "interpreter and broker" when his employer – almost always linguistically unprepared for such tasks – shopped in the native town, as well as guide on trips of any duration. The cook generally had complete control of the kitchen, including all purchases, which his employer understood included his squeeze, or percentage for himself. Cooks with noted specialties were "borrowed" by foreigners for special occasions. Cooks also often borrowed provisions from other cooks on short notice to accommodate unexpected dinner guests – one foreign woman even reported finding her own initialed silverware and napkins while dining at a friend's house. Cooks' wages were the same as those of the boy. Merchants with wives and families often kept an *amah*, or children's nurse, and larger Bluff residences required a *momban*, who functioned as gatekeeper, gardener and general handy-man.[61]

The term "betto" meant "attendant groom", or "hostler", and no foreigner who owned horses did without at least one. Bettos performed the routine chores relating to the care and feeding of their employers' horses, as well as accompanying his mounted employer by running beside his horse while holding the bridle. William Elliot Griffis described their duty "to harness the animals, yell at the people on the road and be sworn at". Griffis continued, "He is not only an expert at driving and drinking, but such an adept in the theology of the bar-room is he, and so well versed in orthodox profanity, that the heathen betto regards his master as a safe guide, and imitates him with conscientious accuracy". Bettos' dress was only one garment, "a loose blue coat coming to a little below the hips, with socks on his feet, and the usual white loin-cloth around his waist". He described one betto as "my Mercury in bronze [who] runs before my horse ... tattooed from neck to heels with red and blue dragons" and observed that bettos were "of a very low social grade", that "like other working-classes, form an hereditary guild".[62]

One directory of foreign residents in Yokohama from 1861–62 listed the names of the master of the house as well as his principal employees. Most foreign merchants lived "in or above their offices, the same building often serving the joint purposes of an office, a warehouse, and a place of residence". In most cases, the directory listed a betto. Of the seventy-nine masters, fifty-two had bettos residing with them in their employ. This suggests that the majority of masters owned horses, and since many foreign residents raced their ponies at the Yokohama track, this is not surprising;[63] during the treaty port years, "any foreigner of importance kept one or more horses, and maybe a buggy, a brougham, a phaeton or a landau". Bettos often provided more personal service to their employers as well. While afoot, Westerners could rely on the services of atoshi, servants who allowed the "fat and lazy" to climb hills on Sunday hikes without effort by means of pushing them along with a pillow attached to a pole.[64]

"How Japanese can serve a certain class of foreigners at all", Lafcadio Hearn noted, "I can't understand".[65] But serve they did, and with a deference toward superiors natural in Japanese culture that reinforced foreigners' ideas of their own separateness and superiority, and lessened foreigners' anxiety over their vulnerability to those servants. One foreigner, for example, described hiring a servant named Yasu:

> Having made his obeisance, he stood respectfully, now glancing at Marshall and now at me. As Marshall explained to him that I was willing to have him as my boy and that he must be obedient ... he responded every now and then with a 'He,' a short emission of breath barely above a whisper, which seemed to denote the very essence of deference, each emission being accompanied by a bow; and his eyes the while kept glancing at me with an expression in which gratification, curiosity and respect were curiously blended.

Indeed, one observer wondered whether foreigners were "served with almost too much formality and elaboration". Established servants were, of course, not without some power over their employers; cooks, for example, were responsible for purchasing all food and utensils, and supplemented their usual wages of five to eight yen per month with squeezes.[66] Yet the numerous and cheap servants of treaty port society in many ways reinforced on a daily basis the hierarchy in which merchants occupied the highest position. Little served American psychic needs as well as a servant, like Yasu, who was perceived to know his inferior status in relation to his employer quite well. On the mud sill of Asian service, Westerners built their society.

Other features of merchant life offered the comfort of routine and the flavor of home. One of the lynchpins of the social system was, in the words of an American naval officer, "the blessed hour of our dinners". The day's only purpose, he claimed, was to have dinner, and the "winter is spent in an exchange of these evening meals". Many social obligations were fulfilled by dinner invitations, whose "formality and solemnity" assumed religious proportions.[67] Griffis' commentary on the social dinners in Yokohama reveal something of the awkwardness, self-consciousness and stiff formality of treaty port society:

> In Yokohama, dinner is the test of success in life .... A dinner to be given must be studied and exquisitely planned, as a general plans a battle, or a diplomat a treaty. A dinner to be attended must be dressed for, anticipated, and rehearsed as a joyful hour on a higher plane of existence, or – as an ordeal for which one must be steeled and clad in resignation .... Real enjoyment is doubtless to be obtained a these dinner parties; but such an idea is not necessarily included within the objects sought by an orthodox giver of a dinner. There are a great many "brilliant flashes of silence" at these dinners, and meditations on crockery are common.[68]

Such gatherings, if sometimes awkward, were nearly always elaborate, with "certain rigid minimum standards ... for entertaining" that pertained to "nearly all white men in the ports of Japan, and the widely criticized Oriental requirements of 'face' applied amongst them as strictly as amongst the Japanese themselves". The non-white were excluded and spared.[69]

There was no native food eaten with chopsticks at such affairs. A substantial part of the volume of foreign imports into the ports were goods intended for foreign, not Japanese, consumption. In May, 1869, the China and Japan Trading Company expanded its operations by purchasing the store and auction portions of H. Fogg and Company in Shanghai, the auction and storekeeping portion of Case and Company in Hyogo and Osaka, and the general storekeeping business of Inglis and Company at Nagasaki. The company then began advertising imported items such as wines and liquors for foreigners yearning for a taste of home.[70] Another paper shows the availability of New York cheese, Sill's butter in kegs, California lard, Oregon bacon, fresh tomatoes, fruits, jams, pickles, claret and champagne. The Hyogo Hotel called residents' and visitors' attention to its table, which could "be relied on as equal to any in the East, and the other luxuries to be unsurpassed".[71] Assuming visitors' tastes to be the same as residents', one merchant in Kobe recommended that two globetrotters take a "large stock of tinned meats and a dozen bottles of claret" into the interior. While local markets sold meat, fruits, vegetables and fish cheaply, transportation costs ensured that foreigners' usual fare was not inexpensive.[72]

When E. Peshine Smith attacked the foreign communities in the treaty ports, the *Japan Weekly Mail* responded by defending the foreign establishment as one of "orderly and excellent life, much strict and honorable conduct, much cultivation and even refinement".[73] But even the most enthusiastic booster of the cultural life of the ports would have admitted to a certain strained quality to the ports' efforts at refinement. Occasionally during the winter, "fourth-rate theatrical troupes come limping through India, up the coast of China to Japan. Then the poor starved foreigner dons his evening dress, and religiously attends the performances, and sighs for the theaters of home". Because of the paucity of even such professional entertainment, port residents watched amateur theatricals, which got in "their deadly work". Japan was simply too far away to attract better troupes, so the ports had to be satisfied with local talent. The Yokohama Amateur Dramatic Corps, for example, presented two English plays, *Raising the Wind* and *Slasher and Crasher*, at the Gaiety Theatre in Yokohama in 1876.[74]

Theatrical performances were divided between "select nights" for the upper strata of port society and "ordinary nights" for the shopkeeper and tradesman. One story – with a distinct ring of the apocryphal – has it that on one select night a tenor, having sung a sustained high note, drew in a great breath and, incredibly, "sucked his false moustache down his throat" whereupon a physician fortunately in attendance saved the man before a stunned audience by performing an emergency laryngotomy with a penknife.[75] On one occasion, a Japanese acrobatic troupe performed before a foreign audience of two hundred. Though most were pleased with the show, the *Mail*'s comment on one performer underlined the treaty port's steady racist stereotyping: "the little boy dressed in brilliant red, who displayed so much agility on a hanging bamboo was very clever, but his gymnastic maneuvers were very suggestive of that well-known child's toy – a moveable monkey on a stick".[76]

Public entertainment was frequently connected with philanthropy in the ports. On February 5, 1873, Abell's American circus opened on Lot 41 in Yokohama, and at least one subsequent performance was a benefit for the victims of a recent fire in the settlement. Three years later, half of the proceeds from a performance of *La Fille de Madame Angot* were given to the Yokohama General Hospital.[77]

Learned societies in the ports included the Asiatic Society of Japan, founded in 1872 for "the collection of information and the investigation of subjects relating to Japan or other Asiatic countries", and boasting two chapters in Tokyo and Yokohama. Entry and yearly fees were ten yen; lifetime membership was available for the entrance fee and a lump sum payment of ¥100, and candidates were elected by the council of the society. Benefits of membership included the *Transactions of the Asiatic Society of Japan*. Papers read before the society varied in quality from valuable to pedestrian, and treaty port merchants were not noted for their attendance at such gatherings.[78] The intercourse at the Asiatic Society were driven, of course, by the need to understand Japan in its various aspects, and since pursuit of this goal would have necessarily at some level diluted merchant ethnic and professional solidarity, merchants showed little interest.

Other amusements included dances, usually given in the Public or Masonic Hall, of which the Bachelor's Ball was "the event of the season". These were usually "subscription affairs", and the German Club gave three winter balls. Life so far from Western society was not without its perils for the relatively few women in the ports. In the winter of 1886 a craze for foreign dress swept over Japan, and Tokyo dealers came to Yokohama and purchased the whole season's stock of dresses. The increased demand led Japanese and Chinese dressmakers in the ports to emigrate to Tokyo, where Japanese ladies paid them far more than had the foreign women in the settlement.[79] Scandal occasionally enlivened society. A certain Mrs Carew, the wife of the manager of the Yokohama United Club, poisoned her husband with arsenic and was sentenced to death. Though her sentence was later commuted to imprisonment, Yokohama society became so absorbed with the case that a "special card game was introduced to divert the conversation and thoughts of society".[80]

IV

O. Henry, in his 1904 story "Cabbages and Kings", wrote, "In all the scorched and exotic places of the earth, Caucasians meet when the day's work is done to preserve the fulness of their heritage by the aspersion of alien things".[81] Another commentator remarked that the "average workaday mortal craved, in the evening, a hearty recognition of his merits as a man as well as lively intercourse with persons of his own social standing, bantering conversation, laughter and song".[82] Indeed, the foreign clubs were among the most compelling and graphic expressions of merchants' need to satisfy two equally compelling imperatives: separation from the frequently ominous world of Japan and convivial fellowship with each other. It was here that merchants rubbed elbows on a daily basis, reaffirmed that they were governed by a different and identifiable heritage, and fortified themselves against the vicissitudes of life and trade in their exotic setting.

Three months after the port of Hyogo opened to foreign commerce, Paul Frank wrote to the American Minister in Japan asking for $300 allowance for office rent. The minister agreed to his request, adding that he hoped the money would allow Frank to rent a respectable place; he could only imagine the hardships Frank endured in what was then an "almost barbarous town".[83] Van Valkenburgh's comment is revealing; the difference between civilization and barbarism in the ports depended on the replication of Western, primarily English, society in what most Western residents considered a distant outpost of civilization.

Among the crucially important remedies to barbarism was the club – an exclusive domain where none but the Caucasian, English-speaking and male tread. It is tempting to view these clubs – so central to treaty port society – largely as expressions of racism, and surely to some extent they were. Yet merchants in the treaty ports did little that men of their class back in the U.S. were not already doing. In mid-century New York City, "a delightful social life existed among many of the merchant princes and their friends of the old New York society" redolent of "ordered good living".[84] All-male middle-class associations such as San Francisco's Olympic Club had been part of American urban life for some time. But even more numerous at mid-century

were the exclusive patrician male enclaves, such as Boston's Somerset
Club, New York's Knickerbocker Club, Philadelphia's Rittenhouse Club,
and San Francisco's Bohemian Club. These were places where … "a
gentleman found his peculiar asylum from the pandemonium of commerce and the bumptiousness of democracy".[85]

Men's clubs for the élite "reached full flower after the Civil War, pervading high
society in every major city by the 1890s", places where "men could define and
reinforce their identity as men".[86] Merchants in the ports would have defined the
twin plagues as the "pandemonium of commerce" and the "bumptiousness of the
concessions", but felt the need for escape from them just as intensely than did
their commercial brethren back home.

The Yokohama United Club, an imposing edifice at Number four Bund,
sported similar amenities: a bowling alley, an extensive library, reading and billiard rooms, and "every luxury the climate could suggest", including an excellent
table. The governing committee of the club included American members, and a
U.S. consul general served at least once as its president. Inside the club, one found
"a very agreeable and genial set of members, American as well as English",
American papers, magazines, billiards and drinks in abundance. One part of the
verandah of the boat club was known as the American corner because American
boots had left their imprint on the railing.[87] The Kobe club was a large, rambling,
red-brick building equipped with "every luxury, and situated within an extensive
garden", situated next to a cricket field and lawn tennis courts. The club boasted a
large reading room, a well-stocked library, a bowling alley and a huge billiard
room with nine tables.[88]

Club libraries in the Chinese treaty ports were well stocked with "current
newspapers and magazines from home, and popular novels". Harold Otness'
research has shown that as early as 1832, the English factory at Canton possessed
4,000 publications "classified in six categories", and by 1867 one visitor
described an "excellent Library and Reading Room, supported in part by subscription from members of $9 per half year" at that port.[89] While relatively little is
known of club libraries in Japan, they were probably similar: Samuel Pellman
Boyer, a young surgeon attached to the U.S. Asiatic Fleet, recorded withdrawing
Washington Irving's *A History of New York* from the Yokohama club library, and
read the *Atlantic Monthly* while visiting.[90]

Beyond such ancillary amenities of the foreign clubs lay their central value to the
merchant community – the fellowship of the bar. One of the salutary functions of
saloons in the U.S. was to allow "urban newcomers from foreign lands and
American's hinterlands to preserve their pre-immigration cultures in congenial sur-
roundings", and many saloons had distinctly particular ethnic clientele. In the minds
of some contemporary reformers, such a function was essentially illegitimate, promoting "an un-American spirit amongst the foreign-born population of our
country". Reformers emphasized the need to "'assimilate American ideals and
embrace the dominant Anglo-American culture".[91] But immigrant workingmen,

heedless of such reforming, assimilationist zeal, throughout the Gilded Age flocked to saloons where they could share a fellowship based on their shared ethnic heritage.

American merchants in the treaty ports did precisely what American reformers instructed – after creating it, they enthusiastically "embraced the dominant Anglo-American culture" of the ports. They did so as intensely and consistently as American ethnic immigrants because they felt themselves isolated at least as dangerously. Because of their anxiety, they insisted upon non-negotiable standards for club admission that bespoke their need to define "fellowship" with enormous precision. Qualification for admission to the treaty port clubs was on strictly enforced racial, gender and occupational terms. A hall porter at the front door screened out undesirables, including women and any Japanese. All merchants not engaged in the retail trade qualified for club membership "providing the chiefs of his firm qualified",[92] and members preserved exclusivity by voting on new admissions. Samuel Pellman Boyer was "proposed a visiting member" of the club on April 14, 1868, and elected on May 2.[93]

In many ways the heart of club life was the bar. Madelon Powers has creatively "examine[d] how saloongoers promoted the process of community building in urban America from 1870 to 1920" and many of her findings shed light on the club and drinking culture of Americans in the ports. She argues that "the barroom was an intensely conservative and traditional place" and seeks to "show that saloon clublife ... far from being trivial or detrimental, constituted instead a major stepping stone along the road to cultural integration, self-organization and cooperative effort within the working class".[94] Though Powers' focus is on the American working class (and American merchants in the ports would have been horrified at any such association), her work sheds considerable light on the male bonding that daily occurred along the club bars of the treaty ports.

Here the merchants gathered at lunchtime and after hours, where "rightful topics" of conversation in the club were the interpretation of treaty clauses concerning imports and exports, "the moral turpitude" of the American consul's "unappreciative partner, and the probability of another naval officer rolling his ball off the alley thirty consecutive times .... Good feeling, mutual charity and common ignorance triumphed".[95] This was the "all-male environment of amiable sociability". With the help of alcohol, merchants "could escape from the pressures of ... their work ... find camaraderie with others who shared the same situation, call each other by nicknames, and reinforce class, ethnic, and perhaps most importantly, gender identities".[96]

The "pecking order" once inside placed senior members of the firms at the top. Members seated themselves according to social rank in the dining room and at the bar, juniors sitting near the door, more substantial members at the far end. Drinking, except on Washington's Birthday when American members entertained, was always with coats on. Some clubs in the Far East affected unique customs. Members of the Kobe club always shook dice to determine who paid for each round of drinks, and daily attendance was mandatory, the penalty for absence being raised eyebrows and a reputation for "unsocial traits or stinginess". As one newspaper put it, "Popularity in Yokohama can only be purchased at the cost of 'being sociable".[97]

Back home in the U.S., the definition of a full-fledged "regular" at the bar depended on three criteria: willingness to "conform to the laws of barroom drinking"; a reasonably "convivial" personality; and "sharing some common ground ... such as an occupational or ethnic tie".[98] The prescribed ideal of merchant club behavior suggested above precisely describes two of the three criteria. First, rotation among those paying for rounds of drinks was an integral and extremely important part of nineteenth-century saloon behavior. The code of drinking was clear – "once a man joined a circle of treaters, naturally he couldn't desert them. That would be the trick of a short-sport, a quitter – unmanly, in fact". Reciprocal treating was an essential prerequisite to gaining the "acceptance and fellowship" of one's peers[99] and, in Yokohama and Hyogo, an important way all members of the group could judge the quality of an individual's sustained intent to remain a member of a group. Second, if popularity in that peculiar treaty port society could be purchased only by sociability, this reality only underlines the truly collective, and in some ways actually defensive, nature of merchants' social endeavors.

As the case of E. Peshine Smith illustrates, if one was not "for" the social order of the ports, one must certainly be "against" it. Hence, the emphasis on regular attendance to continually confirm its value and symbolically restate membership. Though the dues for most clubs were only six yen a month, the obligations membership carried were heavy. Beyond the individual's obligation to "keep up his end", the clubs required considerable cash outlay for maintenance, mostly from the club bars – the main source of their revenue.[100] In all of this one senses a rigid insistence on protocol that was, again, consistent with the behaviors in such clubs in the U.S. Interactions in the clubs were meant to sustain the group's identity, but the group also "pressured each member to act 'as a gentleman' – or 'as a clubman' – and reprimanded, often in prescribed ways according to club by-laws, those who behaved in an objectionable manner and to the annoyance of their fellow members".[101]

This reality certainly implies that American merchants might, occasionally, seek escape – even from a world that provided them with such predicable comfort. The lower social orders of the ports might seek drunken release in the seedy sailor bars of Bloodtown; the respectable merchant sought his release in more appealing and bucolic settings. Foreign merchants frequently escaped the hot summers, and country excursions to Ikegami, Kamakura and Futago were popular, as were surrounding areas for flower-viewing. Well-off merchants sometimes "took a temple" (rented a small temple) and temporarily installed their household goods. Many went to Enoshima, a popular weekend spot noted for fish dinners, two good swimming beaches and quality inns, just twenty-two miles from Yokohama.[102]

If Yokohama's "high society" stressed propriety some merchants, away from the clubs, displayed a distinct lack of any "delicacy or decency". One appalled visitor described one such excursion in 1870:

We encountered parties in our own tea-house, and in others close at hand, that had come down from Yokohama to pass the Sunday, and the members of which were celebrating their arrival by thwacking the "coolies", aggressively flourishing their sticks and whips, flinging the female servants about, and handling them with revolting grossness; and generally deporting themselves in a manner sufficiently offensive to the eyes of their own countrymen, and utterly abominable to a Japanese of any cultivation.[103]

Such raucous, insensitive release denotes that merchants behaved entirely with reference to their own social world; the larger world of Japan was merely the setting. Indeed, the logic at work, like that in much of the travelogue literature of the period, "render[ed] indigenous peoples as mere fixtures of [the] landscape" and "effaced the 'natives' as sentient agents in their own right, and denied the import of their own languages, laws, customs, mores, intellects, histories and world-views".[104]

The system of credit – readily adapted to the requirements of businessmen firmly committed to sustaining their peculiar solidarity even at the cost of solvency – was the mainstay of personal and professional life in the ports. Salaries of young American bachelors were about $150 per month, or slightly more than ¥300, an amount one source described as "almost wealth".[105] The typical foreign resident carried little if any cash; in payment for goods and services received, he wrote and signed chits. Accounts were settled up, at least in theory, at the end of each month, but the system encouraged living on borrowed money.

Beyond its role as daily financier, the chit book was a means by which residents recorded most of their personal correspondence, each note sent and received duly recorded. Foreign residents betrayed their social standing even by the appearance of their chit books: the thick, leather-bound variety belonged to the "Big Taipan", while the "unpretentious clerk" owned the small, neat one. A gold border, initials and an image of Cupid decorated that of a junior clerk in a large hong who fancied himself a ladies' man, and the matted, dog-eared and smeared mess of blotting paper belonged to the "wild young spark, given to frolic and spree". Chit book correspondence might include dinner invitations or notes from the Saibansho (the local Japanese judicial office). Most residents regarded their chit book as "a trusty and well-beloved friend".[106]

One resident, describing the defects of the system, noted that "chits in Yokohama constitute one of the pleasantest curses known to man". Port residents were

always "good for a drink" or anything else, and if you do not look too much like a sailor – "a Damnyoureyes San", as the natives say – and are able to write your name, you are "good" for whatever you may wish …. Chits, being interpreted, means "drinking made easy", – drinking and other things.

Most merchants, except around steamer days, worked a leisurely schedule, "coming down to work at 10 a.m. and quitting usually at 3", with an hour off for lunch at one of the hotels or clubs, and had ample free time to indulge the popular passion for credit. Those receiving chits sometimes lost them, rendering an already loose system even looser.[107]

The economic benefits of the trading business of the treaty ports were, like the fruits of most capitalistic endeavor, necessarily unevenly distributed. Some merchants were able to sustain the costs inherent in holding up their end at the bar week after week; others' budgets underwent significant strain. The chit system was, above all, a creative solution to the problem of including as many merchants as possible in the social system (thereby making it easier to sustain), and for a time pretending that all could afford to be included. It was a form of financial procrastination that, for a time, served to buttress the clubs and the security they represented to merchants.

V

Merchants' behavior reflected other elements of their cultural sensibilities as well. Explanations of the upsurge in the popularity of sports in the years after the American Civil War are various and over-lapping but all, to some extent, emphasize sports as part of a redefinition of American manhood. Athletics, seen before the Civil War as "a form of physical culture that strengthened the body, refreshed the soul, and increased a man's resistance to luxury and vice" came increasingly to be associated with competition, replication of the rigors of war, cultivation of masculine character traits such as steadiness of "nerve", and overcoming the debilitating tendency of modern life to produce flaccid and "luxury-loving individuals". Some also argued that athletics, with self-denial a prerequisite for success, were an antidote to self-indulgent vice.[108] More the province of bachelors than of married men in the U.S., the sporting culture was, not surprisingly, an important place where males established their identities. Unlike in Europe, where sporting males were usually upper class, American cities, beginning in the 1820s, spawned a sporting life comprising men of all social classes.[109]

Among such activities Westerners pursued was the gentleman's sport of horseracing. Many pursued it passionately; one of the badges of social rank in the ports was to own horseflesh. On the high ground beyond the Bluff lay the Yokohama racecourse. Merchants brought in ponies from Hokkaido and China, and often rode their own entries in hurdle and flat races and steeplechases.[110] A regular column in the *Japan Weekly Mail* called "Training Notes" denoted the importance of horseracing to the foreign community.

Around the center of the main social clubs spun the galaxy of athletic clubs.[111] While a fire was consuming part of Tokyo in 1879, one visitor observed wryly that foreigners were "chiefly interested … in the preservation of the boats" of the local rowing club.[112] Boating was indeed one of the most popular sports in the ports, and the competitive and social aspects all took place in the context of clubs. The Kobe Regatta and Athletic Club was typical. Alexander Cameron Sim, a Scottish pharmacist who became a thirty-year resident of Kobe, founded the club on September 23, 1871. The club held races of many kinds on land and water and promoted friendly rivalries by sponsoring inter-port competition. Sometimes company teams competed against each other, including American ones; Carroll and Company, Warren Tillson and Company, and Board and Company, for example, all competed in one 1876 regatta. After such exertions, members could retire to the club itself, where a pier with a diving board for swimmers jutted fifty yards from the beach in front of the club.[113]

Many of the sporting gatherings were extensive affairs. The Yokohama Amateur Athletic Association Meet in May 1876, included 100, 150-yard and one-mile races, throwing at wickets, throwing the hammer, high jump, one-mile walking and hurdle races, long jump, pole jump and vaulting; England stood all comers in a tug-of-war, but lost. The meet lasted two days and the *Japan Weekly Mail* reported in great detail the performances of all the participants.[114] The Yokohama Athletic Club was founded by a British subject, James P. Mollison, in 1868, to promote the sport of cricket. Initially given sixty square yards of land known as the Swamp, the club eventually doubled the size of its field in the 1870s, and built a single-storied clubhouse for its members.[115] Both Yokohama and Kobe had cricket and baseball grounds, and by the 1880s sufficient numbers of Americans had joined the Yokohama Athletic Club for baseball to supplant cricket in popularity.

The treaty ports offered – at least to merchants of sufficient means – a tolerably good life, even a very desirable one. Merchants' schedules left plenty of time for a social life comprising teas, tiffins (lunches), card-parties, dances, amateur entertainment and club life. In its physical setting, its club and broadly stratified social and sporting life, treaty port society partially satisfied merchants longing for stability.

VI

As hard as merchants tried to insulate themselves against attacks from various quarters and to replicate the institutions, associations and security of home, the equilibrium they prized above all else proved at least somewhat elusive. Patterns of behavior among those in the upper strata of treaty port society were rigidly defined, and this brittle quality, coupled with established patterns of trade and the smallness of the society, left merchants no safety net, economically, socially, or psychologically, when their fortunes went sour.

The most well-adjusted residents could not escape their peculiar social demands of treaty port life. We have seen that, to maintain his social standing, the treaty port merchant of Japan was expected to belong to a number of clubs which reduced his working time and cut a "big slice out of his earnings" in membership fees and entertainment bills. The appearance, not the substance, of material wealth and success was essential:

> All that is required of him is that he shall keep up the show, wear new clothes, new ties, new hats, and take part in, or be seen at every show or amusement in town, and that he shall go to the country in the summer and leave his business to Japanese boys in the mean time.

In the increasingly challenging business environment of the 1880s and 1890s, some merchants failed to reduce time and money spent in clubs and on appearances, arguing that their bank and business credit would suffer if they failed to "keep up appearances". The insistence on preserving treaty port society intact through the end of the century led some to the inevitable conclusion: "sport, drink and amusements send business begging", while the Japanese took the business foreigners could not hold.[116]

On occasion the ports exacted a heavy toll from the profligate, careless or the overly ambitious; the liabilities of trying to sustain the kind of camaraderie isolation in the ports seemed to demand could sometimes be devastating. In the U.S., clubs and drinking occupied a position both chronologically and thematically to a broader culture

> such clubs were, after all, a function of the age and drives of the plea-sure-seekers who formed them, young men whose primary interests in life were carefree carousing and courting the girls .... In most cases ... when young men reached a certain level of age and maturity and respon-sibility, and especially when they settled into marriage, the pleasure club died a natural death.[117]

A unique feature of the clubs in the treaty ports, of course, was the lack of women to eventually lure men away from them. Since marriage was so unlikely, some young merchants became middle-aging merchants while falling deeper and deeper into debt, relying on the chit system of credit to delay a final reckoning for as long as possible. Nearly all merchants were constantly in debt; the conscientious settled up once a year or paid off chits on a rotating monthly basis.

Most merchants paid up within three years on average, but some had no intention of paying until after they were dead – life insurance policies freed them from concern about either the number or chronology of the chits they signed. Indeed, some merchants lived "luxuriously on the fringe or ragged edge of the crazy quilt of chits" until, assuming they lived long enough, they became a ward of their consul or were "sent home steerage at government expense". The last stop before deportation for a merchant buried in debt was "fleeing to the natives", where, "for a modicum of seaweed fish and rice beer, [he] teaches Peter Parley's History of the World".[118] The connection between credit and status was clear; some club members refused to leave even after exhausting their savings. The more fortunate had friends who contributed to purchasing financially depleted colleagues "a second class steamship ticket back to their native land".[119] In 1905, *Eastern World* noted that "there have been the usual quiet departures, and the community at large still looks upon people who candidly admit that they have to work for their living as criminals who are a disgrace to good society".[120]

Here again we see the relentless demands of masculine barroom fellowship at work, and the need of at least some Americans to remain loyal to a group (and to enjoy the benefits of membership) even after their financial means to support that loyalty had vanished. The consequences of not "holding up one's end" in the U.S. ranged from loss of face, to failure to attain full membership or respectable status, to expulsion from the bar.[121] In the treaty ports it meant all of these things, but also intensified embarrassment in a community where all such developments were public knowledge. Often it meant simultaneous admission of business as well as social failure. The fear many must have had of both help explain why they delayed their related social and financial reckonings for as long as possible.

The delicate equilibrium of the ports can in some ways be measured by merchants' response to criticism by outsiders. That response frequently bespoke an extreme touchiness born of insecurity – the old hands generally endured rather than welcomed globetrotters. Permanent residents considered their hospitality often violated by some passers-through who understood little of the foreigner's problems in Japan; it was easy for someone to drop in on Yokohama or Kobe, pass judgement, enjoy a moment's notoriety in the foreign language press, and move on.[122] Perhaps the most notable example of this was the firestorm of protest that followed the publication of a letter by Henry Norman, a British newspaper correspondent, in the *Japan Weekly Mail* in 1888. Norman painted a less than flattering portrait of Yokohama society, emphasizing the insularity and intolerance of the mercantile community in particular. Merchants, he argued, lived a life entirely cut off from things Japanese, and offered up evidence including laziness, business complacency and extreme racial prejudice; one English merchant explained to Norman how he referred to some Japanese: "When you've seen something of the East you'll know that everything that's not white there is a nigger".

The reaction to Norman's article was immediate and vehement. Basil Hall Chamberlain first took up the gauntlet on behalf of Yokohama's merchants by listing the achievements of the foreign community in "civilizing" Japan. "Not the loosest of European *viveurs*", he wrote, "not the lewdest grogshop-haunting English Jack-ashore would have blushed at the flaunting immorality, the really unimaginable indecency which preceded our advent in this country". Lauding the removal of "phallic emblems" at Nikko and the modification of indecent childrens' toys as examples of "the greatest decency ... in the foreign settlements of Yokohama and Kobe", Hall concluded that Norman – a species of "*Globe-trotter Journalisticus*" – was merely an ignorant "self-elected sermonizer". Another response focused on the shrillness of others' responses to Norman: "Blundering defenders" such as Chamberlain attributed a "womanish sensitiveness" to port merchants that was inappropriate.[123] One can imagine the conversation about Norman's indictments at the club bars, merchants defending with vigor the social arrangements that provided them with security, social arrangements to which they could imagine no alternative.

One foreign newspaper called Yokohama a "slanderer's paradise", a place where "unlimited license of tongue is considered to indicate frank independence of character".[124] In the narrow, circumscribed world of the treaty ports, petty hatreds and prejudices were exaggerated, and there is no better example of mutual recrimination than the mud-slinging between merchants and missionaries. At best, the two groups regarded each other with cold hostility; at worst, open disgust. One explanation for the missionaries' dislike of merchants was simply that the latter were, in their terms, immoral and failed to set a good example of civilized, Christian behavior for the Japanese. Failure to attend church, working on Sunday, visiting brothels, keeping Japanese mistresses, and indifference and hostility to missionary goals were all tangible evidence of merchant degradation and spiritual deficiency.

By 1870 three churches – Union, Episcopal and Roman Catholic – were holding services in Yokohama. Clergymen of different denominations conducted services at the Union church on a rotating basis, and this bespoke a basic condition of the missionary presence in Japan: M.L. Gordon stated that it was "a striking exhibition of the absurdities of Christian denominationalism" that more than thirty different societies were working in one small country.[125] In spite of the substantial effort, mission results were meager. One source stated that by 1894, there were over 600 foreign missionaries in Japan, yet Christians numbered only 105,000 out of a population of 40 million; one American missionary in Hakodate acknowledged that his five years of labor in Japan yielded "scarce half a dozen souls".[126] Equally irritating to treaty port missionaries was merchant non-attendance at services; a representative congregation numbered twenty or thirty souls throughout the treaty port years.[127]

Mary Pruyn, an American missionary who worked and lived in Yokohama in the American Mission Home on the Bluff from 1871 to 1875, embodied something of the holier-than-thou attitude that merchants despised. She lamented that the Japanese were "so totally ignorant of the true God", but castigated foreign residents: "Most of those who have come from Christian lands are so wicked that they do not care any more for [Sunday] than the heathen do". Indeed, merchants' lives, especially on Sunday, were an affront to the missionaries. E. Warren Clark wrote of Yokohama that "There is no more Sabbath here than if the Ten Commandments were never written. The sounds of labor are heard in every direction, and sin and corruption abound in their worst forms".[128]

Contradictory racial views abetted in fomenting merchant–missionary hostility. Whatever the elements of condescension in the missionary view, the group saw the Japanese as humans whose souls were equal before God, while many merchants were convinced that evangelical effort was wasted on a people who could never be "honest and trustworthy". They responded by calling missionaries "wife-beaters, swearers, liars, cheats, hypocrites, defrauders, and speculators", and would inform any newcomer to the ports that missionaries occupied "an abnormally low social plane" and deserved the scorn of the respectable. The merchants of Yokohama served missionaries "up whole at the dinner table" and devoured their reputations, suggesting that missionaries lived in hotels spending money meant for the conversion of souls. So pronounced was the antipathy between the groups that missionaries usually vacationed at Hakone, where they were less likely to see their "lay brethren", and went to some lengths to avoid contact even in the tiny foreign settlement in Osaka.[129]

Especially irritating to merchants was the sight of the large American missionary community living comfortably on the Yokohama Bluff.[130] Japan was a congenial field of operations for missionaries because of its climate, progressive government and economy, and determination to win the respect of the Western world.[131] Many thought that missionaries had it too easy in Japan. M.L. Gordon, an American missionary, complained that some in the eastern ports were content with a superficial judgement of missionaries: "They assume the identity of the missionary life with physical discomfort, and that missionary funds are raised to relieve the suffering missionaries; and so, if they find them living in comfortable houses and decently clothed, they rate them all hypocrites, as they certainly would be were the above assumptions true".[132] Newspapers often reflected the merchants' anti-missionary bias. One typical article observed the difference between the hard-working merchant and the lazy missionary who "potters around for a year or two, gets into the country as often as he can, or wishes to go, if the souls of the settlement won't bite, and then he comes to the conclusion that he is 'breaking down,' that he must go home for a year or two".[133]

Definitions and meanings of nineteenth-century American masculinity offer a way of understanding merchant–missionary enmity more deeply. A key component of masculine endeavor was work, defined as participation in a newly emerging, highly economic environment. Work inconsistent with such definition was often described as "feminine", and the career choice of the ministry was often so regarded. Thomas Wentworth Higginson's 1863 essay "Saints and Their Bodies" suggested that "one of the most potent" causes of the public alienation between ministers and the public was ministers' "supposed deficiency of a vigorous, manly life". One way of resolving the problem was "through a strategy that merged the worldly with the godly, the 'male' with the 'female'" – clergy could associated themselves with aggressive Christian warfare against paganism.[134] Indeed, the merchant critique of missionaries residing in or near the ports emphasized missionary sloth, with the implicit comparison to merchant diligence, usefulness and respectability. That merchants concentrated their criticism on missionaries close at hand suggests that merchants differentiated between the "treaty port bound" variety and the presumably more "masculine" clergy who aggressively went into the Japanese hinterland in search of converts.

Merchant attitudes toward missionaries offer an interesting reversal of the majority/minority relations *vis-à-vis* marital status in the U.S. At home, bachelors had frequently been defined and to some extent discriminated against as a minority group who challenged social stability by refusing to domesticate themselves through the institution of marriage. Defined from colonial times on as "rogue elephants" and encouraged to "become whole" through marriage, bachelors as a minority population in the nineteenth century encountered legal problems, especially in cases where women claimed that bachelors had reneged on promises to marry them. Judges came to view such cases as violations of "female purity" and sometimes awarded damages to female litigants.[135] In the treaty ports, however, the merchant bachelor population found itself the majority, and attacked its missionary critics with as much vigor as the married majority at home attacked bachelors. Each attack was leveled for the same reason – the majority group believed its stability threatened by the minority group.

Issues concerning manhood and marital status, however, do not fully explain the shrillness of the merchant critique of missionaries. Missionaries earned the undying and especial enmity of merchants by advocating the unthinkable: treaty revision. The treaties stipulated, of course, that foreigners were to reside in the foreign concessions, and, with the exception of diplomatic personnel, were to have the privilege of travelling inland only the distance of ten *ri*, or about twenty-five miles, without having to obtain a permit from the Japanese government.[136] To reside elsewhere, foreigners had to enter into the employ of the Japanese government, a Japanese company or a private individual. Japan's official proscription of Christianity ended in 1873, but restrictions on travel in the interior remained. Many missionaries, eager to evangelize the Japanese interior, chafed under this constraint on their movement,[137] and many reluctantly entered into contracts to teach English, accepting the loss of time for their real work, in order to obtain access to the hinterland.[138]

The American Board of Commissioners for Foreign Missions had urged treaty revision in a memorial to President Ulysses S. Grant as early as 1872. Fundamentally uninterested in questions of tariff autonomy and consular jurisdiction except as they bore on the issue of access to the interior, missionaries would have happily submitted to Japanese law "if permitted to reside in the interior". One contemporary stated that "all [missionaries] will heartily welcome the revision of the treaties"[139] The U.S. consul in Hyogo solicited the opinions of prominent missionaries and reported in 1890 that "many, perhaps the majority, favor [treaty revision] as a matter of wise, prudent and just policy".[140] It was clear, however, that the Japanese government would not open the interior of Japan to residence and trade for any reason without some sort of quid pro quo. Since extraterritoriality and control of the tariff were basic underpinnings of the foreign community in the ports, merchants regarded any attempt to disturb the status quo with grave misgivings. As the prospect of treaty revision loomed closer, with the certainty that all foreigners in Japan would eventually be subject to Japanese law, and the favorable tariff structure would be repealed, merchants resented missionaries as one of the agents by which their status as privileged residents would be irretrievably lost.

Foreign merchants, though enthusiastic supporters of all the trappings of treaty port society, were still only imperfectly compensated for residence on the fringes of the "civilized" world, and this imperfect compensation took the form of the gender imbalance. Though some treaty port residents – especially missionaries and some employees of the Japanese government – brought families to Japan, the vast majority of the Western merchant population was single; as trading communities established on the outskirts of the "civilized" world, the treaty ports did not attract large numbers of women who were not missionaries.[141] The few unmarried Western women in the ports were apt to be missionaries, and all British and most American firms in the Far East frowned upon marriage of their junior members, as "experience showed that if men married young, when their salaries were low, peculations were apt to result".[142] The relatively few merchants who were married occupied the upper echelons of established trading firms. In at least one case – that of Augustine Heard and Company – junior employees were strongly discouraged from marrying, in part because the firm paid for their room and board.[143]

In spite of this significant difference between their society and the larger one they strove to recreate, merchants engaged in relationships with Japanese and Western prostitutes and with other Japanese in all the ways that their circumstances made possible. Though one historian has explained sexual contact in colonial settings "almost as an act of baffled despair",[144] in reality American behavior toward women in the ports provides evidence of the community's quest for order and stability, and of the often exploitative nature of the relationships that quest produced. That behavior also seems to confirm that Victorian American men had been subjected to two powerful messages about sexual conduct. The first was the well-known set of Victorian admonitions in favor of restraint, including doleful warnings against masturbation. The second, suggested by the "very existence of an ideology of self-control – and the vehemence with which it was asserted – might have suggested long ago to historians that an opposite doctrine existed" was an "ethic of male aggression".[145]

When foreign sailors debarked from their ships in Yokohama, they had but to get into a jinrikisha and ask for "Number Nine", a well-known house of prostitution, to satisfy urges pent up for months at sea. Permanent residents' arrangements, if they did not wish to be seen frequenting the brothels in Bloodtown, were only slightly more complicated. Missionaries frequently commented on the immorality of merchants keeping Japanese mistresses, and while the records contain few individual indictments, some evidence suggests the nature of their relationships with Japanese and Western women.

In the 1850s and 1860s, the Bakufu was divided on the issue of how to respond to the Western challenge, but it recognized the need to take the *joi* (expel the barbarian) elements seriously, and tried therefore to offer protection for the general population from "contaminating influences". The policy of making foreigners comfortable in their isolation manifested itself immediately in its arrangements for the sexual entertainment of the foreign community. One visitor to Yokohama noted that "where heathen women are cheap, and wives from home are costly, chastity is not a characteristic trait of the single men".[146] In response to this reality the Japanese took measures to make Yokohama more attractive to traders already satisfied with their isolation. In an area called "The Swamp", one observer noted that the authorities endeavored to render Yokuhama an attractive locality to young, unmarried foreigners by establishing at the edge of the settlement and on a site approached by a narrow drawbridge over the canal, one of those infamous public institutions ... containing its two hundred female inmates dispersed over a spacious series of apartments and all under government regulation and control.

This establishment, called the Gankiro Teahouse, was destroyed by fire in 1866, but was eventually replaced by what euphemistically became known to the foreign community as "Number Nine", supervised "by a madam whom the foreigners of Yokohama had profanely nicknamed 'Mother Jesus.'" The Bishop of Hong Kong, George Smith, reported with horror that native officials, not satisfied with "these flagitious methods" of keeping foreigners satisfied, "contributed every facility for the perpetration of domestic vice and impurity. Young men were encouraged to negotiate through the customs-house the payment and selection of a partner in their dissolute mode of living". Smith condemned the foreign community's enthusiastic response and the "deplorable scene of demoralization and profligate life" he observed in the port.[147]

Respectable American males reluctant to engage in sexual contact with women of their own class had growing access to prostitutes throughout the nineteenth century. E. Anthony Rotundo suggests that one way American men attempted to reconcile the twin messages of restraint and self-control on one hand and aggression and conquest on the other was to "practice self restraint with one class of women" but "enjoy erotic pleasures and give vent to their natural passions with another".[148] Many sexual relationships in the ports, of course, were with prostitutes, and the scattered evidence available suggests that the skin color of the fallen woman made little difference to American merchants. Practicing self-restraint with the respectable class of foreign women in the ports was easy – they were either unattainable as wives of missionaries or wives of important merchants and, one presumes, to be trifled with at considerable professional risk.

Eager foreign bachelors without a taste for longer-term commitment did not look far to express their "natural passions" with the less respectable and had ample opportunity for contact with Western women of the evening. One source states that "much bedizened and bejewelled 'China Coasters'" – white prostitutes who plied their trade on tours including "all the ports of Japan", China, Hong Kong and Manila – attended events at the Kobe Club and the Kobe Athletic and Regatta Club. Kobe sported two foreign brothels – both of which barred Japanese – known as "Dawn's" and "Virginia's" and their owners advertised newly-arrived girls by showing them off at club events and by taking them on "sight-seeing tours in rickshaws through the foreign settlement ... always held between five and six o'clock in the evening" after Japanese coolies circulated "'to whom it may concern' notices of the forthcoming parade to all of the foreign firms". Merchants signed chits for these services, and every month "regularly employed chit coolies presented these I.O.U.'s for payment", rendering any man's monthly sexual indiscretions visible to any "inquisitive gossip" alert enough to notice who visited his office. Houses with Japanese women, such as "Fat-Arsed Jane's" in Kobe and "Mother Jesus's" at Number Nine in Yokohama were more numerous, and equally well patronized by foreigners.[149]

Certainly merchants had the financial means that allowed them to take advantage of Japanese women attracted to the ports out of economic necessity; some must have chosen a more libertine attitude than might have been possible for them at home, but relationships between Japanese and Americans often did not end after a single, physical act, suggesting a deeply felt need to recreate, however imperfectly or merely symbolically, the order and restraint that Victorians associated with a feminine presence.

By the standards of an emerging male middle class at home, the "disreputable" would surely have included all available women in the ports – Japanese and foreign alike. Merchants, if they were interested in anything more than simple exchanges of money for sex with prostitutes, were forced to consider what their counterparts in the U.S. would have considered unacceptable alternatives. These other women were unacceptable because of the racism of the age, but also because American bachelors at home (if sufficiently well-off) had, in the late nineteenth century, access to a robust culture of urban leisure populated by growing numbers of men and women of independent means. The young and unattached came together in this new, urban matrix of social opportunity in ways that gave them new and fulfilling opportunities to explore levels of intimacy and commitment that satisfied a wide range of personal sensibilities.[150] Such opportunities were, of course, denied residents of the ports, but they expressed the same needs for intimacy, often engaging in longer-term relationships with available women.

One contemporary observed that "public prostitution" was responsible for the extent of venereal disease around the ports. Any young bachelor merchant in search of a 'musume' (daughter or girl) needed only to "call on the young lady" – whose mother had earlier decided to make her available for such liaisons – and give her four dollars, with which she purchased a license from the Japanese customs house entitling her to be his mistress for a month, as well as to have "a daily bath in the public bathhouse". If the relationship proved satisfactory, the foreigner hired a room and servant for her at about ten dollars per month, and paid her an allowance of fifteen to twenty-five dollars per month to buy her faithfulness. If the foreigner found that his musume had "carnal communication" with others, he could return her to the customshouse, where she would be flogged, then sent to serve for seven years "as a public whore".[151]

Missionaries pointed to some merchants who kept "several mistresses and change[d] them every month", and there is little doubt that long-term port residents maintained Japanese women in this way. As late as 1899, one newspaper referred to merchants' common practice of taking "one or half a dozen prostitutes out of a Japanese brothel". The openness and acceptability of such practices from the beginning is clear in a Yokohama directory for 1861–2 that listed seventy-nine residents, of whom thirty cohabited with musume; where two single men shared quarters, the directory listed two musume.[152]

These arrangements, where foreigners could exercise such control over Japanese women, were possible in a system supported by the Japanese to control the foreign community. Nevertheless, Western men could and did enthusiastically use such mechanisms to achieve the desired end of female companionship. A contemporary establishment in the U.S. that served an analogous purpose – female companionship, even if purchased – was the taxi-dance hall. Unique to the bachelor sub-culture of post-Civil War America, taxi-dance halls were "the dominant type of dance hall in the business centers of [the] largest cities".

> Designed explicitly for male patrons only, the taxi-dance hall employed women who sold tickets that entitled purchasers to the privilege of dancing with them. Each female employee was expected to accept any man who selected her for as many dances as he was willing to buy, and she was paid on a commission basis, depending on how many tickets she sold.

The primary function of the taxi-dance hall was to provide "immigrants ... however tenuously and temporarily, female companionship, with the sexuality hinted at by dancing, free from the risk of rejection". Paul Cressy, the sociologist who closely studied the halls, believed that "the taxi-halls could conceivably facilitate the emotional adjustment of certain men by providing 'their only opportunity for affectional ties of a heterosexual character'".[153] If Filipino and other Asian immigrants used taxi-dance halls for their emotional adjustment, American merchants used Japanese government-sponsored brothels – and the longer-term liaisons they sometimes produced – for the same purpose.

Such practices were common and did not evoke criticism from a community where many daily felt the liabilities of the Western gender imbalance. Rather

> The keeping of Japanese mistresses, often slightly camouflaged as "servants" by young bachelors involved little or no social censure .... This loose sex life was so prevalent that it resulted in large revenues for the foreign doctors, and the ordering of a non-alcoholic drink at the club bar always led to damaging conjectures. Barley water, in particular, provoked jocular comment, for it was popularly supposed to be a soothing irrigant.[154]

Some American treaty port residents, after long relationships with particular Japanese women, decided to marry them or, having had arrangements with several women, finally decided for one reason or another to settle down with one. Examples of Americans marrying Japanese include William Copeland, aged 46, who married Katsumata Ume, 21; J.J. McGrath, 51, who married Sunoda Rhew (Ryu), and Arthur Otis Gay, at age 71 one of the most distinguished American residents of the ports, who married Hida Toyo, 27. Edward Lake, a Nagasaki merchant, never married, but he probably long cohabited with a Japanese woman, with whom he had a child whose tombstone read "Lily Ito Lake".[155]

Some longer-term relationships grew out of chance encounters. In February 1879, the U.S. consul at Kobe received a poignant petition from Yamada Cho, then seventeen years old, who had borne the child of Matthew Scott, an American employee of the Kobe customshouse. Yamada was living in Yasaku's Eating House in Yokohama, and stated that Scott came to her house in September 1878, where she waited on Scott and became acquainted with him. She stated that Scott "often made indecent advances" toward her, to which she was "once compelled to submit". After two more visits to Yamada's residence, Scott returned to Kobe in October 1878. After this encounter with Scott, Yamada explained that "the state of my health gradually changed .... My parents soon became aware of it, so that it was impossible for me to hide the result of my connection with Mr. Scott ... from them any longer. For a time, my parents were very angry with me, but after satisfying themselves that nothing could be done, they agreed that I should take the best possible care of my health".

Yamada bore a daughter on June 20, 1879, and in August, Scott returned to Yokohama. She informed him of his status as the parent, but apparently made no overtures toward marriage, and accepted thirty yen from Scott, which "lessened [her] anxiety to some extent". Before leaving for Kobe in September, Scott asked that the child be named "Omachi", gave Yamada another fifty yen, said he would send more money if necessary, and promised to bring Yamada to Kobe as soon as he could make suitable arrangements. Yamada wrote to Scott in Kobe twice, and finally received twenty yen and a promise to send more money if necessary. This "perfectly satisfied" Yamada. While waiting for Scott to make "suitable arrangements" for her move to Kobe, Yamada sent him a picture of the child, but discovered shortly thereafter that Scott had died on November 15, 1879, naming his brother in San Francisco to receive his property. Scott's death made Yamada "very unhappy and sorry, for there is now no one to whom I can look for support, and I do not know how to bring up the child".

Yamada described her child as "far different from any ordinary child, she is really very clever", and spoke of her "great hopes for the child's future". Asking the consul to find some means of support for herself and child, and "not thinking of [her] own shame", Yamada expressed the hope that she and her child "may be allowed to remain together until Omachi grows up to be a young woman, when she can go abroad, and pray on the tomb of her beloved father". Yamada closed by asking for the address of Scott's nearest relatives in the United States "for the use of Omachi", though it seems clear that she restricted her plea for support to the American consul in Kobe and did not expect Scott's relatives to send money.[156]

The story of Scott and Yamada suggests the anguish, or at least the complexity, that could result from such liaisons, but also illustrates that Americans – at least sometimes – considered their relationships with Japanese women in a context beyond a simple exchange of sex for money. That Scott suggested the child's name and considered bringing Yamada to Kobe is telling – particularly in light of the frequency of such arrangements among other Westerners and Americans. If Yamada's liaison with Scott was at all typical, it seems clear that Americans, like other foreigners in the ports, had the privilege of dictating the terms of their relationships with Japanese women.

Merchants took advantage in sexual relationships that fulfilled basic desires according to available circumstances, but Scott's relationship with Yamada suggests that doing so must have caused them to think wistfully about the more permanent marital stability for which their frequently temporary liaisons substituted. Twenty years after the opening of Yokohama, one resident wrote that the "mildew of inaction" had grown over the port, subjecting its residents to a "weariness, staleness, [and] unprofitablness of existence compared to men at home". Japan had not proven to be an El Dorado, and the feeling of excitement and novelty that infused the settlement in the early years was gone. Steam routes and telegraphic communications imposed new demands, forcing merchants to remain in their offices longer. Travel to the interior was inconvenient and expensive, and Western women had less voice in domestic affairs, because the kitchen was the "abode of the heathen".

The answer was a less formal society in Yokohama, one where sincere and enjoyable social relations among foreigners would be possible. Turning inward for a solution, this resident suggested that women – wives of senior members of the Western trading firms – should open their homes and take the lead in creating a more informal society, which would "give a taste of home to the aimless wandering herds of the unattached" foreign men of the town. In this way, bachelors could enjoy the "magnetic power of feminine refinement". A move away from "champagne and supper" toward "grace and good humor" would enliven the sterile social environment.[157] Yearning for the benefits of such a "cult of domesticity" indeed suggested the strong connection to home. A hemisphere away the same imperatives obtained. In the mining camps of the American west, "deeper commitments to place… waited for women to turn bivouacs into settlements"[158] and reforms like prohibition awaited the arrival of women in cattle towns.[159] Speaking again of the domesticating power of women, "one observer of Chicago pool halls stated that 'Women not being present and there being no restraint of any kind, often the lowest and foulest expressions are heard. Obscene stories are related by small groups who do not engage in the game, but congregate in the corners and smoke cigarettes.' To this and other observers, an environment without women lured men down the path of dissipation".[160]

VII

One resident in the 1880s suggested that "the contents of the mail-bags, social events, and the perfection of physical comfort comprise the interests of most of the residents" of the ports. Most residents were nearly completely indifferent to their host country; the "old hands" of the ports shrugged with "superiority, amusement and fatigue" at anything new.[161] But the circumstances of residence in Japan changed. In the early years, few foreigners ventured far outside of the ports because of the danger involved – little real knowledge of their host country was the norm. By 1890, however, Japan's great questions of government and modernization were decided, and the host country was one with a stable political structure and an increasing trade with the West. Now foreigners could – if they so chose – individually or collectively enjoy a wider scope of contacts,[162] and consider modifications of their society in the light of the great changes taking place in their host country.

Yet treaty port merchants, including Americans, remained insular and largely uninterested in change of any kind. Merchants sought to preserve a social status quo which positioned them comfortably, if uneasily, at the top of port society. Americans gained easy entry into the British-dominated port society, and, once comfortably inside, made no critique of the social structure because it served their needs well, though they, like their British neighbors, considered their way of life under siege from a variety of forces. Globetrotters and missionaries, by criticizing merchants' social and moral pretensions, highlighted the fragility of treaty port life. Lacking the cultural flexibility with which to see any social or business potential beyond the island communities of ports, merchants largely ignored greater Japan while continuing to support a system whose rewards focused on the moment.

3

FORMAL POWER, ACTUAL DEPENDENCE

Consuls as intermediaries

> The local government ... in their relation to the foreign consuls
> have the character of being civil, courteous and yet obstructive
> withal.[1]

We have seen that American merchants were part of a society whose chief purpose was the preservation of order – they strove to sustain a world in which their solidarity was constantly reinforced. In this world, relations to groups perceived to be dangerous to the maintenance of that order were well defined. In this, merchants in the ports replicated larger patterns in the American experience. The startling growth in American power after the Civil War and into the early twentieth century revealed fault lines in the American consciousness in new and profoundly disturbing ways:

> In the period between the Centennial Exposition in 1876 (in which the
> United States announced its power on the international scene) and
> World War I (in which it demonstrated that power) the dynamics of
> industrialization rapidly accelerated the rate at which Americans were
> coming into contact with foreign peoples, both inside and outside U.S.
> borders. American political culture in these years was characterized by
> a paradoxical combination of supreme confidence in U.S. superiority
> and righteousness, with an anxiety driven by fierce parochialism.[2]

The treaty port society merchants built, while it served many essential functions well, contained some fault lines born of imperfect construction. In the process of conducting business in the ports merchants discovered new, related tensions whose resolution was complicated by the presence of groups on whom their dependence became increasingly clear; relations with their consuls, Japanese and Chinese employees and Japanese merchant counterparts progressively exposed these tensions. The resulting anxiety stemmed from conflict between "fiercely parochial" Americans and an unfamiliar landscape, and from the imperfect tools merchants found available to impose control on that landscape.

In their attempts to impose order and control on the business landscape of Japan, American merchants found their consuls to be at least partially effective proxies on behalf of merchant interests. Although the control the merchants exerted was largely defined by the level of Japanese cooperation, it was nevertheless sufficient to sustain in merchants' minds a sense that they themselves could and did help define the contours of their business success or failure. It must be remembered that, in the process of negotiating problems and challenges of the day-to-day operations discussed here, American merchants dealt directly with their consuls – men of their own race and language, who provided a welcome buffer against the more threatening and alien entity of the local Japanese government. When the consuls carried the day, merchants could be satisfied to have been part of cooperative progress. When their consuls failed, they could and did bemoan Japanese intransigence, bureaucracy and officiousness to the consuls, with whom they could at least comfortably commiserate on the fight well fought. Merchants, dependent on a variety of groups, were least threatened by their dependence on this group of fellow countrymen.

I

Ralph Waldo Emerson's essay "Wealth" applies the concept of individualism to the realm of economic endeavor:

> Wealth is in application of mind to nature, and the art of getting rich consists not in industry, much less in saving, but in a better order, in timeliness, in being at the right spot. One man has stronger arms, or longer legs; another sees by the course of streams, and growth of markets, where land will be wanted, makes a clearing to the river, goes to sleep, and wakes up rich.[3]

Later, Lester Frank Ward's *Dynamic Sociology* made a similar claim for man's ability to control his environment, stating that "society is simply a compound organism whose acts exhibit the resultant of all the individual forces which its members exert".[4] This attractive view of man in imagined, fortuitous control over his world appealed to the aggressive, entrepreneurial Victorian sensibility, and summarized something of the robust opportunities a rapidly growing economy offered. While the vision no doubt remained attractive throughout the Gilded Age, the reality of work for most Victorian men involved more compromise than conquest, more detail than dominance.[5] The Japanese "gold rush" ended in the late 1850s, and merchants who wanted to carve a living out of the strange marketplace of Japan faced in their daily lives obstacles large and small. In overcoming some and succumbing to others they measured their identities as men and their success as businessmen.

The formal political context in which Western businessmen operated in the treaty ports guaranteed them the advantages inherent in foreign control of Japan's tariff. The unequal treaties clearly stated that foreigners could "freely buy from the Japanese and sell to them any articles that either may have for sale, without the intervention of any Japanese officers in such purchase or sale, or in making or receiving payment for the same".[6] In practice, however, foreign merchants frequently complained that the Japanese government adhered to the letter rather than the spirit of the treaties.

On April 23, 1868, just four months after the opening of the port at Hyogo, the *Hiogo News* expressed its disappointment that Paul Frank, who had operated as consular agent since the opening of the port, had not been appointed as U.S. consul. The paper noted that Frank would be missed at Hyogo, "where in every instance in which he has had a controversy with the native officials, he has invariably sustained his position, and gained his point". This brief article accurately summarized the American merchants' definition of the function of the appointed officialdom in the ports.

What, in fact, did American merchants want? Their demands fell into several broad if often overlapping categories. They constantly asked for help with physical aspects of the ports – buildings and other improvements, for control and punishment of theft, and for swift and fair resolution of property and personal disputes. All of this implied the need for the Japanese authorities to sustain a presence in the ports capable of keeping order and distributing resources reasonably. At the same time, merchants wanted to be left alone, free from interference, to evade the modest tariff duties, to manage their cargoes as they saw fit and, on occasion, to smuggle. Clearly, Japanese priorities and very hands-on management would support some merchant aspirations and activities, while restricting others.

But American consuls' effectiveness – from the merchant point of view – was severely limited by two factors. First, American consuls, though carelessly chosen and ill-prepared for their duties abroad, nevertheless demonstrated an even-handedness in dispensing justice that disappointed any merchant expectations of consular extension, at Japanese expense, of their political rights and economic advantages under the treaties. Second, firm Japanese control over treaty port trade – in spite of the unequal treaties – further limited the power of consuls already overburdened with the minutiae of their jobs. American consuls clearly recognized that their effectiveness depended on the Japanese, whose general fair-mindedness reflected their commitment to living with the *fait accompli* of foreign merchants' "protected" status, while Japan both secured substantial control over the foreign trade and communities in its ports and demanded treaty revision to regain unambiguous sovereignty. So the control that Americans sought was possible only when their goals comported with Japanese goals.

What was the nature of the consular service that merchants called upon so frequently to do battle on behalf of their interests? General accounts of American diplomatic affairs in the late nineteenth century have made clear the broad limitations in the nation's consular services. The post-Civil War era saw the U.S. occupied with the great internal challenges of reconstruction, urbanization, immigration and industrialization, and with its attention focused inward, the nation paid relatively little attention to foreign policy. This indifference to foreign affairs applied especially to East Asia, which seemed exotic and unimportant and where the U.S. government perceived no vital political or economic interest.[7] By the late 1860s American consuls were appointed to Japanese posts from the U.S. as political rewards for loyal party service. One authority on the U.S. consular service labeled the period between the Civil War and the Spanish-American War "the nadir of U.S. consular system". Beginning with Ulysses S. Grant, who had no real concern for consular appointments other than to reward friends and veterans of the Union army, U.S. presidents' attitudes toward consular appointments reflected the general Gilded Age apathy toward foreign affairs.[8]

In the early days of the treaty ports, the U.S. government recruited American consuls from the ranks of businessmen already living in Asia. In many cases, these men did not distinguish between their official duties and their mercantile activity, often treating one as an adjunct of the other. Eben Dorr, for example, was both agent for Augustine Heard and Company and U.S. consul at Yokohama, and his employers were quick to take advantage of his official position in their business ventures.[9] The case of an American clipper ship calling at Hakodate, where its captain decided to stay and begin trade as a merchant, illustrates the blurring of trade and consular duties: the American consul there fought a duel with him over who would enjoy trading privileges at the port.[10]

The selection process later was hardly an improvement. An acquaintance of Grant's secretary of state Hamilton Fish described the period of appointments as "the rutting season among stags, with the amenities and decencies of civilization forgotten". Office seekers desirous of a consular or diplomatic appointment went to Grant, from whom they obtained cards which contained the president's recommendation for specific posts; "Apparently the procedure was to drop in at the White House, remind Grant of auld lang syne, get one of the scribbled cards, and present it at the State Department – as at a teller's window – as a voucher good for one diplomatic office".[11] On one occasion, Grant recommended a particularly unfit man for an overseas post; when Fish asked him about it, Grant responded that he simply "wanted to get him out of the country".[12]

As late as 1897 Mahlon Pitney, a New Jersey Congressman, endorsed the candidacy of Samuel Lyon for a consular post in Japan by stating that "Mr. Lyon is, and always has been, an earnest Republican", frequently elected as such, and that he was "strongly supported by influential Republicans" in Pitney's district.[13] Thomas Jernigan, who gave up an "uncongenial" position as a commission merchant in Norfolk in favor of the U.S. consulship at Osaka and Hyogo in 1885, initially wrote to the State Department asking for an appointment to "some consulship of respectable grade" at some unspecified location. One of his letters of support identified him as "a sterling democrat, a gentleman of the highest integrity and probity" who would no doubt discharge his duties competently; another mentioned that he "canvassed his district well" in the recent presidential election; two others asked that he be appointed as consul at "one of the leading cities of England or Scotland" or some other English-speaking location as a reward for life-long effective work on behalf of the Democratic party.[14] Another longtime consul was unusual in that he requested Japan first, but he noted that a position at Shanghai, Calcutta, Rio de Janeiro, Melbourne or Honolulu would also be satisfactory.[15]

Indeed, political appointees cared little for their overseas destinations beyond sometimes whether the host country was English-speaking. Realizing that tenure in consular posts was dictated by how long their party remained in office, consuls knew or cared little more than merchants about learning the Japanese language or any of the intricacies of doing business in Japan. Certainly their interests did not extend to advocating any reform of the established methods of doing business in the ports.

In July 1870 Congress approved an act to examine the accounts of American consuls abroad and to investigate how they managed their consulates. As a result, De Benneville Randolph Keim visited American consulates throughout the world from August 1870 through September 1871. What he found suggests precisely how unimportant consular appointments were to the U.S. government. Keim noted that:

> Almost every consulate had some defects in its history, owing to the incompetency, low habits and vulgarity of some of its officers, during the endless round of evils incident to official rotation .... Indeed the most important feature of my investigations was the ingenuity displayed by consular officers ... in defrauding the government and grasping gains from various outside sources beside.[16]

At Kanagawa, Keim "found an officer [Lemuel Lyon] in charge who was not only utterly incapable, but had established for himself a considerable reputation for ill manners and gross habits", whose consulate, reflecting his personal style, contained a "rude table, bookcase, and improvised desk, and a few chairs, the worse for rough treatment".[17] Tyler Dennett, a historian of U.S.–Japan relations, echoed Keim's assessment, stating that American consular officials were political "hangers-on" without legal training who succumbed to the "constant temptation for peculation" while abroad.[18]

Problems were not only the fault of the consuls. Once out of the country, consuls frequently had to operate on shoestring budgets, sometimes all but forgotten in remote outposts of "civilization" such as the Japanese treaty ports. Consular functions in East Asia included "general service and protection of interests" of American citizens. In this category was support of Americans' right to trade, use land and buildings, travel inland, secure burial grounds and worship freely. In addition, consuls were expected to guarantee fair trial to Americans, issue their passports, settle their estates and aid shipwrecked sailors[19] – heavy obligations for undermanned and poorly financed consular operations.

Consular requests to the State Department for larger allowances to pay for more clerical help became a constant refrain, but appropriations were hardly a priority in

Congress. Throughout the period, the incessant cry for more money and more manpower demonstrated a clear lag between funding and need. On one occasion, the Hyogo consulate noted that it was "entirely out" of such basic items as "ink and inkstands, sealing wax, quills, India rubber, tape, twine, plain official envelopes large and small ... blotting paper, office knives, erasers and mucilage", all unavailable locally except in "inferior quality and at exorbitant prices". Some requests suggest an almost pathetic need: T.M. Patton requested $100 to buy a "letter-copying press, a desk, a bookcase and a few office chairs. Such of these articles as are now in use here are more or less dilapidated and inadequate to the requirements of the office".[20]

Space was also a serious problem. In 1889, for example, E.J. Smithers, the consul at Osaka and Hyogo, wrote to the State Department describing how he heard numerous cases dealing with American seamen in the consulate's general office, which often caused "inconvenience and delay to the merchants having business at the consulate". He asked for an additional $200 to fund construction of a consular courtroom.[21] Indeed, the increasing numbers of American seamen passing through the treaty ports took an enormous amount of the consuls' time. By 1890, E.J. Smithers wrote plaintively to the State Department that "the work of this consulate has increased to such an extent" as to make acute his need to hire an "experienced assistant as vice or deputy consul" to assist with paperwork. Police cases of seamen and the constant demands for passports to travel into the interior from travelers and missionaries consumed Smithers' time as well as that of his interpreter.[22]

A dearth of competent interpreters hindered American consuls as well. One authority on U.S. consular affairs in East Asia correctly described the government's handling of translating and interpreting as "linguistic mendicancy". Often borrowing the linguistic expertise of "English colleagues" or "busy missionaries", American consular officials were, especially in the early years of the treaty ports, frequently embarrassed by their inability to provide basic services.[23] In September, 1868, for example, the State Department denied Thomas Stewart's request for a salary appropriation for a staff interpreter, suggesting that Stewart hire one "as needed". By 1870, the Hyogo consulate had an interpreter on staff, but again in 1877 the consulate requested a $500 yearly allowance for an interpreter.[24]

The quality of these interpreters was often suspect; in 1883, the Kanagawa consulate requested $1,500 per year for a "first class Japanese interpreter" as he was "making do with a Japanese at $35 per month" who was not satisfactory.[25] In fact, interpreters rarely remained with the consulates for long periods and consequently the quality of communications suffered; consuls were often at the mercy of whomever was in the port and claimed to speak serviceable Japanese. The case of the Japanese interpreter K. Agaya, who in 1883 "absconded ... after an unsuccessful attempt to obtain money by forgery from the Japanese Judicial Court", highlights the problem of reliability.[26] Competition over the small pool of competent and experienced personnel demonstrates the manpower shortage that plagued the consulates. For example, when Julius Stahel left his post in Hyogo for

Shanghai in 1884, Thomas Van Buren, the U.S. consul at Kanagawa, persuaded George Scidmore, a competent "Old Japan Hand", to remain in Japan, but he accused Stahel of maneuvering to have Scidmore transferred with him to Shanghai.[27]

Clearly, consuls laboring under such difficulties and hard-pressed to meet even their own official needs were unable to provide adequate interpreting or translation services to merchants who were frequently confused over the provisions of contracts, or who needed assistance when appearing in Japanese court, or who were unable to understand the mechanics of specific business transactions except through their Asian employees, who often had reason to withhold their knowledge from their employers.

II

Whatever their prejudices in favor of their own nationals, American consuls' usually took a balanced approach to settling conflict in the ports, in part because there was some political sympathy for the Japanese and in part because consular effectiveness in fact depended heavily on Japanese help. John A. Bingham, U.S. Minister to Japan from 1873 to 1885, made no secret of his disdain for the unequal treaties and the humiliation that U.S. consular jurisdiction inflicted on Japan; some consuls sympathized with Bingham's position and meted out justice fairly to Japanese and American alike in their consular jurisdictions. Julius Stahel, who served as in the Kanagawa consulate, 1866–69 and as U.S. consul at Hyogo from 1877 until 1884, displayed consular competence that attracted wide respect.

Stahel's life spanned many countries, causes and careers. Born in Hungary in 1825, Stahel attended school in Budapest and joined the Austrian Army, where he was promoted to lieutenant. He sided with the revolutionary cause during Hungary's struggle for independence, but had to flee the country when the movement was suppressed in 1849. For the next ten years he worked as a teacher and journalist in London and Berlin. In 1859 he came to the U.S., and until the outbreak of the Civil War he edited a German-language newspaper in New York City. When the war broke out, he and Louis Blenker recruited the 8th New York regiment, of which he became lieutenant colonel and later colonel. In 1861 he was promoted to brigadier general, and to major general of volunteers in 1863. In November of that year, Stahel led the escort from Washington to Gettysburg when Lincoln made his famous address. In 1864, he was severely wounded while leading a division, for which action he was eventually awarded the Congressional Medal of Honor in 1893.[28]

After the war, Stahel secured an appointment as consul at Kanagawa and served there from 1866 to 1869, but was recalled when Grant entered office. Although Stahel had other prospects, one of which was a position with the Equitable Life Assurance Association, he sought and obtained the post at Osaka/Hyogo in 1877, and discharged his duties with an integrity that earned him the respect of the State Department, which promoted him to the position of consul general at Shanghai seven years later. One China merchant considered him "so different from the ordinary run of consuls that I am anxious to do anything in my power to help him". Another supporter stated that he was much impressed with Stahel's operation in Hyogo, and that Stahel had the solid backing of the business community.[29] Yet Stahel was no merchant lackey. In 1879 he noted that the Kobe consulate lacked the proper legal books for reference in cases heard in his court and admonished the State Department that:

> The consuls in the East who have Judicial Power are often called upon to give decisions and pass judgement on cases of more than ordinary importance. In many cases their duties are of a very perplexing nature, having to deal with intricate and knotty points calculated to puzzle the mind of even an expert jurist. To find one self in this position without even the benefit of even a proper book of reference at hand is by no means an enviable situation for one, who is actuated by feelings of responsibility.[30]

Stahel's attitudes reflected those of his superior, John A. Bingham. As U.S. Minister to Japan from 1873 to 1885, Bingham consistently opposed the treaty port system which deprived Japan of judicial and tariff autonomy. A constant foe of British Minister Sir Harry Parkes, Bingham emphasized that the treaties humiliated the Japanese, and he urged their immediate revision.[31] Tyler Dennett characterized Bingham, as "one of the most determined and uncompromising American friends of Japan which the last half of the nineteenth century produced in abundance .... He was a characteristic American of the period".[32] Bingham complained bitterly and constantly of the irony of the U.S. – ostensibly a republican example to the world – imposing its will on a weaker nation. Implicit in Bingham's attitude was a willingness to deal directly and equally with Japan as a rapidly industrializing and "civilizing" nation which deserved the equal treatment accorded Western nations. Bingham firmly believed that American participation in any cooperative policy that deprived Japan of its tariff autonomy was inappropriate and contradictory to republican principles. In 1876 Bingham labelled the Convention of 1866, which set tariff rates at an even more favorable rate than had the Harris treaty

> a manifest injustice by the confession of every Treaty Power with Japan, each of which claims for itself what it denies to Japan, the right to control its foreign commerce by commercial regulations of its own enactment, fettered by nothing save reciprocal conventions[33]

and argued that the artificially low tariff made Japan "a tributary to Great Britain".[34]

Bingham was an Ohio Republican who had authored Reconstruction legislation, and his idealism was reflected in his position toward Japan. The U.S., he argued, should lead the way in welcoming Japan to the fraternity of "Westernized" – read "civilized" – nations, the inevitable result of which would be long-term goodwill between the nations, as well as the benefits accruing from American access to Japanese interior markets. The "simple justice" of treaty revision would redound to America's favor as Japan continued to develop. Bingham argued that Japan was "[b]y the ordinances of nature the gate to the commerce of America and all western Europe with Eastern Asia, and therefore it is of moment that our government … should deal justly with Japan".[35] Because Bingham emphasized Japan's readiness to enter the comity of civilized nations, the Japanese came to regard him as a warm friend and ally in their long fight to revise the treaties. The Americans employed by the Japanese foreign office reflected Bingham's attitude toward Japan's status *vis-à-vis* the treaty powers. E. Peshine Smith, Eli T. Sheppard and Henry W. Denison, *oyatoi* recruited by the Japanese government as advisors in the process of treaty revision, all supported Japan's drive toward equality.[36]

Keim's report would suggest an officialdom that was corrupt and clumsily greedy; certainly they were political appointees with little preparation and inadequate financing for their jobs. Yet American merchants came to rely on certain consuls and expressed sincere regret when they were recalled or left their posts for other reasons. A group of Hyogo residents, including five prominent American merchants, presented a memorial to Grover Cleveland in 1885, asking him to retain Thomas M. Patton as consul in Osaka and Hyogo, arguing that he was "in the relations of life – public and private – a fit representative of an enlightened Christian country, whose removal we would deeply regret".[37] When Julius Stahel left after three years at Kanagawa, he noted that "the American Merchants and Citizens at Kanagawa united in a memorial to the State Department, requesting my retention as Consul at that Port", and again when he left for a post in China after seven years in Hyogo, the foreign citizens there gathered in sincere appreciation of his efforts on behalf of the foreign community and its mercantile interests.[38] Thomas Van Buren, the U.S. consul at Kanagawa, earned the trust of Yokohama merchants, who expressed "unqualified praise as to the manner in which [Van Buren] performed his arduous duties as Consul General; he made indeed a very, very good Consul and an excellent judge".[39] Both the British and American mercantile communities expressed sincere regret at the departure of Paul Frank, who was acting consul, from Hyogo.[40]

What accounts for these expressions of merchant approval, despite the weakness of the general system? One possible explanation would involve the kinds of judgments that American consuls rendered in their courts.[41] If merchants perceived that their property interests were particularly well served by American consuls, their often favorable attitude becomes more understandable, and indeed there is some limited evidence to suggest that American consuls' decisions in mixed cases – where the plaintiff was Japanese and the defendant American – occasionally favored merchant business interests.

One example of a pro-merchant court decision concerned some Americans' plans to lease property to businessmen. In 1870, the American J.M. Batchelder purchased the leases of four lots in Tsukiji, the small foreign concession in Tokyo, with the expectation that the Japanese government would strictly enforce provisions forbidding any foreigners to live outside the concession area – thereby increasing the rental value of his lots to foreign businessmen. When foreigners moved into areas outside of Tsukiji, leaving it little more than a backwater, Batchelder refused to pay his ground rents to the Tokyo government, which then sued him in the U.S. Consular court for ¥3,500 in unpaid rents. Batchelder responded by asking for a judgment against the Japanese for $10,000 in damages to compensate him for the improvements he made in the properties and for lost income.

The testimony at the trial revealed that other foreigners – John Hartley, William Rangan and Caspar Bennwald – had rented land at Tsukiji for the same speculative purposes, and that twenty-four other original purchasers of land had petitioned the American Minister in 1875, bringing to his attention the "wrongs and injuries" done their property by the Japanese. Van Buren dismissed the case of the city of Tokyo against Batchelder, saving him the ¥3,500 in unpaid rentals. With regard to Batchelder's counter-suit, Van Buren agreed that Batchelder had suffered $10,000 in damages, but recognized that he had no authority to compel the city of Tokyo, which had voluntarily submitted itself to U.S. consular jurisdiction, to pay damages. The commentary of the *Japan Weekly Mail*, an English language newspaper in Yokohama, was decidedly sympathetic to the position of foreigners whose land depreciated in value because of the "connivance of the authorities".[42] Such cases buttressed the Japanese conviction that foreign consular courts always gave the "profit and advantage to the foreigner and always hurled on the head of the Japanese the loss and injury".[43]

The picture of injustice in foreign consular courts, however, derived more from the Japanese desire to escape the thraldom of the treaties than from fact. Richard T. Chang has argued persuasively that Western consular court injustice to the Japanese was little more than a myth. Chang estimates that the U.S. consular courts heard approximately 659 mixed cases, of which possibly one – the case of Batchelder and his Tsukiji "investment property" – was adjudicated unfairly.[44] Working on the assumption that sustained consular injustice would surely have resulted in some public outcry, Chang tested his conclusions by looking at Japanese newspapers throughout the forty years of extraterritoriality and discovered only nine instances where newspapers referred to "unpublicized" cases.[45]

There is a certain logic to the proposition that incompetent and unprofessional consuls were liable to dispense questionable justice, but such a "conclusion is contrary to the facts as it applies to Japanese litigants at the American courts".[46] Chang noted that the bad reputation of foreign consular courts derived from five highly publicized cases – not one of which involved the American court. Chang correctly points out that the problems manifest in Keim's report – insofar as they reflected the official behavior of the consuls he encountered – show clearly that "none of the individuals who complained were Japanese or speaking on behalf of any Japanese"; all related to "civil suits or disputes" among Americans.[47]

While diplomatic officials addressed the nation's interests, consuls were expected to care for "separate and individual concerns".[48] Consuls were part of the workaday mercantile world of the ports. Sharing the club and sporting life of the ports with merchants, and rubbing elbows with them in a hundred ways, one might reasonably expect consuls to sympathize with merchant concerns and to express such concern by using their authority as judges in consular court to protect their property interests. Such decisions, however, were apparently extremely rare; Batchelder's case was exceptional in its unfairness.

Men such as Stahel, whose notions of justice more closely resembled the moral high ground of Bingham, were upright public servants, who never wholly catered to merchant interests at the expense of justice to the Japanese. If American consuls did not consider it their duty – at least in court – simply to favor American business interests, the seeming anomaly of merchant affection for consuls who played no particular favorites in court persists. One compelling explanation is that merchants simply depended on their consuls on a daily basis. Merchants' interests were served in essential ways by maintaining social and professional relationships with consuls who could intercede on their behalf in the countless business details of mercantile life in the ports. After a seasoning period, consuls developed skills in dealing with the mechanics of recovering stolen property, passing on merchant complaints and other routine requests common to the treaty ports. In addition, merchants were doubtless well aware that consuls could do little when Americans wanted to recover property from the Japanese, a circumstance not provided for under extraterritoriality, and did not hold them responsible for doing the impossible.

American merchants' definition of "doing business" in the treaty ports seldom included direct contact with Japanese customers or markets. Isolated from Japanese merchants and officials and the Japanese marketplace, American merchants turned the inevitable misunderstandings over to the increasingly overworked and undermanned American consulates. One of the most striking features of the material in the archives of Osaka/Hyogo and Nagasaki is the frequency with which merchants called upon consular officials to intercede in the day-to-day affairs of the business community.

Earlier, on the China coast, "the extension of the consular system meant the grafting of a restrictive political element upon what had been primarily a commercial and social situation". In this strained state of affairs, merchants long accustomed to independent action resented political consuls and often regarded them as little more than a "nuisance".[49] In Japan, however, the foreign presence proceeded from a diplomatic event – the signing of the Townsend Harris treaty in 1858 – and merchants never established any real independence of action. When their Japanese customers failed to fulfill contracts or pay their bills, or when local authorities arrested their Japanese employees, American merchants turned to their consuls for assistance.[50] Culturally insulated in the ports, merchants depended upon those whose responsibility it was to buttress the political structure that ensured their "favored" status.

III

The nature of the male culture of the Victorian workplace sheds some light on the salutary relationship between merchants and their consuls in the ports. First, the world of work and the world of relaxation overlapped considerably for nineteenth-century men. In their time away from work, they frequently associated with men they knew from the workplace, and conversation frequently turned to topics of mutual professional concern. This form of bonding was quite common in the U.S. and, as chapter two suggests, even more common in the social structure and activities common to the treaty ports. Consuls and merchants lived together in the very narrow society of the ports, shared a common language, memories and heritage. Men in the U.S. gathered together according to geographical origin, such as "men from New Hampshire who moved to Boston tending to settle in the same neighborhoods and boardinghouses",[51] and merchants in Japan did the same. While the merchant and consul treaty port population may have been more diverse (with men from far-flung areas of the country), it is clear that in the context of the port, where an automatic solidarity with other white men obtained, they bonded together coherently and often productively. The lives of these merchants and consuls were as "narrowly circumscribed" as those of folks back home "who considered the next town or the next city block alien territory". Among such people, "deeply felt loyalties served both as a defense against outsiders and as a means of identification within".[52]

Second, merchants quickly realized that they needed help to negotiate the business world they had chosen. The nineteenth-century mythology of the self-made man has obscured the obvious – that the "work world created by the market economy was a fundamentally social one .... The work of the merchant ... was usually interpersonal and some of it was unrelentingly so. Many men had partners, most had subordinates, some had face-to-face rivals, all had clients, and, in differing degrees, all of them were clients themselves".[53] This more complicated world, in which the individual needed to subordinate various individualistic impulses and rely on the expertise of others, was the workaday world of the treaty ports. Though the individual remained the primary "unit of action", the world of male work was one of "profound interdependence". American merchants recognized this, and the many contingencies on which their success or failure, measured daily, would depend.[54]

Merchants' requests involved consuls in several kinds of issues. The first was petty crime in the ports. In 1871, the American merchant Jonathan Staples wrote to the U.S. consul at Kobe complaining that his Japanese gardener, "one Chuyamon of Osaka, ran away from my house where he has lived in my employ for the past year, stealing a small amount of my money, and, I think, sundry other articles. I now beg you to request the native authorities to apprehend the thief, restore my stolen property and have him punished according to his crime".[55] On another occasion, an American merchant stated that his servant, the Chinese woman Ah-Ho, stole several items and an unspecified amount of money from his residence; another case involved a "vulgar person named Kumazo", who confessed to stealing two pieces of light green blanket from a foreign house in the settlement.[56] Other reports deal with the theft of clocks, drinking glasses, flower pots, table linen, boat sails and small amounts of kerosene oil and charcoal.[57] Throughout the treaty port era, the Japanese responded strongly to such requests, motivated by a strong desire to make their control manifest.[58]

Other routine services to merchants involved acting as go-betweens in land disputes. In 1871, Walsh, Hall and Company held a promissory note on a house mortgaged by a Japanese named Nakamura. When the note fell due and Nakamura failed to pay the balance, the American firm wrote to its consul, "We wish … to be placed in possession of the property secured to us and will feel obligated if you will take whatever steps may be necessary for the purpose".[59]

Merchants also depended on consuls to settle the large volume of petty disputes among foreigners. Packed together tightly in the confines of the foreign concessions and immediately surrounding areas, frequent squabbles, occasionally erupting into violence, arose between foreigners. In 1869, for example, an American merchant named Simon went to the beach at Hyogo for a swim with two of his dogs, which he tied up on a hillside behind the beach. There they began barking, and another American, William Nivers, shot one of the dogs while Simon swam. When Simon confronted Nivers, he admitted killing the dog, which he claimed had earlier killed some of Nivers' cattle. In the ensuing argument, Nivers threatened to shoot Simon, who later sued in consular court for $100 and damages.[60] Disputes among foreigners of different nationalities were more frequent and required tedious exchanges of notes among various consuls to determine whose consular court had jurisdiction and an appropriate means of enforcing judgment.[61]

A typical problem between foreigners of different nationality was that involving two Englishmen named Johnson and Walsh, who in 1872 published the Hiogo News, the local paper in Kobe. In their June 5 issue, they referred to the American assistant surgeon of the U.S.S. Colorado, J.R. Tryon, as "Dr. Spindleshanks" and as a "Legation Lackey". The paper further noted that Tryon had won a sum of money in a recent poker game and was "reveling in the proceeds". Tryon took grave offence, and demanded an apology, which Johnson and Walsh printed, but which Tryon considered inadequate to retrieve his soiled reputation in the narrow social world of the ports. Considering the original item an "unpardonable insult" and "cowardly in the extreme", Tryon stated that he could not, "with honor to myself, allow anyone to brand me, through public print, as a gambler and a blackleg with impunity". On his next visit to Hyogo, Tryon recruited a comrade from his ship, a lieutenant Emory, and found Johnson in the Public Garden. There, Tryon stated, he

> took redress in my own hands and caned him to the best of my ability. Being disarmed by breaking my own stick over his head and shoulders, I stooped to pick up a "Penang Lawyer" thrown to one side by Lt. Emory. In doing this Mr. Johnson struck me with his cane. I turned upon him

with my weapon and struck fairly at him, when he turned to run halooing "Murder Help" etc. I pursued him through the garden, where the crowd interfered and I lost sight of him.

This case involved Americans and British citizens, and was further complicated by the question of where Tryon, if found guilty, would be punished as he was attached to the U.S. Asiatic Squadron. The incident was followed by a tedious exchange of notes among the commander of the squadron and the British and American consuls.[62]

IV

While many consuls acted with integrity in the cases they handled, their fairness owed most to the fact that they generally depended on the Japanese to accomplish anything. Consuls' limited success in prodding the local Japanese authorities into action accurately reflected their limited power. Though some consuls may have agreed with merchants' assessment of their role in the treaty ports, the practical consideration of weighing merchant interests against Japanese resolve to take an active hand in controlling treaty port trade defined consuls' limitations and strategies in defending merchants' interests.

Compelled by circumstances to open the ports, the Bakufu allowed trade but regulated it informally. American merchants entered a country whose government was accustomed to an active economic role. Throughout the Tokugawa period, the state had played a major role in the economy of Japan, exerting "some degree of control over almost every aspect of economic life". As foreigners took up residence in the treaty ports in the late 1850s and 1860s, such controls became "increasingly detailed", and, though their effectiveness was declining, they nevertheless continued to influence the economy. The shogunate controlled the large financial and commodity markets of Osaka, and regulated them through chartered trade associations. It issued a wide variety of decrees in the 1860s to control prices, supervise foreign trade, control all main highways, regulate freight rates, operate mines and encourage certain industries. Some "han" (feudal domains of the *daimyo*) also participated in "production and marketing" on a smaller scale. In Choshu, for example, "almost all commerce in the more important products was handled from producer to final sale by official marketing boards".[63]

But central control emanating from the Bakufu itself was an over-riding, if declining, reality throughout the Tokugawa period. The Bakufu held almost twenty-five percent of the nation's land, including all cities of high economic importance, and almost half of the urban population. It controlled silver and gold production, monopolized coinage, and "could issue orders to the *daimyo* ... who tended to follow its lead".[64] The Japanese economy in which foreigners found themselves involved was one in which the precedent of central guidance had been firmly set. However, even those in the Bakufu who favored the opening of the country in the 1850s were inclined toward restriction and monopolization of foreign trade to secure its advantages to the government by using it to strengthen the Japanese military. The British diplomat Rutherford Alcock defined the Japanese approach to foreign trade by labeling its policy as one of "negation, accepting the letter, but determined on resistance *à l'outrance* to the spirit of the treaties".[65]

William Beasley has noted that "from the beginning the Bakufu attempted to restrict trade by every means short of breach of treaty. It countenanced obstruction by customs officials, at one time imposed an embargo on silk exports, at another refused to supply foreigners with Japanese currency". By May, 1860, the Bakufu decided to exercise more permanent control of foreign trade by "ensuring that all exports of certain selected goods (including silk thread, wax and rape seed oil) must pass through the hands of the great Edo wholesale houses, which were under bakufu patronage and supervision …. While bakufu intentions remained restrictive, the attractions of wealth and profit proved stronger than the machinery of enforcement. Large-scale evasion made the regulations ineffective".[66] Foreigners, then, functioned in the face of official opposition, but they were able to function because of the acquisitive aspirations of some Japanese individuals.

From the very beginning of American mercantile activity in the treaty ports, a frequent and shrill complaint was that the Japanese threw too many obstacles in the way of doing business. What was intolerable to merchants at the beginning seemed to them to grow more odious and conspiratorial as time wore on. Japan's social order had been frozen since the seventeenth century into the class divisions of samurai, peasant, artisan and merchant. This social hierarchy – with merchants at the bottom of society – though considerably eroded by the mid nineteenth century, still remained a reference point for judging social status in Japanese consciousness. American merchants, assuming the ameliorative effects of the trade they brought to Japan, blamed the Japanese government for failing to recognize the importance of its own merchants. "Agents of the customs house", one observer noted, "leave no means untried of establishing a check on the movements of foreigners and restraining within their own power the extent of native intercourse with the new mercantile establishment" (see Figure 5, page 108). He continued:

> Native officials appear to retain … the contemptuous depreciation of the mercantile class which prevails in the country, where traders and merchants, however prosperous and wealthy, occupy one of the lowest steps in the social scale and stand some degrees below artisans, carpenters and stonemasons in popular estimation. It is probably this feeling which leads them to underrate the importance of commercial privileges and to misunderstand the policy of European nations in seeking new outlets for our trade. They throw many impediments in the way of foreign commerce by the same custom-house restrictions as sometimes occur in Nagasaki, and by employing intimidation against native sellers to deter them from bringing their produce direct to the foreign merchant.

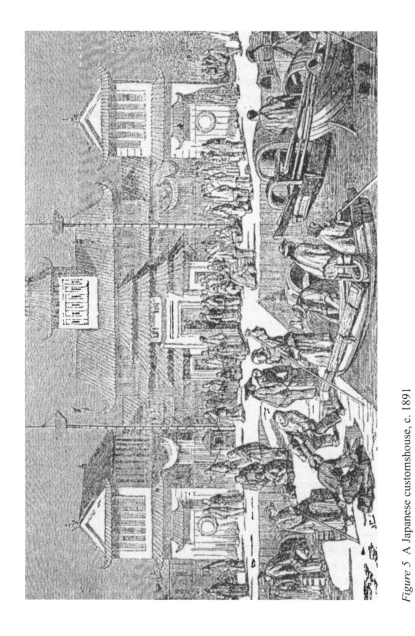

Figure 5 A Japanese customshouse, c. 1891

Source: Edward Rand, *All Aboard for Sunrise Lands* (Chicago: Donohue, Henneberry & Co. 1891).

He also noted that a Japanese silk-dealer came to an English merchant and "in my presence complained of the native officials laying three percent secret duty on all the bales of silk which he had ready to be transported for sale" at Yokohama, and that "another merchant had a superior pair of quality lacquered folding-door screens which he was willing to sell by private contract to a foreigner at his own house, but which he was prohibited to remove from his warehouse without a special permit and previous payment of a percentage value to the Japanese custom-house". Native authorities had complete control over the "ferries, roads and all means of approach" to the foreign settlements and functioned as "an effective curtailment of foreign commerce". The Japanese government, fearing that large silk exports would produce scarcity and drive up prices, "laid on an impost of three percent on silk ... in ignorance of the fundamental laws of political economy and thus helped to close up a source of national profit and imperial wealth, instead of encouraging native industry and promoting the material prosperity of the country".[67]

This component of the foreign response to Japanese interference in trade – that a malicious and short-sighted Japanese government willfully deprived the Japanese public of the benefits and prosperity that trade would bring – recurred often. Describing Nagasaki in 1860, George Smith wrote that:

At one time the Japanese officials give an arbitrary high conventional value to the native gold and silver coin, in which they compel all transactions of barter to be made, thus depreciating the silver Mexican dollar which forms the general medium of exchange ... and proportionately raising the price of every article purchased. At another time they endeavor to limit all foreign trade to licensed native buyers and sellers, who are known to be mulcted in a percentage of the moneys received, and to find relief in a necessary addition to the prices charged by foreigners.

He continued, "Sometimes all native boatmen are prohibited from hiring themselves to foreigners except those who bear a written permit from the custom-house", adding that "large stores of Japanese produce are bargained for, and at the last moment the transaction is delayed or frustrated by the withholding of the requisite sanction of the native authorities". "The ordinary mercantile classes of the Japanese", he wrote, "if left to themselves, would gladly enlarge their dealings and bring down from the interior districts almost any desired amount of merchandise".[68]

The emphasis on control continued under Meiji leadership after 1868. Given that most Meiji reforms and Japan's emphasis on *fukoku-kyohei* was designed to preserve the independence of the country, the Meiji leaders understandably perceived Japan's treaty requirements and the relatively small group of foreign merchants controlling the great bulk of foreign trade as an embarrassment and a threat to national sovereignty. Japan after 1858 was, for better or worse, incorporated into the world economy. As the foreign merchant presence was an accomplished fact – supported by the structure of the unequal treaties – the Meiji government determined that trade would go forward on its own terms, and its regulation of Western merchants reflected the imperative of Japanese control of Japanese trade by the means left at its disposal.

Foreign merchants in the treaty ports felt the controlling hand of local authorities almost daily; Japanese authorities worked through the foreign consuls to regulate many of the details of treaty port life. No business was transacted on Japanese public holidays, for example.[69] Because foreigners' dogs often roamed the concessions "defiling the streets and causing great injury", the local Japanese authorities required each foreign dog owner to display a wooden registration ticket without which dogs would be subject to impoundment.[70] On one occasion, the Japanese government reminded the American consul to admonish Warren Tillson Company, which supplied the pork requirements of the Hyogo settlement, to control its pigs, which were sometimes "left at large on the streets and entered the compounds of some houses". The local authorities even notified the foreign consuls that a "ploughman" named Kisoyemon was designated as "sweeper and duster" of the streets in the foreign concession".[71]

The Japanese commitment to promoting trade on their own terms can be glimpsed in the attitude toward physical improvements in the ports. The Japanese prepared each of the ports for foreign residence and trade, but foreigners – with the exception of those in Hyogo – proved generally unwilling to manage their own municipal affairs.[72] Failing to fund necessary improvements themselves, merchants were forced to rely on the Japanese to provide the physical improvements essential to a growing trade. Three years after Hyogo opened to foreign trade, the local foreign chamber of commerce complained that the docking place at the far eastern end of the settlement was not deep enough to accommodate ships for loading, because it was "gradually filling with sand ... and a considerable portion of it is already useless for the purpose for which it was intended". The chamber observed that "ladened ships have to wait as much as a day for tides to get them through" and requested that the consuls prevail upon the Japanese to "remedy the evil without loss of time".

The Japanese authorities responded by starting work in August 1871, but soon abandoned the project for over five months. By January of the following year, foreign merchants remained unsatisfied, and resolved in a meeting: "Consuls are again asked to press the matter upon the attention of the authorities". The consuls dutifully passed on the merchant concern, and the Japanese government office responded that its mechanical dredger had proved ineffective, and that the job now would be done by manual labor. Because the coolies could not work in the water in cold weather, labor would recommence in the warm season.[73]

Six years later, J.D Carroll and Company complained that storms threatened to flood their godowns because the drainage in the settlement was insufficient to carry off the water coming over the bundwall.[74] Sometimes merchants appealed to their consuls in high-flown terms that disguised their dependence on the Japanese. Complaining that a pathway to his property was not constructed in accordance with his lease agreement, Charles Wiggins of Carroll and Company commented bitterly that "in all civilized countries in the world where a man buys or leases a piece of property he is entitled to a roadway to same …. If you think my demand unreasonable, I am willing to pay the full amount, having learned another lesson of putting faith in Japanese verbal promises and just treatment".[75]

When Japanese interests coincided with those of Western merchants, expensive construction could go forward with alacrity. No doubt with an eye to the day when Japan would take control of its foreign trade, the Japanese government subsidized the Kobe Pier Company, which in 1884 completed a modern pier 500 feet long in the harbor at a cost of ¥100,000 ($87,000) which allowed ships to unload directly without using the small and unwieldy native boats. Connected to the pier by a tramway were four fireproof warehouses totaling 17,000 square feet. The structure was completed "entirely under the supervision of native engineers" and its opening was accompanied with the publication of detailed regulations and pier and storage charges for all shipping.[76]

One focus of American merchants' complaints involved irritation at what they judged to be the overzealous behavior of the individual Japanese customshouse employees. The American commercial treaty of 1858 specifically provided that the "Japanese Government shall have the right to place custom-house officers on board of any ship in their ports".[77] Since Japanese customs officials until the 1870s were two-sworded samurai accustomed to social deference, tensions ran high at times as they inspected the cargos of sea captains accustomed to having complete authority at sea. John Baxter Will, a ship captain who was in and out of the Japanese treaty ports extensively in the late nineteenth century, described a visit to the port of Hakodate in 1860:

> The first people to come on board were the customs officials, each wearing two long swords at his side. They brought a little wooden house with them; it was a little over six feet square. It was put up on deck for them to live in. The wood was all jointed and was put up in half an hour, roof and all …. This held the two mats on which they squatted and slept at night. They had a box with a charcoal fire, which was used for making hot water for their tea in the daytime but was put out on deck at night when they slept. Everything about the house was neat and clean.[78]

Such procedures, though permissible under customs regulations, sometimes led to misunderstandings.

When the inevitable conflicts concerning the mechanics of trade occurred, Japanese authorities showed a willingness to compromise after having established the principle of their own essential control. In April, 1868, William Jones, master of the American barque *Despatch*, complained to Paul Frank that a squad of two-sworded men boarded his ship and, after establishing an irregularity in its cargo seals, began removing its cargo of tea. Coming on deck, Jones observed a gang of coolies unloading the tea, and immediately forbade them to "touch a single package", while at the same time pointing emphatically to the American flag flying from the mast. Jones instructed the mate to take the cargo tackle from the customshouse officials, but one man made as if to draw his sword, whereupon one of Jones' crewmen pointed a pistol at him, forcing the Japanese to retire. Finding he "had not sufficient force to keep them from further insulting the American nation", Jones signaled the American warship *Oneida*, which sent a party to help. Now outnumbered, the Japanese left.

Jones immediately wrote to Frank stating that he would not allow Japanese on his ship and demanded an apology from the Japanese as well as "ample compensation for threatening the lives of myself, officers and men". He concluded by leaving "the satisfaction of the insult to the flag to your own judgement and discretion". Two days later, Jones, still indignant, wrote Frank again that he was "still annoyed and put under great delay and inconvenience by the rudeness and insults of the Japanese officials ... notwithstanding there were proper [inspection] permits".

Frank, whose service in the American Civil War would suggest a sensitivity to issues of national honor – now manifest in the "violation" of American mercantile rights in a foreign port – wrote a strong letter of complaint to R.B. van Valkenburgh, the American minister at Kanagawa, demanding an official apology from the Japanese government. Though he sympathized with Frank's position, van Valkenburgh replied that such a demand was "not advisable" and that he did not believe he was justified in demanding that the Japanese "discontinue boarding merchant vessels while wearing swords". Retreating to the text of the treaty, van Valkenburgh insisted only on "our undoubted right that in all cases of complaint against American citizens, no action whatever shall be taken by the Japanese authorities without the knowledge and consent or at the request of the Consular Officer of the United States". [79] Van Valkenburgh's response suggests something of the power relations in the treaty ports: while American interests were to be safeguarded when possible, the reality of Japanese control effectively limited the range of American action.

V

Soon after the port of Osaka/Hyogo was opened to foreign residence and commerce in 1868, the U.S. consul Paul Frank wrote to the local Japanese authorities expressing the American hope that the mercantile relationship between the Japanese and Americans in the ports would be mutually beneficial. "Believe me", he wrote, "I will always use my official authority to prevent any American here to do injustice or take unfair advantage of any Japanese subject but that I shall in return most earnestly request that the Japanese authorities act upon the same principle". The following month, Ito Shunske (later known as Ito Hirobumi), the vice governor of Hyogo, wrote to Frank:

> I have the honor to beg you will be pleased to notice to American subjects that the customhouse shall come into effect from 5th day tomorrow and the officers in charge of the customhouse, being all engaged, the

commerce will be treated without obstruction and also the import and the export duties will be required according to the trade regulations of treaty.[80]

The rhetoric of goodwill notwithstanding, the customshouse was to become an unhappy location for each side – a conduit for voicing disagreement and mutual recrimination which reflected the differing expectations of Japanese and Americans. An examination of the endless controversies surrounding the customshouse sheds light on the processes of trade, the expectations of the American merchant community, and the realities of power in the ports.

The Japanese, struggling throughout the late nineteenth century toward the goal of treaty revision and mercantile as well as diplomatic equality with the West, saw the customshouse as a point of intersection with foreigners whereby an extremely narrow interpretation of the treaties could limit foreign penetration of the Japanese economy. American merchants, when it was to their advantage to do so, insisted on adherence to the "spirit" of the treaties and trade conventions with equal persistence and stridency. The original Harris treaty and the Convention of 1866 were quite specific with regard to duties, but there were nevertheless many points of contact on which the agreements were subject to interpretation.

For the mercantile communities of the treaty ports, the customshouses occupied a central place geographically as well as institutionally. From the first, the Japanese authorities issued specific regulations that were to govern the details of how foreigners went about doing business. On the day after the port of Hyogo opened, the U.S. Minister in Kanagawa transmitted to Paul Frank a copy of "regulations for the trade and residence of the foreigners at Hiogo and Osaca", which he expected Frank to distribute to American citizens engaged in trade. Included were guidelines governing the establishment of a tow boat, lights and passage boat service between Hyogo and Osaka. Another set of regulations governed specifics such as limits on charges for hiring boats transporting cargo, (including a "small distinguishing flag with Japanese and European figures") and the rates and distances for which coolie labor could be hired to carry goods to warehouses. By April, the customshouse informed foreign merchants that they could land or ship goods only from one of the two specially constructed jetties in the harbor, and only after securing permits from the customshouse. The regulations were clear that "any violation" meant the merchandise could and would be confiscated and that penalties for non-compliance would be enforced.[81]

Upon arriving at Yokohama in 1878, Isabella Bird observed, "At the customshouse we were attended to by minute officials in blue uniforms of European pattern and leather boots; very civil creatures, who opened and examined our trunks very carefully, and strapped them up again, contrasting pleasingly with the insolent and rapacious officials who perform the same duties in New York".[82] Perhaps Bird's comments on the demeanor of the officials reflect that she was a traveler. Merchants rubbed elbows with Japanese officials constantly, with profits at stake, and judged their behavior and attitudes by different criteria.

Japanese and Americans were, in a practical sense, working out what the treaties meant, and there were some instances for which the treaties did not and could not make adequate specific provision. Customshouse officials, for example, insisted on collecting the export duty on all coal taken on board foreign steamers. Though this practice technically complied with the treaties, foreign merchants complained that portions of the coal were intended as fuel for the vessels and not to be sold abroad. The first complaints met with resistance – the governor of Hyogo prefecture responded that "the export duty on the every Japanese production, even in the smallest part of it, when shipped on board the foreign vessel, is to be received". Some ten months later, after repeated requests from trading firms such as Walsh, Hall and Company, the Japanese government relented and accepted a proposal "according to which coal taken on board of steamers shall hereafter be duty free", but which was careful to exclude that taken on board sailing vessels, where "the full duty in accordance with the tariff shall be levied, irrespective of quantity".[83] Indeed cooperation, once the principle of control was established, served the Japanese interest as well.

Such zealous enforcement of trade regulations sometimes extended – according to the merchants – to extremes. In 1870, for example, Walsh, Hall and Company received a visitor on his way to Shanghai who intended to stay only a few hours at the company's Hyogo compound. The company sent his servant to fetch the visitor's baggage which contained "two boxes of wine and a small package of cigars", but the customshouse officials would not allow the goods carried onshore because the visitor held no permit to land them. Japanese officers dutifully impounded the offending merchandise at the customshouse, where it remained until after the gentleman left Hyogo. Enraged that his hospitality could be violated by such a proceeding, the company agent wrote, "We look upon the conduct of the customs officers as extremely vexatious, and particularly so as the gentleman referred to is not a resident in Japan, and could have no knowledge of any custom pertaining here different from the [ways] of other Japanese ports he had visited", and demanded the immediate release of his visitor's property.[84]

Though such behavior seemed nettlesome and excessively restrictive to Americans, it was mainly a nuisance and an irritant. Foreigners expected, even welcomed, certain organizational and procedural guidelines, and issues such as surly customshouse employees, coal export, and violations of their hospitality, hardly threatened their livelihood. Moreover, Western merchants' reactions to Japanese attempts to stifle trade in the early 1860s and the later efforts to manage the growing trade essential to modernization and self-strengthening suggest commitment to a static ideal of what they considered their political right to profit.

Americans were always eager to point to the text of the treaties as the only written safeguard of their interests and the only guideline for conducting trade; merchants and the Japanese authorities frequently interpreted the specific provisions of the tariff convention of 1866 differently. The Convention listed gold and silver, coined and uncoined, as Class II, duty free goods, and in May, 1873, Walsh,

Hall and Company imported an amount of gold leaf on the ship *Oregonian* from Shanghai. According to the convention, the gold leaf was subject to an import duty because it was not, strictly speaking, "coined or uncoined". When the company complained, the superintendent of Customs at Hyogo stated to Turner that gold leaf was a manufactured item and therefore legally subject to a 5 percent *ad valorem* duty. Walsh objected to the consul, who instructed him to pay the import duty under protest "whilst by cooperative action we seek to obtain a satisfactory understanding with the Japanese authorities". Walsh responded by observing that on June 24, 1873, "an entry of gold leaf [was] made by the Oriental Bank Corporation at the Hiogo Customshouse" duty free. Walsh further stated that "We claim of course to be put on an equal footing with others in such matters, and as we have suffered inconvenience and loss in consequence of the decision of the Customshouse, we ask as compensation interest upon the value of the box of gold leaf … at the rate of 1% per month until such time as it may be passed free of duty".

The customshouse responded by stating that the gold imported by the Oriental Bank Corporation was in fact "gold pieces of about 5 inches long by 3 inches … and therefore an entirely different article from that generally known as gold leaf", and that the duty would stand. In late December of that year, the customshouse declared the gold leaf duty free, and Walsh took delivery and paid the storage charges that applied, but did so under protest and stated that he would continue trying to recover his costs of $638 – interest and storage charges – that arose from the original decision on the part of the customshouse. The customshouse felt no responsibility, however, to compensate Walsh for his loss because the delay was caused by Walsh, Hall and Company's "refusal to allow the customs authorities to examine the case [of gold leaf] at the time of importation". As late as February of the following year, Walsh was still pressing his claim for compensation with the U.S. Minister in Yedo.[85]

On another occasion, Walsh, Hall and Company imported a large quantity of hemp bags, and hoped to pass these at the customshouse duty free as provided in Class II of the tariff. Customshouse officials, however, considered hemp bags to be on the list of goods subject to an *ad valorem* duty of 5 percent. The company paid the duty under protest, but demanded a remedy to what it considered arbitrary behavior on the part of the Japanese officials. Daniel Turner, the American Consul, carefully considered the case and consulted with Matthew Scott of the Imperial Customs at Hyogo, and decided that the goods were liable to payment of the duty.[86]

The safe storage of kerosene was of particular importance to American merchants, who imported virtually all petroleum to Japan. One visitor in Yokohama in March, 1880, remembered seeing a blackened hulk – an American ship laden with kerosene, burnt down to the water's edge.[87] Because of this wharf accident, the Japanese suggested that all kerosene be stored in government godowns for safety. American merchants were receptive to this idea because of their own limited facilities and, at their request, the Japanese authorities built limited additional accommodations, which were subject to government regulation. Fraser and

Company and the China and Japan Trading Company complained of the "long and tedious delays" in their construction and of their inadequate space and location, and though constructed at the expense of the Japanese, the merchants nevertheless vehemently objected to the Japanese right to regulate storage at the godowns and set storage fees, observing that storage rates there were "*six times* greater than at the storehouses of American merchants".

Merchants viewed such rates as a "tax for the benefit of the Japanese, without any advantages to the community". The American Consul further noted that the Japanese had promised fifteen years before to erect suitable storage facilities for explosives, but had done nothing, forcing Americans to store gunpowder inconveniently in different parts of the settlement.[88] The American Minister, John Bingham, supported the merchants, and the Japanese responded by reducing "the storage to so low a rate that it would not be profitable for importers to establish their own warehouses". Payson Treat commended "this astuteness of the Japanese in maintaining their regulations, while removing all criticism of them".[89] Indeed, such flexibility while maintaining the principle of control was a hallmark of Japanese management of the treaty ports.

Problems of storage persisted into the 1890s, however. Merchants continued to face the problem of persuading the Japanese to construct adequate facilities to keep up with the demands of a rapidly growing foreign commerce. In 1895, nineteen Western merchants wrote letters of complaint to the American Consul at Hyogo, detailing their difficulties with the customshouse. By far the most common complaints concerned the shortage of covered space in the customs facility and long delays in having goods inspected. Walsh, Hall and Company observed that it was

> insufficient either in extent or stability to protect from the inclemency of the weather the merchandise which by treaty the Japanese Government requires to be deposited there pending examination and the collection of duties, and as foreign merchants have protested in vain for years past, they are obliged, being quite helpless in the matter, to take risks of weather which often result disastrously.[90]

Western dependence on the Japanese was no less obvious at the end of the treaty port years than at the beginning.

In 1868, some nine months after the opening of the port at Hyogo, a committee of foreign merchants – including the agents of four American companies – outraged by what they considered to be willful Japanese obstruction of their trade, wrote a long memorial to their consuls. It is worth considerable attention, as it expressed much of the foreign critique of Japanese interference in foreign trade. The memorial stated in the strongest possible terms that the Japanese government was exerting its influence behind the scenes by levying transit duties on Japanese merchants who transported goods to the ports for resale to foreign merchants. The memorial declared that, although Article XVI of the commercial treaty of 1858 and Article V of the Tariff Convention of June, 1866 clearly stated that imports were "declared free of all internal duties, and produce intended for sale to foreigners is placed upon the same footing as other Japanese commodities in the transit from the producer to the consumer", the government imposed transit duties for the use of public roads, or, in effect, a tariff in addition to that specified by treaty. The merchants decried the illegality of such duties, whose "ill effects [were] aggravated by reason of the amount of the tax being left entirely to the caprice of the native authorities, instead of its being defined like that collected under the foreign tariff".

The merchants declared these duties a "distinct tax on foreign trade". Aware that the Japanese authorities argued that this tax was intended to be borne by the "native consumer, and that foreigners had no interest in the matter", the merchants responded:

> If the right of the government to impose such imposts is once admitted, we have no guarantee that it will not be abused to a very serious extent. In the present unsettled state of Japanese politics, the party in power may be in urgent need of money and not overscrupulous as to the means of obtaining it. To a people singularly deficient in the knowledge of financial rules and the laws of political economy, heavy duties upon foreign commerce must offer a tempting method of refilling the treasury and our trade with Japan would, during the process, be ruined. It was probably such a contingency the framers of the treaties had in contemplation when they inserted the articles that are now being infringed.

Regarding native Japanese merchants, the committee stated that "the rule requiring permits for the admission of foreign goods is carried out to an almost ludicrous extent, affecting the smallest article purchased even in retail shops at Kobe", and added that "since the so-called opening of the port, the hindrances to trade have increased *ten-fold*".

The committee concluded with a number of observations concerning the "discourteous" behavior of customshouse officials, which "cause[d] much dissatisfaction and annoyance". Noting that a "guardhouse [was] built where the contents of all boats are examined", the merchants reported

> numerous instances of foreigners and natives subjected to great inconvenience and detention at this station. Personal baggage has been seized and only released after special application to the custom house. Permits are demanded for the most trifling articles, such as curios, furniture, and other Japanese ware of small value, and when not forthcoming the articles have been confiscated.

Irritated that "foreign merchants are not treated with the consideration and civility which at the other ports they have been accustomed to receive", the merchants complained of the "general tone of indifference to our interests and

other disregards of the value of our time that seems to pervade the establishment", while the "conduct of important business appears to be too often left
entirely in the hands of some ignorant and inexperienced interpreter". They concluded, "We believe that a strong remonstrance from the consuls might induce
the authorities to insist upon their servants treating foreign gentlemen with at
least as much politeness as is shown to their own countrymen".[91] On behalf of
American merchants in Hyogo, one U.S. consul pointed out in 1872 that the

> Japanese Government has and does, in numerous ways, interfere with
> the trade between its own people and ours. Only certain Japanese sub-
> jects are permitted to deal in teas, silks, silkworm eggs, etc. the charge
> for such privilege materially enhancing the cost of those products to our
> people. The treaty ports have been constantly surrounded by guard-
> houses in which armed guards have been kept whose duty has been to
> compel all passing Japanese who have any articles of merchandise to
> stop and submit the same to inspection and assessment and been com-
> pelled on his return to pay the arbitrarily duty affixed, which duty of
> course in all cases falls as a tax on the foreign purchaser.

Restrictions on attendance at foreign auctions further damaged merchant interests
and resulted in "the direct injury of the foreign salesman".[92] Such discussion
served little purpose other than to camouflage irritation at Japanese control that
merchants' insular attitudes promoted.

Merchants' expectations of treaty port arrangements were clear in such complaints. On the one hand, they sometimes appealed to their consuls to accomplish
the impossible, though they did not expect miraculous results. The treaty powers
could not possibly enforce any restrictions on the Japanese right to impose transit
duties on public roads, and any appeal based on foreign "rights" to promote trade
by demanding their abolition was utterly unrealistic. On the other hand, Western
assumptions of racial superiority and frustration with their lack of control showed
up in complaints about "civility"; control by "inferior" Asians, especially interpreters who alone could understand the situation, was particularly irritating.
Equally clear is that merchants feared the uncontrollable – beyond the limits of
the ports – that they believed threatened their businesses.

All American companies in the ports felt the heavy hand of the Japanese customshouse. One of J.D. Carroll and Company's operations, a ship's chandlery,
complained about permits for several containers of paint and some coils of rope
sold to the captain of a ship then in port in Hyogo. Since the goods were of foreign
manufacture and were imported earlier by Carroll, the company paid the regular
import duties when it received the goods from abroad. But when company
employees brought the items to the hatoba, the Japanese officer refused to let
them on board, saying that an export permit was required. Carroll's explanation
that the goods were in fact ship supplies did not satisfy the officials, and Carroll
could "not understand why the customshouse should interfere [by] demand[ing]

permits for everything they sold from their store". Carroll observed that such interference made the routine supply of ships in the harbor difficult: "If a ship wants to buy items during the time that the customshouse is closed", he wrote, "how are we expected to get a permit to sell? We lose the sale of our goods and many good customers".[93]

More than one observer commented that it was easier to deal with higher Japanese officials than lower ones. Minor officials' concern with petty matters, literalism and "unwillingness to sacrifice the letter of the law to its spirit", as merchants saw it, was a constant irritant: "The more insignificant the business, the greater seems to be their tendency to magnify it .... Often a gnat is strained out at the very time when a camel is being swallowed". The *Japan Weekly Mail* once featured a fictional portrait of a Japanese official emphasizing the traits merchants had come to despise – rigidity and arrogance.[94] One historian attributed merchants' difficulties to a new class of customs officers appointed after the victory of the imperial forces in the civil war. The new government, unable to "spare its best men", appointed inexperienced men, who slowed an already lethargic institution "almost to a standstill".[95] Yet these were the officials whose decisions affected a wide variety of foreign business concerns. One longtime resident recorded a skit entitled "The Consul and the Sangi, A Brief Comedy of Manners", a humorous rendition of the mutual politenesses and flattery that went with formal encounters between Western and Japanese officials.[96]

One major point of contention involved the simple mechanics of loading and unloading ships. Once again, the commercial treaty of 1858 was specific on this matter: "No goods shall be unladen from any ship between the hours of sunset and sunrise, except by special permission of the custom-house authorities".[97] In January, 1871, Smith, Baker and Company wrote to Paul Frank asking him to apply for a permit to continue loading goods on the S.S. *Meneka* after sunset. The Japanese customshouse responded that such permission would be granted on a "case by case" basis. One month later, the customshouse finally responded with a denial of permission. It rapidly became clear that customshouse officials intended to exert control by refusing to grant night permits and, under pressure from the merchants, Frank formally complained on their behalf to the American legation in Kanagawa. In July, DeLong wrote back to Frank informing him that the Japanese government was considering the protest and that, whatever the Japanese decided, it would "at least be more satisfactory to have some general rule about the matter than to have it left as it was before for their customs officers to discriminate between applicants or positively refuse any accommodation upon any terms whatever". Nine months later, the merchants had a preliminary response: night-loading and unloading would be permitted only for mail steamers.[98]

One effect of this regulation against night-loading was to slow outgoing ships, and merchants frequently complained about such loss of valuable time. The agent for the Pacific Mail Steamship Company pointed out that, because of the nature of navigating on the Inland Sea, "our steamers almost invariably leave this port for Nagasaki and Shanghai at the break of day". The advantages of loading cargo at night were obvious, as "many bills of lading which must necessarily go forward by the steamer carrying the goods are signed only a short time before her sailing". If the exact meaning of the restrictions on night-loading were adhered to, shippers would be "prohibited from sending the necessary documents along by steamer after the consulate is closed at 6:00 PM".[99]

The final ruling, which came in June, 1873, permitted unloading at "unusual times" only after the duty on goods landed or shipped was paid during regular custom's hours, and after the captain of the foreign vessel reimbursed the Japanese customs officers for the extra work.[100] One result of this was to burden the Pacific Mail Steamship line with the overflow of goods forced to wait. Even when Americans loaded at night onto mail steamers, the Japanese government sometimes interfered. In 1874, Henry Wilson, the agent of the Pacific Mail Steamship Company, complained that, while loading cargo onto the ship *Golden Age*, customshouse officials interfered on the grounds that Wilson had not obtained proper permits, delaying loading by several hours. The proper permits usually cost about $30, and American firms often paid the fees under protest, placing them with the U.S. consular office while appealing the expense. When the Japanese government denied the appeals, the U.S. consulate remitted the monies to them.[101]

Japanese motivation for such measures was twofold. First, restrictions on night-loading of cargo acted to reduce the theft of which Americans themselves frequently complained. One American merchant, for example, protested that thirteen cases of kerosene oil were stolen from a boat he hired one night. He noted that he had been "repeatedly robbed in this manner" and demanded a thorough investigation. Another observed that an unidentified thief stole "all the sails from his two sailboats" at night. Since many of the Japanese coolies worked not directly for the American merchants but in labor pools controlled by the Japanese government – which made the Japanese responsible for any theft they committed – restrictions on activity at night lessened crime for which the Japanese accepted general responsibility. Moreover, such restrictions, when violated, provided the Japanese recourse to deny certain claims. For example, the Pacific Mail Steamship Company claimed a $1,000 loss in 1874, which the customshouse denied on the grounds that the loss was sustained while in violation of the restriction on night-loading.[102] Second, banning night-loading made harder the illegal importation of opium. Observing the effects of opium importation on China and the war that Great Britain fought to preserve its right to continue opium trade in that country, the Japanese insisted on a ban on opium importation in the commercial treaty of 1858. Strict control of night-loading also helped prevent smuggling of other kinds.

In addition to influencing the mechanics of trade, the Japanese also sought to restrict certain imports and exports. Because of the behavior of off-duty American sailors in the ports, the Japanese understandably undertook to prevent the sale of *sake* to the crews of U.S. men-of-war, giving "strict orders" to native dealers producing it. Even though the Japanese customshouse lacked jurisdiction over Americans violating such restrictions, it sought enforcement through the appropriate foreign authorities. In February 1868, for example, Paul Frank received an official notice from the customshouse concerning the American merchant Charles Sloos, who along with another American, Thomas Decker, had failed to comply with an order to place in bond all liquors in their possession, and continued selling it to the crews of men-of-war anchored in Kobe. At the request of the customshouse, Earl English, the commander of the U.S.S *Iroquois*, detached a detail to destroy Sloos's liquor and took Sloos into custody and held him until a regular courts martial could be convened.[103]

Much of American merchants' irritation with "restrictions on trade" was grounded in the desire to avoid paying the required duties. "It is the religion of some men in the world", wrote the *Japan Weekly Mail*, "to evade the payment of customs duties in any conceivable manner".[104] Western merchants quickly discovered that some Japanese customs officials required bribes to oil the gears of trade.[105] One observer in Yokohama in the early years noted that "between August, 1859 and January 1860, as reported in the commercial statistics and prices current of Shanghai, raw silk exports from Yokuhama exceeded 3000 bales, but that during the same period duties equivalent to only 500–600 bales were paid to the customs house", and that a "respectable American merchant" corroborated this by declaring that he could show customshouse receipts of "export duty for his own shipments of silk during the same period exceeding this aggregate in the official return". It seemed certain that "mercantile representatives of Christian nations [were] pursuing the selfish, suicidal and wicked course of corrupting by bribes the official agents of the Japanese government".

The same observer noted that the export of copper coins was expressly forbidden by treaty, but reported an occasion where the British consul in Yokohama saw a cask labeled "oil" on board a foreign vessel burst because it was packed with copper coins. The consul remonstrated with the customs official, who chose to ignore the infraction. "The fact is notorious", he wrote, "that the Japanese officials each have their price; and the flagitious corruption which has necessitated at the Chinese consular ports the system of foreign inspectorships of customs as a protection to the honest trader, is likely to be reproduced in Japan".[106]

John Baxter Will described smuggling in the early years when "invoices of cargo were not examined very particularly". He remembered that

> our long boat was put out and rigged, and as the *Eva* had three large stern windows which would let through gin or brandy and even larger cases such as ... boot cases, after dark, when the hatches were closed, the crew got quietly into the hold through an opening made in the forecastle bulk head and carried the selected cases aft and through the bulkhead to the cabin. A man was detailed to keep the [Japanese] customs officers in their house on deck to see they did not come aft to look over the stern. This job fell to the mate. Chiefly a bottle or a little drop of rum or gin generally sent them to sleep.[107]

More frequently Americans encountered Japanese efficiency in preventing the entry of unauthorized goods. All the major American trading companies in Hyogo smuggled to a greater or lesser extent, and much of the correspondence between the local Japanese officials at Kobe and the American consuls concerns unauthorized imports. In January, 1871, for example, an American merchant took delivery from the quay at Hyogo boxes containing what he claimed were books. Noting that the shipment lacked a landing permit, an alert Japanese customshouse official opened the package and found 59lbs of cotton yarn.[108] The Chinese in the treaty ports were sometimes involved in the smuggling of opium for use in the Chinatowns of the foreign concessions. Once, a Chinese compradore named Chun Kin, a man of some wealth, had several long, private consultations with the captain of the American schooner *Halcyon*, a known opium smuggler.[109] Some firms shipped silk handkerchiefs in tea-chests, lacquer boxes, bales of silk or concealed in other products.[110]

Merchants' irritation frequently appeared in the form of complaints against Japanese control in the ports. Having surrendered municipal control of Yokohama to Japanese authorities in 1867, residents expressed regret in 1879 and wistfully observed that Hyogo governed itself in cooperation with the Japanese. The Yokohama arrangement gave the Japanese what "they love even better than dollars – the control of the principal foreign settlement of this country". In the minds of some, Yokohama paid more than it should in land tax and municipal rates to a usurious and alien Japanese municipality, and did not get its money's worth. Maintaining that drainage, police and lighting would improve if the foreign community controlled its own finances, some complained that funds were diverted to projects which did not serve the foreign community. One road, on which the Japanese spent foreign money, had "turned into a series of mean villages, the haunts of the many rascals who prey[ed] upon Bluff residents". The $50,000 annually spent maintaining the Bluff, ran the argument, was twice the necessary cost, and two advisory committees, one for the Bluff and one for the settlement, would introduce an element of foreign control over future improvements.[111]

Since the Japanese were not accountable to the foreign community for land rent expenditures, Westerners were irritated at Japanese resolve to control them. One correspondent to the *Japan Weekly Mail* posited that, of total rents of $54,000, settlement residents contributed $30,000, and Bluff-dwellers $24,000. Estimating total maintenance costs, including the police force, he determined that receipts exceeded expenditures by $15,000 per year, and asked that the imperial government maintain the Bund and the Canals. Further, the paper accused the Japanese of ill-conceived improvement projects. Instead of repairing main roads, foreign money was used to repair "some wholly unimportant hillpath … leading either to a dirty village inhabited by thieves and receivers of stolen goods or to a rice swamp, furnishing it with elaborate gutters, carefully finished stone steps and a handsome stone faced embankment".[112]

Two and a half years later, the *Mail* soberly pointed out to foreigners still complaining about their ground rents that their tax was 11 percent less than that levied on the Japanese in the native town, and that the municipal government had in fact spent more money on the upkeep and improvement of the settlement than it had received in ground rents.[113] Concern over Japanese omissions also animated merchant discussions. One observer criticized the Japanese government for the precedence it gave to repairs on military roads and the roads leading to shrines and resorts over investment in the commercial arteries that transported goods and services.[114]

Merchants were sometimes as disgusted with general Japanese honesty and thoroughness as with their officiousness, and their frustration with Japanese management sometimes flared into violence. In 1872, the Hyogo government office complained to James Harris, the acting U.S. consul, that two foreigners carried three cases of goods from the premises of Smith, Baker and Company to a boat in direct contradiction of a notice prohibiting using private landings to load goods. When a Japanese customshouse official tried to intercede, employees of the company "violently assaulted him" and conveyed the goods to a German steamer. Undaunted, the officials followed the men, who then turned around and "beat them with sticks".

On another occasion, a Mr Staples, an employee of the same company, brought a four-dollar box of European paper, ostensibly for use in writing, into Hyogo without paying an import duty. Though Staples had obtained a landing permit, a customshouse official physically blocked his path, stating that he had not paid, and instructed him to go directly to the customshouse with the paper. Enraged, Staples "struck the face of the officer so [hard] that blood came out and took the box home".[115] During a dispute over how and where a duty would be paid on two packages, W.A. Wood, an employee of the International hotel at Yokohama, struck one customshouse official in the face with his open hand, and punched another in the chest with his fist, knocking him down[116] Such examples of violence showed American discomfort with the wide disparity between their sense of racial superiority, their own putative power in the ports – and actual Japanese authority.

The Japanese, emphasizing control and the drive toward equality and national independence, laid a heavy hand on foreigners' attempts to circumvent the machinery of tariff collection. With its revenue already limited by low tariffs, the Japanese government was loathe to surrender its just due of revenue or the principle of control in the ports. Americans held tightly to their own notions of trade privilege – closely if paradoxically associated with their assumptions of racial and cultural superiority and feelings of dependence – and reacted plaintively, critically and occasionally violently to Japanese efforts to control both the mechanics and substance of their trade.

VI

In 1879, the State Department addressed itself to its Far Eastern consuls, who, it believed "have allowed themselves to fall into the habit of communicating with the dept only when necessary".[117] If consuls launched less than the requisite amount of paper at Washington, D.C., they scribbled more than their share of notes to the Japanese and the merchants in their consular jurisdictions, but the Japanese responded only to the degree they thought appropriate.

U.S. consuls provided what assistance to American firms they could in the context of Japanese power. Crude operations, ill-supported by the home government and manned by political appointees, gave some limited but essential support to American merchants groping for the assistance that their own imperative of cultural separateness made necessary. With no more language ability than the merchants whose interests they represented, beset with the minutiae of their jobs, and burdened with ever smaller staffs relative to their workloads, but nevertheless dispensing justice fairly in their capacity as judges, consuls had neither the time, inclination nor resources to intercede aggressively or particularly effectively on merchants' behalf.

Merchants daily confronted evidence of Japanese control, and consuls, though imperfectly equipped to deal with merchants' needs, routed their correspondence and did what they could to address merchants' fundamental problems. In the resulting fellowship, consuls earned a measure of merchants' trust and appreciation in spite of the limits on their ability to effect the kind of change merchants wanted. Conduits, confidants and sometimes victors in small battles over Japanese regulation, consuls were merchants' best, most recognizable, allies.

When stolen property was recovered, or when the Japanese authorities – in their own time – made good on promises to improve the settlements, consuls received the credit from the merchants. In what merchants considered the threatening world of treaty port business, even modest victories were doubtless savored. Merchants clearly recognized that the intercession of their consuls, though often ineffective, was essential.

4

BUSINESS BY PROXY

Bantos and compradores

The Yokohama merchant does not enter into direct relations with his Japanese customers.[1]

Foreigners' simultaneous disdain of and dependence on Japanese servants can be glimpsed in the description of one Westerner who left a record of her ties to a Japanese employee. As steam travel shrank the world in the late nineteenth century, Japan became an increasingly popular destination for a leisured class of globetrotters. Many such visitors to Japan were content to shop for curios, visit Mount Fuji, Hakone and perhaps take in the temples at Kyoto after a cruise on the inland sea. Isabella Bird, a British traveler who arrived in 1878, was ambitious enough to risk the rigors of travel beyond the world of tourist attractions and international hotels. Though her plans suggested interest in things Japanese far beyond her contemporaries, her travels nevertheless illustrate that element common to many travelers in Japan: the native "servant interpreter" who accompanied the Westerner to purchase food, make travel arrangements and generally intercede in the event of any difficulty.

Before striking out for the interior, Bird interviewed four candidates – all bearing recommendations from acquaintances – in Yokohama. Regarding "intelligible English" as a "sine qua non" for the job, Bird rejected the first two applicants on the basis of language. She was prepared to hire the third when she suddenly opted for the services of a young Japanese named Ito with, she said, "a round and singularly plain face, good teeth, much elongated eyes, and the heavy droop of his eyelids almost caricatures of the usual Japanese peculiarity". Though she thought him "the most stupid-looking Japanese" she had seen, his qualifications – employment on the Osaka railroad and the American legation, and a familiarity with her destination – made her decide to engage him at twelve dollars per month. Realizing how much of the success of her journey would depend on her guide, Bird referred to Ito as "my good or evil genius for the next three months".[2]

Bird's condescension was not unrelated to her dependence. She, like most Westerners, found servants absolutely essential to negotiate unfamiliar geographic and cultural ground, and her wry recognition of her dependence was widely shared in the American merchant population in the treaty ports. As much as Bird, these merchants relied on their Asian servants and employees, but for much longer than three months.

Generally shared ethnicity, language and culture rendered merchant dependence on their consuls reasonably palatable to them. As merchants continued to seek ways to order their business world however, they were forced further toward the unknown, and their chief solution to this problem was to arrange their operations around the indispensable services of Japanese and Chinese employees who were at the very heart of treaty port trade. Again merchants attempted to exert control, and again it was done by proxy, but this time the element of dependence on Asians (not fellow countrymen) complicated both the process and the result. Anxiety was still the by-product, however, as American merchants fell into a pattern of reliance on the Japanese and Chinese in the ports that persisted until the repeal of the unequal treaties in 1899.

I

An examination of the relationship between American merchants and their Japanese and Chinese employees in the treaty ports sheds considerable light on the nature of these American enterprises. Americans depended heavily on both groups in the mechanics of their day-to-day business operations, but their personnel policy was to have only Western partners and employees in key inside positions. With the exception of Joseph Heco, a naturalized American citizen of Japanese birth, there are no examples of Asians in partnership with Americans in the major business enterprises in the treaty ports of the late nineteenth century.[3]

For Westerners in trading firms in Japan, work primarily meant office duties. Business hours began at ten and ended at five, and the midday break was sacred. After lunch, work was more leisurely, unless a mail day – around which the rhythms of work in the ports centered – approached. Correspondence – usually "long handwritten letters" – with other branches needed to be ready for posting by mail day, as did all detailed communication with purchasers of Japanese exports in Europe or the United States.[4] One Heard and Company official expressed the concern that one employee would not be able to handle the books alone, especially on steamer days, when the work came "all in a lump".[5]

Shorter but much more frequent written communication with local consuls about a wide variety of topics might use up the morning hours. Trade issues, of course, predominated. Complaints about Japanese interference, problems relating to currency and shipping and Japanese detention of employees were common to all American trading firms throughout the period. Other matters requiring constant written communication included those problems only solvable by the Japanese. The consuls were buried under repeated requests regarding such items as lot drainage and sanitary conditions, improvements to lots promised but not yet completed, customs duties collected in error and a thousand other details. Merchants spent other hours attending meetings of local chambers of commerce.

Account books reflecting frequent price fluctuations and transactions in numerous kinds of products, including goods consumed by the firms in Japan, food and transportation costs accounted for tedious hours.

Throughout the treaty port years, the search for competent employees remained a constant concern for American companies. The correspondence of Augustine Heard's manager in the company's Yokohama branch provides a glimpse of that company's internal operations. Albert Farley, the manager of the Yokohama branch of the company, described one of his employees at the Yokohama office of Augustine Heard and Company: "One can buy plenty of men, but when you get hold of a good one, I think it best to treat him well. Time servers are not worth their meat! Gillingham is a useful office man, steady and a good bookkeeper".

Gillingham had agreed to a contract of two years and lived at the company's Yokohama compound at company expense while in Japan. If he chose to move to another residence, the company provided $65. The value of good office employees to Heard and Company is further illustrated by J.K. Cunningham's observation that "I know from my experience of lst season that tea-firing requires constant overlooking to have it done properly; without a really good office-man my attention would be constantly called away from it and we should lose in having my attention constantly called away from it".[6]

Such internal concerns left untouched the problem of finding employees who had even minimal control of Japanese to deal with the "outside" concerns of the company. Fifteen years after Heard and Company began operating at Yokohama, no employee was sufficiently competent in Japanese for business purposes. In February, 1873, Cunningham wrote to the Canton office of Heard and Company: "I must say that a new man from Hong Kong would be of little use, as we want someone who understands the Japanese and their language. Livingston is still persevering ... and he seems to be progressing, though slowly".[7]

The office work for companies such as Augustine Heard expanded in the years after 1859, and as American companies faced increasing workloads and personnel needs, they sometimes showed a preference for hiring from the pool of English-speaking workers nearest at hand – the numerous American and European seamen discharged from foreign vessels in port. Though such men were ordinarily initially without the skills necessary to work for the trading companies, and their character was sometimes open to question, companies hard-pressed for Western employees turned to these men after careful screening. The U.S. government required that companies interested in the services of such men guarantee that they had been discharged voluntarily and to put up their return passage money to the United States, ensuring that the ex-sailors would not become charges upon the government as destitute seamen. The China and Japan Trading Company, for example, hired W.H. Stevens off the American barque *William Hales* and promised to pay $80 within twelve months for his return passage.[8]

Trading companies went to additional expense to secure the services of these seamen. Upon discharge, the U.S. government usually owed sailors several months wages, and sometimes American trading companies eager for help paid these wages to the American consulate at Yokohama to obtain the necessary workmen. Walsh, Hall and Company, for example, sent a draft to Yokohama in the amount of $281.31 Mexican – the wages due J.C. Cooper, late mate of the ship *Goldstream* – to obtain his services.[9] By the late 1870s, when business was brisk at the port of Hyogo, Walsh, Hall and Company hired three discharged sailors, George Schott, C.H. Kent and Thomas Coin, for a total outlay of U.S. gold $229.35, the amount of wages owed them at discharge.[10]

Americans recruited from ships were hired into an established method of operation. They were clearly intended for inside office work; among their qualifications were the language and culture they shared with their employers, and their ability with words and numbers. The line between office and outside work was clear and reflected American convictions concerning the proper role of Westerners and Asians. But these employees were incapable of engaging the larger world of treaty port business; no matter how efficiently books were kept or how well or promptly letters were written, the world of treaty port business required interaction with the wider marketplace.

II

Of course, Japanese employees, in a very different sphere, were an integral part of the business lives of foreign merchants in the treaty ports. Western business depended on a class of Japanese employees, bantos, whose formal position was beyond the pale of the office, but whose work was nonetheless crucial. One source defines a banto as a "chief clerk, buyer, intermediary, or factor in a mercantile house", a definition which exaggerates the formal position but not the services of these necessary intermediaries. Another definition – shipping clerk – also fails to capture the essence of the services bantos provided.[11] Bantos' duties included all those activities where the office had to meet the Japanese community: collecting money owed, carrying messages to the docks and customshouses and generally running personal and business errands. At times learning enough English to act as translators, they became intimately familiar with their employers' customers, and, in the tightly-knit business context of the ports, came to occupy extremely important positions in foreign firms. Harold Williams, describing of the role of bantos in the hongs, wrote that "at least one of the office rooms [in the company compounds] was in Japanese style where the *banto* interviewed Japanese merchants".[12]

Beyond their role in the ports, bantos were foreign merchants' link to Japan's interior markets. Since "foreigners could not distinguish between types of Japanese merchants", bantos crucial task of investigating customers' status fell "entirely to bantos, instead of being made a practical study as in Europe and America".[13] Otto Keil, the American secretary general of Yokohama Chamber of Commerce, observed in 1886 that there was no "regular" way of doing business in the ports, since the merchants rarely ventured out and had little knowledge of the hinterland. Commission merchants receiving an order usually gave it to their bantos, who went into the market on their employers' behalf. This necessarily involved a series of "squeezes" for all with whom the banto dealt, sometimes adding as much as 30 percent to the cost. Keil summed up common business practices succinctly, emphasizing the centrality of

> native servants called bantos whose duty it is to make purchases for export, or sales of imports .... By certain houses it would be considered a breach of dignity for a member to condescend to negotiate a bargain with a native merchant. The order, being placed in the hands of the banto, is contracted with a merchant who is either a friend, or is willing to pay a "return commission", known to us here as a squeeze. It is needless to say that the lowest prices are not paid by the banto.

Since this system applied to "all goods of export", Keil correctly concluded, "Few firms are really in the trade and know what they are doing", leaving the details of business to "their Japanese or Chinese employees who always manage to squeeze a few percent of extra commission".

Because merchants depended on the Japanese coming to them and had to tolerate the squeezes of the bantos, selling prices in the ports were inflated and merchants could rely on "no stated or settled price for anything". In many instances, contracts for future deliveries were made, and the "goods were not brought to the purchaser for some months". In general, the quality and cost of silk goods varied significantly because the bantos got the work done in many different places. Embroidery of designs on handkerchiefs, for example, could be done for anywhere between 0.60 to more than $1 Mexican, depending on the personal connections, obligations or whim of a banto.

Keil reported that any merchant specializing in one product and making large purchases direct without going through the agency houses would have a real advantage because he would not pay the costs of the commission merchant, and cited one American exporter of silk handkerchiefs as a rare exception to prevailing business practices. This anonymous merchant, in violation of restrictions against conducting trade beyond the treaty limits, actually went into the silk districts to purchase piece goods from Japanese weavers. He made contracts months ahead to secure their manufacture, then contracted with handkerchief manufacturers for about 100 dozen each, and delivered them the piece goods. These manufacturers in turn distributed the pieces to their workers for finishing – often fifty to one hundred families working in their homes. One typical transaction showed his cost for fifty-six dozen handkerchiefs as $5.30 per dozen. The merchant's cost in such an operation was lower and much more predictable because he performed the contracting work himself and was not subject to the inevitable squeezes that accompanied business as usual in the ports.[14]

Merchants' insularity compelled them to give large advances to their Japanese bantos to conduct their trade. "Merchants", observed the *Japan Weekly Mail*, "are

obliged to violate the treaties in order to elude the monopolists that invest the settlements". The system forced Westerners to take all the risk, considering that the
Japanese "could not be held legally accountable to money entrusted to him under
such conditions". Perhaps the *Mail* was correct in asserting that "there are not
many parts of the world where commercial confidence goes to the length of trusting round sums to men against whom no legal claim could be established if they
chose to default".[15] Theoretically, the only escape from dependence of this sort lay
in repeal of the unequal treaties that would give foreigners access to Japan's interior markets.

In other isolated cases, foreign merchants did go outside the ports in pursuit
of trade. The *Mail* noted in 1876 that two foreigners made "considerable purchases of silk in the interior, in contravention of the clause in the passports which
forbids all trading out of the foreign settlements" (see Figure 6, page 131).[16]
Considering the enthusiasm with which the Japanese government enforced most
regulations concerning foreigners, it seems reasonable to assume that such activity was not widespread. But it is also clear that the vast majority of Americans
and other foreigners lacked the interest to move beyond the ports. The consequences of dependence on bantos for most merchants, while unpredictable and
perhaps unprofitable, at least had the virtue of sustaining treaty port society:

> They had things all the easier as the "bantos" made them a "name" with
> their masters, who thinking that they had so far only dealt with slow, cau-
> tious folks, were very glad that they could get business without much
> work, could go about cricketing and racing, while their "bantos" worked
> for them, and secured contracts all the time ... the banto's commission,
> being payable on the amount of sales, was a sure incentive![17]

Such harsh critiques emphasized merchant complacency as much as merchant
anxiety over lack of control.

American merchants were locked into business patterns dictated by their
reliance on bantos; to initiate new business relationships on their own would have
been difficult or impossible. If bantos – given license to move through interior
markets on foreigners' behalf to purchase exports – did not cooperate, foreign
merchants were hamstrung. Bantos almost certainly dealt with the same Japanese
merchants over time, and would have little incentive to disrupt established habits,
especially to buy smaller quantities of new products from unfamiliar sources.

A survey of the complaints American merchants made when deprived of bantos' services even for a short time highlights their dependence. The local Japanese
authorities rigorously enforced the law in the treaty ports with regard to their own
subjects, and this practice, while giving merchants help in recovering stolen property, often irritated merchants by lessening their control – that desperately sought
commodity – over key Japanese employees. Americans so depended on their
Japanese bantos in their business, that, when these employees became subject to
Japanese military service, violated Japanese law, or became involved in disputes

Translation of the Directions Printed in Japanese on Back of Passport, and to be Borne in Mind by Citizens of the United States of America, Travelling in the Interior.

I. — The bearer of this passport must obey all local regulations while travelling in the interior.

II. — This passport must be returned to the Kanagawa Koncho as soon as possible after its expiration.

III. — The bearer, while travelling in the interior, must produce this passport for inspection upon the request of any local official or police officer, or of the landlord of the inn at which he may lodge. Refusal for any reason so to produce it renders the bearer liable to be sent back to the nearest Open Port.

IV. — The passport is not transferable.

V. — The bearer of this passport is not permitted to trade or make contracts while in the interior.

VI. — The bearer is not permitted under this passport to rent houses or to reside in the interior.

VII. —Even those who have licenses to hunt are not permitted to discharge fire-arms or hunt game outside of the Treaty Limits.

Note. — The local regulations, above referred to, forbid the following and similar acts

1. — Travelling at night in a carriage without a light.
2. — Attending a fire on horseback.
3. — Disregarding notices of "No Thoroughfare."
4. — Rapid driving on narrow roads.
5. — Neglecting to pay ferry and bridge-tolls.
6. — Injuring notice boards, house signs and mile-posts.
7. — Scribbling on temples, shrines or walls.
8. — Injuring crops, shrubs, trees or plants on the roads or in gardens.
9. — Trespassing on fields, enclosures or game preserves.
10. — Lighting fires in woods or on hills or moors.

Figure 6 Directions carried by passport for travel in the interior of Japan, c. 1885
Source: OHMC, National Archives, RG 84, 6-6-85

with other Japanese, they could not carry on their business – and so wanted a selective application of law.

The passage of a new law for universal conscription into the Japanese army became effective in January 1873, and created particular problems for merchants. Popular Japanese dislike for this "blood tax" led some Japanese serving foreigners to try to use their jobs to escape military service.[18] On December 21, 1874, A.O. Gay, an American then employed by Augustine Heard and Company, noted that the foreign office requested that his banto, Yamada Shintaro, report the next day for military duty. He observed that "the man in question expresses much unwillingness to enter the service, but I have urged him to make his appearance without resistance".[19]

Most commonly Americans reacted to the prospect of losing their servants by arguing their indispensability. One striking example is the case of Asai Katsutaro, who was employed by J.D. Carroll and Company, an American firm in Hyogo. In January, 1876, the local Japanese authorities requested that U.S. consul Nathan Newwitter inform Carroll and Company that "Asai Katsutaro ... is, in accordance with our military law for the enrollment of soldiers, of such suitable age as to serve as imperial soldier", and to prepare to release him from their employ. In February, Carroll and Company complained bitterly to Newwitter, arguing that the loss of Asai would deeply damage its business interests, and asking Newwitter to point out to the Japanese authorities "the difficulty we, as well as all other merchants, will be under if our servants, after being trained and intrusted with confidential business, are to be taken from us at any time without ours or their consent". The complaint was dutifully passed on to the Japanese military, which emphatically stated that Asai deserved no exception and required his presence for military duty on June 2, 1876.[20]

American merchants' feared losing their bantos' services to more than the Japanese military. Schultz, Reis and Company complained in 1869, for example, that the Japanese government "imprisoned [their] Banto on the charges of a Japanese merchant, apparently without anything to sustain the charge", causing the firm "much inconvenience". The company implored the U.S. vice consul at Osaka to "please endeavor to have him released immediately unless there be some evidence of fraud against him".[21]

The same year, Japanese authorities seized another Japanese banto employed by Schultz, Reis and Company and imprisoned him on the charges of a Japanese merchant who claimed that he had received money from him "without giving the equivalent in merchandise". In spite of the possibility of their employee's guilt, the American firm claimed that "his imprisonment while charged ... proves a very great inconvenience and may involve considerable losses to us" and asked Stewart, the American consul, "to use [his] influence and have him speedily released", adding that "we need not say that we consider it very arbitrary of the Japanese authorities imprisoning a servant of ours without advising you or us of the circumstances".[22] These cases illustrate the control the Japanese wielded over their citizenry, even those central to foreigners' business. The government never heeded such pleas. Merchants might fume and consuls request, but with little expectation of result.

American merchants readily submitted to the liabilities and inconveniences associated with their reliance on bantos as servants. Though granting these essential agents formal status as employees might have resulted in greater loyalty and given Americans more control over the mechanics of their businesses, this would have run counter to merchants' racial assumptions of superiority.

III

In one area, however, the Japanese government responded strongly to merchant complaints, that of crimes against Western merchants by Japanese lawbreakers. Though this suggested an abstract commitment to justice and did much to reconcile the foreign community to the Japanese government's exercise of authority, it was in fact further proof to those Japanese who had most contact with the Euro–Americans that they were subject not to their employers but to their government. That mechanism of control is clear in the government's insistence that to offer protection it had to know precisely how many of its citizens worked for foreigners in the ports, purportedly to aid in its law enforcement activities. Throughout the treaty port years Japanese officials reminded the American consuls to send it complete lists of Japanese in foreign employ, including name, age and birthplace.[23]

The volatile, transient social context of the treaty ports provided an ideal milieu for petty thieves and a variety of illegal operators. Theft, heightened by the bantos' inside knowledge and outside status, provoked outrage in Western newspapers almost on a daily basis. Even a cursory reading of the internal consular correspondence reveals descriptions of stolen goods, complaints, and requests for action so numerous as to be numbing. The *Hiogo News*, for example, referred to "the almost daily announcement of some house being robbed, and under circumstances that lead almost positively to the conclusion that the perpetrators were the servants in the employ of the parties who were the sufferers ... as in the matter of Messrs. Browne and Co., where their own Banto and servants decamped with a large amount of cash".[24] The *Japan Weekly Mail* ran a regular column entitled "Today's Burglaries".

There is little question that Japanese support of foreign businessmen's complaints about theft was adequate, even enthusiastic. The Japanese were scrupulously systematic in handling such cases. Typically, an American victim of theft reported the incident to his local consul, who then reported it to the local Japanese authorities, usually the governor. The governor then referred the case to the Saibansho, or local Japanese judicial office. The Saibansho conducted inquiries, and, if necessary, instructed the local Japanese police to apprehend the perpetrator. If found guilty, the Japanese informed the American consul of the conviction and the punishment.

In 1878, for example, Walsh, Hall and Company was engaged to carry rice to the American ship Mount Washington, and under the boards of two of its boats, a company official discovered concealed lots of rice. They immediately informed the Japanese police, who took the suspected boatmen into custody and returned the rice. The company stated that "officers in charge of the police department request that we make application through you [the American Consulate] for the punishment of the offenders". Later, the company withdrew its claim against one of the boatmen when it collected 200 *rios* from him in settlement.[25]

When employees were suspected of wrongdoing, the Saibansho notified companies in advance that their employees must appear for questioning.[26] After arresting Japanese employees, local Japanese authorities scrupulously informed the companies that their employees had been detained and explained why. A typical example is the Saibansho's notice to the American consul in Kobe that the Walsh, Hall and Company employee Matsuda Minedjiro was being held in the Saibansho prison for questioning about his theft of kerosene oil.[27] When the Saibansho recovered stolen property, it frequently notified the American consulate that the rightful owners could recover their goods at the local Japanese government office. In September, 1873, for example, the Saibansho notified the American consul Daniel Turner that a representative of Walsh, Hall and Company could come to their office to recover some kerosene oil stolen by their employee Takibaru Torukichi.[28] Scores of recorded instances show that Japanese thieves were punished, sometimes severely, for stealing from American residents. A frequent punishment for convicted Japanese offenders was anywhere from twenty to 100 "blows". The Japanese Genkichi, for example, stole several pieces of cloth on a Pacific Mail Steamship Company steamer and was sentenced to eighty blows. Kimura Kumakitchi, who stole meat from the American merchant A. Fobes, was convicted and received forty blows, and Mizuwara Kichinosuke, employed by the China and Japan Trading Company, was convicted of stealing kerosene oil and sentenced to fifty blows.[29]

The Japanese carried out punishments promptly and sometimes publicly, especially when the crime was against foreign trading houses, to make manifest both their justice and their control. For example, two Japanese employed by a Mr Cotsner, an American merchant, were sentenced for having stolen three pairs of shoes, six caps, and one piece of cloth to be beaten 100 times after being held and humiliated in "the public view during three days in the settlement".[30] On another occasion, the Saibansho reported to the American consul that a Japanese named Masataro, employed by the American merchant Mr Lyons, had died from some sickness while in jail, but had been sentenced to "public exposure in the settlement for three days", after which he was to have "received 50 blows and serve 100 days at hard labor as punishment for having stolen a watch and revolver from [his] shop".[31]

Beyond recovering stolen goods and punishing offenders, the Japanese authorities often followed up with legal action to recover money from Japanese employees guilty of larger thefts. A. Fobes of the China and Japan Trading Company, for instance, asked the American consul Daniel Turner to initiate legal action to recover money its banto Honda had embezzled. Honda had confessed to stealing $109 collected from the imperial railroad, eighty-two dollars collected from the Osaka Saibansho and thirty-seven dollars from sundry other parties. When he could not repay the amounts, the company asked for legal action.[32] Sometimes in cases such as this, the Japanese authorities confiscated the guilty party's estate and divided the proceeds on a *pro rata* basis among all claimants, foreign and Japanese alike.[33]

Occasionally the Japanese authorities acted without the stimulus of a foreign merchant complaint. In July, 1879, the government office instructed Julius Stahel to notify the China and Japan Trading Company that a Japanese boatman, one of its employees, had been arrested in possession of fifteen gallons of kerosene oil. Thomas McGrath, the agent for the company, gratefully acknowledged the efforts of the Japanese, and noted that the oil having leaked out into the bottom of the ship during shipment, was mixed with seawater and was ruined.[34]

Japanese justice was effective with regard to servants who had broken the law. In fact, merchants, who could have neither asked a Japanese-speaking person a question nor understood an answer, were no doubt relieved that the Japanese handled their own lawbreakers. Yet each incident, whether the guilty were punished or went undetected, accentuated the merchant sense of vulnerability. Merchants could take care of themselves in this basic area of irritation and loss no more than could Isabella Bird walk through the Japanese countryside unaided.

In other areas, less demanding of strong action, the Japanese desire to "help", and Westerners' dependence, led to plans which would have put most business transactions under the authority of Japanese officials. To manage the population of servants, the local Japanese government at Hyogo proposed a system by which headmen were be in charge of labor pools and given responsibility not only for the performance of the crews, but also for anything that anyone under their supervision might steal. This simplified to some extent the tedious process of pursuing one criminal claim at a time with the consular office, which then in turn had to report the theft to the Japanese authorities and seek restitution on an individual basis.

In May, 1869, some seventeen months after the opening of Hyogo to foreign residents, the *Hiogo News* printed a set of suggested regulations for Japanese servants which Governor Ito Shunske (Ito Hirobumi) had proposed one year earlier.[35] In it he stated that "Servants of Japanese Princes, or Ronins, are entered to the foreign residents in Kobe, [are] changing their appearance. We therefore are fearing that they will perhaps make a hurt to the foreigners". Noting that foreign residents frequently complained of theft committed by their Japanese servants, Ito went on:

> We think, if such complaints are made often in the future, not only would foreigners be distressed, but it would be much trouble for us to inquire into the case; accordingly, I made out a Regulation, as here attached, and therefore have to request you will be pleased to notify to American citizens or subjects that all Japanese Servants who are in the employ of the foreign residents, should be examined and questioned, to see them safe or unsafe ... if the foreigners wish to have a Japanese Servant, they will go to the office, where they can obtain any Japanese Servants to employ to them as prescribed in the attached Regulations.

The regulations provided for the creation of an office where servants could register for work and where a headman would broker the labor to foreigners as needed. When an individual could no longer work or became "diseased", the servant could be removed by the headman and replaced. All wages were to be collected by the headman, "who may be held responsible for any loss or robberies conducted

by them". Moreover, a ticket was to be issued to each servant, and prospective foreign employers could inquire into the "derivation and character of all Japanese
Servants". Ito concluded that the regulations would "avoid any loss of property".

The foreign community, realizing its vulnerability to loss of property through
squeezes and outright theft, seized upon Ito's proposal as a solution. The editors
of the *Hiogo News* argued strongly for the adoption of Ito's proposal and
addressed itself to the consuls: "Now! why should this state of things exist? ....
When the remedy is in our own hands, shall we supinely fold our arms and permit
unfaithful servants to rob us right and left?" The paper noted that the office would
be "under the control of the Government, who would *become responsible for all
losses* sustained through unfaithful servants, thus creating in fact *an insurance
office in which all could secure policies, without the payment of premium*". The
paper was aware that some had argued against the adoption of Ito's plan because
it would provide "means for the authorities to squeeze the servants of foreigners
out of a portion of their wages", and the editor proposed that any "truly valuable
servant" could be protected if his employer would "add a little to his salary".[36]

The rhetoric here, in support of a plan that would have given the Japanese government direct control of "servants" who were in fact crucial selling and
distributing agents of the firms, is significant. Contrary to its robust insistence on
action, the plan implied that foreign merchants would not do the hiring of "servants", on whom their essential economic work depended. That Western
merchants were enthusiastic about such a proposal reflected how much they recognized their dependence, and how much they sought at least to formalize that
dependence in predictable patterns.

Some evidence suggests that a shadow of the plan Ito proposed – and the
American community so strongly supported – was actually implemented. In
February 1879, a Japanese boatmen stole some kerosene from Walsh, Hall and
Company, and the firm did not submit a complaint to recover its stolen property. A.
Fobes, the agent for the company in Hyogo, stated that "the Japanese who employed
the boat and boatmen has repaid to us the value of the oil stolen and if any complaint has to be made, we suggest it be made by him. We held his guarantee and
were paid as above stated and have no complaint to make".[37] Japanese coolie masters were responsible for Chinese employees as well: in 1879 Walsh, Hall and
Company recovered fourteen yen from the Japanese coolie master Shimazu in compensation for three stolen cases of kerosene oil stolen by Chinese coolies.[38]

The Japanese government's commitment to the prompt discharge of justice
regarding Japanese criminals and debts reinforced the wide margin of insecurity for
merchants isolated by language, custom and attitude in the "island communities" of
the treaty ports. Merchant insularity led naturally to dependence on bantos. The by-
products of merchants' reliance on bantos – exposure to theft, manipulation and
lack of control of the crucial mechanics of trade – created a desire for answers that
would have in fact accentuated their dependence.

IV

One group of foreigners in Japan, the Chinese, proved more competent in handling their own business. Though Americans depended on Japanese bantos and servants to carry out many of the day-to-day essentials of their businesses, they were even more dependent on the Chinese, without whom American trading houses would have been hard-pressed to function at all. The Chinese were the most numerous, and in many ways anomalous, foreign nationality in the Japanese treaty ports. They were not there because their government had forced Japan to give them special privileges, but because Western businessmen could not operate without them. They also were the treaty ports' true entrepreneurs, who made substantial profit by knowing their business and the people with whom they transacted it. Chinese had been present in Nagasaki during the *sakoku* period as traders along with the Dutch and lived in the *Tojin yashiki*, or Chinese quarter. A large Chinese community had permanently established itself in the seventeenth century and eclipsed the Dutch in sheer numbers and in the volume of trade it helped facilitate until the 1850s, when the Dutch enclave was swept away by the new treaties. The Chinese continued as an important presence in the ports partly because many foreigners from the China coast treaty ports brought their Chinese servants, clerks and warehousemen with them.[39] Crucial to this study, however, are the Chinese compradores, some of whom had acted as middlemen in the commercial transactions in the China ports. These men came because they saw, as one historian has shown, "the growing opportunities for money making in Japan".[40]

From modest beginnings, the numbers of Chinese grew rapidly after 1868: by 1875, roughly half of the total foreign population of Japan of 5,000 was Chinese, and by 1894, out of 9,800 foreigners, 5,000 were Chinese. Except during the Sino–Japanese war of 1894–5, Chinese always accounted for at least half of the populations of Kobe and Yokohama, and two thirds of that of Nagasaki.[41]

Part of the Chinese business community worked independently; many Chinese owned and operated laundries and tailor shops, ran gaming houses and traded on their own account. The English language press in the treaty ports often complained of competition from Chinese merchants and sometimes hinted at practices which enabled Chinese to make profits when Westerners could not, often because they could and did provide needed services better than others, even in the face of formal attempts – such as restrictions on land rentals – to constrict their activity.[42]

Americans frequently employed Chinese as domestic servants, and Chinese access to the sources of supply for foreign households made them valuable beyond the simple role of servants. The agent for Heard and Company in Yokohama wrote plaintively that "both here and at Kobe we have a China house-boy, the rest of the servants are Japanese. I have tried *all* Japanese and find that they squeeze worse than Chinese. We *must* have Chinese ... or else increase our European staff greatly – and then would not have it done so well or so cheaply".[43] Eugene Van Reed, for a time another employee of Heard and Company, described the domestic arrangements in the Heard compound in Yokohama: "The whole responsibility of catering for the house has been in the hands of the [Chinese] butler, who has, I find, been accustomed to procure from the stores such articles as he deemed wanting. His monthly accounts were never inquired into".[44]

Though important as personal or household servants, Chinese were indispensable in business. The basic mercantile communication problem was not unique to Japan. Foreign merchants in China were no better prepared for face-to-face commercial contact with Asians than were their colleagues in Japan. A key feature of the system of doing business on the China coast was the use of Chinese compradores (from the Portuguese word *compra*, "to buy"); these compradores had increased their sphere of influence over time to a degree well beyond the power merely to decide, skim and on occasion, steal. Foreign merchants, segregated in factory compounds and excluded from most contact with the Chinese, depended on "a special class of compradores"[45] to conduct the Chinese side of their business: doing the purchasing and selling for foreign merchants; guaranteeing the Chinese staff necessary for such trade; and taking responsibility for trade goods while on the foreign merchant's premises, including hiring the labor required for handling the goods. A compradore provided "security for his own honesty in cash", and many firms maintained connections to compradores in one Chinese family for more than a single generation; some compradores in the Chinese treaty ports became wealthy through their handling of foreign trade.[46] In their homeland, Chinese compradores became accustomed to handling a large volume of goods and, as there was no analogous class of go-betweens in Japan, foreign merchants showed a marked preference for using the Chinese in the Japanese treaty ports. One observer noted that

> The Chinese are a much pleasanter people to have to deal with than the Japanese who are to me the very incarnation of Treachery .... While affecting to despise Trade and merchants and only to respect arms and chivalry, the moment the question of money comes forward, they show an amount of greed for gain that far outdoes the much talked of cupidity of the Chinese. And yet in spite of this ... they are too vainglorious to take advice or to admit that they need it: so they are the prey of adventurers.[47]

Another visitor to Japan observed that Japanese merchants were "more dilatory, undecided and unmethodical in business" than the Chinese, consuming as much time "in disposing of a few hundred dollars' worth of oil or vegetable wax, as the Chinese merchants would occupy in disposing of a million dollars worth of silk and tea".[48]

This association of Chinese with certain areas of especial competence or expertise was consistent with broader American thinking on race and labor. In the late nineteenth century, "racial language came increasingly to identify the American workforce" and thinking about race ... became increasingly intricate ... taking on regional shapes and shades in response to regional demographics and regional imperatives of productivity". Certain racial characteristics were linked to jobs or even specific tasks. An early historian of immigration stated in 1912 that "American industry had a place for the stolid, strong, submissive, and patient Slav and Finn ... it needed the mercurial Italian and Roumanian". Even the performance of specific tasks were thought to be race-specific – one American journal stated in 1886: "In the matter of picking and packing fruit" it was hard to locate "any desirable white help who will do this as satisfactorily to the consumer as the trained Chinaman, who, by tact peculiar to themselves mainly, seem to have reduced it to a science".[49]

By associating certain foreigners with specific skills or functions, perhaps Americans rendered them less threatening by identifying a known place for them. But the urge to integrate was clearly subordinate to the urge to exclude back home, where anti-Chinese feeling was virulent:

> No variety of anti-European sentiment has ever approached the violent extremes to which anti-Chinese agitation went in the 1870s and 1880s. Lynchings, boycotts and mass expulsions still harassed the Chinese after the federal government yielded to the clamor for their exclusion in 1882 ... a labor union could still refer to that patient people as "more slavish and brutish than the beasts that roam the fields. They are groveling worms".[50]

In the U.S., fiercely parochial members of their "island communities" reared up in racist unison to preserve their notions of racial uniformity and labor opportunity for whites. Threatened by the Chinese drift toward other occupations after the completion of the transcontinental railroad, white workers decried the "degraded" condition of Chinese labor.[51] Worse, Chinese showed themselves unregenerate. "All attempts to make an effective Christian of John Chinaman will remain abortive in this generation ... ages of senseless idolatry ... have left him without the essential qualities for appreciating the gentle teachings of a faith whose motives and unselfish spirit are alike beyond his grasp".[52]

In the ports, however, Chinese competence somehow needed to be ranked ahead of any threatening Chinese feature and, without apparent contradiction, merchants set about the task of locating the Chinese where their own economic necessity required. At home, the Chinese presence threatened economic security and stirred up racist sentiment in a substantial segment of the population. In the ports, the Chinese presence ensured the economic security of a substantial white majority. Because it did, that majority was happy to put aside the issue of race.

In 1864, A.O. Gay of Heard and Company encouraged the transfer of a Chinese named Akew to Yokohama from Kobe, describing him as "clever" and "valuable" and praising his extraordinarily useful "knowledge of the market here, after a long residence".[53] Nine years later, the agent for Augustine Heard in Yokohama – then without a compradore's services – complained to Heard's office in Canton that "I found last season that all my time was taken up in buying, firing and packing; we have to buy in very small quantities, say 10 or 15 piculs and seldom get a parcel of 100 piculs – there is more bargaining about one of these small lots than about a chop of 800 chests in Hankow".[54]

Often, the compradores were important enough to warrant their own offices in the foreign company compounds – one source described their rooms "with high-backed chairs for [their] compradore staff". The important duty of warehouse superintendent – considering the volume of theft which occurred in the settlements – also fell to the Chinese: "A Chinese godown keeper ... assumed full responsibility for the contents; and unflattering though it may sound to the insurance companies, he seemed to represent a more adequate cover against theft".[55] The crucial responsibility of overseeing tea-firing godowns usually fell to Chinese as well.[56] Western traders received samples, fixed prices and arranged through their bantos for the goods delivered to a warehouse. There the goods were inspected, with or by a compradore. If the goods passed inspection, they were weighed, and the Western merchant paid for them, the Japanese dealer paying the export duty of 5 percent. The Westerner then paid the compradore his due. In the early days when shipments were relatively small, the tea arrived completely dried, but larger orders quickly produced shipments with imperfectly dried tea which could spoil in transport. Chinese "experts from Shanghai" invariably supervised the Japanese women in the tea-firing godowns. One close observer of the tea-firing process noted that:

> One compradore, notified at eleven o'clock at night that tea must be fired the next day to fill a cable order, had four hundred coolies on hand at day-break, many of them summoned after midnight from their villages, distant over seven miles from the godowns. This mysterious underground telegraphy in the servants' quarters is one of the astonishing things of the East.

The women coolies "waited patiently outside the compounds until the lordly Chinaman" decided the necessary labor force for the day.[57]

One consular report on tea observed that the refiring process for the American market actually damaged its quality, and wondered why American consumers demanded the green color the process produced. The Chinese who supervised the refiring process, though aware of its consequences, were unconcerned. The "keen Chinaman", said the report, "does not hesitate to apply the artificial coloring to suit our depraved taste, and would doubtless add arsenic if he was asked to do so and could be shown how it would pay".[58]

By the 1860s it was clear that Chinese were functioning as far more than simply servants of Europeans and Americans in Japan. The prints of the Yokohama *ukiyo-e* (Yokohama floating world) provide evidence that, at least in the minds of the Japanese, the Chinese were associated with the Western community. Common representations of Chinese linked them closely with foreign trade. One picture shows a Chinese looking on with interest as Japanese and American merchants discuss a business transaction. Other scenes show Chinese with foreigners in the sitting room of a merchant ship, inside a merchant's home, around business compounds and supervising the unloading of goods. One telling scene shows the inside of a "flourishing American trading house" with Chinese both inside and outside on the busy street. Numerous street scenes show robed and pigtailed Chinese freely mingling with the foreign population, and scenes depicting amusements sometimes show Chinese both as guests at Japanese establishments and as servants in foreign homes.[59] All of this suggests Chinese integration into the economic life of the ports, and the high degree to which foreign merchants depended on them.

The essentials of finance often bore a Chinese imprint. Western hotels employed Chinese 'shroffs', or cashiers, where they determined the rates of exchange between various currencies, seldom passing up an opportunity to squeeze globetrotters. Almost all banks employed shroffs as well, who tested coins and made payments over the counter. Money changers, too, were Chinese, and one contemporary noted that "every business house has its Chinese compradore or superintendent, through whom all contracts and payments are made". Foreigners sometimes borrowed money from Chinese: the guide to communicating with Chinese in Yokohama pidjin contained the phrase "Anatta go-hakku lio aloo nallaba watark-koo-lack'shee high shacko dekkelloo alloo ka?" (I should like to borrow 500 yen from you if you have them).[60]

William Elliot Griffis, an articulate observer of nineteenth-century Japan, commented extensively and perceptively on the dependence of American mercantile establishments on the Chinese. He noted that "most of the largest and wealthiest business houses are owned and managed by those who were among the first comers to Japan", and that such companies' staffs comprised "from five to twenty young men ... backed by a small army of native porters, coolies, packers, boatmen, etc". Griffis further observed that:

> These large firms control nearly all the export trade of Yokohama, and indeed of Japan. The tea, silk, cotton, rice, etc. is brought from all parts of the country ... and is disposed of by native merchants, through brokers and "compradores". In most cases the native producer, or even the broker, never sees the foreigner with whom he deals. The most important man in many foreign firms, the power behind and before the throne, is the "compradore". This superior being is a Chinaman, who understands enough Japanese, especially with the help of the written Chinese character, to deal with the Japanese merchant, producer or broker. He is the provider and paymaster of the firm in its dealings with the natives. He arranges, by and with the advice of the merchant, the purchase, sale and delivery of merchandise. He hires and pays the Japanese *employes*, and, being the trusted man, is a creature of imposing pretensions, and a quasi-partner in the firm. His facilities, opportunities and never-cloyed desire for "squeezes" from his Japanese clients are equally abundant, and he lives up to his privileges.

Explicit in Griffis' critique of such business arrangements is his admiration for Chinese competence; implicit is a contempt for American merchants' who found themselves so detached from affairs at the heart of their business interests. He continued: "This aristocratic and highly antiquated form of doing business, in which the merchant practically holds himself aloof from his customers, is an inheritance from the foreign merchants in the ports of China". Merchants in China, he noted, depended on Chinese compradores in the same way, and "grew rich without troubling to learn the language of the pigtails around them". Griffis concluded that compradores were a necessary evil in Japan because foreign merchants were determined not to learn Japanese, but he hoped that this situation would improve, particularly if "younger firms, members of which are beginning to learn the Japanese language", refused to employ compradores. He noted that there was no excuse for this failure, as missionaries had provided grammars and dictionaries, which were lacking when the ports were first opened.[61]

Griffis' observations were those of a contemporary who wished to see genuine cultural contact between Americans and Japanese. His comments also suggest a lack of contextual appreciation for the dilemma any merchant would have explained, had he the vocabulary: imposing the known upon the unknown was not a negotiable or a divisible process. Griffis' hope that members of "younger firms" would learn enough Japanese to make the use of compradores unnecessary was simply wishful thinking. In 1878, midway through the treaty port years, Isabella Bird offered this description of the Chinese in Yokohama:

> One cannot be a day in Yokohama without seeing quite a different class of orientals from the small, thinly-dressed, and usually poor-looking Japanese. Of the 2500 Chinamen who live in Japan, 1100 are in Yokohama, and if they were suddenly removed, business would come to an abrupt halt. Here, as everywhere, the Chinese immigrant is making himself indispensable. He walks through the streets with his swinging gait and air of complete self-complacency, as though he belonged to the ruling race.

Bird noted, "He is not unpleasing-looking, but you feel that as a Celestial he looks down upon you. If you ask a question in a merchant's office, or change your gold into *satsu*, or take your railroad or steamer ticket, or get change in a shop, the inevitable Chinaman appears ... he is sober and reliable, and is content to 'squeeze' his employer rather than to rob him – his one aim in life is money. For this he is industrious, faithful, self-denying; and he has his reward".[62] Indeed, the Chinese held themselves above other Asians in the ports, sometimes treating the "poor Japs as though they were no better than dogs".[63] One visitor's account emphasized the Japanese dislike of Chinese: a Japanese coolie averred that the Chinese were "too smart", and that they had "gobble[d] up all the best situations" in the ports. A satiric verse summed up his grudging respect for the Chinese, however:

You can kill a fly and
Smoke out a mosquito,
But you cannot dislodge a Chinaman!
They do not conquer a country
By force of arms, but
By dint of patience and numbers.[64]

These pictures summed up the situation precisely. The Chinese were the business-men most in charge of the profits of treaty port trade and, if their well-fed complacency irritated Westerners – and some Japanese – it was because the Chinese so gently, subtly and firmly ruled the "ruling race".

Few aspects of business avoided the shaping hand of the Chinese. The larger firms' business frequently involved arranging purchases of tea and silk in the interior,[65] and Americans left the arrangements for quantity, transportation, and prices of goods to those who could move beyond the circumscribed ports with comfort. Pat Barr has written that, because Chinese compradores "could read and write both Japanese, and, after a fashion, English, and had good heads for figures, they had early established themselves as reliable and indispensable middle-men in the mercantile world". The Chinese squeezed their Japanese customers, but were "faithful to their foreign masters in their fashion and they exercised considerable behind-the-scenes power".[66] Such status and control attracted compradores to the ports in Japan, where those with any English language ability preferred long-term employment with a foreign trading firm, where their "activity, zeal, anxiety and watchfulness" translated into profit, with the Chinese often deciding the size of their own share.[67] Two Yokohama *ukiyo-e* scenes underline the Chinese role as lin-guistic and business go-betweens. One shows a Chinese in a foreign godown and another shows a foreigner at his desk doing accounts while a Chinese talks with another foreigner and a Japanese.[68] Chinese interest in Western firms sometimes reflected direct financial investment. Some Japanese citizens rented houses in the foreign quarters to conduct business and thereby elude taxes by representing themselves as servants or employees of foreigners; the Chinese did the same thing, investing capital in foreign firms.[69]

The level of their Chinese dependence is clear in the cases where American merchants requested their consuls to intervene when their Chinese servants were detained by the Japanese government. In August, 1877, the Chinese Ah-hun, employed by the American merchant Eugene Gill, was accused of attacking and badly wounding the Japanese citizen Imai Kashichi. The Japanese authorities noti-fied Gill to send the Chinese to the Saibansho, whereupon he was released when Gill posted bond guaranteeing that the Chinese would not leave Hyogo. Though Gill expected his servant's detention to be brief, the Saibansho found Ah-hun guilty of the offence, prompting Gill to write a series of notes to his consul, demanding to know what the nature of Ah-hun's penalty would be. "As my busi-ness is at a standstill without this man", he wrote, "I wish to know if I can get him back, or shall I be obliged to engage another? Please obtain his release as soon as possible". A scant six days without Ah-hun prompted Gill to write ominously that he would take "proper steps for the protection of my affairs" and demand details of the proceedings of the Japanese court.[70]

Foreigners' awareness of their substantial dependence on compradores sometimes showed itself in bitter humor. One piece of doggerel entitled "The Honest Chinee" illustrated the power of the compradore:

> There was a Chinee named Fu Hsing,
> Or Hok – not hic haec hoc – Hing,
> And another named Yeh Shao Ling,
> But, no matter with which of the two
> You may have business to do,
> It has been ordained that you
> And your heirs, executors and administrators as well,
> Shall lose every d — d thing.[71]

A language guide, in explaining some Chinese variations on the pidjin prevailing in the ports, suggested that one translation of "Wok-kallimassing" (a corruption of the Japanese *wakarimasen*, I do not understand) was "It is simply a question of *Mexicans* (Mexican dollars), and if you make it worth my while I will [understand] very quickly".[72]

Augustine Heard's agreement with Chun Min Chee, a Chinese who agreed to come to Japan with four assistants in 1864, clearly illustrates the importance of Chinese compradores to American trading houses in Japan. In his capacity as compradore, Chee warranted a separate contract which specifically spelled out the terms of his employment. Chee agreed to proceed to Japan in "the employ of and entirely under the direction of Augustine Heard and Company", and promised to do nothing for any other firm while in Heard's employ. His contract stated that he was "fully competent to superintend the manufacture of tea", but reserved the right to employ him in other tasks. The agreement further stipulated that Heard and Company would pay the rent for Chee's residence, but that he and his Chinese crew had to pay for their own "chow-chow" (food) and other living expenses. Chee, as headman, received fifty dollars per month, his four assistants each were paid twenty dollars or less per month, and the company advanced each employee three months wages.[73] That Chee and his helpers warranted such a formal, specific contract, and that Heard advanced a considerable sum of money for wages, especially when the company was struggling financially, highlights the importance of the position of compradore.

Just as they sought to protect their key Japanese employees, Americans, along with the British, expressed concern when faced with the possibility that the Japanese government would assume full control of the Chinese community in Japan. The Chinese had originally come to Japan largely as servants or employees of Westerners, and until 1868, their diplomatic status in the Japanese ports was unclear. The new Meiji government began to exert control of the Chinese through registration, expulsion and punishments for lawbreakers. Though welcomed by some members of the Western foreign community, others expressed doubt about giving the Japanese exclusive jurisdiction over the Chinese. Foreign fears were muted when the Japanese agreed that the Chinese and other non-treaty residents would fall under the control of local Japanese authorities, "assisted by the foreign consuls".[74]

The somewhat divided authority over them left the Chinese fairly secure in the treaty ports until the Sino-Japanese war approached, when the American mercantile community became aware of its danger. In the summer of 1894, disturbing rumors ran through the foreign settlements that the Japanese government was planning to take punitive measures against Chinese citizens in the treaty ports that would result – either through outright expulsion or making the Chinese liable to Japanese military service – in a mass repatriation of Chinese. Since almost all merchant houses in the ports depended on compradores, foreigners faced the possibility of the near total disruption of smooth business in the ports. The Chinese and other foreign merchants held a series of meetings to prevent the dislocation of trade that was sure to result from any removal of essential Chinese intermediaries. The Japanese did not engage in any punitive measures against or massive deportation of that segment of the Chinese population most important to foreign trade.[75] Compradores, after all, served the purpose of facilitating foreign trade, the advantages of which the Japanese fully understood, especially in time of war. There was a drop in the Chinese population during the war, but not enough to justify the worst fears of the Western merchant community. The only change in Japanese policy was to require Chinese who remained to register with the government.

The reaction of the Japanese at the crisis suggested their dependence as well on the Chinese for the advantages they gained from foreign trade, despite their own dislike for aspects of the system of doing business. In 1873, the Japanese Saibansho issued two directives aimed at eliminating the squeezes that Japanese wholesalers paid to Japanese and Chinese employees of the foreign firms. The Chinese, for example, squeezed Japanese wholesalers for packing and weighing merchandise for transportation to the ports and a percentage of tea purchases as compensation for firing, packing and shipping charges.

These directives triggered editorials and responses in the *Japan Weekly Mail* that documented well Western merchants' near-total dependence on their Asian middlemen and the occasional self-delusion Westerners needed to soften that reality. Well aware that certain Japanese and Chinese squeezed foreign firms as well as Japanese wholesalers, the *Mail* expressed surprise that the Japanese authorities would attempt to reform the system instead of foreign merchants themselves. The *Mail* noted that foreign merchants had generally accepted the practice since the opening of the ports: when a Japanese merchant bought from or sold to a foreign merchant, he paid "certain fees or percentages to the Chinese compradore or godown-man of the foreigner, or, in the case where there was no Chinaman, to the Japanese banto who was in the same position". Foreign merchants were aware of the capital drain but lacked either the know-how or "the courage to attempt to break it up". The Chinese or Japanese staff of any foreign house, the *Mail* averred, skimmed off $5,000–$10,000 per year as middlemen, a practice tantamount to taxing trade in the ports.

The editor queried, "What does a compradore do in the way of arguing with native import dealers, beating them up, and collecting market information, which a European could not do, or which is not well recompensed by his wages of $50 per month?" The *Mail* observed that the system was inefficient in that it gave the bantos an interest in the foreign merchants' business: bantos wanted their masters to sell and buy large quantities, regardless of the profit margins. The liabilities of such a system were obvious: "As the foreign merchant contemplates his silk boy weighing off a parcel of silk, he has the pleasant reflection that whereas he pays him his $25 per month, the Japanese owner of the silk is about to 'cumshaw' him $50. Surely the silk boy serves two masters". Indeed, Japanese merchants at least partially funded foreigners' compradores, but foreigners paid in the end because the Japanese merchants were adding the cost to the charges for each delivery of goods.[76]

Some suggested that if the system were discontinued, merchants would be forced to raise the salaries of their Japanese and Chinese employees. But the *Mail* argued that their salaries were already fair, and the extra they made in squeezes "goes only to pamper them in luxury and extravagance", to "enlarge the wardrobes, to nourish the rubicund noses, to maintain the harems, to feed the gambling houses of aliens!" But if in fact the "majority of foreigners in Japan" secretly groaned under such tyranny, other defenders of the system argued that the employment of compradores "saved them substantial bother" of bargaining, buying and packing. Indeed, compradores' partial funding by the Japanese allowed smaller firms to afford their services too.

Letters to the editor on this issue revealed a narrow range of responses. Several agreed that the squeezes amounted to a tax on trade. Others agreed that compradores should not receive salaries from those "over whom they are charged to exercise control", but admitted that the system allowed some foreign firms to keep up "a comparatively large native and Chinese staff" at relatively little expense since the Japanese paid a large part of their "salaries". One respondent stated that the issue at stake did not concern the relative value of relying on compradores and bantos, but whether the Japanese had any right to interfere in the "legitimate trade" of the foreign trading houses. "I maintain", he wrote, "that it is infinitely preferable to submit to its continuance than to endure its removal by government interference". No doubt the irony of his last statement was lost on most merchants: "Government ... can never be too chary of charging itself with the management of matters which the persons interested are capable of managing themselves". This conclusion was redolent of merchant self-delusion, in this case to mask, as did the whole debate, who alone was capable of managing treaty port business.[77]

In the event, the Japanese government decree proved unenforceable, in part because the Chinese were not subject to Japanese law. Foreign merchants nevertheless sent a protest to their consuls, resisting one of the reforms that might have measurably increased their independence from Asian middlemen,[78] though in this case they noticed that the gain in freedom could be made only at the cost of increased dependence on the Japanese government. In a subsequent issue, the *Mail* stated the reasons for merchant resistance succinctly:

> No one will deny that it saves trouble and allows merchants to do their business with less annoyance to themselves, that it gives them more leisure, that it relieves them from the tedious processes of haggling over sales or purchases, and that it obviates the necessity for the study of an uninteresting and intractable language.

In a highly competitive business environment with increasingly narrow profits during and after the 1870s, some discussion of reform would have seemed appropriate. By the 1870s, business in the Far East was gradually losing its quality of a "kid-glove occupation", as rapid telegraphic communication and steam transportation changed the pace of business. If Westerners just learned Japanese, the *Mail* observed, they would enjoy "a prestige with the Japanese that the Chinaman lacked". But foreign merchants instead pursued business as usual, avoiding the "tedious processes" that would have violated the assumptions upon which their community was built.

One outraged observer of foreign businessmen in Yokohama called the town "more dead than alive" since businessmen's response to the Japanese proposal and the *Mail's* support was little more than a collective yawn. Merchants did not address it in any public meeting or in their chambers of commerce. His indictment went further than had Griffis' earlier:

> Given sufficient trade to keep a decent table, a tolerable glass of sherry, a pony or two, or a billiard table, a comfortable bungalow with its appurtances ... and it's how we apples swim! Interfere in this life in any way, take away a servant, oblige a man to put the buttons on his own shirt, to brush his own clothes, to ascertain what he has got in his godown the property of himself and those who support him, and it's "What a confounded hole this is", and "What are the Consuls about?" .... Is there a single foreign merchant who has taken the trouble to learn to speak with the men he does business with every day of his life?[79]

A piquant exchange in the *Japan Weekly Mail* in 1888 highlighted the issue of language. In October, an article appeared which stated that the Yokohama community "knows little and cares little about the real Japan and the real Japanese people. Outside the consular service there are probably not half a dozen people who speak Japanese well enough to share an idea with the people they live amongst".[80] In November, an anonymous defender of the merchant community wrote a long response entitled "Yokohama's Real Slanderers". In it he admitted the essential truth of the accusations, stating that with regard to merchants' inability to speak Japanese, the accuser merely repeats what no one would have questioned a month ago. Whether owing to radically different habits of life, or whether because … the Japanese prefer to be left alone, it is beyond question that the barrier separating them from the foreign residents of Yokohama stands today much as it stood twenty-five years ago. No one denies this, nor need anyone be surprised if such a state of affairs strikes an intelligent stranger very forcibly. As to the alleged want of acquaintance with the Japanese language, it seems to us that [he] has not greatly erred in his assertion.[81]

It is notable that the most strenuous defense of merchant behavior contained no refutation of the accusation. Neither is there consensus on the degree to which missionaries, with a much clearer motivation to communicate directly, learned the language. One authority on missionaries in Japan states that "Davidson McDonald was one of the very few Western missionaries who became fluent in Japanese. Because the majority of missionaries failed to master the language, in the 1870s the Japanese needed a knowledge of English before they could be converted" and stated frankly that "the teaching of English was a very important means by which missionaries made converts".[82] Another source suggests that "one of the greatest obstacles was the problem of communication. A number of scholars learned Japanese; so did a few diplomats and missionaries. So far as the bulk of Westerners in Japan were concerned, however, the linguistic hurdle was generally by-passed".[83] Critics of merchant linguistic incompetence might have criticized for the same failing almost all foreigners in – and sometimes beyond – the treaty ports.

The layers of insulation provided by Japanese bantos and Chinese compradores defined the nature of business in the ports. American merchants were reduced to little more than always irritable, if sometimes well-paid, spectators as the Japanese government and merchant strove toward control of their own trade, treaty revision and the inevitable end of the treaty port system, and as their Asian "servants" controlled the essential aspects of their trade, paying themselves largely as they saw fit and as the market allowed.

One visitor, returning to Yokohama in the mid-1890s after an absence of a decade, noted that "still the pleasant life of foreign residents went on, much as it had years before, open port life showing fewer changes than purely native places". She remembered that the "past has perhaps been canonized".[84] Another traveler, explaining why he did not tarry long in Yokohama, noted that merchants' "manner of procedure and idea in business is so precisely identical, that no studying is required".[85] Indeed there was little variety or sophistication to the business practices of men whose "actual sphere of influence … reached out but little beyond the concession itself". Areas beyond the ports remained

little known to the trader and the official clerk, or merchant dwelling in the foreign quarter. To each of them it remains, often for years, a veritable *terra incognita* – a mysterious region possessing for them few attractions; which as their individual taste may dictate, they may or may not enter once a year. Some … have lived half a score of years in the concession without once really penetrating the Japanese town by which they are hemmed in.

Another contemporary remembered that "there is so wide a distinction between the races that to merely cross the line of demarcation between the foreign settlement and the native town was … almost as great a thing as a trip across the Pacific".[86]

The line of demarcation existed on the map – and in the imagination and behavior of American merchants. The world they built functioned as an island of security, but also as a confining cage within which the limitations on their control was daily demonstrated in the form of their extreme dependence on putative "inferiors". That dependence constituted a grave, interior contradiction in the foundational logic of the ports that was never reconciled, but its consequences were ameliorated by compensatory freedom and agency in another area.

Surely hunting provided relief from the boredom and routine of port life, but the frequency and passion with which the foreign community pursued its sporting life can be connected more deeply to the need to defy Japanese control. Jackson Lears has argued that American élites, buffeted by changes in religious life, and feeling their individual autonomy threatened by bureaucratization produced in them a feeling of being "weightless" and "over-civilized" as the world industrialized around them. Such feelings caused these men to yearn for intense experience, for "real life". In the vigorous, competitive world of sport, young men could learn to take control of their lives.[87] Considering the circumscribed nature of life in the ports, and the high degree of reliance on bantos and compradores, Americans in the ports doubtless felt superfluous and "weightless" in spite of their efforts at building a society that they could dominate in some putative sense. Donald J. Mrozek has suggested that the "constituent groups which favored sport did so out of need. In different ways, each found in sport a strategy for regeneration and renewal".[88] In light of their dependence, merchants felt the need to seize upon whatever opportunities for regeneration – and autonomy – they could find.

Such quests for personal autonomy are understandable (from the merchant point of view) in the specific political context of the ports. Foreigners seeking to go out of the treaty ports proper were required to apply at their consulate for a passport to carry with them while travelling in the interior. Article VII of a typical passport (see Figure 6, page 131) stated that "Even those who have licenses to hunt are not permitted to discharge fire-arms or hunt game outside of the Treaty Limits".[89] This warning had little effect on where, when or how many foreigners hunted. One visitor described, (facetiously, one hopes) the result of two Kobe merchants' hunting excursion: "They had started on their trip by shooting a coolie and missing a weasel, whereat they were somewhat depressed".[90] Foreigners' penchant for hunting – if not the callousness (if the story was true) of the two merchants – was a source of constant tension between the foreign and Japanese communities. Foreigners, though not often eager to escape the ports, were determined to hunt the abundant game found in the areas surrounding the settlements, often beyond the treaty limits. Probably at least some of the Americans in Japan had served in the Civil War, and many were familiar with firearms.

In November, 1876, an American citizen named H. Upton, while hunting in the rice fields near Akashi outside of Kobe, fired at a snipe in a rice field without noticing that a group of Japanese were at work there about 70 yards away. Three of his shot struck a woman, one in the eyebrow, one in the lower part of the cheek, and one in the forearm. Upton immediately went to her aid, found her with wounds "bleeding slightly", and, apparently at a loss what else to do, "gave her a rio and departed". A large number of farmers pursued Upton and tried to stop him from leaving the scene. Upton had no intention of allowing himself to be detained by the farmers but wanted no further bloodshed, so he removed the cartridges in his gun. He retreated without further incident, and met a policeman, to whom he gave his name, then returned to his house.

Upton deeply regretted the incident and offered to have the woman brought to Kobe where he would hire a "skillful European physician to attend on her" and pay her board and compensate her for lost work time. The incident was resolved amicably between Upton and the Japanese woman.[91] Nevertheless, this was pre-cisely the type of occurrence that the Japanese government sought to prevent by requiring foreign residents to hunt only within the treaty limits. The difficulty, of course, lay in enforcing any such regulations, since foreigners were not subject to Japanese law. Japanese officials pressured the foreign consuls to enforce restric-tions on hunting by subjecting foreigners to fines for breaking regulations concerning the use of firearms, but a common response was that this would amount to giving up extraterritorial rights – the political guarantee of their sepa-rate status – by administering Japanese justice in foreign courts by proxy.[92]

In the event, the consuls supported the foreign residents by doing little to enforce Japanese regulations; foreigners continued to hunt beyond the treaty limits with rel-ative impunity well into the 1880s.[93] Upton and other foreigners were shielded by extraterritoriality from prosecution in Japanese courts. Whereas the American con-sul considered such incidents to be minor, without the protective shield of extraterritoriality Americans would have been subject to prosecution under Japanese law, with consequences that would have violated every fundamental assumption upon which the American community operated. Immunity from Japanese law was a tangible form of control for Americans, the freedom to defy regulations.

V

Almost thirty years after the opening of Yokohama, the *Japan Weekly Mail* observed that "the Yokohama merchant does not enter into direct relations with his Japanese customers, there being always either a Japanese banto or a Chinese compradore as go between; while in all the banks the actual cash is counted in and out by a Chinese shroff".[94] As Americans, already dependent on their consuls, complained to them about their long-term dependence on their bantos and com-pradores, their lack of agency must have seemed to double. Yet the alternative was unthinkable, and would have involved a complete transformation of attitude and re-examination of the cultural assumptions on which those attitudes rested. Instead, Americans dealt with the uncertainty of business by proxy and willingly, if sometimes with loud complaint, did everything possible to protect the system that ratified the values of their "island community", even putting aside the issue of race when it was inconsistent with the sure-handed economic function of the compradores. Letting bantos and compradores take on the role of buffers freed parochial merchants from direct involvement in the central business of buying, selling, and negotiating in an environment that they suspected as alien and untrustworthy.

Americans acquiesced in Japanese-sponsored attempts to streamline the process of making claims against Japanese servants accused of theft, but did no more. Nothing suggests that Americans sought alternative arrangements; they accepted the presence of layers of insulation, both from Japanese society and business, as a given, and openly resisted the one Japanese effort at reform because they hazily perceived that the shift in influence would go to the Japanese and not to them. Merchants' eagerness to retain the services of those on whom they depended suggests a commitment to social and business stasis, but also reveals the depth of merchant anxiety over their possible loss. Consuls were always reli-ably available; it required work and worry to sustain the services of bantos and compradores. That they could be taken away revealed their indispensability to merchants.

5

THE PRICE OF ISOLATION

External pressures

Trade hardly covers its expenses in Yokohama.[1]

Peter Dobkin Hall, in an analysis of Massachusetts merchant behavior in the nineteenth century, wrote that:

> Few of these merchants had started as wealthy men, so they all knew too well the hazards to which new fortunes were subject. Not many of them could claim deep roots in the city where they had made good – they could not depend on circles of well-established kinsmen to help them out. None could look to the state or to the law as a bulwark to defend their interests …. To maintain their wealth in the face of incredible economic risk and political turbulence … would require remarkable knowledge and skill.[2]

Edward Chase Kirkland's study of Gilded Age business thought opens with an entire chapter devoted to describing the sense of uncertainty that afflicted the American business community in the years 1860–1900. The "panic and pain" of those years was due to intense fluctuations in the American economy; one analyst of "business cycles in terms of contemporary reaction to them" determined that "fourteen of the twenty-five years between 1873 and 1897 were ones of 'recession' or 'depression'".[3]

Businessmen of the period routinely insisted that the vast majority of men in business ultimately failed, and that business was an intensely "precarious" endeavor. Kirkland avers that not even "the titans of the generation, confronted by an era of rapid and disturbing changes and without precedents to govern them, were either as omniscient or omnipotent" as many have suggested. Even John D. Rockefeller, one of the master empire builders of the age, was not immune to feelings of vulnerability, stating that "All the fortune I have made has not served to compensate for the anxiety of that period. Work by day and worry by night, week in and week out, month after month".[4] While Americans may have believed in the existence of certain "natural laws" such as that of supply and demand, those laws offered only abstract consolation – one observer noted that "under the fixed laws of trade, of supply and demand, the employer has really little more control over prices … than over the winds and the weather".[5] Kirkland's incisive commentary goes further:

> Only our habit of writing the history of the era in terms of politics, Supreme Court decisions, and briefs of learned counsel has led historians to interpret the structure of business thought primarily as defense propaganda rather than as explanation or comfort for business insecurity in face of the "facts of life". Panic and perplexity … gave the first occasion for this sort of business thought.[6]

If such perceived vulnerability and uncertainty was endemic in the American business community, it was exacerbated by the additional uncertainty spawned by the arrival of increasing numbers of immigrants.

Historian Matthew Frye Jacobson has observed of the same period in U.S. history that "the soaring numbers of diverse immigrants were welcomed for their labor power and yet resented – even violently assaulted – for the economic competition they presented, or for the element of 'difference' they introduced to the society … the deep American dependence upon these foreign peoples seems to have fueled the animus against them".[7] If the interpretations of Hall, Kirkland and Frye regarding broad national attitudes are at all accurate, they certainly apply to Americans in the treaty ports, who were often bemused by the reality of doing business in Japan – and as aware of instability as any of their counterparts in the U.S. In an environment where they, too, "could not depend on circles of well-established kinsmen to help them out" and where they believed (in Hall's words) they could not "look to the state or to the law as a bulwark to defend their interests", Americans set upon the task of dealing with business uncertainty. The more they realized their dependence on the "inferior" and "untrustworthy" Japanese trader, the more they came to be disturbed by their own inability properly to order their business relations with the Japanese. Indeed, the interventions of their consuls and their bantos and compradores may have salved merchant anxiety to some degree, but those interventions ultimately proved to be a porous barrier against the relentless waves of attack from an ominous Japanese hinterland.

When Americans complained about the Japanese refusal to conform to Western notions of "proper" business procedure, they expressed a frustration at disorder and uncertainty intensified by their assumptions of racial superiority. Americans' daily reminders of their inability to control "inferior" peoples fueled their animus in the microcosm of the treaty ports. The heightened sense of vulnerability, the desire "to bring disorder under control, to substitute order and calculation for confusion" in the American economy led, according to Kirkland, to the consolidation movement in the 1880s and 1890s.[8] In the treaty ports, it led to a nearly unilateral defense of the unequal treaties and the security they provided, the nearest equivalent means by which merchants could fight off the uncertainty brought on by change.

Committed to relative stasis, American merchants were frequently content to accept the inconveniences and liabilities their isolation wrought. As Japan increasingly took control of its own foreign trade, Americans were unable and largely unwilling to make the cultural adjustment on which any adjustment of business practice would need to have been based. Aware of the loss of control associated with isolation, American merchants sought control in the only way they knew – by attempting to impose their notions of "proper" business procedure on the Japanese. When this failed, stability rightly seemed to them more elusive than ever. The resulting discomfort, however, proved an inadequate stimulus to change.

I

One thoughtful observer of Gilded Age business attitudes has written, "Though businessmen of exceptionally bold and speculative temper may have welcomed the high winds and enjoyed steering their craft to fortune through the current hazards of storm and wave, the generation as a whole was more prone to seek security and reassurance than to welcome upheavals".[9] One message Victorian boys and men received about the meaning and nature of work defined it as an individualistic struggle toward achievement, a field of endeavor where manliness could be proved by aggressive action. The dynamic economy of the nineteenth century provided a broad venue for the healthy expression of male competitive instincts, and the individual with the best instincts for survival would naturally rise to the top:

> As the nineteenth century opened, the United States was becoming a nation where no formal barriers prevented white men from achieving positions of wealth, power, or prestige. Now, a man could determine his place in society through his own efforts ... a man could thrill at the prospect of improving his own position and becoming the master of his own social fate through personal energy and determination. Again and again, men described their personal goals as the outcome of their struggle – through their work – for a desirable social position.[10]

Here "a man could thrill at the prospect of improving his own position and becoming the master of his own social fate through personal energy and determination". Men frequently described their goals in specific language, wanting to "arrive at eminence and fame"; "rise to wealth and honor"; "[get] on in the world"; "prepare myself for some station of respectability and usefulness". One middle-class man stated the nature of the challenge and its meaning succinctly: "Man is made for action, and the bustling scenes of moving life",[11] words that accurately describe the career and purpose of Eugene Van Reed, a man seemingly unwilling to let a single identifiable opportunity pass him by.

Van Reed was that exceptional American who seemed to glory in the storm and wave of entrepreneurial opportunity, and his career in Japan suggests the possibilities of activity unconstrained by the quest for stability that characterized almost all American merchants' behavior. Van Reed's colorful story throws the majority of merchants' attitudes into sharp relief in that he was certainly *sui generis*; his activities illustrate opportunities for profitable scheming that the fluid economic and, at least until 1868, political context of the ports created for a motivated, acquisitive entrepreneur.

Van Reed was born in 1835 in Reading, Pennsylvania.[12] In 1851, he sailed with his father to California to participate in the gold rush, where his father became a gold-dust broker. In 1853 the elder Van Reed returned to Reading to bring his wife and two younger children back to San Francisco, where he established himself in the real estate business. It was there that Eugene, then eighteen, became friends with Joseph Heco, a Japanese castaway who had arrived in the United States in 1851. Van Reed learned some Japanese from Heco, and when the latter left for Japan in 1858, Van Reed, "urged by the spirit of adventure", decided to follow him. On the way to Japan, Van Reed stopped in Hawaii, where he observed the foreign community and noted the insular social life of the "Founding Fathers" of Honolulu. He arrived in Japan in the summer of 1859, and secured an appointment as clerk to United States consul Eben Dorr. He remained in the clerk's job for only six months, but there can be little doubt that Van Reed observed, probably with great interest, the currency exchange frenzy, that his appetite for speculation was whetted, and that Dorr's speculations introduced him to the value of holding an official position.

In late 1861, with the help of a Japanese, he published a small book of English phrases and their Japanese translations, written mainly "with a view of facilitating the Japanese in their mercantile intercourse with foreigners". Van Reed's interest in trade was more than simply linguistic, however. He was by now employed by Augustine Heard and Company, and he wanted the job overseeing Satsuma's foreign trade, which, in the atmosphere of the mid-1860s, meant arranging for the export of Satsuma's products to pay for arms imports. Throughout 1863, he engaged in secret negotiations with Satsuma – on his own behalf, not Heard's – to "build men of war, supply him [the daimyo of Satsuma] with the most approved weapons of warfare, regulate his shipment of produce to foreign countries and generally superintend his foreign trade",[13] which came to nothing when the Bakufu learned of the plot and imprisoned Van Reed's go-between.

Stymied in his "personal diplomacy", Van Reed in 1864 joined the expedition to reopen the straits of Shimonoseki to foreign commerce as private secretary to the American Minister, Robert Pruyn. While at Shimonoseki, Van Reed pressed for commercial advantages on behalf of Heard and Company, signing agreements "with Choshu officials granting him and Heard priority in renting large parcels of land at choice locations along the waterfront in the event Shimonoseki was opened to foreign trade". Van Reed's correspondence with Heard and Company while engaged in negotiations with Choshu show him at his wheeler-dealer best. Convinced that the Bakufu was backward and not nearly as amenable to fostering foreign trade as the more "progressive" han (feudal domain) he had dealt with, Van Reed tried to convince his employers to cast their lot with what he shrewdly guessed would be the winning side in the coming civil war. In September, he wrote, "Satsuma's object is to overthrow the gov't and place himself in the chair".[14]

Ever eager for the ready sale, he recommended certain weapons: "If possible and you can do so, I think breech-loading rifled cannon will serve well; pictures, with prices, calibre size named, would be well to send, also, pictures of ironclads, descriptions, cost laid down, etc". He continued, "I am not through with Satsuma yet, and I believe the time is near at hand when a great trade can be safely and quietly done with him". Chastened by his previous experience with the han, he wrote, "I have regulated the rumors in the papers here, to throw the Japanese government off[f] their guard". Hedging his bets if the Bakufu proved victorious, he added that Heard should try to get a certain Mr Mugford appointed Russian Consul at the port of Kanagawa, as there were "many little advantages to be gained by being in with the gov't".[15]

Realizing that Satsuma would need revenue with which to pay for the proposed arms shipments, Van Reed facilitated the import of seeds. In May, 1864, he wrote, "I have procured a small quantity of Tobacco and rice seeds from San Francisco to give to the daimyos. Sea Island Cotton has been sent to me but were you to procure about a picul for distribution to producers it might lead to something .... I will see Satsuma's people and give them the Sea Island Cotton Seed ... I know nothing more acceptable to the Daimyos at present than a present of seeds. When the country is more opened, we may do more in friendship, leading to trade". Van Reed firmly believed that "the gov't alone was our enemy, the daimyos (naturally ambitious) were our friends".[16]

To arrange transport, Van Reed tried to sell a river steamer to Satsuma but, ever mindful of the government at Edo, he recommended caution: "In Japan, owing to the great number of officials, spies, etc, etc, no arrangement can be entered into even of the most trifling character unless all duly investigate and concur as to the course [on which] to proceed". In June, he wrote that, when the "Japanese make up their minds to have a steamer, experience proves that almost any steamer which happens to be on hand can be disposed of". Regarding the possible sale of two men-of-war, Van Reed argued that "as the main object is to commence a large business with the Daimyos, I agreed that if the contract were awarded, that but 5% commission would be satisfactory, and should the vessels prove to their liking, that all business be given to us". Later, he wrote that Satsuma officials asked to see the U.S. man-of-war *Jamestown*, having already shopped among English, French, Dutch and Prussian vessels. Van Reed protested against showing them "our *old vessels*" and showed them instead pictures of newer ships from *Harper's* to demonstrate the "great improvements we were inaugurating in warfare". Almost desperate for the sale, he told Heard that "now is the time to have those views, diagrams, estimates, etc, they are *panting* to possess a man-of-war to startle their countrymen, and I am confident that if anyone can get that contract, it will be an American, and that the House" [of Heard].[17]

Van Reed welcomed the possibility of foreign intervention in 1864 to stoke the fires of civil war in Japan. Eager for trade with Satsuma and Choshu that he thought their victory might bring, he wrote in July that the "troubles in the country are great, Japanese adhering more than ever to the idea of driving us out of this port. We must have a trial of strength with these people before trade will resume its natural channel". Fearful that an uncooperative Bakufu would strangle foreign enterprise if allowed to continue to exist, Van Reed observed the next month that "the war has now been deferred for 3 months, but the end must come, we *must* have a war and that soon, or there will be no trade here to pay house expenses even". He viewed the punitive expedition against Choshu as a catalyst for Japanese civil war, and stated that "good results must ensue from this war, and we hope that now that the Tycoon's perfidy is manifested that he will be polished off without mercy".[18]

The final confrontation between the rebellious han and the Bakufu did not occur until 1867, and Van Reed's ambitions for quick sales and profits went unrealized. Even while negotiating with Satsuma, he turned his attention to a scheme to export Japanese labor to Hawaii.[19] The Hawaiian government, concerned over the decline of the whaling industry, turned to sugar to buttress the Hawaiian economy, and was looking for a source of cheap labor for its plantations. Once again, Van Reed sought to do business under the official aegis of the U.S. government. In April, 1865, he wrote, "I may get the appointment of commissioner to Japan from Sandwich Islands. Official position with the Japanese I consider imperative, in order to make an impression on the people – and besides it will alight something handsome".[20] After securing the appointment as U.S. consul for Hawaii, Van Reed requested a leave for reasons of "ill health" from Heard and Company to visit Hawaii to finalize arrangements. Though the Bakufu refused to authorize his plan, Van Reed, with a "substantial" sum of money from the Hawaiian government, proceeded in 1868 with his plan and recruited 350 Japanese laborers, about 150 of whom ultimately were transported to Hawaii.

By early May, the imperial forces opposing the Bakufu had occupied Edo, and though they refused to issue passports for the workers, Van Reed nevertheless sent the laborers to Hawaii on May 17. The foreign press in Yokohama condemned Van Reed's scheme as "equivalent to slavery". Later, an unofficial envoy of the Japanese government determined that the workers had been gravely mistreated, and forty decided to return to Japan.[21] Hawaii did conclude a treaty of commerce and friendship with Japan in 1871, but Van Reed's soiled reputation and his history of being "troublesome" barred him from the negotiations. Though Van Reed was appointed U.S. consul in Hawaii in 1872, it was on the condition that he "never again try to take part in diplomatic affairs". The following year, Van Reed was taken ill and died at sea on his way back to the United States.

Doubtless Van Reed's career in Japan suggests an emphasis on short-term profit, speculation and adventurism. Some of Van Reed's freedom of action can be attributed to the timing of his presence in Japan and the unique opportunities the turbulent political scene presented. Moreover, his shady dealings concerning contract labor for Hawaii suggest the possibility of unsavory opportunism. Nevertheless, certain features of his career in Japan make for interesting comparison to those of almost all other American merchants. First, he demonstrated an aggressive entrepreneurial spirit, manifested most clearly in personal contact with those he regarded as potential customers. Though his Japanese ability is unclear, the publication of his "phrase book" demonstrates at least an awareness that communication and profit were somehow related. Second, the variety of his activities, the breadth of his interests and his willingness to experiment with new approaches clearly separate him from the vast majority of treaty port denizens. Though most merchants did not share Van Reed's penchant for intrigue and adventure, neither did they share his willingness to move beyond the restricted world of the ports.

II

Victorian boys and men received a second message about the nature and meaning of work, one that emphasized the need to balance cooperation and competition. The "male domain, although it was based on the individual as the unit of action, was a world of profound interdependence .... Men's days were often spent in intense social interaction, and they did their work within dense networks of collaboration, contest and mutual influence".[22] No man functioned alone, and negotiating the dangerous shoals of the chaotic world of nineteenth-century economic life required a judicious recognition of the need for allies as one faced the world's danger and complexity.

The world of treaty port business proved a complex and unpredictable one and, while merchants could take solace by commiserating about the mysteries of trading with the Japanese at the club bar, such commiseration was only talk. A good portion of the "interdependence" these Victorian men must have sought in their work was simply absent. Instead of a web of understandable, balanced competitive and cooperative relationships, Americans in the ports confronted a largely alien and unknowable culture and business world. As they sought to make sense out of the foreboding world of elusive profits, and lurking, malicious Japanese "opportunists" beyond the ports, their frustration increased almost in proportion to the energy they expended to somehow rationalize their transactions.

One of the most nettlesome consequences of merchants' isolation was an inability to exercise any choice with regard to the Japanese merchants on whom they depended to bring goods to and take goods from the treaty ports. Western merchants, according to the treaties, and by their own inclination, remained within the ports. This basic reality of treaty port business rendered Westerners vulnerable in a variety of ways to the Japanese merchants on whom they depended to conduct their trade.

Merchants handling goods in the domestic American marketplace were hard-pressed to meet the challenge of remaining profitable. Business historian Thomas

Cochran noted that one essential of "business success in general trade with remote areas" was "buying, where prices were low, commodities that had a good market in the home or in some other port ... the business called for good judgement regarding ... the movement of commodity prices in distant markets ... and above all else, the shrewd handling of credit. American merchants of the early period [who had much in common with the merchants in the ports] had less access to capital" than European merchants, and the "amount of such credit that a merchant could command depended greatly on his reputation for caution, wealth and probity".[23] Knowledge of the credit worthiness of one's counterparts was equally important – "Business conducted in many places across vast distances had to be based upon faith in one's creditors, for the forceful collection of overdue bills was difficult if not impossible. The merchant's traditional solution to this problem was to restrict his dealings to a network of people known to be trustworthy".[24] But these basic prerequisites to the conduct of known and comfortable business were not available to American merchants.

Many Japanese merchants were much like the Westerners who first came to the treaty ports. Japanese "yamashi" – a particularly opportunistic kind of "Boeki-sho" (men engaged in foreign trade) – were often in a good position to take advantage of Westerners, frequently ordering goods but taking possession only if the market on delivery was favorable. They became "invisible" if the market was not, leaving the importer stranded with goods his limited storage capacity forced him to unload as quickly as possible. In merchant parlance, the numerous Yokohama yamashi were "speculative rogues" who damaged the business of the foreign firms as well as that of reputable Japanese dealers. When yamashi were summoned before the Japanese court, they frequently professed a legitimate inability to pay, sometimes owning little more than a "hibachi or pair of chopsticks for a foreign creditor to attach".

Such difficulties led one Western merchant to lament that "the probable fact is that, by the great majority of Westerners living in Japan, Japanese character is counted a profitless study". Japanese yamashi, taking perverse advantage of Japan's traditional animus against its own mercantile class, could take much advantage of foreign merchants, since most of their countrymen assumed all merchants were equally suspect. Japanese merchants saw how foreigners lived, assumed they were making huge profits and felt no compunction about taking advantage of them.[25] Western merchants deemed it shrewdest and safest to distrust what they could not apprehend clearly, though they took no steps to change their business practices.

Otto Keil, the secretary general of the Yokohama chamber of commerce, noting the complaints of Yokohama silk merchants, stated that "the Japanese, like all Eastern nations, will *never* give the real price of their goods, unless forced thereto by long bartering" [italics added]; they would also always try to deliver goods inferior to the contracted quality.[26] A second strategy was to contract for certain goods, and, when they arrived months later, to negotiate with the foreign merchant according to the new prevailing prices and demand. Often this was

accomplished on the basis of some trivial difference between the actual and contracted goods, with the foreign merchant obliged to accept the terms because no
other Japanese merchant aware of the procedure would touch the goods.[27] Foreign
merchants responded by demanding warehouse deliveries "unsecured by any
down payment or receipt ... often regarding the merchandise as collateral for
bank loans. He often canceled orders and awaited market quotations from home
and rejected the goods if they were unfavorable". Only a few of the foreign firms
– one of which was Walsh, Hall and Company – could pay in cash, and many others quarreled with the Japanese over payment.[28]

Such problems were even more severe than ones encountered by merchants at
home, where "much of the merchant's success ... depended on his estimates of
the terms he should grant. Around his home city, he could keep some track of
what his debtors were doing".[29] Indeed, there was nothing in the ports that at all
resembled the integrated social and economic world of the American frontier
merchant somewhat earlier in the nineteenth century. Such a merchant was "a
general locum tenens, the agent of everybody! And familiar with every transaction in his neighborhood. He is a counselor without license, and yet invariably
consulted, not only in matters of business, but in domestic affairs".[30] Americans
dealing with yamashi in the ports, however, had no way of knowing with any precision with whom they dealt. Western merchants were not in any way integrated
into the marketplace that made their presence possible, and their experience with
Japanese of varying business intents was often a hit-or-miss affair.

A Japanese contemporary observed in 1888 that, although Yokohama was a
flourishing port with increasing business, merchants' profits were generally
declining and indeed, threatened "to vanish altogether". In the early days of the
ports, demand for exports and imports almost always exceeded supply, but this
ideal situation did not last long. Spurred on by competition among themselves in
the commercially crowded ports, foreign firms watched their profit margins on
transactions decline, partly because of their lack of knowledge about their
Japanese markets. Often willing to import "any goods at the shortest notice,
regardless of the existing demand, and under [the] most ridiculous conditions",
merchants, "in spite of bitter dealings with the Japanese, repeated over and over
again", were "still determined to place implicit trust in the word of every Japanese
who comes to them in the guise of a customer" because of their reluctance to look
beyond the ports. Business transactions over which Westerners' control was
severely limited thus tended to beget an even larger volume of similar business.
Many foreign firms did not import unless the goods were ordered by Japanese
merchants; others imported entirely at their own discretion, trusting intuition or
past experience to guide them.[31]

Westerners were equally vulnerable in transactions involving the purchase of
goods for export from Japanese merchants. American merchants routinely
accused their Japanese counterparts of commercial immorality – frequently for
reneging on business contracts, when it was not favorable to take delivery of
goods ordered. One representative example of this was the case of Sujibayashi

Naokichi, a Japanese merchant who sued the American firm of Chipman, Stone and Company for breach of contract to recover money he deposited with the firm for four orders of kerosene lamps and accessories. The contract called for the delivery of the goods within ten months, and though most of the accessories arrived well before the expiration of the contract time, Naokichi refused delivery because some of the accessories were missing. Stone offered to produce the accessories in fulfillment of the original contract, but the Japanese refused and brought suit.

In court, Thomas Van Buren, the U.S. consul at Yokohama, dismissed the case and assigned court costs to Naokichi, arguing the real reason for his refusal to take delivery was that the market price of the goods in Yokohama was lower when the goods were delivered than when originally contracted for. As evidence, Van Buren cited Stone's later sale of the goods at a loss and concluded that many Japanese entered into contracts hoping to find "some trifling difference" in the goods that would allow them to speculate in damages or in large price reductions; Stone claimed to have been victimized by Naokichi for $300 earlier.[32] One commentator observed that "not a bale of silk, not a chest of tea, not a roll of matting, would be received" from such merchants "until every hank, pound and yard had been submitted to the closest expert inspection" since the "most formal contracts are unblushingly repudiated, or at best their execution postponed when their prompt fulfillment involves a loss of even contemptible insignificance".[33]

Yet foreign merchants were not in a position to demand advance payment from their Japanese counterparts who, concealed from foreign view outside the ports, often determined how and when business transactions occurred. In the case of those importing goods already ordered by Japanese merchants, American firms ceased taking even the partially effective precaution of requiring bargain money or cash deposits. The absence of bargain money, which at least formalized business agreements to some degree, meant that any Japanese merchant, with or without capital or the intention to follow through on the agreement to take delivery of imported goods, could order from foreign merchants and then refuse delivery. One disgruntled merchant pointed out that in early days of the ports, the traders coming into the settlement were samurai, worthy of trust, but after the Meiji government abolished that class in 1872, the foreign merchant became subject to the "tender mercies of men entirely unknown to him". The bar of public opinion did not embarrass the Japanese trader, because "the ears of his countrymen were accessible to himself alone" and lax bankruptcy laws often let him escape pecuniary responsibility.[34]

After September 1872, a new Japanese bankruptcy law went into effect, and foreign merchants observed bitterly that it seemed more concerned with protecting defaulters' property than with creditors' rights to collect. One foreign merchant complained, for example, that he received an insulting fraction of a claim for $3,780 after waiting five years for settlement. The same merchant lost a $1,000 advance he had paid to a Japanese merchant for a copper delivery; the Japanese declared bankruptcy, was thrown into prison and committed suicide while there, and the foreigner's claim was never satisfactorily settled. One outraged foreigner cited a case of a Japanese holding an official position who two months previously had been sentenced to two years imprisonment for fraudulent bankruptcy.[35]

The *Japan Weekly Mail* pointed out that "lax bankruptcy laws" often let irresponsible Japanese escape, forcing foreigners to sue in Japanese court, but noted as well that if treaty revision went through, those courts might be more sympathetic to foreign claims.[36] Yet treaty revision was anathema to American merchants, and they refused to consider any potential good that might come of it. Instead, they continued to rely on a consular system that was not particularly well positioned to defend their interests, and in any event was incapable of effective action beyond the limited scope of its own courts. The consular correspondence is littered with merchant complaints, which simply caused consuls to write to the Japanese Saibansho, or turn certain cases over to the American Minister, who then appealed to higher Japanese authority; commonly, appeals proved futile.

Other difficulties often stemmed from the fact that some daimyo dealt with the same Japanese middlemen as some American merchants. When those middlemen experienced financial difficulties, recovery of debts owed to Americans sometimes became an issue. In March 1874, Walsh, Hall and Company advanced $5,000 to Yamanaka Yeizaburo, Yamanaka Matahichiro and Okada Iwashi of Osaka, with which they promised to purchase white wax and tobacco for export before May 30 of that year. The Japanese merchants provided Walsh with fifty boxes of wax as per the contract, but failed to deliver the promised amount of tobacco, bringing only 5,000 piculs to Kobe.[37]

Later, the Saibansho declared Yamanaka and his associates guilty of breach of contract with Walsh, Hall, and forced them to declare bankruptcy. When Yamanaka's estate was settled, the Saibansho offered the company thirty-four yen in compensation for the bad debt.[38] But Walsh claimed that this amount was "very much less than Yamanaka and his friends ought to be forced to pay", and stated that he was owed ¥4,483. He argued that an unspecified daimyo, indebted to Yamanaka, owed Yamanaka a substantial amount of money and that the amount of this indebtedness would be enough to pay them off in full. In effect, Walsh was asking for a daimyo's debt to a Japanese merchant to be transferred directly to an American firm for payment. The Saibansho, however, stated that the transfer from han to prefecture rendered the indebtedness of the daimyo to Yamanaka void. Claiming that this was unfair, Walsh stated that "our debtors have assets which, while valueless, are so only because of an arbitrary act of the government", and asked for Newwitter's help in recovering a larger share of the debt.[39]

Some attributed such losses to foreign merchants' failure to insist on bargain money. One merchant who had done business in Japan for twenty-five years stated that the demand for bargain money was common early on, but that an unidentified English firm began accepting contracts without it and the rest of the firms followed suit. Reputable buyers were hard-pressed to compete with the larger orders of the fly-by-nights, and the merchant lamented further that Japanese buyers have made of the foreigner such use as ought to be made of every man who makes a fool of himself; they take delivery – one and all – if the goods leave a profit, and refuse delivery on some pretext or other if they do not, or, at least, force the foreigner to act as godown-keeper for them, without rent, interest, fire insurance, or guaranty of exchange, until doomsday, as hardly anybody ever ventures to lose the good graces of such a class of men, for fear of not getting any more of the "beautiful business".

This merchant had contracts printed up, limiting the time of delivery and liability, but Japanese merchants quickly informed him that other houses would accept orders without any contracts at all. Put off that his modest attempt at reform was stillborn, he suggested that some foreign firms were less concerned with putting their own business on a solid foundation than in trying to "get at their neighbors" to damage them, insensible to the damage they did to themselves, as they built a "house of paper".[40] In all such complaints was indication of what this merchant made explicit: Japanese merchants often decided the essential terms on which business was conducted.

A Japanese observer noted that merchants' thirst for more and more orders without checking on the solvency of their customers hurt them severely, and suggested that foreigners unite and uniformly require 10 percent bargain money on all transactions to prevent those without capital from entering into agreements with foreign agency houses. Foreigners, by this method, would lock themselves into having to deliver the goods, even if prices rose in the supplying country, but reasonable business practices included this precaution anyway. Current business practices, he concluded, were covering the "reputation of Japanese commerce with black disgrace". The *Mail* suggested the possibility of foreign merchants combining with reputable Japanese traders to exclude the adventurers to create an agency which could broker information on the solvency of Japanese merchants, but foreign firms, competing with each other for larger – though paradoxically more costly – orders were unable to cooperate except in the rhetoric of accusation.[41] Japanese were "cunning enough" to exploit foreign firms' hunger for business: by "going from one agent to another", they were "able to work the cash guarantee down toward the vanishing point".[42]

Yet such reform would almost certainly have been largely cosmetic. American merchants in the earlier period had fairly routinely required bargain money, but this practice had not solved the fundamental problems generated by merchants' lack of knowledge about the world beyond the treaty ports; receipt of bargain money was rarely a deterrent to broken contracts and foreign losses. In 1875, for example, the China and Japan Trading Company contracted to deliver to three Kyoto merchants 3,500 cases of kerosene oil. When the kerosene arrived, the Japanese did not take delivery, and the firm appropriated the bargain money of ¥700 and stated that it would hold the Japanese "accountable for the loss of interest at 1% per month, for cost of insurance at 1½% per month, for rent of godown at 1½% per case per month for any delay since the due date of December 4, 1875". The Japanese merchants – probably yamashi who simply decided that taking delivery would be inconvenient and unprofitable at that time – claimed that the American firm had violated its part of the agreement by shipping oil designated for other customers on the same ship.[43]

On another occasion, Schultz, Reis and Company complained that it had made a contract with an Osaka merchant to deliver 10,000 piculs of cotton rags. Three thousand were due to be delivered in April, 4,000 in June, and 3,000 in August. But by November, the company claimed that they had received "only 5,000 bales of a quality inferior to that contracted for". The company claimed a loss of $2,000 Mexican and gave notice that it was claiming the bargain money.[44] Seven years later, the China and Japan Trading Company complained to the American consul at Kobe that the Japanese merchants Kangimoto and Okamoto refused to take delivery, per their agreement, for a shipment of kerosene oil, prompting the company to threaten to initiate legal proceedings to recover interest, insurance and storage; the two Japanese observed that the delay was due to Okamoto's absence from Kobe when the goods came in. Though the problem was eventually resolved, such cases required an inordinate amount of follow up with the consuls.[45]

In 1875, the China and Japan Trading Company complained that it had entered into an agreement with the Japanese merchant Shonin of Osaka to deliver 1,440 carbines, accouterments and ammunition, at the price of six yen per carbine. The Japanese paid 1,000 *rios* as a deposit, but did not take delivery. There was no written contract to prove duplicity, but the American firm offered to produce witnesses to the agreement and asked the American consulate to compel Shonin to take delivery.[46] Nor were such incidents isolated: local Japanese authorities observed that Americans complained of a "great number" of cases involving verbal contracts that resulted in misunderstanding, and suggested that written contracts might reduce such difficulties.[47] But written contracts, too, could obfuscate as much as they clarified, since foreigners usually needed their Japanese "office boys" to translate them.[48]

From their vantage point inside the treaty ports, many American firms were forced to rely, through their Asian intermediaries, on the good faith and assumed sound financial status of Japanese merchants of whom they knew nothing. Merchants' only recourse in this and dozens of similar cases was an anguished or outraged series of notes to the consuls, who could do little more than pass complaints along to an unsympathetic Japanese government, which made decisions often based on its own interests. Merchants expressed their frustration by lashing out at the Japanese. One Westerner who had been in business over twenty-five years claimed that he "had not found one native merchant trustworthy".[49]

Because they were at the mercy of Japanese merchants who took delivery only when convenient, American businessmen were unable to coordinate the volume of their imports with anticipated demand. As a result, foreign traders were frequently left with large volumes of unsold merchandise. Reporting on foreign tea purchases in 1875, the *Japan Weekly Mail* pointed out that, in spite of heavy arrivals, "the

eagerness of teamen to purchase kept stocks from accumulating, and the consequence was that the prices were well maintained".[50] But doing business with
yamashi much more frequently meant business uncertainty and the added cost of
maintaining unsold merchandise. With regard to kerosene imports, the *Mail* noted
in July 1883 that 2,408,000 cases were already either in godowns in Kobe and
Yokohama, en route from U.S. or on U.S. docks. After deducting consumption until
December, the *Mail* projected that a whole years' supply would be on hand by
December 31, and observed that such a large volume – which consumption figures
did not support – seemed inexplicable.[51] Some evidence suggests that foreign merchants either lacked or did not apply knowledge of their own home markets as
well. One report estimated that foreigners held unsold in their godowns some
12,000 bales of cotton yarn, valued at $1,200,000, costing the merchants "interest,
rent and insurance" because there were no buyers outside of Japan.[52]

Merchants sometimes sustained business losses because of developments in
Japan they could not have predicted, and over which they could exercise no control. In early 1868 the imperial forces defeated the Tokugawa and established a
new government. In their quest to establish central power, the new Meiji leaders
recognized that the continued existence of the anachronistic han was an impedi-
ment to central control. The process of abolishing the han began in March, 1869
and the former han, numbering about 270, were finally replaced with prefectural
units headed by governors appointed by the central government in 1871. Though
this process meant that many of the daimyo surrendered the power they had previously enjoyed, many welcomed this move because of severe internal weaknesses
and financial problems. The central government now assumed the debts of the
former han and became responsible for their paper currencies.[53]

In theory, any American merchant who had lent money to a daimyo or delivered merchandise and accepted a promissory note in payment was protected, and
merchants' difficulties collecting from former han or their agents were sometimes
resolved to their satisfaction. The China and Japan Trading Company, for example, sold ten plates of iron to Tsukamotoyu Sennosuke, an agent for Choshu han,
who promised to pay for them when he sold the plates. Fobes complained that
Sennosoke instead sold the plates immediately at a lesser price; when the plates
appeared in the foreign settlement, Japanese authorities seized the plates and
returned them to the company.[54]

At other times, however, numerous complications arose. In December, 1870, a
Japanese named Yamaoka Goro, whom Schultze, Reis and Company and Smith,
Baker and Company assumed to be the legitimate agent and treasurer of the
daimyo of Yodo han, arranged with both companies for substantial loans.
Yamaoka contracted for "loans in the shape of merchandise" for 10,100 *rios* from
Schultz, Reis and 8,100 from Smith Baker, both payable within 180 and 200 days
respectively. When the notes came due in June, payment was refused on the
grounds that Yamaoka, then imprisoned by the daimyo of Yodo, had had no power
to undertake liabilities on behalf of the han. Both American companies stated that
in fact "Yamaoka *was* known and acknowledged as managing agent and treasurer"

of Yodo han by "foreign and Japanese merchants" and that Japanese officials at Kobe validated the seal of the daimyo of Yodo [italics added]. As evidence that Yamaoka was in fact the duly appointed agent of the han, Edward Behncke, an employee of Schultze and Reis, noted that a signboard at the entrance to the commercial department of the Prince of Yodo in Osaka clearly identified Yamaoka as the agent and treasurer for the han. Translated copies of the promissory notes clearly indicated that the transactions were legitimate.

Behncke further noted that the "Japanese Government is known to be exceedingly keen-sighted to discover any irregularities in the doings of the commercial concerns of the Princes [daimyo] and would obviously not allow Yamaoka to be publicly declared treasurer of the Prince if he had not really held that position". Behncke stated that Schultze and Reis had acted with "honest and straightforward purpose" and that the daimyo's claim that Yamaoka had had no power to act for him "must be taken for what it is worth coming from an Asiatic who finds himself called upon to make good the results of, or take over transactions entered into on his behalf by a servant, confidence in whom turns out to have been misplaced".[55]

Beyond Behncke's personal criticism of the daimyo of Yodo, this case has additional meaning. In May, 1872, the U.S. vice consul in Hyogo wrote to the Assistant Secretary of State in support of Schultze, Reis's claim and expressed deeper concerns. Observing that "the principle point on the part of the Japanese Government [was] to state that the said Yamaoka Goro was no agent for the han", the American consul believed that the claim was legitimate. Before the consolidation of the han under government control as prefectures, the central Japanese government had acted as a neutral arbiter in cases of dispute between merchants and daimyo. After the consolidation, however, the Japanese government acted as "judge and defendant. By deciding a claim not to be a claim against ... a former han, the responsibility of the general government ceases". Though he admitted that some claims against the former han had been settled without difficulty, he stated that:

> Very serious complications are dreaded by our countrymen to arise from this power of the Japanese Government, which by the peculiar local circumstances in dealings between foreigners and former Japanese Princes and by the difficulty to receive from Japanese subordinate authorities proper information as to local matters, has led to slight omissions in regard to form in contracts and agreements between foreigners and Princes, which omissions, beyond the control of foreigners, are now brought forward by Japanese General Government as reasons for non payment.[56]

The claims of the two American companies were never paid. The Japanese government held firm to its contention that the loans had been fraudulently contracted and refused to make restitution, while admitting the impropriety of the transactions and that Yamaoka in fact had sold the merchandise acquired from the

American companies and spent the money himself. Instead, the Japanese government agreed to confiscate Yamaoka's properties and divide the proceeds among creditors according to the quantity of each debt. In addition, Yamaoka was sentenced to fourteen years hard labor, two other employees of Yodo han received seven years hard labor, and a third was sentenced to thirty blows.[57] The Japanese government thus sought to discharge the financial obligations of the former han. Perhaps to prevent a reoccurrence of similar problems, the Saibansho in November 1873 notified American consulates that it was required by the central Japanese government to inquire into debts incurred by the han.[58]

Doing business in the Far East was characterized by a certain informality. Business, even among those who shared a common language and culture could sometimes be problematic – foreign merchants extended credit freely, sometimes carelessly, as in the case of three American merchants doing business under the name Hall and Holtz in both Yokohama and Shanghai. John Gargan, another Yokohama merchant, purchased $200 worth of goods in Shanghai, which his clerk selected and shipped back to Yokohama to set up Gargan's sister in business. After the order was filled, Hall and Holtz's Shanghai salesman persuaded Gargan to send considerably more merchandise, which he thought "would suit the Yokohama market", and Hall and Holtz shipped an equal amount of extra merchandise with every succeeding order until Gargan accumulated a large debt. Unfortunately, a fire at Gargan's premises in Yokohama consumed a large portion of the goods received on credit. Since he had no insurance, Gargan sought to avoid liability for the debt by arguing that the goods rightfully still belonged to Hall and Holtz. The *Japan Weekly Mail* called the case "another illustration of the careless and extraordinary mode of doing business in the East".[59]

The informal business style made for some interesting accounting discrepancies. In September 1871, for example, the Japanese merchant Ito Hachibei entered into a business agreement with the American merchants John Walsh, S.K. Lothrop, R.W. Irwin and A.O. Gay, with Ito depositing $20,000 with the Americans for joint business ventures. There was no written agreement, no time limit on the partnership, no joint account book, and no precaution against fraud or disagreement; the entire affair was conducted on a "principle of mutual childlike trust". Hashimoto Benzo, a Japanese broker, and "Shincoi", a Japanese employee, purchased goods on behalf of the partnership. After the partnership was informally dissolved, the Americans' records showed that Ito owed them $39,999.21, whereas Ito's indicated that the Americans owed him $108,715.24. Understandably, the case ended up in U.S. consular court in May, 1876.[60]

Confusion and mutual recrimination were common by-products of a business environment characterized by mutual isolation. In the U.S., an American lady was once visited by a young Japanese and an American merchant who had lived in Japan for several years. When the man boasted of having profited by taking advantage of the "ignorance of the natives", the Japanese, instead of being offended, asked his hostess for the man's address, stating that "My object in coming to this country was to learn from your merchants how to cheat, and this is the very man to give me the information I want".[61] Any line of inquiry whose aim is to determine who learned to cheat from whom is, of course, useless.

More useful is a cursory discussion of the advice dispensed by Gilded Age success manuals so popular in the U.S. While no direct evidence suggests that such manuals found their way across the Pacific (though indeed they may have) the nature of merchant complaints about their Japanese counterparts suggests that American merchants had internalized some composite notion of what constituted proper business behavior, and the relationship between that behavior and a just reward. Such manuals advised men to "work hard, to save, and to lead a sober, responsible life. In other words, they were exhorted to cultivate the tried and true economic virtues of pre-industrial America". The manuals also made sure that "the careful reader learned not to be a greedy capitalist. Success manuals taught that in business, good guys won ... not only be employing honesty, frugality, and hard work, but by an ethic of decency, fair-mindedness, conservative investment, and patient contentment with modest returns".[62]

American merchants found themselves in a situation where mutual mistrust and desire to take advantage could bloom, but one that also revealed – even showcased – their vulnerability to their Japanese counterparts. Moreover, they were constantly confused and irritated by Japanese failure to play by the rules suggested by an inherited tradition that was quite irrelevant to them. Satisfaction with modest rewards was difficult in business transactions conducted with and through men whose mendacity often seemed certain, and whose intent to defraud seemed clear. These were men with hazily understood but eagerly applied notions of right behavior confronting their racially different, economically threatening counterparts, with profit and livelihood at stake. That merchants might feel disconnected, or even "weightless" (as Lears might suggest) would not be improper speculation.

American merchants were not unaware of the difficulties that their own dependence and isolation created, and turned to alternative business devices over which they believed they could exert more control, and demanding less involvement with the Japanese merchants whose depredations they feared. Frustrated in their attempts to control and rationalize their mercantile activities with the Japanese, merchants turned to forms of business activity in the ports in which their control could be more clearly manifest.

III

One way foreign merchants made profits unrelated to import/export trade was by lending money to individual Japanese entrepreneurs. In the uncertain years just before and after the Restoration, some Japanese borrowed from foreign companies. Iwasaki Yataro, for example, borrowed substantial amounts from both Walsh, Hall and Company, his business agent in Yokohama, and the British firm of Alt and Company, fearing that loans from Japanese would make his financial status known and cause him to lose his credit. Iwasaki's extensive short-term loans did not damage his credit because he always paid them back on time, and the foreign press sustained his reputation.[63]

The volume of shipping, large and small, passing along Japan's coasts insured ample opportunity for salvage operations. Merchants could and frequently did engage in the buying and selling of wrecked vessels to dismantle and sell for parts. The American John Linsley, for example, purchased the whaling barque *Lagoda* from the Japanese for $2,600 to "strip and dismantle". On another occasion, a Russian dispatch vessel was driven aground in northern Japan, and the American firm Carroll and Company bid money on behalf of John Baxter Will, an American pilot then living in Yokohama. Will wrote of the transaction, "I telegraphed down to Mr. Frank Spooner of Carroll and Company at Yokohama to bid as high as 1,000 dollars for the *Rupak* on my own account", and, though Spooner bid $50 more than Adams authorized, Spooner assured Will that if he was "not pleased he would take her himself".[64] Other, smaller scale salvage operations attracted American firms as well. When the English steamer *Sakura* lost its anchor in the Awaji Sea, the American firm of Board and Niven hired a number of Japanese coolies to raise it, an operation involving considerable expense and planning.[65] Even when not involved directly in such operations, the U.S. consulate made arrangements through American firms to dispose of shipwrecked cargoes, transactions on which they earned a commission.[66]

American firms also engaged in provisioning and repairs for the large number of ships plying Far Eastern waters. One of many examples of this type of activity were the repairs Smith, Baker and Company performed on the British Schooner *Clio* in 1869.[67] Occasionally, American merchants acted as go-betweens for the Japanese government in times of need. When the Japanese government wanted to use American ships to transport troops to Taiwan, the U.S. government's neutrality forced the Japanese to employ foreigners familiar with East Asian shipping. An American merchant named J.M. Batchelder purchased the *New York* from the Pacific Mail Steamship Company, which was later used to carry out intelligence missions in China.[68]

A fourth means by which merchants made profits while avoiding depredations of the yamashi was the sale and recycling of goods within the foreign community itself. Warren Tillson and Company, for example, though active in regular trade with Japanese merchants, also functioned as bakers, storekeepers and navy contractors in addition to their role as general commission merchants.[69] Tillson's bakery supplied "fresh bread daily" to a foreign population not interested in the more austere Japanese diet dominated by rice, and Carroll and Company sold house fittings to build Western-style houses in the ports. Other companies, American and European, were engaged in the auction business. As companies and individuals went bankrupt or left Japan, their effects were auctioned off to older, established firms, or to newcomers seeking to establish themselves. Such auctions of used and sometimes damaged goods, held frequently throughout the entire treaty port era, served as a way of "recycling" Western goods, and provided an alternative means of making money, as well as underscoring the separateness of the foreign community.[70]

One ship captain recalled that around 1870 an unidentified merchant "bought up anything that was unsalable in the auction rooms at Hong Kong, chartered this vessel and sent her to call at all the ports in Japan. After calling at Kobe and Yokohama, selling all they could, they came to Hakodate with the balance". The captain himself purchased "two or three casks of spirits, some cases called champagne, some cases of brandy and gin, beer and porter, and a miscellaneous lot including some six gross of finger rings with stones".[71]

Merchants also rendered other services for which the degree of the compensation was unclear. One of these was the funding of Japanese students' stays in the U.S. In January, 1869, "certain Japanese government officials" sent a Japanese student named Shirane to the U.S. for educational purposes, and William Morse of the China and Japan Trading Company furnished him a letter of introduction to the company's New York agents and advanced him $1,228 while he was there. In a note to the U.S. consul at Kobe, Morse complained that he had been reimbursed for neither the principal nor "interest at 7% per annum" promised by Shirane's sponsors.[72] Another example was that of seven Satsuma students, on whose behalf Kagoshima han remitted $3,300 through the U.S. consulate to the China and Japan Trading Company's agents in New York for financial support for a five-year stay in the U.S.[73] A third instance of such activity involved Eugene Van Reed's arrangements to send Japanese students to the U.S. Two Japanese students went to Reading, Pennsylvania, in September 1867, and two others went to San Francisco to live with Van Reed's parents to improve their English.[74]

Another service was caring, for a commission, for American pauper seamen who took ill and required care while in port. Because of limited facilities, U.S. consuls sometimes paid American merchant firms out of their fund for the relief of destitute seamen to provide for seriously ill patients. The commander of the U.S.S. *Colorado*, for example, left a sailor named Vauley who was stricken with smallpox and another to act as his nurse in the care of Paul Frank, who arranged with Carroll and Company to provide for their needs until the sick sailor recovered.[75] Yet all such peripheral activity did not silence the complaints about dependence on "inferior" Asians.

From time to time, American consulates in Japan received inquiries from American companies in the United States concerning the potential distribution of their products in Japan. In 1878, for example, the U.S. National Association of Stove Manufacturers sought information about the possibility of importing their products; in 1896 one American member of the National Association of Manufacturers inquired about the possibility of selling brass lamps in the Japanese market, and other requests occasionally inquired after the nature and quality of Japanese manufactures.[76] Such requests, had they been more numerous, might have represented an opportunity for some relief from the pattern of Japanese control that so frequently made Americans uncomfortable. But since the U.S. was mainly "an exporter of raw materials or semimanufactures on order, little attention was paid to overseas marketing .... This situation is not surprising, considering the size and rate of growth of the American domestic market. In almost every line the rewards seemed greatest for successful marketing at home".[77] Americans in the ports would not become distributors of American goods.

IV

As the male and female spheres separated as a result of industrialization in the U.S., the male world of work and the female sphere of home largely defined each other. "In a society where values changed frequently, where fortunes rose and fell with frightening rapidity, where social mobility provided instability as well as hope, one thing at least remained the same – a true woman was a true woman, wherever she was found".[78] The home was a place of female virtue, a haven in which the moral compass of men sullied by the competitive, tumultuous world of work could be daily reset. The home stood in stark contrast to the public world, where "we behold every principle of justice and honor, and even the dictates of common honesty disregarded, and the delicacy of our moral sense is wounded; we see the general good, sacrificed to the advancement of personal interest". This was "a harsh place where cruelty and deceit held sway".[79]

The language with which Victorian Americans described the differences between the female and male worlds approximated the language with which American merchants described their own business practices and those of the Japanese. As American missionaries accused the Japanese of sexual immorality,[80] so American merchants accused them of commercial immorality, claiming that Japanese merchants were not on the "moral level" of their Western counterparts.[81] Seeking to explain their vulnerability to "predatory" Japanese merchants, foreign businessmen often argued that Japanese import dealers were a group "distinct in many respects from the rest of the mercantile class in the country". The Boeki-sho were associated, they said, "in popular fancy with whatever is most disgusting in the character of Japanese merchants – dishonesty, unscrupulousness, unfaithfulness" and were not respected by their colleagues in the interior. Japanese port merchants, "originally desperate adventurers" who had failed in the interior, made good through the foreign trade in the ports, where they went as a last resort. Since many reputable merchants were either "timid or ignorant" of foreign trade, the unprincipled Boeki-sho eventually came to dominate. In addition, the great hereditary commercial houses of Japan were extremely conservative, and unwilling to enter into foreign trade.[82]

Probably this stereotype of the immoral Japanese bore less relation to reality than to Western merchants' frustration with the vicissitudes of their business world, and the need to explain them in language that cast the treaty port itself in the role of the comforting "female", safe from the predatory "outside" world of predatory Japanese. Being "equally ignorant of the language, the social conditions, and

the customs and resources of the Empire", merchants were, at least in some significant measure, "incapable of judging either the commercial or social status of those
with whom they were dealing".[83] Many were confident that they had to deal, as one
merchant complained, with the unscrupulous classes of Japanese. "We are
regarded", he wrote, "by every enterprising rogue in the country as proper and easy
subjects for deception and plunder". That the Japanese press denounced foreign
merchants for trying to hold their own against Japanese rivals increased his outrage. Foreigners, he argued, would take a more liberal view of the Japanese
character if only they had some tangible evidence that such better character
existed.[84] Hence, a Japanese merchant class of which "no standard of either honesty or truth was expected" confronted foreign merchants who, Westerners told
themselves, "presented to the Japanese models of commercial honesty".[85] This
complaint of Westerners that they were wholly honest, and thus at the mercy of
unscrupulous Japanese, moralized merchant failure, but in a larger context.

The assumption of Anglo-Saxon racial superiority was a crucial component of
the Western imperialist impulse. Americans had commonly invoked this idea to
justify frontier Indian conflict and in arguments in favor of maintaining slavery in
the south and white dominance in the post-Civil War period.[86] Convictions of
Anglo-Saxon superiority readily found expression abroad as well. Eric Seizelet
has suggested that Western countries in the nineteenth century were characterized
by a "strong feeling of superiority, supported by their industrial and economic
dynamism. They commonly shared the same vision of a Western cultural and
political supremacy".[87] Such confidence led to inevitable justifications of expansion and dominance. W.J. Mommsen observed that the West saw itself as bringing
"civilization, justice, and Christian codes of conduct to still-undeveloped regions
of the world".[88]

In his widely-read book, *Our Country*, Josiah Strong summarized notions of
Western cultural superiority succinctly in 1885:

> If human progress follows a law of development, if "Time's noblest off-
> spring is the last", our civilization should be the noblest; for we are "the
> heirs of all the ages in the foremost files of time", and not only do we
> occupy the latitude of power, but *our land is the last to be occupied in
> that latitude* .... If the consummation of human progress is not to be
> looked for here, if there is yet to flower a higher civilization, where is the
> soil that is to produce it?[89]

Such rhetoric implied that the robust products of Western civilization could overcome any resistance that "inferior" peoples might offer. Such an easy sense of
superiority had an uneasy application in the treaty ports, where assertions of
Western moral and cultural superiority were contradicted by the failure of
Westerners to produce the order basic to the "education" they wished to provide
the Japanese. Such assertions were further subverted by merchants' own definition of themselves in terms of the victim of aggressive Japanese, a role far more

"female" than could possibly be consistent with their notions of appropriate male behavior.

Such rhetoric also assumed that responsibility for merchant woes lay outside the treaty ports, in a world darkened by deceit and disorder. Because Western merchants had no social intercourse with Japanese merchants, no "first-rate Japanese merchant" wanted to deal with them. Westerners separated business and social concerns, and contributed to a situation where able but what they preferred to label disreputable Japanese merchants – who themselves were happy to sacrifice the niceties of sipping *cha* after concluding a mutually profitable business transaction – did not hesitate to take advantage of foreign merchants they neither saw nor cared about. Such Japanese merchants did not "lose face" by cheating foreigners.[90]

One Japanese historian writing just after treaty revision claimed that the "low tone of commercial morality among the Japanese merchants must also be counted as one of the causes which are hampering the development of direct transactions with foreign countries".[91] A contemporary observer echoed the view, noting that foreign merchants

> were called upon to deal not only with a degraded class, but with the very worst specimens of that class. Timidity was too deeply ingrained in the hearts of the Japanese traders to allow those of substance or reputation in their own sphere to embark on an entirely novel career, to risk the secure position which each had in his own district by tempting fate in unknown aspects. Those who did so, who flocked to the newly-opened ports in numbers, were, without exception, adventurers, with neither name nor money to lose, with keen wits and the determination to exploit to the utmost, by any means fair or foul, the El Dorado that was suddenly placed before them.[92]

When foreign merchants discussed "native business ways", they often used "language more vigorous than polite". Such responses stemmed from frustration born of isolation in the treaty ports; Japanese traders freely changed their minds after ordering merchandise, frequently leaving Westerners with large amounts of unsold merchandise. One observer described the practices of some Japanese:

> So the merchant who has ordered a thousand bolts of flannel at the agency of some foreign house is likely to appear a few days later ... to say he does not care for flannel, but thinks he will have a dozen cows to start a health farm with. On the morrow he may have changed again and be eager for Waterbury watches or "mustache-producing elixer". Should the agent say it was too late to change, as he had ordered the flannel, the gentle native would say, "O kino doku sama", ... freely translated, "the joke is on you".

Contracts were useless instruments against Japanese merchants who refused to accept the Western premise of business "good faith".[93]

V

For some, the frustrations inherent in treaty port business may simply have been too much. One newspaper suggested that a rash of suicides in 1896 was attributable to the dissipated lifestyle of the mercantile class. Some merchants tended toward "reckless extravagance" far beyond their means, such as drinking, gambling and "intrigues with women", and became indebted to Chinese and Japanese servants and moneylenders, or fell in with swindlers or speculators in an effort to sustain their habits. Unsuccessful, some drifted out of the ports, others turned to the treaty port version of "white collar" crime, and some ended their downward spiral beyond the pale in Bloodtown.[94] A sense of brooding uncertainty born of dependence on the still unknown lurked behind the pleasant facade of Yokohama society. One observer attributed it to "something in the climate or the life that plays havoc with a foreigner's nervous system, destroying first his temper and in an alarming number of cases, his reason afterwards". Some residents admitted to certain symptoms of long-term port residence – ill temper, headaches and general "crankiness".[95]

Some had higher thresholds than others. On January 31, 1899, Oscar Otto Keil, a respected American of long residence, put a gun to his head and pulled the trigger. The coroner's jury reported that Keil was driven to suicide by temporary insanity, but the editor of the *Eastern World* suggested that Keil died of the maladies more common to port residents: "Anxieties and apprehensions, disappointed ambition, envies and jealousies". Indeed, it seems that the treaty ports retained a hint of their original promise as an El Dorado, where riches, on which all success depended, seemed just around the corner. Though popular in Yokohama society, Keil was a driven man: "It is the first consideration in Yokohama", ran the paper's argument, "that a man shall make money"; Keil had not acquired enough capital to enter into the "luxury" of matrimony, and attempted to take the shortcut of engaging in speculative ventures.[96]

The malaise was identified in 1869 as a disease called neurasthenia, an episodic affliction attacking men in youth and early middle age. Though the disease had appeared earlier in the century, it was reported to have reached "near-epidemic proportions in the northern United States" by the 1880s. Professional men came to see a direct, causal connection between overwork and breakdowns such as those Keil experienced:

> The basic structure of the illness, with overwork, tension, fatigue, breakdown and extended rest, amounted to a rejection of work. The fact that this cycle was repeated over and over in so many lives only adds to the sense that neurasthenia involved men's negative feelings about their work. The comments of male neurasthenics and their doctors and friends

also make it clear that the sickness could be a response ... [to] the nature of the work itself. One gets a stronger sense of the connection between work and male neurasthenia by noting that breakdowns often happened at times of vocational crisis.

Anthony E. Rotundo suggests that cases of neurasthenia were clustered among men "in callings – the ministry, the arts, scholarship – typed as feminine", and "exceptional among men of business".[97] But the world of the treaty port was inhabited by businessmen, at least some of whom probably exhibited symptoms of neurasthenia as a response to the frustrations of doing business in the ports. Indeed, if a man was unable to deal effectively with the challenges of work, at some level his basic manhood was being revealed as suspect. The far-ranging symptoms of the affliction were unified by "a common effect: A paralysis of the will. Tortured by indecision and doubt, the neurasthenic seemed a pathetic descendent of the iron-willed Americans who had cleared forests, drained swamps and subdued a continent". Whether overcivilized or simply, cumulatively enervated, treaty port merchants suffered consequences as severe as those throughout the Western world.[98]

Other expressions of merchant frustration turned outward and took on a violent character. The Japanese outside the ports were shadowy, avaricious and elusive targets beyond merchant reach, but their Asian servants within the ports were easily accessible. Having moved away from the concession areas in search of social order and stability, merchants' frustration at crime in their elevated suburbs could be extreme. A deeper explanation relates to their lack of agency in their businesses and the intense response that lack generated. Believing themselves victims of an incomprehensible and dishonest marketplace outside the ports, but lacking the means of redress, merchants reacted with punitive violence when their servants – or someone else's – victimized them inside the ports. The resulting violence may have been a form of compensatory control, but it also was an example of precisely the disorderly behavior their hierarchical social order was designed to eliminate.

One day a long-time resident of Yokohama was coming down into the settlement from the Bluff in his carriage when he accidentally drove into a jinrikisha driver coming the other way, so that one of the shafts of the jinrikisha wounded the man's horse. The man lost his "temper and struck the [driver] over the head with the butt of [his] whip".[99] Such physical expressions of anger against Japanese and Chinese were all too common in the ports. In a world ordered separately from its Asian environment, foreigners punished their servants with nearly complete impunity.

References in the travel literature to corporal punishment of Japanese servants are quite common,[100] but the information in the Hyogo archive suggests an even greater degree of violence toward servants than was visible to the traveler passing through. One American at Kobe, a Mr Papechas, employed a servant named Kisaburo who stole a fork, a knife and two dollars from him. Papechas brought his servant to the Saibansho for punishment, but only after he had tied and flogged him and "cut off his hair". The Japanese authorities pointed out that beating his servant was a violation of the treaties, but such warnings had little effect on servants' treatment. On another occasion, two American citizens, H.W. Livingston and J. Staples, went to the house of a Japanese named Kintaigo and broke the door, window and part of a wall. Once inside, they attacked three Chinese servants whom they suspected of stealing from them, tied them with ropes, dragged them to the Bund and threatened to throw them into the bay. Fortunately, the Japanese police interceded before they could be harmed.[101]

A most poignant incident in May 1873, involved a Japanese servant named Seikichi. His Japanese employer found a small puppy crying in the street, brought it home and the following day instructed Seikichi to return to where he had found the dog to try to locate its owner. Seikichi could not find the puppy's owner and was preparing to take it to the police station when two Americans, one of whom was a Kobe merchant named Ferrier, "took hold of him violently by the chest" and called him a thief, apparently thinking that Seikichi had earlier stolen one of their dogs. When the Japanese denied any wrongdoing, the two Americans took him to their house, where they tied his hands behind his back and fastened him to a tree in the backyard so that he hung on tip-toe. They "continually struck him with their fists" in spite of his repeated cries for mercy. At some point later on, two other foreigners came to the house, one of whom, a woman, loosened the ropes that bound him to the tree. Seikichi explained his innocence to this woman, who left to confirm it with his employer. Even after her return, Ferrier and his accomplice would not release the Japanese, until the Japanese police came to the house. After freeing Seikichi, the Japanese went to the American consul to complain.[102] These violent incidents bespeak the intense frustration of American merchants who saw themselves besieged from all sides and sought to exercise whatever forms of control they found available – even at the cost of disturbing the tranquility they sought to create and sustain in their little suburbs away from the blight of the concession areas.

VI

The Japanese government continued its long, sustained attack on the unequal treaties in 1871, when the Iwakura Embassy began its tour of the Western powers in the United States, and continued with formal conferences with the treaty powers in Tokyo in 1882 and 1886.[103] The foreign reaction to the threat of treaty revision – which would have simply given political expression to Japan's growing economic power – was telling. The Japanese government made clear in 1886 that access to Japan's interior markets, with at least its promise of escape from the fixed routine of business in the treaty ports, could only be purchased at the price of the repeal of the unequal treaties with their provisions of extraterritoriality and foreign tariff control.

Merchants' arguments against treaty revision began immediately, and clearly indicate that they reacted with horror at the possibility of eliminating the barrier between their world – even with its fragile security – and the threatening land-scape beyond. In spite of the tightening commercial noose, Westerners preferred "unsocial isolation and permanently unprofitable trade" to submitting directly to Japanese law and surrendering their control over tariffs. Merchants, wrote the *Japan Weekly Mail*, were "prepared to submit to anything, not excepting total defeat of [their] purpose in coming to Japan", rather than withdrawing from the protection of the treaties. Westerners, who still enjoyed the social life and the rel-atively easy profits of the ports, wanted to keep their shrinking part of Japan's trade for as long as possible.[104]

The hand-wringing led to tortuous arguments in favor of delaying treaty revi-sion. Western merchants frankly admitted that the Japanese goal of managing their commerce independently was perfectly rational, and a comparison of their critique of Japanese designs to contemporary descriptions of the Chinese sheds some light on merchant attitudes. Throughout the nineteenth century, the American stereotype of China held that it was backward, possibly beyond redemption, and lacked most of the fundamental prerequisites for development into a modern state whose people would consume American products. Chinese characteristics, according to missionaries and merchants, included "torpidity, a remarkable fondness for stasis whose underside was an equally remarkable resis-tance to innovation and change, and a stubborn scientific and technological backwardness". All of this pointed to a civilization "lamentably stunted".[105]

Obviously, no reasonably alert observer could apply such a critique to Japan. Americans observed the coming of new trade patterns in which Japanese mer-chants would obviously play a much expanded role, but crafted their defense of the status quo in terms that differed in its essence from the American critique of China, but served the same purpose. They pointed out, for example, that Japan was too anxious to gain control of her foreign commerce as a matter of national pride and as a badge of independence and civilization. Japanese eagerness for independence led the government to support inexperienced merchants, and the resulting business "incompetence", born of rushing unprepared into sophisticated commerce, might lead to disaster. Merchants, who depended heavily on their consuls in many aspects of their trade, argued that the only "true" merchants were those who managed without governmental assistance. Hence the logical recommendation (though it ignored precisely such Japanese efforts) that twenty or thirty Japanese youths be placed "in merchants' manufacturing centers in the West", where they could "devote nine or ten years to a careful study of the methods that have made Western merchants what they are". Earlier action would reflect "an inconsiderate and reck-less impatience". This line of reasoning rendered "every fresh evidence of Government interference in commercial matters" another reason for delaying the creation of a new political structure where their governments would not provide them business privileges at the expense of Japanese sovereignty.[106]

Soon after Yokohama opened, George Smith observed that relations between the Japanese and the rest of the world would improve when "the true representatives of the Christian civilization of Britain and the United States shall have flocked to this land in greater number".[107]

Such typical rhetoric in opposition to treaty revision often involved declarations that the Japanese, while making progress toward civilization, would be embarrassed by the premature abolition of extraterritoriality; not only would foreigners expose the barbarous Japanese legal system for what it was, foreign merchants would rapidly leave the country, interrupting the growth of foreign commerce, a process by which somehow foreign merchants imparted "light and knowledge". The *Japan Weekly Mail* observed innocently that:

> A moderate tariff will be most instrumental in assisting [Japan] to find out what it can, and what it cannot, do, with greatest advantage to itself, and this discovery will best promote its growth in wealth. It can only grow rich by increasing and improving its exportable produce, and developing its mineral resources. Why should it be anxious to make dearly what it can buy cheaply, instead of selling dearly what it can produce cheaply, we are wholly at a loss to know.

The Japanese, "new-fledged with the mere down of Western knowledge ... cannot even see to the bottom of one of MILL'S translucent sentences, imagine they have mastered his whole political economy". The paper then continued to lambaste the Japanese government for imposing a heavy land tax,[108] when in fact a major reason for the heavy burden on the Japanese peasantry was to fund the heavy costs of self strengthening (*fukoku-kyohei*) by creating a reliable basis for revenue collection.[109]

As early as 1879, the Yokohama Chamber of Commerce reported that giving tariff control to the Japanese would be a mistake because Japan's civilization was of "short growth", and "limited in its effects". Since the country's rulers did not possess a high understanding of political economy, frequent changes in the tariff would confuse trade. As the Japanese government took an active interest in trade, its tariff policy was bound to be unduly biased and would divert trade from its "legitimate channels". Instead, the Japanese government should "discourage any kind of combination tending to hinder the natural and healthy development of trade ... which will prove of highest value to the case of Japanese enlightenment and civilization".[110]

Another argument held that if Japan opened up the interior to residence and trade, "lower class" foreigners would flood in, forcing the Japanese to deal with a "revolutionary and turbulent element" in her interior, a "rabble" that the government could neither control nor expel; the difference between port residents and such *hoi polloi* was similar to that between the average educated Japanese and the aboriginal people of Formosa. One outraged response to such arguments accused foreigners of wanting to monopolize Japan's foreign trade and subordinate world commerce to the "Yokohama clique". Another respondent verified that most foreigners were "indifferent or hostile" to the idea of opening the country up to commerce, since their "interests inclin[ed] them to the concentration of business at the ports rather than to its expansion through the country".[111] All the arguments against treaty revision, to a greater or lesser extent, were based on the assumption that Japan was making progress but still needed Western tutelage, or that Japan's progress was somehow mutated or inappropriate. In either case, no precipitous action in terms of treaty revision was needed or advisable.

Of course, all of the arguments were also based on the assumption that Western definitions of civilization were the essential reference point that subjected Japan (and other non-Western areas) to "a powerful double-edged imperative: If we know the savage's proper path of development, then surely they should remain under our tutelage and stewardship; and if they are so dramatically behind us on that path ... then we are not beholden to treat them as equals ... in this long process of helping them along".[112] But the Japanese imperative of *fukoku-kyohei* required little from foreigners in the way of such advice.

One Japanese newspaper suggested that Westerners wanted to delay the abolition of extraterritoriality because foreign merchants did not expect that profits from trade in the interior would justify giving it up; they were content to live in the "narrow and circumscribed limits of the foreign settlements". But if rich gold fields were discovered, foreigners would rush in. "At present", the paper observed:

> native merchants bring silk and tea to the settlements and there offer their goods to foreign merchants. But if a number of men of independent spirit were to agree to sell nothing to foreigners unless the latter go to the native merchants, if the silk dealers of Iwashiro and Joshiu were to combine to keep their goods in the interior and invite foreigners to come to them, we should hear no more about the imperfection of Japanese laws.[113]

The hope that foreigners could be somehow forced out of the treaty ports, however, proved unrealistic; the silk boycott of 1886 proved that the Western merchant community could outlast a serious attempt to disrupt established trade patterns. But the reference to a gold rush was appropriate: while it may not have brought Westerners out voluntarily, a gold rush would certainly have struck a resonant chord among treaty port "old-timers" who remembered the easy profits of the currency exchange frenzy of late 1859 and early 1860.

As treaty revision approached, merchant expressions of fear grew more frantic. On September 9, 1890, more than three hundred foreigners of all nationalities – the largest single gathering of the foreign community up to that time – assembled at Yokohama's public hall to protest the proposed treaty revisions. The chairman of the meeting put three resolutions to the group. First, he proposed that extraterritoriality should remain in force, and that the time was not yet right to promise even an estimate of when such a change might be considered. Second, the conditions of foreigners' land tenure in Japan should not be altered without their consent. Third, the group should create a standing committee to represent the community and work for the other two resolutions. All three resolutions were carried unanimously.

The chairman stated that Japanese proposals aimed at treaty revision had been of a very "shifty character", and pointed out that the Japanese had enjoyed justice in foreign consular courts for years. "We are asked", he exhorted, "to surrender a great deal of that which we know we possess". The Japanese proposal contained no provisions for *habeus corpus* and jury trials, and the supervision and surveillance common in Japan would certainly prove intolerable to foreigners. The Japanese race had "never breathed the breath of freedom" and "has always been more or less servile". Another speaker felt sure that a "very large number of cases will arise of difficulties which do not now exist", and encouraged the attenders to contribute money, because "you cannot carry on a war, on paper or otherwise, without money".[114]

Western merchants were well aware of the Japanese impatience with the slow pace of treaty revision. By the late 1880s, dissatisfaction showed itself in public demonstrations, and there were occasional reports of stoning of foreigners in public places. The *Japan Weekly Mail* reported that the mood of Kobe – always noted for its relatively harmonious relations with the Japanese – had turned black because of some incidents between foreign sailors and Japanese mobs, and some Westerners charged Japanese police with "willful failure" to protect foreigners. "Kobe's mood of resentment", the paper noted, "is not purely fanciful".[115]

To soften the hard reality of a declining share of the market and the inability to see beyond the protective structure of the treaties, the Western merchant draped himself in the cloak of civilizing agent. One contemporary noted enthusiastically that "there is nothing which tends more effectually to break down artificial barriers between different nations than trade ... commerce becomes one of the great civilizing forces in the world".[116] Another foreign observer noted that kerosene was a great boon to the Japanese people, "granting to both the artisan and the upper classes a good light by which to spend their evenings profitably ... instead of wasting their time in idle gossip". The *Japan Weekly Mail* echoed this sentiment, stating that "if the opening of Japan to foreign trade has conferred upon the Japanese the sole boon of the kerosene lamp ... it would have amply justified itself".[117]

Correctly noting Japan's concern with *fukoku kyohei*, merchants failed to distinguish – as did many missionaries – between modernization and Westernization. In the case of missionaries, many of whom moved beyond the insular world of the treaty ports with enthusiasm, the failure to make such a distinction was perhaps more understandable. Their investment in time, energy and commitment to evangelizing a pagan nation logically made them, in their own minds, bringers of Western light to the spiritually dark East.[118]

Yet merchants claimed something of the same role, perhaps understandably casting themselves as a stabilizing influence, a compass point by which Japan could steer. Akira Iriye has suggested that to Americans in the U.S., "It seemed only natural that Asian countries be brought into contact with advanced countries of the West. Trade would serve as a harbinger of change, and through exchange of goods new ideas would be introduced and enlighten the hitherto dormant populations".[119] Noting missionaries' small number of converts to Christianity and the declining numbers of foreign specialists employed by the Japanese government, merchants argued the centrality of their civilizing role. One observer reflected merchants' assessment of their contribution, stating, "The only foreign element which has had much effect on the Japanese is that of the commercial settlers. They have done their work in the country manfully and well. They are, I fear, the class of foreigners who have made themselves respected by the Japanese".[120] In return for their presence and its imagined benefits to the Japanese, merchants received, according to this line of reasoning, little in return. Foreign merchants consistently claimed that they were enriching the Japanese without themselves enjoying the benefits of the trade. The *Japan Gazette* noted in 1881 that:

> Calm impartial reflection confirms the decision that the benefits arising from commerce have been all on the side of the Japanese people, foreign merchants who originated and conducted it being, so far as their worldly wealth is concerned, poorer now than at the commencement of these operations.[121]

Eastern World claimed in 1900 that Yokohama never produced millionaires, "even in two-shilling debased yen" and that in fact Yokohama merchants, and those of Nagasaki and Kobe, never even made clear profits.[122] Even Basil Hall Chamberlain, a man with an unsurpassed understanding of Japan's language, culture and people, agreed. In return for giving Japan a civilization, he argued, foreign merchants got "a pittance". Foreign companies' employees who got "what would in Europe or America be deemed large salaries can be counted on the fingers of one hand, and the merchants making fortunes cannot be counted at all, for the simple reason that there are none".[123]

Except in the 1870s, and especially in the 1890s, Westerners benefited from an expanding trade that their loud complaints largely ignored. Convinced of their right to profit in the ports by virtue of their race and culture, they expressed their irritation at their dependence on "inferior" Asians by emphasizing the difficulties of trade in the Victorian language of *streben*, and by arguing that their best effort could not overcome the immorality ranged against them. When the Japanese rejected Western merchants as bringers of civilization and commercial prosperity, whose benefits – according to Westerners – were self-evident to all, merchants could easily cast themselves in the role of enlighteners, spurned by an unappreciative and "uncivilized" Japan.

The Japanese accepted half of the Western equation, desiring commercial prosperity and the national power it brought. The Japanese obviously had reservations about Westerners' self-definition as bringers of civilization, and took advantage of Western ignorance and isolation when they could, thus providing Westerners with material on which to base their accusations of Japanese immorality. The cycle could not be broken because neither side had, or wanted, a vocabulary with which to explore another way.

VII

Merchants' business isolation – and its inevitable concomitant of exposure to the yamashi – mirrored their social isolation. Whereas their society ratified their racial and cultural assumptions, their business arrangements left them increasingly helpless spectators to the dramatic erosion of their market share by the 1890s. Merchants' reluctance to leave the "protection" of the ports was a testament to the sustained power of their urge to recreate the familiar in a stable environment.

Given the cultural disposition of the vast majority of American merchants, the linguistic challenge of learning Japanese to any level was simply irrelevant. Missionaries recognized that some measure of linguistic skill was desirable considering their evangelical purpose, and some struggled with Japanese's lack of cognates and its hair-splitting levels of respect because they were preparing to work among the Japanese people. Daniel Crosby Greene, a missionary who lived in Osaka in the 1870s, communicates something of the size of the linguistic task. Even after basic grounding in Japanese during his stay in Tokyo, still felt the need for "one good solid year of study in the language" to increase his ordinary Japanese vocabulary. He hoped to achieve this by spending "good long forenoon[s]" with his teacher and afternoons "visiting house to house with a view of correcting the tendency of the study of books to remove my vocabulary too far from the people".[124]

M.L. Gordon, speaking of the enthusiasm of the young missionary eager to spread the word of God in Japan, stated, "When he reaches his destination, however, his complacency receives a terrible shock. Geographically speaking, he is now near the people whom he hopes to teach; but ... a broader ocean than the Pacific still rolls between him and them .... The language, the language – what an Alpine barrier to all communication with the people he would teach".[125] One authority claimed that "one can learn to understand as much Spanish in six months as he can of Japanese in six years", and an older missionary advised younger ones to "stay twenty years in the country" to learn the language. The Protestant missionaries of Central Japan unanimously resolved that new missionaries should be given no responsibilities in their first three years in the country, but should "give [their] whole time and strength to the work of securing a knowledge of the language and people".[126] Upon his arrival in Japan in the 1880s, the missionary Sidney Gulick was "shocked to learn that there were only about a dozen missionaries out of all the denominations who had achieved true fluency in Japanese, and none who had totally mastered the language and could work without a teacher or translator".[127] These descriptions of the daunting size of the linguistic challenge came from those who saw purpose in learning Japanese.

Few men engaged in trade made any effort to learn Japanese, a reality that most merchants would have explained in terms of their society, whose order was centered on the recreation of the culturally familiar, not the embrace of the linguistically confusing. Francis Hall, an American associated with Walsh, Hall and

Company until 1866, apparently learned the basics of the language, and the entrepreneurial merchant Eugene Van Reed's collaboration on a small book of English phrases and their Japanese translations in 1861 suggests more interest in the language than characterized the vast majority of treaty-port denizens.[128] Yet Hall and Van Reed were most exceptional; evidence illustrating nearly universal merchant ignorance of Japanese is overwhelming.[129] Even for men who lived years in Japan, one observer recorded, "the mere order of words in a grammatically correct sentence of any but the baldest import is a standing difficulty".[130]

Rather, they were content to communicate by means of the pidgin so prevalent as the *lingua franca* in the Asian ports. Japan's variety was dubbed the "Yokohama Dialect", and this utilitarian language served well enough the needs of merchants who usually restricted their contacts with Asians to their own servants or employees. A tongue-in-cheek guidebook to the Yokohama dialect advertised itself glibly but accurately: "It is easy to see the advantage of getting at the dialect actually used in Yokohama, rather than learning by laborious study the Samurai dialect ... which nobody understands beyond a few teachers". Its five lessons reveal a linguistic ingenuity born of Western merchant concern with minimal utility and maintaining the integrity of their own society by preserving the English language as one of the chief means by which separateness from Asia could be measured. Communicating essential actions such as removing, taking away, carrying off, clearing the table and getting out of the road all were simply and forcefully expressed as "Piggy", while urgency was expressed by adding "jiggy-jig". Many of the phrases translated deal with services Westerners expected: "Give me a cigar" (Mar key tobacco sinjoe), "Take good care of the child" (Babysan ah booneye), "Pass the wine around the table" (Sacky maro maro), "Tell the tailor to come tomorrow and I will have plenty of work for him" (Start here hanash meonitchi maro maro tacksan so so arimas), or "Tell the laundryman to wash the clothes" (Sin Turkey hanash kimmono a row). One also needed to know how to threaten punishment (Pumgutz) for failure to execute instructions properly.

Food and amusements were another large concern: Beer (Beer sacky), Claret (Ah kye sacky), bread (pan), beef (Ooshee), fresh milk (Ooshee chee chee), canned milk (bricky chee chee), and translations for stove, roast, chicken, eggs, potato, plate, fry, cook, boil and hot water were all listed. Much of the vocabulary was specific to the horseracing so popular in the ports: stopwatch (Matty toky), racing pony (high high mar), and many more specialized words; after a race and a rubdown a Westerner might instruct his groom to feed his horse by saying "Mar chobber chobber sinjoe".[131] One noted authority observed that the Yokohama dialect was the "*patois* in which newcomers soon learn to make known their wants to coolies and tea-house girls, and which serves even as the vehicle for grave commercial transactions".[132] The "Yokohama Dialect" was a kind of linguistic expression of the social structure of the ports, its vocabulary reflecting only areas where merchants found interaction with Asians unavoidable.

Merchants' failure to take advantage of Japanese-sponsored efforts to provide them with trade information was another demonstration of their commitment to the treaty port status quo. In April 1872, a fifty-day commercial exhibition in Kyoto provided foreign merchants the opportunity to display their products and view those of native manufacture. Charles Shepard, the U.S. Minister, considered it a "great concession" that the Japanese would allow American merchants to attend. He reported that the exhibition was "not exactly a government affair", but seemed a way for the Japanese government to test "alike the feelings of the Japanese people and the conduct of foreigners". Shepard was hopeful that "further general privileges" would be forthcoming if foreigners attended and conformed to the regulations governing the exhibition. The *Hiogo News* of April 9, 1872 stated that interested parties should apply to the consul for proper passes, exhibitors were permitted to come a week early to set up, and the exhibition committee facilitated hotel arrangements. Exhibit rules stated that prices should be attached to items for sale, and that "new discoveries and strange machinery should have their description and mode of use attached". Judges were appointed to decide on the various articles exhibited.[133]

Shepard was concerned that Americans be on their best behavior and do nothing that would jeopardize future business opportunities beyond the treaty ports, even suggesting that some American appointed by the Hyogo consul "act as a sort of Deputy Marshall during the Fair, having power and instructions if necessary to arrest" any miscreants. Few foreign merchants attended the exhibition, however.[134] One journal reported sadly that "there were rarely more than twenty foreigners in the city at a time, very often not more than ten", though "preparations had been made to receive [foreigners] by the hundreds". One visitor to the exhibition reported seeing silk weavers and machinery, spinning machines and looms, and chided "those gentry who *affect* (italics in original) to compare the present Exhibition ... to a mere curiosity shop". Indeed, foreigners seemed to look upon the exhibition with disdain from a distance, though *The Far East* suggested that the event might "lead to some increased export trade". In its detailed descriptions of the exhibition, the journal did not mention any foreign goods on display, further suggesting foreign merchants' indifference to this venue.[135]

The Far East suggested one explanation for such indifference, complaining that the Japanese had given insufficient notice, just over two weeks, to allow foreigners to prepare for the event.[136] Yet interested merchants could surely have come to gauge the exhibition's potential to promote trade, even if they were not displaying goods themselves. Conceivably, merchants were nervous about the possibility of attack by *ronin* (samurai without masters), but this danger was minimal by 1872, and the Japanese offered to escort and guard foreigners. The exhibition was expanded to 100 days and held every spring at least through 1877, presumably because the Japanese found it valuable for increasing their trade, but Western merchants' apathy continued.[137]

Perhaps foreign merchants were disdainful of Japanese technology of any kind, but it would seem that common sense and curiosity would lead them to want to see better what the Japanese made, and how well. But reluctance to leave the ports on this occasion denotes more than lack of interest in any single venue for the promotion of trade. Such a refusal suggests merchants' willingness to generalize negatively about any business possibilities beyond the protective ramparts of the ports. If merchants were victimized with such regularity in their existing trade, what new difficulties might await them further in the interior?

VIII

In 1876, seventeen years after Yokohama opened to foreign trade and well after the establishment of the basic pattern of treaty port trade, the *Japan Weekly Mail* observed that the commercial conditions of the treaties were sound, and Japan's "free trade" well supported by a low tariff. Nevertheless, trade was depressed, with "no revival in sight", and the paper called on the ministers of the treaty powers for a diplomatic solution to the commercial ills.[138] Indeed, the unequal treaties had deprived Japan of the right to set its own tariffs on imports and exports and set the tariffs at a low rate to facilitate foreign trade. American merchants continued to assert that restoration of tariff control to the Japanese government would spell the end of "profitable" foreign trade.[139]

Such complaints were perhaps understandable during a relatively brief period of economic stagnation, but Westerners clung to the unequal treaties ever more desperately as the most visible expression of (and protection of) their Victorian coherence abroad. Tied viscerally by their racial and cultural assumptions to an increasingly fragile system of trade, merchants watched as the economic underpinnings of the treaty port system began to crumble. Though Van Reed's experience suggests business possibilities that might have led merchants to support the repeal of the unequal treaties, thereby giving them access to Japan's interior markets, the vast majority of traders remained committed to a system of trade that was intimately linked to their need to hold the unfamiliar at bay.[140]

The only means of escape from this system of trade and its obvious liabilities was for foreigners to "open their eyes", support treaty revision, obtain access to the interior, and rid themselves of their dependence on Japanese merchants who dictated the terms on which trade was possible. Westerners, who refused to accept restrictions on hunting game outside the treaty ports, readily accepted the restrictions on their businesses that their cultural prejudices imposed. This seeming contradiction was no contradiction at all for the treaty port merchant. Alternatives to his patterns of behavior were unthinkable. One contemporary summed up the merchants' dilemma succinctly: "If foreign merchants choose to remain in the settlements, the present state of affairs is, in one sense, a just reward for their conservatism and race prejudice".[141] But the "present state of affairs" – expressed as the political structure of the unequal treaties – protected Americans and most Westerners as they wished to be protected, and rewarded them with mixed but ultimately palatable quantities of profit and anxiety.

CONCLUSION

The highest manifestation of life consists of this: that a being governs its own actions. A thing which is always subject to direction of another is somewhat of a dead thing.

St Thomas Aquinas

As if to signal the change in Japan's position as an emerging world power, with all that this implied for her foreign merchants, some Japanese took up the Western sport of baseball with enormous enthusiasm, and confronted the West symbolically on its diamond. The First Higher School of Tokyo issued its first challenge to the foreign team at Yokohama in 1891, but the club refused it, and several subsequent challenges, because baseball was an American game and because of the Western claim of physical superiority to the Japanese.[1]

When the two teams finally clashed in a series of games beginning in 1896, the Japanese won with ease, and their victories, though appreciated by the entire Japanese nation, were particularly heralded by what Donald Roden has termed the Japanese "*Lumpenproletariat*" in the service or employ of foreigners at the ports. Playing the first game on a field previously designated for Westerners only, "many spectators greeted the Ichiko students with jeers and howls when they entered the park for pre-game warm-ups", but they were quickly silenced by a 29–4 thrashing. Of a total of twelve games Japanese and foreigners played, the Japanese won all but two.[2] To save face after these demonstrations of Japanese prowess, foreigners naturally searched for a way to devalue the games. After the first defeat, the Japan Weekly Mail was quick with an explanation: the Japanese, "with their daily opportunities for practice, their constant matches, and *sparer figures* have always the advantage over a team of grown men".[3]

The baseball games were a cultural expression of the changed political and diplomatic reality of two years earlier. In 1894 Great Britain had finally agreed to treaty revision, and the United States, officially sympathetic, was quick to follow the British initiative. By the early 1890s, Japanese judicial reform was sufficient to give Great Britain an excuse to recognize the deeply changed realities. Japanese popular opposition to the continuation of the treaties involved risking serious domestic repercussions in Japan and the real possibility of endangering foreign lives and property. Moreover, failure to revise the treaties meant that Japan might repudiate them – and thus force a range of undesirable options into consideration. For these reasons, Great Britain and Japan signed the Kimberly-Aoki accords in 1894, and officially the unequal treaties came to an end five years later in July 1899.[4]

Akira Iriye marks the middle of the decade as significant, suggesting that "after 1895... one begins to note a slight strain in Japan's official relations with the United States. Partly this was because of Japan's new sense of power". Flushed with its victory over China, and "self consciously emerging as an imperial power",[5] Japan was rapidly coming of age and, as a matter of course, rendered its foreign merchant community an anachronism.

I

In the early 1860s, one Western visitor to Japan, perhaps anticipating what was to become Western self-willed isolation in the ports, implored:

> Let our traders indulge in no boasts of superiority or professions of disinterestedness, but be content to establish friendly commercial relations with the Japanese; to introduce all that they will accept of ours; to receive all that we require of theirs; and, while gradually developing the incalculable resources of a new and splendid country, reap a golden harvest from their energy and enterprise.[6]

The experience of American merchants over the following forty years showed that this picture of mutually helpful and respectful intercourse was utopian. Throughout the treaty port years, diplomatic representatives of the U.S. had ranged themselves against Great Britain in favor of treaty revision. As early as 1878, John A. Bingham argued that early recognition of Japan's complete sovereignty would give the U.S. a commercial advantage over its European rivals. If the U.S. would revise its treaty unilaterally, he argued, Japan would respond gratefully by enlarging commercial opportunity.[7] Bingham's premise, while logical considering the Japanese desire for release from the thralldom of the treaties, failed to take into consideration the nature of American trade as it was practiced in the ports, and Japanese nationalism expressed as *fukoku-kyohei*. For four decades, merchant attitudes toward treaty revision ran contrary to American official thinking; American merchants of 1890 possessed most of the characteristics and trade practices that had defined them in 1860.

In the early 1880s, another contemporary recognized that "true understanding and intercourse between Japanese and foreigners" would only come when the country was thrown open to Western commerce, and when foreigners came under formal Japanese control. The unequal treaties, he knew, situated Japan and the outside world as adversaries, and he suggested that Westerners pass "beyond the limits of our consular island, [to] rescue ourselves from our anomalous position in the country" and "cease to be a community of strangers holding aloof from the whole nation, a continual reproach to its institutions, an insult to its independence and self-respect". This, he argued, would open up a new field for the "disappointed energies" of the foreign merchant population and enable the West to work its ameliorative influence on Japan.[8]

Other observers recognized that the treaty port system – from the Western mercantile point of view – was seriously flawed. One welcomed treaty revision, arguing that both sides would benefit from the abolition of the treaties:

> From a completer mingling a better mutual understanding will necessarily follow, and that curious distrust and dislike which each side seems destined to feel for the other at the point of contact of two races in a treaty port – just like the corrosion which occurs at the meeting point of the two carbon poles of the electric light – will disappear forever.[9]

A visitor opined that "free intercourse with the interior of Japan should have immense attractiveness".[10] Responding to the statement of a foreign merchant who feared that treaty revision would force him to "perambulate the country" to conduct his trade, another observer styling himself "Libertas" welcomed freedom from confinement in the ports. His tongue-in-cheek critique was telling. There would be, he argued, "no forcible suspension of trade in the treaty ports" that would drive Western merchants "out into the byways and villages to dispute the vantage ground of local market places with their native competitors, to buy at cottage doors the skeins of milk fresh from the reeling basins" and disposing of their wares "face to face with the consumers". But foreign merchants, happily freed from the drudgery of Yokohama, might do well to "sing a ditty to interest some native buyer".[11] Some Japanese observers agreed. After treaty revision became an accomplished fact, they claimed that foreign manufacturers would reap large profits after the demise of the agency house system.[12]

With the end of the treaties came the formalization of Japanese control, and the Imperial government soon decided to impose a 2.5 percent tax on foreigners who rented land in the concessions. When Alfred E. Buck, then the U.S. Minister to Japan, suggested that Americans pay the tax, reaction was swift. One American responded, "Let all good Americans retire to their closets, sprinkle ashes on their heads and humbly pray that who represents their interests in Tokyo, will soon receive orders from his paternal government in Washington, to pack up his carpetbag and start for Georgia".[13] Such responses to Japanese control had been common since the 1860s, but now each American had to decide whether to stay or go.

II

Describing one aspect of the nineteenth-century international merchant community, Charles A. Jones has suggested that in Buenos Aires, Britons, Germans, Yankees and Argentine businessmen "did business together" and "formed partnerships" in a robust and cosmopolitan commercial setting.[14] This community, Jones argues, collapsed after 1890, "sending firms and individuals racing from the apron strings of newly assertive states. Nationalism and regulation, imperialism and racism were the hallmarks of the *fin de siècle*" and produced the resulting "catastrophe of cosmopolitan liberalism".[15] The American community in the treaty ports was cosmopolitan, if a fairly narrow definition is applied. American merchants would have automatically and enthusiastically defined themselves and their purpose as cosmopolitan in the sense that they lived in multi-national communities far from home, had integrated themselves into the social world of those communities, handled goods across large distances, and dealt with Asians on a daily basis.

It is true that Americans had insulated themselves as much as possible from the threatening and challenging realities of business in Japan, but the distinction between themselves and a British merchant enjoying cordial relations with the native, landed élite of Buenos Aires would have been quite minor. Without doubt, these Americans had far more in common with a German or British counterpart anywhere in the world's international commercial community than they did with a Japanese merchant living and trading three miles from Yokohama or Hyogo. For this reason, perhaps Jones' "catastrophe of cosmopolitan liberalism" was less a Western retreat from Japan (where Western traders had little long-term impact) than an atomizing of Western interests in new patterns of competition with each other.

If American merchants understandably failed to live up to twenty-first century notions of cosmopolitan behavior, on what grounds might they be indicted? W.J. Reader, in a thoughtful analysis of businessmen's motives, observed that "No man but a blockhead, it is to be hoped, ever went into business without intending to make money .... But money is raw material: a means to an end. It is not usually, to the creative businessman, an end in itself. It comes closest to being an end in itself when the end to which it is a means is security".[16] Real estate could not constitute security in the treaty ports, as foreigners could not own the land on which their agency houses sat. The sustained reluctance to engage the unknowable and the malign that defined their community, while understandable, came at a high cost – the suffocation of the spirit of innovation, and of any genuine sense of optimism about their circumstances. Vernon Parrington sought to define "the most characteristic qualities of the American temper" and listed Puritanism and optimism as the two central ones.[17] With a narrower focus, David Dary, a historian of the U.S. frontier, argued that there a "silent army" of entrepreneurs was characterized by "imagination, optimism, self-reliance, initiative, ingenuity, individualism, and resourcefulness".[18] If "optimism" defined the American response to challenge or adversity, the treaty port merchants found their environment too alien and inhospitable to sustain anything but a reactive, deeply conservative (even pessimistic) response to the particular challenges of the treaty ports.

Indeed, one striking feature of the merchant community was its lack of leaders. In part, this is attributable to merchants' high degree of dependence on their consuls, who naturally occupied positions of leadership in the ports. But because almost everyone agreed on the need to repeat the conservative mantras supporting the status quo, it seldom occurred to the "prominent men" of the ports to suggest adjustments in business practices that the end of the treaty port system seemed to require.

Yet the context of nineteenth-century American economic development must be considered. Throughout the century, the rewards associated with the rapidly expanding domestic American marketplace were "greater than those offered by distant opportunities". Since trade with other nations was of secondary importance to Americans, it received "perhaps less attention, less creative energy" than in nations where foreign trade was pursued more aggressively. The resulting "historical American indifference to cultures and markets abroad" was certainly played out in the attitudes of the American merchants in the ports. The "huge and expanding [domestic] market was, on the whole, relatively free of the entanglements and uncertainties of dealing with different cultures, different languages, different rules of the economic game, the risks of shifting exchange rates, the problems of securing foreign exchange, and the myriad other challenges of cross-national trade".[19] Certainly these realities suggest that foreign trade attracted neither the most competent nor, necessarily, the most daring of American entrepreneurs in the last half of the century.

One visitor wrote, "If most residents did not affect indifference to things Japanese, life would be much more interesting".[20] But against the shores of their island community, American merchants saw the lapping, eroding waves of change and the attendant challenge to their social and economic worlds. Hence they found stasis and security far more appealing than the "interesting" life of change in their alien setting. The idea of community in the treaty ports was crystal clear – and intimately bound up in the cultural assumptions of its entirely Western membership. Western merchants were powerfully bound by ties of language and ethnicity, and their sense of community derived equally from its need to present a united front against the malign forces they believed threatened it.

This response was typical on the American frontier in the late nineteenth century. Robert V. Hine spoke directly to the experience of American merchants in the ports when he described the "ethnic colonies" in the American West:

> In assessing community among ethnic colonies, the fit between the colony and the prevailing culture would ultimately determine persistence. The larger the ethnic colony, the higher were the barriers raised around it; the more distinct the differences between colony and prevailing

society, the greater its longevity. Hardship generally aided the cooperative community, but sometimes economic decline forced the breaking of
ties with the old ways in order to survive in the new. If self-sufficiency
could be attained, isolation was a binding agent. But whatever the envi-
ronmental interactions, the basic bond within was ethnicity, intensified
by frontier conditions.

The shared bonds of ethnicity that allowed German Lutherans to cooperate with
German Catholics and even with German socialists[21] on the American frontier
allowed Americans to cooperate readily and enthusiastically with the British in the
ports. If the ports are considered as "ethnic colonies", their size helps explain the
barriers raised around them, and the "distinct" differences between the ports and
the "prevailing society" of Japan (to say the very least) certainly help explain the
persistence of merchant solidarity for four decades. Americans in the ports differed
from some of their frontier cousins in the U.S. in that economic decline did not
"force the breaking of ties with the old ways". Instead, economic decline hardened
their defense of the unequal treaties into a repetitive canon of conservatism.

Another observer of foreign business at the end of the treaty port period noted
that whatever increase in foreign business might accrue to foreign merchants
from the opening of the interior would be "more apparent than real, and that competitive native firms will in the not far distant future practically drive out the alien
merchants". In light of Western attitudes and Japanese determination for national
independence, that "this should ultimately happen [was] not ... a cause for won-
derment".[22] Noting how Westerners' attitudes had contributed to their business
limitations, another contemporary noted, "It is even possible that the Western
world may in the distant future find in Japan a formidable and unmerciful rival,
animated by the ancient national spirit, which will brook no barrier to triumph
and advancement".[23] These observations articulated the American merchant's
worst fear – a world in which he was elbowed aside by a Japanese, leaving him no
place as a man, or as a businessman.

It is as businessmen that these merchants were subjected to peculiar strains.
The American Business Creed, a study attempting to define and explain American
business behavior, argues that:

> the content of the business ideology can best be explained in terms of the
> strains to which men in the business role are almost inevitably subject.
> Businessmen adhere to their particular kind of ideology because of the
> emotional conflicts, the anxieties, and the doubts engendered by the
> actions which their roles as businessmen compel them to take, and by the
> conflicting demands of other social roles which they must play in family
> and community. Within the resources of the cultural tradition ... the con-
> tent of the ideology is shaped so as to resolve these conflicts, alleviate
> these anxieties, overcome these doubts.[24]

Though this thesis was advanced more than a half century after the demise of the treaty ports, it speaks directly to the American experience there. The peculiar American cultural tradition, with its deep emphasis on the "structure of logical argument and empirical description which attempts to explain and direct the workings of society according to humanly understandable principles",[25] was the reference point for these Americans, and their frustrations grew from the difficulties associated with trying to apply this approach in Japan.

Americans came to the business world of the treaty ports armed with two powerful components of their cultural and intellectual tradition: individualism and the importance of work. As they attempted to apply these values to their world, they found that both values were undercut by an alien environment that understood neither American goals nor the reason applied toward realizing those goals. The dual realization – of their profound dependence at various levels, and of the irrelevance of their central values – made the "island community" the only place from which they could derive security. The withdrawal was even more complete when the American tendency to "view issues in moral terms and to stress the importance of moral character in the functioning of society",[26] further defined their admittedly self-righteous response to Japanese business practices. With each criticism leveled at an intractable Japanese official, Americans reaffirmed their belief in reason; with each loud complaint about a "dishonest" yamashi, they defined themselves as honest. Tension resulted when they realized that their success was not based on the application of their values, and high anxiety resulted when they realized that their failure was equally irrelevant to those values.

John Higham has advanced one broad explanation of the meaning of sports at the turn of the century:

> From the middle of the nineteenth century until about 1890 Americans on the whole had submitted docilely enough to the gathering restrictions of a highly industrialized society. They learned to live in cities, to sit in rooms cluttered with bric-a-brac, to limit the size of their families, to accept the authority of professional elites, to mask their aggressions behind a thickening facade of gentility, and to comfort themselves with a faith in automatic material progress. Above all, Americans learned to conform to the discipline of machinery.

Americans, then, sought release from their various confinements, and found it in sports and recreation, nature, music and "an unsettling of the condition of women".[27] Though many of the particulars of Higham's argument do not apply to merchants in the ports, his general approach does. Americans there felt themselves trapped – in the sense that their own, deeply held cultural values left them ill-equipped to deal proactively and creatively with their business circumstances. If a longing to escape different kinds of entrapment characterized the male response to both the broader American world and to that of the treaty ports, both were expressed, perhaps, in the release of physical, outdoor activities. Through hunting and through their sporting lives, merchants demonstrated their need for renewal, control and competition acted out in terms comprehensible to Americans.

W. Somerset Maugham once wrote that "ideas do not grow on a gooseberry bush and few people in a generation can devise new ones".[28] Living with half-understood contradictions is often easier than devising new ideas – or making adjustments in deeply ingrained patterns of thought. American merchants, eager for the profits that expanded trade would bring, once abroad jealously guarded their "rights" to the detriment of their original purpose. Thus the paradox: while clutching at the framework that supported their special status, they complained bitterly of limitations on their trade that only the repeal of the treaties might possibly have improved. But treaty revision meant the symbolic and actual destruction of the barriers surrounding their island community.

It is true that the Japanese took pains to keep foreigners sexually gratified when Yokohama began trade operations, and this denoted a clear intent to keep foreigners happy with the status quo. When Yokohama's original location was determined, early Western officials had expressed fear that the Japanese were attempting to create "another Deshima" – where Westerners could be managed and controlled as they had been since the early Tokugawa period. This concern was legitimate, but gravely misdirected, as American merchants were determined to create that isolation themselves. In this they required little help from the Japanese, and in fact would have resisted any Japanese attempts to draw them from the secure island communities of the ports.

What of merchants' status as men, and of the relative absence of women in the ports? If American men in the U.S. were threatened by women seeking a place in the public sphere, and sought to reaffirm their masculinity through the fashioning of new, more strenuous lives, such a threat could not, of course, apply in the ports, where the gender imbalance rendered this irrelevant.[29] But since failure, or at least the looming possibility of failure, in business was challenge enough to Victorian notions of manhood, a further challenge to such notions from women was in any case superfluous in the ports.

If there was some sort of crisis of masculinity among American merchants, what form did it take? Margaret Marsh has challenged the "crisis" thesis by suggesting that "masculine domesticity" may well have been an expression of voluntary and constructive male accommodation to societal changes. Marsh suggests the need to "supplement the image of the dissatisfied clerk with a picture of the contented suburban father, who enjoyed the security of a regular salary, a predictable rise through the company hierarchy, and greater leisure".[30] But of the benefits Marsh lists, merchants enjoyed only leisure in the ports, and would have regarded few features of their professional or personal lives as predictable or reassuring. This may explain the heavy use of credit and the lives of dissolution into which some merchants fell. Viewed this way, treaty port society looks like an entity constructed largely on the basis of racial, ethnic, class and linguistic solidarity, but one lacking the interior elements to underpin that solidarity – home, family, and reliable employment and professional prospects. Hence the plaintive articulation of need for the domestic influence of women as a solution to the problems of Yokohama society. At the root of treaty port anomie was a crisis of domestic instability – in addition to the anxieties brought on by the vagaries of work.

Merchants expressed the anxieties about the health and success of their businesses (and any attendant threat to their manhood) in a variety of ways. They fought off the effects of routinized work, like their American counterparts, in vigorous sports competitions; they violated the treaty limits by hunting with impunity; they complained vigorously to their consuls when they believed their interests were threatened; and they sometimes took out their frustrations violently on servants. Above all, they waged a high-pitched, sustained battle to retain the unequal treaties as the only way the playing field of economic endeavor could be properly leveled, the only way a gentleman could know the rules by which (and the context in which) he should balance his dual instincts toward cooperation and aggression.

On the issue of Victorian racism, we are given pause. I have argued throughout that one of the defining features of the American community was its dependence. Because of merchant dependence, particularly on bantos and compradores, one can reasonably deduce that the kind of racism enunciated by Josiah Strong did not stand up perfectly or even well considering the day-to-day requirements of business in the ports. The enthusiasm with which Americans sought to protect their Chinese and Japanese employees suggests the tempering of racist condescension with commonsense respect for their indispensable business competence.

Americans in the U.S. might see "immigrant ghettos ... populated not by individuals, who might speak for themselves and whose recognizable humanity might make a claim on our sympathies, but by crowds, throngs, masses of unindividuated and unspeakably odd folk whose very numbers overwhelmed the capacity for empathy".[31] Certainly to a large degree, American merchants in the ports shared this reaction to the unfamiliar world beyond the ports. But even as they feared and generalized about the collective, alien Japan, they must have trusted the particular, known banto or compradore. Likewise, the (admittedly scant) evidence of merchant relationships with Japanese women suggests an ambivalence about the dangers or rewards of miscegenation, and American merchants fled the concession areas to escape contact with Asians, but also to escape contact with less desirable members of their own race. Class, treaty port style, mattered as much as race.

The ports were recognizable as America, and American responses to the unfamiliar were indeed familiar ones. The new immigrants of eastern and southern European ethnicity who began arriving in the U.S. in great numbers in the 1880s sparked a strong nativist response. "From early on, the new immigrants were the targets of nativist intellectuals concerned with such issues as how best to preserve political democracy, defend individual liberties, maintain respect for the law, and preserve the purity of the Anglo-Saxon race". But a deeper and more ominous response to these new peoples came from

> rank-and-file nativists who deplored the threat they believed newcomers posed to their economic and social position. These were not wild-eyed

reactionaries, but a broad spectrum of sober, middle-class Americans who dreaded job competition from alien workers, bemoaned the congestion of cities crammed with foreigners, and distrusted strangers who spoke other languages and lived lives that seemed so peculiar.[32]

The American merchant response in the ports was more circumscribed, but the essential contours of the broader American attitudes toward threatening immigrant peoples are well represented here. American traders steadfastly supported the unequal treaties as the political structure they believed was their only protection against the threat to their "economic and social position". Neither were these merchants "wild-eyed radicals"; they dreaded unprotected competition with Japanese yamashi, and moved to the Bluff and Kitano-cho from whose heights they bemoaned the congestion and chaos of the concessions. They certainly refused to learn Japanese, the language of the outside, of those they distrusted, of those who preyed upon them.

In a pronounced historical irony, the very racial assumptions that fueled Euro–American imperialism toward Japan were intimately related to the limits of that imperialism's efficacy. But again merchants' racist expressions can only be understood in the context of their dependence. When Japanese efforts at treaty revision challenged their privileged status, merchants cast themselves in the role of civilizing agents, but this was little more than a temporary palliative, a way of masking their own insecurity with the comfortable rhetoric of racist condescension, rhetoric that assuaged the anxiety that their fundamental dependence produced.[33] Likewise, increasing Japanese control of Japanese trade proved an inadequate stimulus to change; Americans considered their rights to profit in the ports self-evident and displayed none of the flexibility that characterized the Japanese response to their presence.

But what of the issue, identified in the introduction to this study, concerning the way in which Japan acted upon these men, and how these men acted upon Japan? Neil Harris identified three reactions to the Japanese exhibition at the Philadelphia Centennial Exhibition of 1876: Americans responded to Japanese art and craft work, to specific aspects of Japanese artistic expression, and responded with "anxiety and concern" that "Western patronage might destroy the distinctive Japanese characteristics" admired by America. At Chicago in 1893, Americans were struck by the seeming paradox in what they perceived as the combination of Japanese "industry and docility".[34] Such responses, even born of brief and contrived encounters with Japan, indicate as much sophistication as many merchants in the ports would have displayed.

Were American merchants "particularistic" in that they viewed Japan in terms of their own self-interest and prejudices? Certainly to some extent, this was the case. But American attitudes can more completely be explained in terms of ignorance and fear of their host country. Twenty-five years ago Akira Iriye suggested that:

this was the case with an overwhelming majority of Americans during most of the nineteenth century when (if at all) they considered Japan. Apart from those few who were affected by ideas about power politics, cultural concerns, nationalistic considerations, or specific personal interests, the attitude of most of the population was one of indifference.[35]

Americans in the ports cared, of course, about the process of their business operations. And they cared enough about Japan to level specific charges against her in their arguments against treaty revision. But this study, in its comprehensive contours, suggests that these men were far more intent on sustaining the essential centripetal force of their society than they were in engaging any essential aspect of Japan. All or nearly all of their energy – necessarily, they would have argued – was expended on security and replication of the familiar. American provincialism was on display for forty years, representing "an attitude of disdain, ignorance, or indifference toward things external to the United States".[36] In the U.S., the attitude toward Japan was indifference; in the ports it was an odd combination of indifference and fear due to closer proximity. Both attitudes rested upon a bedrock provincialism.

III

While the Japanese moved toward national independence in their diplomatic and business initiatives, American merchants remained quiescent observers, and their insistence on isolation meant tacit acceptance of the consequences of those Japanese initiatives. Merchants were only the conduits through which flowed – for a time – the foreign trade necessary to Japan's modernization. "The farsighted amongst the Japanese" foresaw that they would "ultimately rid themselves of the haughty and overbearing Westerners" by simply waiting until they could take over their trade themselves. Foreign traders "mistook … the patience of the Japanese for easy-going indifference, and a forgetfulness of past injuries and past injustice".[37] American merchants' tenure as imperialists was brief, imperfect and ultimately salutary – for the Japanese.

Ironically, American merchants' insistence on maintaining their isolation played directly into the hands of the Japanese, who wanted on-going control of the foreign population and restriction of its activities, while expanding and gaining control of its own trade. The Bakufu, while understandably reluctant to suffer the indignities of the treaties, was content with certain features of the treaty port system: it isolated foreigners from the Japanese population and gave the Bakufu the opportunity to control trade with the West. After 1868, the Japanese response to the challenge of the West was flexible, strong and determined. Unhappy with the Japan's status *vis-à-vis* the unequal treaties, the Meiji leaders changed their country's economy and polity to reflect the priority of self-strengthening that was imperative to survival. The Western merchant presence on Japanese soil was the most visible sign of Japanese inequality and formal Western dominance, but it in fact became part of the process of essentially building Japan's strength.

Though the nature of the Japanese government changed dramatically over the course of the last half of the nineteenth century, official Japanese attitudes toward foreigners in the ports until 1899 remained fairly constant. Japan, unlike China, benefited from a linguistic, ethnic and cultural homogeneity and, after 1868, a talented leadership and a centralized government that permitted a much more focused response to the unequal treaties and the presence of foreigners on Japanese soil. By 1886, the Japanese had made the price clear: access to interior markets would come only with the repeal of extraterritoriality and return of tariff autonomy.

In 1890 the foreign trade of Japan was essentially that of a "non-industrial society, in effect a 'colonial' economy, mainly providing raw materials to the somewhat more industrialized states of Europe while receiving manufactured goods from them". But "by 1914 Japan had established many of the basic political and economic elements of an industrial order",[38] including nearly full control of its foreign trade.

The combination of Japanese determination to control Westerners while waging its sustained and ultimately successful attack on the unequal treaties, together with the insularity of merchants in the ports, determined the contours of this episode of imperialism. With neither strong support from the home government nor the flexibility to adjust to changing circumstances, American merchants looked inward as the Japanese developed the *de facto* hegemony that rendered the treaty port system first a shallow façade of Western power, and then obsolete.

IV

After the revision of the treaties took effect in July 1899, the foreign settlements and the treaty ports themselves ceased legally to exist. Few of the fears and even fewer of foreigners' dire predictions proved warranted. Some Americans left, as did some British, but most remained with a social and economic life that was increasingly constricted by Japanese industrial growth. Among the genuine (and most nettlesome) questions remaining was that of perpetual leases, an issue not settled by the treaties. This divisive issue persisted until the Japanese unilaterally and simply cancelled all perpetual leases in 1937.[39] The *Kobe Chronicle* spoke for most when it stated in January 1900:

> Looking back upon the six months that have now almost been completed since foreigners came wholly under Japanese jurisdiction, we think it will be admitted by impartial persons … that to a very considerable extent the apprehensions felt were groundless. On the whole the transition from Consular to Japanese jurisdiction has been effected with tact and discretion, and the authorities have throughout shown an earnest desire to avoid friction, and to encourage good relations between the foreign and Japanese communities.[40]

More significantly, following the trend already begun some twenty years earlier, the foreign trading community continued to diminish in importance as Japan industrialized. By the outbreak of World War I, Western trading companies were no longer pre-eminent, "more and more Japanese shops and services replaced Western ones" and "even the foreign press was affected", with the Japanese securing control of some papers.[41] The inexorable trend was toward full Japanese control of its own economy, though Japan did not recover full tariff autonomy in 1899, a right that was delayed until 1911, when the last discriminatory tariff would be abolished.[42]

When a newspaper reporter asked John LaFarge if he was in search of Nirvana in Japan, he responded, "It's out of season!"[43] Indeed, any "business Nirvana" was out of season for American merchants as well. Just before treaty revision, one Western Yokohama scribe expressed something of the irony and sadness of merchants' experience in the treaty ports:

The Merchant at Yokohama

When I first came to live in Japan,
My duty was simple and plain:
To dazzle the nation with civilization
Implying more money than brain.

In a mansion as big as the Bluff
I had servants and horses enough,
While the native possessions
Outside the concessions
Appeared to me very poor stuff.
I shall live on a different plan,
When I mix with authentic Japan.

You may have guessed
That East and West
Have a difficult gulf to span;
We shall cross on a golden bridge,
When we mix with the real Japan.[44]

For forty years the treaty ports continued to exist – an offspring of the West implanted for a time in the East, and the gulf was indeed "difficult to span". Japan faced the new century with growing power, and the American firms once dominant in her trade faded gently into the fabric of history as the underpinnings of their home abroad vanished.

NOTES

INTRODUCTION

1 For a thoughtful discussion of Western imperialism and the treaty port system in China, see Rhoads Murphey, *The Outsiders, The Western Experience in India and China* (Ann Arbor: University of Michigan Press, 1977), 80–234.

2 F.G. Notehelfer, *Japan Through American Eyes, The Journal of Francis Hall, Kanagawa and Yokohama, 1859–1866* (Princeton: Princeton University Press, 1992), 22.

3 To obtain the trade concessions embodied in the commercial treaty of 1858, Townsend Harris pointed out that Japan would be better off making a treaty 'with a single individual, unattended' rather than with England or France, who would 'bring fifty men-of-war to these shores'. Payson Treat, *Diplomatic Relations Between the United States and Japan* (Gloucester, Mass.: Peter Smith, 1963), 1: 51–2.

4 Japan at mid-century is described in W.G. Beasley, *The Rise of Modern Japan* (New York: St. Martin's Press, 2000), Chapters 2 and 3, and Conrad Totman, *A History of Japan* (Malden, Mass.: Blackwell Publishers, 2000), Chapters 11 and 12.

5 In the event, Yokohama was substituted for Kanagawa in 1859, the opening of Hyogo and Osaka was postponed from 1863 to 1868, and that of Tokyo from 1862 to 1868. The commercial treaties the Bakufu reluctantly signed in 1858 with the United States, the Netherlands, Russia, Britain and France provided for the opening of the country to foreign trade at the ports of Kanagawa (Yokohama), Nagasaki and Hakodate in 1859, Niigata in 1860, Hyogo (Kobe) in 1863 and the cities of Osaka and Tokyo in 1862 and 1863. For the political background see W.G. Beasley, ed., *Select Documents on Japanese Foreign Policy, 1853–68* (London: Oxford University Press, 1955), Introduction.

6 Exports duties were 5 percent with gold and silver coins and copper in bars duty free. Exceptions to the 20 percent rate on imports were 5 percent *ad valorem* on coal, timber, rice, steam machinery, zinc, lead and raw silk, and 35 percent for intoxicating liquor of any kind. Opium importation was prohibited, and there were no duties on the import or export of coined or uncoined gold or silver. Both Japanese and foreign currencies could be used to pay for goods, and the treaty set exchange rate of ichibus (Japanese silver coins) to Mexican dollars (the common currency of Far Eastern trade) at 311 to 100. For the entire text of the treaty, see William M. Malloy, comp., *Treaties, Conventions, International Acts, Protocols and Agreements between the United States of America and Other Powers, 1776–1909* (Washington, D.C.: Government Printing Office, 1910), 1: 1000–1010.

7 Because of Japan's failure to open the port at Kobe as promised in 1863, and because of its refusal to show good faith through imperial ratification of the 1858 treaties, the

Western treaty powers forced Japan in 1866 to revise the tariff to favor Western merchants even more. In the only instance of its type in the nineteenth century, the United States, in ratifying the Convention of 1866, entered into a joint treaty with the other European powers in Japan. The agreement contained no provision for terminating this arrangement, suggesting only that it would be subject to revision in 1872. The Convention had the effect of making Japan an economic and diplomatic prisoner of the treaty powers. One historian has suggested that this treaty was the most "thoroughly un-American ... ever ratified by the American government," that the United States had failed to influence the policy of the combined powers, and that the policy of cooperation was tantamount to handing leadership over to Great Britain, whose military and commercial presence in Asia was pre-eminent. How "un-American" this treaty was depended upon one's perspective. But there is no doubt that the U.S. participated in cooperation with European treaty powers. Rates were fixed at an average of 5 percent on all commodities exported from and imported into Japan. In July of that year, both import and export duties were fixed at 5 percent ad valorem, reducing the previous duty of 20 percent on the non-enumerated imports substantially. The value of the goods imported was calculated from the average export price in the exporting country over several preceding years, rendering import duties immune to Japanese currency fluctuations. Export duties remained extremely favorable to Western merchants. Tyler Dennett, *Americans in Eastern Asia, A Critical Study of United States' Policy in the Far East in the Nineteenth Century* (1922; reprint, New York: Barnes and Noble, 1941) 403–5; Malloy, *Treaties and Conventions*, 1: 1012–21.

8   G.C. Allen and Audrey G. Donnithorne, *Western Enterprise in Far Eastern Economic Development*, (1954; reprint, New York: Augustus M. Kelley, 1968), 197. The American commercial presence increased dramatically between 1859 – when eleven merchants set up in Yokohama – and 1895, by which time American companies numbered seventy-three. For an estimate of the merchant population, see Chapter 1. It is clear that Americans were the second most numerous group in the ports after the British, who outnumbered them by roughly two to one until 1890. See Shinya Sugiyama, *Japan's Industrialization in the World Economy, 1859–1899* (London: The Athlone Press, 1988), 41.

9   T. Scott Miyakawa, "Early New York Issei: Founders of Japanese–American Trade" in Hilary Conroy and T. Scott Miyakawa, eds, *East Across the Pacific, Historical and Sociological Studies of Japanese Immigration and Assimilation* (Santa Barbara: Clio Press, 1972), 158.

10 W.G. Beasley, *The Meiji Restoration* (Stanford: Stanford University Press, 1972), 377, Chapter 14.

11 Sugiyama, *Japan's Industrialization*, 215–16.

12 Ibid., 51.

13 F.G. Notehelfer, *American Samurai, Captain L.L. Janes and Japan* (Princeton: Princeton University Press, 1985), 6–7.

14 Ibid., 270; 272–3.

15 Sandra C. Taylor, *Advocate of Understanding, Sidney Gulick and the Search for Peace with Japan* (Kent: Kent State University Press, 1984), xi.

16 Hazel Jones, *Live Machines: Hired Foreigners and Meiji Japan* (Vancouver: University of British Columbia Press, 1980).

17 Ardath W. Burks, ed., *The Modernizers: Overseas Students, Foreign Employees and Meiji Japan* (Boulder: Westview Press, 1985).

18 Robert A. Rosenstone, *Mirror in the Shrine, American Encounters with Meiji Japan* (Cambridge: Harvard University Press, 1988), ix, xi.

19 Lawrence W. Chisolm, *Fenollosa: The Far East and American Culture* (New Haven: Yale University Press, 1963), 51.

20 Donald Roden, "Baseball and the Quest for National Dignity in Meiji Japan" *American Historical Review* 85 (June 1980): 511–34.

21 Notehelfer, *Japan Through American Eyes*.

22 Examples include Akira Iriye, *Across the Pacific: An Inner History of American–East Asian Relations* (New York: Harcourt, Brace and World, Inc., 1967); William L. Neumann, *American Encounters Japan, From Perry to MacArthur* (Baltimore: Johns Hopkins Press, 1963); Robert Schwantes, *Japanese and Americans, A Century of Cultural Relations* (New York: Harper and Row, 1955) and, to some extent, John Hunter Boyle, *Modern Japan, The American Nexus* (Fort Worth: Harcourt Brace, 1993).

23 Robert W. Rydell, *All the World's a Fair* (Chicago: University of Chicago Press, 1984), 48–9. See also Neil Harris, "All the World a Melting Pot? Japan at American Fairs, 1876–1904" in Akira Iriye, ed., *Mutual Images, Essays in American–Japanese Relations* (Cambridge: Harvard University Press, 1975), 24–54.

24 Rydell, *All the World's a Fair*, 48.

25 Mark Wahlgren Summers, *The Gilded Age or, The Hazard of New Functions* (Upper Saddle River, NJ: Prentice Hall, 1997), v.

26 General treatments of the period include Ray Ginger, *The Age of Excess: The United States from 1877 to 1914* (New York: Macmillan, 1965); Robert Wiebe, *The Search For Order, 1877–1920* (New York: Hill and Wang, 1967); John A. Garraty, *The New Commonwealth, 1877–1890* (New York: Harper and Row, 1968); Alan Trachtenberg, *The Incorporation of America, Culture and Society in the Gilded Age* (New York: Hill and Wang, 1982); Nell Irvin Painter, *Standing at Armageddon: The United States, 1877–1919* (New York: Norton, 1987); Vincent P. De Santis, *The Shaping of Modern America: 1877–1920* (Wheeling, IL: Harlan Davidson, 1989); Sean Dennis Cashman, *America in the Gilded Age, From the Death of Lincoln to the Rise of Theodore Roosevelt* (New York: New York University Press, 1993); Summers, *The Gilded Age*.

27 T.J. Jackson Lears, *No Place of Grace, Antimodernism and the Transformation of American Culture, 1880–1920* (New York: Pantheon Books, 1981), 38, 46–7.

28 Matthew Frye Jacobson, *Barbarian Virtues, The United States Encounters Foreign Peoples at Home and Abroad, 1876–1917* (New York: Hill and Wang, 2000), 5.

29 These developments are dealt with in John Higham, *Strangers in the Land: Patterns of American Nativism, 1860–1925* (1955; reprint, New York: Artheneum, 1978), Chapters 3 and 4; Dale Knobel, *"America for the Americans": The Nativist Movement in the United States* (New York: Twayne, 1996).

30 Jacobson, *Barbarian Virtues*, 56.

31 Ibid., 4.

32 Wiebe, *The Search For Order*, 3.

33 Ibid., 12.

34 Ibid.

35 With the exception of the *Tokio Times*, owned by the American E.H. House, practically all of the newspapers published in the ports were British owned. For a lengthy discussion of the English language press in the treaty ports, see James Edward Hoare, *Japan's Treaty Ports and Foreign Settlements, The Uninvited Guests 1858–1899* (Sandgate, Kent: Japan Library, 1994), 141–67, and Olavi K. Falt, *Clash of Interests: The Transformation of Japan in 1861–1881 in the Eyes of the Local Anglo–Saxon Press* (Rovaniemi: Historical Association of Northern Finland, 1990).

36 The miscellaneous correspondence received at the Kobe archive for the years 1868 to 1900 consists of sixty-two volumes.

37 The dispatches from Osaka/Hyogo in the years 1868–1900 occupy five reels of microfilm; those from Yokohama twenty-two reels.

CHAPTER ONE

1 Clive Holland, *Old and New Japan* (London: J.M. Dent and Co., 1907), 266.

2 Charles A. Jones, *International Business in the Nineteenth Century, The Rise and Fall of a Cosmopolitan Bourgeoisie* (New York: New York University Press, 1987), 29–65.

3 Ibid., 28.

4 David M. Pletcher, *The Diplomacy of Trade and Investment, American Economic Expansion in the Hemisphere, 1865–1900* (Columbia: University of Missouri Press, 1998), 21.

5 West African trade is discussed in George E. Brooks, Jr., *Yankee Traders, Old Coasters and African Middlemen, A History of American Legitimate Trade with West Africa in the Nineteenth Century* (Boston: Boston University Press, 1970).

6 For one example see Thomas A. Bailey, *A Diplomatic History of the American People*, 6th ed., (New York: Appleton-Century-Crofts, Inc., 1958).

7 William Appleman Williams, *The Tragedy of American Diplomacy* (1959; reprint, New York: Dell Publishing, 1972). See also Walter LaFeber, *The New Empire, An Interpretation of American Expansion, 1860–1898* (Ithaca: Cornell University Press, 1963).

8 Pletcher, *Diplomacy of Trade and Investment*, 4.

9 Ibid., 13.

10 Ibid., 23–4.

11 For the nature of the traffic, see M.E. Fletcher, "The Suez Canal and World Shipping, 1869–1914," *Journal of Economic History* 18 (1958): 556–573; C.K. Harley, "The Shift from Sailing Ships to Steamships, 1850–1890," in D.N. McCloskey, ed., *Essays on a Mature Economy, Britain After 1840* (Princeton, N.J.: Princeton University Press, 1971), 21; Francis E. Hyde, *Far Eastern Trade, 1860–1914* (no location: Harper and Row, 1973), 21–41.

12 Allen and Donnithorne, *Western Enterprise*, 123–5; Sugiyama, *Japan's Industrialization*, 37. An excellent description of the Pacific Mail Steamship Company's role in the development of passenger service and trade across the Pacific appears in John Curtis Perry, *Facing West, Americans and the Opening of the Pacific* (Westport: Praeger, 1994), Chapter 14. A good overview of Americans in the Pacific is Arrell M. Gibson, *Yankees in Paradise, the Pacific Basin Frontier* (Albuquerque: University of New Mexico Press, 1993).

13 Francis E. Hyde, *Far Eastern Trade, 1860–1914* (no location: Harper and Row, 1973), 62–3; Allen and Donnithorne, *Western Enterprise*, 269.

14 The extent to which early traders with China dealt with these problems is discussed in Allen and Donnithorne, *Western Enterprise,* particularly Chapters 2 and 6. Western traders' dependence on western banks in providing Mexican dollars, issuing bank notes and buying and selling bills of exchange is discussed in Sugiyama, *Japan's Industrialization*, 38.

15 To form the China and Japan Trading Company, five individuals pooled their capital and business skills, but the interests of the company were more than three fourths American, so it functioned under the protection of American law. F.E. Haskell was the general agent in Shanghai and A.S. Fobes in Hyogo. The firm also employed, in the capacity of general agents, English citizens in Nagasaki and Osaka and a Dutch national in Yokohama. All had entered into agreement to do business under American protection. OHMC, Fobes to Turner, November 4, 1873.

16 Shinya Sugiyama, "Thomas B. Glover: A British Merchant in Japan," *Business History* 26 (July 1984): 115–38; Allen and Donnithorne, *Western Enterprise*, 197.

17 Richard H. Peterson, *The Bonanza Kings, The Social Origins and Business Behavior of Western Mining Entrepreneurs, 1870–1900* (Lincoln: University of Nebraska Press, 1971), 15–17.

18 Ibid., 18–19.

19 Ibid., 21.

20 Ibid., 7, 8, 10.

21 Hoare, *Japan's Treaty Ports*, 18.

22 Ibid., 19–20.

23 Beasley, *Rise of Modern Japan*, 68–9. The policy implementation of *fukoku-kyohei* is discussed at some length in W.G. Beasley, *The Meiji Restoration*, 350–78.

24 Quoted in Masao Maruyama, *Studies in the Intellectual History of Tokugawa Japan*, trans. Mikiso Hane, (Princeton: Princeton University Press, 1974), 338–9; 338n23. The response of two Japanese intellectuals is described in Richard T. Chang, *From Prejudice to Tolerance* (Tokyo: Sophia University Press, 1970).

25 Marius B. Jansen, *Sakamoto Ryoma and the Meiji Restoration* (Stanford: Stanford University Press, 1971), 99.

26 One observer recalled "every foreign resident was accompanied by an armed escort furnished by the Shogun's government." William Gray Dixon, *The Land of the Morning* (Edinburgh: James Gemmell, 1882), 90. Francis Hall, never hesitant to venture outside the foreign concession, was lucky enough to avoid such attacks. See Notehelfer, *Japan Through American Eyes*, passim.

27 Joseph Heco, *Narrative of a Japanese*, ed. James Murdoch (Yokohama: Yokohama Printing and Publishing Co., n.d.), 1: 237, 248–9; Edward Barrington De Fonblanque, *Niphon and Pe-che-li; or, Two Years in Japan and Northern China*, 2d ed., (London: Saunders, Otley and Company, 1863), 101. Contemporary accounts of such killings include J.R. Black, *Young Japan, Yokohama and Yedo, 1858–1879* (Tokyo: Oxford University Press, 1968); Sir Rutherford Alcock, *The Capitol of the Tycoon, A Narrative of a Three Years' Residence in Japan* (New York: Harper Brothers, 1863); and Ernest Satow, *A Diplomat in Japan* (1921; reprint, Tokyo and New York: Oxford University Press, 1968). One resident reported that "two samurai, apparently intoxicated, "placed themselves directly in our path, and, grasping their sword hilts, looking full in our faces, saluted us with the word 'Baca' [idiot]" and later observed that "almost every European … attended the funeral of the poor Dutchmen" and that the price of 'revolvers rose one hundred percent'" after their murder." De Fonblanque, *Niphon and Pe-che-li*, 16, 99–100.

28 Mosco was also charged with attacking Governor Ito before he was subdued and arrested. Mosco was sentenced to one year in jail, then deported. OHD, Stewart to Seward, November 20, 1868.

29 Heco, *Narrative of a Japanese*, 1: 207.

30 The arrival for the audience with the shogun brought further humiliation. When the words "Hollanda Captain" were spoken, the director "crawled on his hands and knees to a place between the presents and then kneeling he bowed his forehead quite down to the ground and so crawled backward like a crab without uttering a single word." On later trips, the Dutchmen penetrated further into the shogun's palace and were required to put on shows for court ladies. This "perfect farce" included being ordered to remove cloaks to be inspected, "to dance, to jump, to play the drunkard, to speak broken Japanese, to read Dutch" and other debasing acts. "With innumerable such other apish tricks," Kaempfer concluded, "we must suffer ourselves to contribute to the court's diversion." Engelbert Kaempfer, *History of Japan* (Tokyo: Yushodo Booksellers, 1979), 2: 174–5, 275–316, 3: 73–101.

31 Beasley, *Select Documents*, 184.

32 George Smith, *Ten Weeks in Japan* (London: Longman, Green, 1861), 251.

33 Notehelfer, *Japan Through American Eyes*, 68. The 1865 plan of Yokohama shows how the foreign settlement was cut off by a swamp and a canal at the rear. Later maps of Yokohama from *The Chronicle and Directory for China, Japan, and the Philippines* shows the limits of the original settlement.

34 Quoted in Treat, *Early Diplomatic Relations Between the United States and Japan 1853–1865* (Baltimore: The Johns Hopkins Press, 1917), 131.
35 Heco, *Narrative of a Japanese*, 1: 201.
36 Ibid., 1: 216–7.
37 Alcock, *Capitol of the Tycoon*, 2: Appendix B, "Minutes of a Meeting of British Residents at Yokohama, February 19, 1861," 377.
38 Pat Barr, *The Coming of the Barbarians, A Story of Western Settlement in Japan, 1853–1870* (London: Macmillan, 1967), 85–6.
39 Heco, *Narrative of a Japanese*, 1: 250.
40 Barr, *Coming of the Barbarians*, 86–7.
41 Harold Williams, *Shades of the Past, Indiscreet Tales of Japan* (Rutland, Vt. and Tokyo: Charles E. Tuttle Co., 1958), 249–50; Black, *Young Japan*, 2: 36.
42 Smith, *Ten Weeks in Japan*, 252–3. Smith stated that he had met "some few English and American gentlemen" who had not joined in the frenzy of exchange.
43 Notehelfer, *Japan Through American Eyes*, 70–1. Payson Treat recorded that "the climax was reached by Thomas Tatham, who asked exchange for '$1,200,666,777,888,999,222,321,'" and mentions that the Japanese customshouse could exchange ichibus only "to the capacity of their mint, or $16,000 a day." Treat, *Early Diplomatic Relations*, 135, 156–7.
44 Heco, *Narrative of a Japanese*, 1: 242, 250.
45 Barr, *Coming of the Barbarians*, 87; Black, *Young Japan*, 36.
46 Heco, *Narrative of a Japanese*, 1: 234.
47 For Alcock's statement, see Satow, *A Diplomat in Japan*, 25.
48 AHC, HM–54, Franklin Field at Nagasaki to A.F. Heard, October 30, 1859.
49 AHC, case 11, folder 13, Letters re Japan trade, Field to Albert Heard, January 16, 1860.
50 It was not unusual for local commercial agents to hold the position of consul. The Heards had been consuls for the Russian government in Shanghai and Canton.
51 AHC, HM–54, E.M. Dorr to Albert Heard, November 11, 1859; Ibid., "Private and Confidential" letter, E.M. Dorr to A.F. Heard, September 21, 1859.
52 AHC, HM–54, E.M. Dorr to Albert Heard, November 12, 1859.
53 That Dorr proved to be somewhat untrustworthy and still received substantial sums from Heard and Company for exchange suggests that the enormous profits were worth the risk of dealing with a dubious official. See AHC, HM–54–1, Franklin Field at Yokohama to Albert Heard, December 20, 1859.
54 AHC, HM–57, HM–54, letters of T.H. King and Franklin Field to Albert Heard.
55 Appleton Collection, Dexter Letters, vol. 64, F.S. Dexter to Appleton and Co., November 4, 1859; December 3, 1859; January 5, 1860. The "Walsh and Co." referred to later became Walsh, Hall and Company after Francis Hall joined the firm. McMaster has argued that the gold rush was something of a fiction: $300,000 in total gold exports, he suggests, "would be on the high side." While he correctly points out that most subsequent accounts relied on Rutherford Alcock's version of the incident, and speculates intelligently on why Alcock labeled the merchants "speculators," he bases his account largely on the Jardine Matheson archive, and neglects the information available on Augustine Heard and Company and from other contemporaries. Outside the scope of his article is the effect of the perception of quick profits, which doubtless led many to Japan who would have otherwise stayed away. See John McMaster, "The Japanese Gold Rush of 1859," *Journal of Asian Studies* 19 (1960): 273–87.
56 Notehelfer, *Japan Through American Eyes*, 74, 80–1, 100–101. It is not clear how much Hall was able to exchange. While it is not likely that he received his funds from home in time to take advantage of the exchange rates, he may well have been advanced money by Walsh, his partner.

57 *Japan Gazette*, March 12, 1881.

58 Smith, *Ten Weeks in Japan*, 263.

59 Harold Williams, *Foreigners in Mikadoland* (Rutland, Vt.: Charles E. Tuttle Co., 1963) 85; Barr, *Coming of the Barbarians*, 86.

60 Barr, *Coming of the Barbarians*, 144.

61 Smith, *Ten Weeks in Japan*, 258.

62 Algernon Bertram Freeman–Mitford Redesdale, *Mitford's Japan: The Memories and Recollections, 1866–1906, of Algernon Bertram Mitford* (London and Dover, N.H.: The Athlone Press, 1985), 31–33. On observer noted that "the so-called pioneers of civilization are ... more noted for physical energy than for gentler or more refined qualities." It was not "the liberal, enlightened, prudent and educated merchant" who came to Japan, but "the daring, money-seeking adventurer." De Fonblanque, *Niphon and Pe-che-li*, 69.

63 Heco, *Narrative of A Japanese*, 1: 235, 241–2.

64 OHMC, Sloos to Turner, October 16, 1873; Gower to Turner, January 5, 1874; Saibansho to Turner, September 16, 1874; Saibansho to Turner, October 14, 1874. Sloos later brought counter charges against Hirabayashi, but never received satisfaction. See Saibansho to Turner, February 14, 1875; Sloos to Turner, April 27, 1875, June 4, 1875; Saibansho to Lewis, September 7, 1875. With regard to the abortion, Sloos referred to the statement of a Western doctor who examined the mother and said that "there was a mystery about ... how the child died as there [were] no marks on the mother." Charles Sloos to Turner, January 30, 1875.

65 OHMC, Charles Baldwin to Turner, January 26, 1875; Sloos to Turner, April 17, 1875; Watanabe, Gon-chiji of Osaka to Newwitter, March 9, 1876; Van Buren to Newwitter, March 31, 1876; Van Buren to Newwitter, April 3, 1876; Van Buren to Newwitter, July 25, 1876; Bingham to Newwitter, August 14, 1876.

66 Lane R. Earns and Brian Burke-Gaffney, trans. Fumiko Earns and Sachiyuki Taira, *Across the Gulf of Time, The International Cemeteries of Nagasaki* (Nagasaki: Nagasaki Bunkensha, 1991), 128. See also National Archives, RG 84, Nagasaki Land Records, American Land Renters, Nagasaki, 1867. Lake's deportation was delayed until he appeared for "several actions" pending against him in U.S. consular court. See OHMC, Willie Mangum to Frank, July 25, 1871; Shepard to Frank, September 26, 1871.

67 *The Chronicle and Directory for China, Japan and the Philippines*, 1866, 1871.

68 Smith, *Ten Weeks in Japan*, 263.

69 By 1867, on the eve of the opening of Hyogo, the Japanese fixed the aggregate price of available leases high enough to cover the cost of preparing the settlement for foreign residence.

70 JWM, July 22, 1882. By March 1865, land in the foreign settlement was controlled in the following amounts: British, 44,339 tsubo; American, 19,550; French, 13,205; Dutch, 8,008; Prussian, 7,591; Portuguese, 3,139; and Swiss 872. One tsubo is equivalent to about 3.8 square yards. Cortazzi, "Yokohama: Frontier Town, 1859–1866," 8.

71 Heco, *Narrative of a Japanese*, 1: 249.

72 The foregoing discussion of land policy rests on Robert Karl Reischauer, "Alien Land Tenure in Japan," *Transactions of the Asiatic Society of Japan*, 2d ser., 13 (July 1936): 1–48; Paul C. Blum, *Yokohama in 1872* (Tokyo: The Asiatic Society of Japan, 1963), 19. For the standing committee at Kobe, which elected three members who sat for three years, see OHD, M460/1, Turner to Hale, No. 26, January 28, 1873; Eliza R. Scidmore, *Jinrikisha Days in Japan* (New York: Harper Bros., 1891), 342. See also OHMC, "Minutes of a meeting held at the house of J.E Leguis, French vice consul at Osaka," December 19, 1868, which discussed the election of foreign representatives. Each landowner had one vote.

73 Some suggested that the word was of Malay origin. One visitor to Japan stated that the term originated from the Chinese, "from constantly hearing the expression to 'go down' to business." JWM, October 6, 1888.

74 Subscription rates were $25 Mexican for six months in the late 1860s. OHD, M460/1, Stewart to Fish, No. 22, October 12, 1869, enclosing "Minutes of the Ordinary Half-Yearly General Meeting of the Hyogo and Osaka General Chamber of Commerce, July 30, 1869," 1–25, passim; OHMC, A.O. Gay, Chairman of Hyogo and Osaka General Chamber of Commerce to Stewart, December 24, 1868.

75 Hoare, *Japan's Treaty Ports*, 20–22.

76 Sugiyama, *Japan's Industrialization*, 41. Sugiyama's figures are calculated from British consular reports, and exclude those living in Niigata and Tokyo. A contemporary source, also relying on British consular reports, claimed that the western total in the three major ports by the late 1890s was 3,527. See D.W. Smith, *European Settlements in the Far East* (New York: Charles Scribner's Sons, 1900), 27, 31, 35. It remains unclear how British consuls obtained their total population figures. I have found no record of British consuls asking their U.S counterparts for American population totals; probably they got them from the Japanese government, who constantly solicited the information from the American consuls. But since the U.S. consuls often did not know precisely how many Americans resided in their consular districts at any given time, Sugiyama's totals should be regarded with suspicion. James Edward Hoare, relying on scattered references to treaty port population in a variety of sources, arrived at higher figures. By 1894, he suggests, the total foreign population of the ports stood at 9,800, of whom 4,800 were western, figures substantially higher than Sugiyama's. Hoare's sources do not reflect any consistent means of counting and are unreliable. See Hoare, *Japan's Treaty Ports*, 20–6. F.V. Dickens, without citing any sources, states that the total Western population of the ports was 3,260 in 1890, of whom 1,400 were British, also figures substantially higher than Sugiyama's. See F.V. Dickens, *The Life of Sir Harry Parkes* (1894; reprint, Wilmington, Delaware: Scholarly Resources, 1973), 2: 445.

77 KD, M135/20, Filletson to Wharton, No. 121, January 13, 1893; House of Representatives, 55th Congress, 2nd session, Consular Reports, Vol. 57, Doc. 435, 625–6. Numerous other sources agree that the British were roughly half of the western population in the ports. See Eustace B. Rogers, "Life in the Foreign Settlements of Japan," *Harper's Weekly* 38 (December 29 1894): 1234, who observed in 1894 that of 1,605 Westerners in Yokohama, 808 were English.

78 *Hiogo News*, September 3, 1868; Otis M. Poole, *The Death of Old Yokohama in the Great Japanese Earthquake of 1923* (London: George Allen and Unwin, Ltd., 1968), 25, 37. Yokohama was roughly three times the size of Kobe throughout the treaty port period. In 1890, there were at least fourteen American firms and slightly more than 100 adult Americans in Kobe, and just under 400 U.S. citizens in Yokohama the same year. See OHD, M460/4, Smithers to Wharton, No. 42, October 4, 1890.

79 OHD, M460/4, Smithers to Wharton, No. 6, January 22, 1891, Register of American Residents at U.S. Consulate at Osaka and Hyogo, December 31, 1890. The Yokohama consular reports include only the names of American residents. The 1889 report shows that 257 Americans (125 men, seventy-one women and sixty-one children) occupied eighty-six houses in Yokohama. There were seventeen American business firms in the port. KD, M135/18, Greathouse to Wharton, No. 228, Feb. 7, 1890.

80 Sugiyama, *Japan's Industrialization*, 41. Another source agrees exactly with Sugiyama's total of 30 American firms by 1875: Yokohama had twenty firms, Kobe seven and Nagasaki three. See JWM, July 22, 1876. The major American firms operating in the ports were Walsh, Hall and Company; the China and Japan Trading

Company; Smith, Baker and Company; Schultz, Reis and Company; J.D. Carroll and Company; Frazar and Company; Fraser, Farley and Company; the American Trading Company; Case and Company; Board, Niven and Company; Warren Tillson and Company; Chipman, Stone and Company; Winckler and Company; Augustine Heard and Company (until the 1870s); Russell and Company; Bush and Company; C.P. Low and Company; and Lake and Company.

81 *The Chronicle and Directory for China, Japan and the Philippines*, 1893. Other key American trading firms included Browne and Company, twelve employees; The American Trading Company, seven. As early as 1870, Schultz, Reis and Company, employed nine and Augustine Heard and Company six. *Chronicle and Directory*, 1870.

82 For example, see *Hong Kong Directory*, 1891, Smith, Baker and Company, which lists R.B. Smith, D.B. Taylor, and G. Bayfield, none of whom appear in the register of American citizens for that year. OHD, M460/4, Smithers to Wharton, No. 116, January 15, 1892. For firm registration and nationality, see G.H. Scidmore, *Outline Lectures on the History, Organization, Jurisdiction, and Practice of the Ministerial and Consular Courts of the United States of America in Japan* (Tokio: Igirisu Horitsu Gakko, 1887), 227.

83 Francis C. Jones, *Extraterritoriality in Japan and the Diplomatic Relations Resulting in Its Abolition, 1853–1899* (1931; reprint, New York: AMS Press, 1970), 66; OHD, M460/2, DeLong to Turner, No. 112, April 28, 1873. See also OHMC, Bingham to Newwitter, August 14, 1876, in which Bingham stated, "There is no law requiring citizens of the U.S. to register at our consulates in Japan, as such registration cannot be considered conclusive evidence of citizenship." See also OHD, M460/2, De Long to Turner, No. 112, April 28, 1873.

84 OHMC, Stahel to Osaka Chamber of Commerce, October 16, 1879; Chamber of Commerce to Stahel, October 29, 1879.

85 KD, M135/12, Van Buren to Blaine, No. 603, January 25, 1882. Most, but not all residents of Osaka and Tokyo were missionaries. See, for example, OHD, M460/2, Stahel to Payson, No. 41, October 25, 1879, which lists fifteen American missionaries residing in or near the Osaka settlement. That the Japanese government did not strictly enforce residence in the two cities to the foreign concessions made an accurate census even more difficult.

86 *The Chronicle and Directory for China, Japan and the Philippines* does not, unfortunately, provide the nationality of the firms it lists. I have identified these firms as American by their correspondence with the American consulates, references to them in consuls' and ministers' dispatches, and in newspapers.

87 The group staying in business twenty-four years comprised Smith, Baker and Company, The China and Japan Trading Company, Walsh, Hall and Company, Browne and Company, Lake and Company, and J.D. Carroll and Company; those staying in business for twelve were Fraser, Farley and Company and Schultz, Reis and Company. Though Schultz, Reis and Company dissolved in the 1870s, Reis and Schultz remained in trade separately at Yokohama until at least 1893. The retention figures do not reflect the careers of men such as Drummond Hay, who left a trading firm to work as secretary for the Osaka/Hyogo Chamber of Commerce. Some others, such as Gustavus Farley, left one firm and appeared later with another. *Chronicle and Directory*, 1870, 1881, 1893. Poole confirms that some families were in business in Yokohama for many years. Poole, *Death of Old Yokohama*, 27.

88 "Yankee Traders," *Fortune* 32 (November 1945): 132–6, 269–76.

89 *Chronicle and Directory*, 1881; The earliest reference to the company is OHMC, Tillson and Company to Turner, October 18, 1873.

90 *Chronicle and Directory*, 1881, 1891, 1893.

91 KD, 135/20, Tillotson to Quincy, No. 155, May 22, 1893. Another American merchant, Charles Merriman, died in October 1890 at age 36 after "many years at Yokohama." His brother took over the business. KD, 135/18, Greathouse to Wharton, No. 281, October 30, 1890.

92 Harold Williams, *Tales of the Foreign Settlements in Japan* (Rutland, Vt.: Charles E. Tuttle Co., 1958), 175.

93 Bantos' roles are discussed at length in Chapter 4.

94 AHC II, Case 27, folder 9, plan of Schultze, Reis and Company; Ibid., folder 56, Augustine Heard property, Japan, Kobe, 1868–1874. Schultz was an American citizen, and Reis was the consul for the North German Confederation.

95 *Hiogo News*, September 3, 1868, May 6, 1869.

96 OHD, M460/4, Smithers to Wharton, No. 6, January 22, 1891, enclosing Register of American Residents at U.S. Consulate at Osaka and Hyogo, December 31, 1890.

97 Yasuzo Horie, "Modern Entrepreneurship in Meiji Japan," in William Lockwood, ed., *The State and Economic Enterprise in Japan* (Princeton: Princeton University Press, 1965), 191.

98 Allen and Donnithorne, *Western Enterprise*, 197; Yukimasa Hattori, *The Foreign Commerce of Japan Since the Restoration, 1869–1900* (Baltimore: The Johns Hopkins Press, 1904), 29.

99 William D. Wray, *Mitsubishi and the N.Y.K., 1870–1914, Business Strategy in the Japanese Shipping Industry* (Cambridge: Harvard University Press, 1984), 248–9. As late as 1890, English ships carried more than half of Japan's foreign commerce. Until the late 1880s, Japan's trade was almost entirely limited to England, the U.S., China, France and Germany. Yukimasa Hattori, *The Foreign Commerce of Japan Since the Restoration, 1869–1900* (Baltimore: The Johns Hopkins Press, 1904), 70. In 1883, a Japanese newspaper, Jiji Shimpo, lamented the fact that no ships were built in Japan, allowing commerce to remain, partly for this reason, in foreign hands. Translated in JWM, May 5, 1883.

100 Calculation in tonnage avoids the difficulties of monetary irregularities and inflation in estimating growth. See Hattori, *Foreign Commerce of Japan*, 8–9, 28.

101 The company opted for the paddlewheel means of propulsion because wooden ships were cheaper to build, lack of maritime infrastructure, and because the company operated far from the nation's technological centers. See Perry, *Facing West*, 138–9.

102 Perry, *Facing West*, 140.

103 Totman, *A History of Japan*, 305.

104 Hattori, *Foreign Commerce of Japan*, 34–60. For the increase in silk exports due to European demand, see JWM, September 2, 1876.

105 For evidence of merchants importing on their own account, see OHD, M460/Stahel to Payson, No. 82, August 26, 1880.

106 Tea exports from Japan grew from just over 6,000,000 lbs in 1862–3 to 37,000,000 lbs in 1882–3. Henry Gribble, "The Preparation of Japan Tea," *Transactions of the Asiatic Society of Japan* 12 (1883–4): 21–22.

107 The four firms purchased about 29 percent of tea brought to Yokohama in 1885, with Smith, Baker and Company second by a small margin to Mourilyan, Heiman and Company. By 1895, Smith, Baker was far and away the leader in tea purchases. Though the number of Japanese dealers declined sharply to twenty-nine in ten years, the volume in transactions increased. See Keishi Ohara and Tamotsu Okata, *Japanese Trade and Industry in the Meiji-Taisho Era* (Tokyo: Obunsha, 1957), 172–4, 188–90.

108 Warren E. Clark, *Life and Adventure in Japan* (New York: American Tract Society, 1878), 123–7.

109 British Parliamentary Papers, Commercial Reports, "Reports on the Production of Tea in Japan," 9, 18–19, cited in Sugiyama, *Japan's Industrialization*, 152–4;

Scidmore, *Jinrikisha Days in Japan*, 352. For the details of the entire process of harvesting tea and bringing it to market, see MD, M133/20, Shepard to Fish, No. 49, June 20, 1872.

110 Hattori, *Foreign Commerce of Japan*, 60–9.

111 William Elliot Griffis, *The Mikado's Empire* (New York and London: Harper and Bros., 1899), 600. By the late 1880s the U.S. was buying about $7,000,000 in tea, $11,000,000 in raw silk and cocoons and lesser amounts of camphor and curios from Japan. In return, Japan imported less than $2,000,000 in kerosene oil, and about $1,000,000 in leather, clocks and watches. As the Japanese economy began to industrialize, American imports such as raw cotton increased substantially. See Hattori, *Foreign Commerce of Japan*, 73; Ohara and Okata, *Japanese Trade and Industry*, 10–12. For a discussion of the role Japanese and Chinese middlemen played in treaty port trade, see Chapter 6. Consular reports during this period, which reported the volume of trade, not merchants' profits, confirm the general increases. See, for example, OHD, M460/ Stahel to Payson, No. 99, November 4, 1880; Ibid., No. 102, November 22; Ibid., No. 107, December 20, 1880. For merchant skittishness concerning any tampering with the export duty on important items such as silk, see OHD, M460/1, Stewart to Fish, No. 22, October 12, 1869, enclosing "Minutes of the Ordinary Half-Yearly Meeting of the Hiogo and Osaka General Chamber of Commerce," July 30, 1869, 13, which stated that "any increase in the duties on silk would be highly injurious to the growing trade of this port" and urged that "the Chamber take every step in their power to obviate such an evil."

112 JWM, June 3, May 13, 1876. Western merchants in China had similar complaints: 1872 marked the year in which British merchants there sent back the "last glowing accounts of the potentialities latent in the China market." Quoted in Nathan A. Pelcovits, *Old China Hands and the Foreign Office* (New York: King's Crown Press, 1948), 102.

113 Sugiyama, *Japan's Industrialization*, 150–1; Hattori, *Foreign Commerce of Japan*, 37–8; Gribble, "The Preparation of Japan Tea," 22–3.

114 Allen and Donnithorne, *Western Enterprise*, 201.

115 KD, M135/14, Van Buren to Davis, No. 798, May 15, 1884.

116 Total imports and exports for 1886 were $79,161,000 and $16,221,000; for 1887, $94,502,000 and $19,365,000. JWM, February 25, 1887.

117 JWM, February 25, 1887.

118 Miyakawa, "Early New York Issei," 158.

119 Hattori, *Foreign Commerce of Japan*, 10.

120 Compiled from statistics in Hattori, *Foreign Commerce of Japan*, 40–49.

121 Hattori, *Foreign Commerce of Japan*, 40–7. See also Kazushi Ohkawa and Henry Rosovsky, "A Century of Japanese Economic Growth," in Lockwood, *State and Economic Enterprise in Japan*, 66–76. After Japan's victory of China in 1895, trade greatly expanded due to a greatly extended sphere of influence, "with the government and the people concentrating their energies on overseas economic expansion." *Japan Year Book*, 1933, 391. For economic expansion after the war, see also United States Tariff Commission, *The Foreign Trade of Japan* (Washington, D.C.: Government Printing Office, 1922), 2.

122 Wray, *Mitsubishi and the N.Y.K.*, 248–9; Hattori, *Foreign Commerce of Japan*, 72, fn 1. In 1880 only 22 percent of the tonnage of vessels entering Japanese ports was Japanese; by 1899 the figure was 35 percent. Hattori, *Foreign Commerce of Japan*, 30. Okuma made clear as early as 1875 that Japan was interested in encouraging home industries. Junesay Iddittie, *The Life of Marquis Shigenobu Okuma* (Tokyo: Hokuseido Press, 1956), 169–70.

123 Hattori, *Foreign Commerce of Japan*, 28–29; Ohara and Okata, *Japanese Trade and Industry*, 175, 190–1. The *Japan Weekly Mail* noted that 300 cases of exhibit material weighing 1,600 tons were sent to the Philadelphia Centennial Exhibition. JWM,

March 18, 1876. For the 1885 exhibition, see JWM, July 25, 1885. For Japanese participation in the Columbian Exhibition at Chicago in 1893, see OHD, M460/4, Smithers to Wharton, No. 140, August 6, 1892. Japan "invested more than $630,000" in its exhibits at the Chicago Columbian exposition in Chicago in 1893. For Japanese participation in expositions in the U.S., 1876–1916, see Rydell, *All the World's a Fair*, esp. 48–52, 200–05 and Neil Harris, "All the World a Melting Pot?" Some Japanese entrepreneurs such as Morimura Ichizaemon and Okura Kihachiro engaged in foreign trade directly. See Horie, "Modern Entrepreneurship," in Lockwood, *The State and Economic Enterprise in Japan*, 191–3. Japanese efforts at establishing direct trade were not without their special character. A New York merchant received the following order for fishing tackle: "We shall present to your company the bamboo fishing rod, a net basket and a reel, as we have just convenience; all those were very rough and simply to your laughing for your kind reply which you sent us the catalogue of fishing tackles last, etc. Wishing we that now in Japan there it was not in prevailing fish gaming, but fishermen. In scarcely therefore but we do not measure how the progression of the germ of the fishing game beforehand. Therefore, we may yield of feeling to restock in my store your countries fishing tackles, etc. Should you have the kindness to send a such farther country, even in a few partake when we send the money in ordering of them should you." Henry T. Finck, *Lotos Time in Japan* (London: Lawrence and Bullen, 1895), 275.

124 *Japan Year Book*, 1933, 390. One source suggests that many foreign trading houses "seem merely to have charged exorbitant commissions or abused privileges under the unequal treaties. For example, before the Sino–Japanese war (1894–95), sugar merchants in Osaka bought sugar through Chinese trading companies, which took a 5 percent commission. As the Japanese merchants opposed this high commission, they established the Sato Goshi Kaisha (Sugar Co. Ltd.) to import sugar directly. This company entrusted Yasham Yoko with a 1.2 percent commission rate … thus there arose a movement among Japanese merchants to protest the unjust practices of their foreign counterparts, culminating in the incident involving the Joint Freight Office for Raw Silk at Yokohama." Shin'ichi Yonekawa and Hideki Yoshihara, eds., *Business History of General Trading Companies* (Tokyo: University of Tokyo Press, 1987), 73.

125 William W. Lockwood, *The Economic Development of Japan Growth and Structural Change* (Princeton: Princeton University Press, 1968), 94, quoted in Lillian M. Li, "Silks by Sea: Trade, Technology, and Enterprise in China and Japan," *Business History Review* 56 (Summer 1982): 197–8.

126 Li, "Silks by Sea," 201. In the 1850s and 1860s, with the opening of the treaty ports, several new centers of sericulture emerged. Fukushima and Gumma prefectures, the traditional sources of the best raw silk, were now joined by Nagano, Gifu and Yamanishi. Ibid., 205–6.

127 Li, "Silks by Sea," 210.

128 Haru Matsukata Reischauer, *Samurai and Silk, A Japanese and American Heritage* (Cambridge: Belknap Press, 1986), 207. Also see Miyakawa, "Early New York Issei," 171–8.

129 Reischauer, *Samurai and Silk*, 208–11.

130 Ibid., 214.

131 From a partner in Japan, Arai received the following in November, 1879: "Perhaps you know that it is quite hard thing for Japanese silk man to get good and reliable report from foreigners in Yokohama … Even the ablest silkman who is not accustomed in foreigner's way of business can hardly ascertain their full report." Ibid., 216.

132 Reischauer, *Samurai and Silk*, 222–3. Another direct trading company was the Boeki Shokai "capitalized at 200,000 yen and founded by Iwasaki Yataro, Fukuzawa Yukichi, and other members of their group." Reischauer, *Samurai and Silk*, 223.

133 Li, "Silks by Sea," 215.

134 KD, M135/12, Van Buren to Blaine, No. 572, October 10, 1881. The boycott began in September, lasted two months and involved twenty-seven Japanese wholesalers. The association was supported by the Japanese government by a low interest loan of ¥1,000,000. As the impasse progressed, silk began accumulating in the silk manufacturers' warehouses, the government loan proved inadequate to handle a sustained boycott, and some wholesalers were forced to sell to the foreign merchants. Ohara and Okata, *Japanese Trade and Industry*, 238. American merchants complained directly to Secretary of State James G. Blaine about monopolies in the Japanese Silk Guild. But when Bingham investigated at Blaine's request, he found the merchants' complaint unjustified and a protest from the United States government unnecessary. MD, M133/45, Bingham to James G. Blaine, No. 1387, October 22, 1881.

135 KD, M135/12, Van Buren to Blaine, No. 572, October 10, 1881.

136 KD, 135/22, McIvor to Rockhill, No. 277, April 1, 1897.

137 Yuzo Kato, *Yokohama Past and Present* (Yokohama: Yokohama City University, 1990), 88.

138 The first graduating class was three students in 1886, and the school sent out graduates every year after 1890. Ibid., 89.

139 *Japan Year Book*, 1933, 391. Shipping followed the same pattern. Until 1890, for example, the great majority of Japanese trade was carried under foreign flags, but by the turn of the century, Japanese ships carried one third. Hattori, *Foreign Commerce of Japan*, 30–1.

140 Sugiyama, *Japan's Industrialization*, 43. The American consular trade reports corroborated this pattern. In November 1883, for example, import trade in yen broke down as follows: the value of dutiable articles imported by the government was 4,335; by Japanese merchants, 61,281. Foreign merchants imported 1,925,160. The value in yen of dutiable articles exported by Japanese merchants was 939,088, while foreigners exported 2,986,026 in goods KD, 135/14, Van Buren to Davis, No. 774, January 19, 1884.

141 Wray, Mitsubishi and the N.Y.K., 84–5. The Pacific Mail Steamship Company's assets in Yokohama in 1872 were $62,000. Another source corroborates the Japanese government's subsidy of the Mitsubishi line to get the carrying trade along coast. See Ohara and Okata, *Japanese Trade and Industry*, 436. In one fictionalized account of Americans travelling in Japan, a Japanese character observed, "We now build our own railroads and steamships. The day has passed for foreign adventurers to make fortunes out of us." Edward Greey, *Young Americans in Japan, or the Further Adventures of the Jewett Family and Their Friend Oto Nambo* (New York: John R. Anderson, 1902), 259.

142 "The New Tax," JWM, March 25, 1876.

143 The British firm accepted the financial loss involved in the compromise it worked out with the Japanese firm, a decision that "struck dismay in the settlements." One writer noted that "at last foreign traders woke up to the fact that they were not only in for keen competition, but that they were at last very much at the mercy of the Japanese firms, the possibility of whose successful commercial rivalry they had pooh-poohed and ignored until it was too late. Guilds of far-reaching influence had, in the years when Japanese traders had been supposed to be asleep or to be quietly submitting to foreign browbeating and dictation, been founded by all the great industries in Japan, and the moves and organization of these could be regulated and set into motion all through the land if necessary by telegraph." By this means "the opposition to Japanese interests could now be successfully and even speedily beaten down." Holland, *Old and New Japan*, 282–3. For a typical American complaint regarding Japanese guilds and their cooperative action, see MD, M133/45, Bingham to Blaine, No. 1387, October 22, 1881.

144 Robert S. Schwantes, "Foreign Employees in the Development of Japan," 201–17, and Hazel J. Jones, "Live Machines Revisited," 20, in Burks, *The Modernizers: Overseas Students, Foreign Employees and Meiji Japan*; Allen and Donnithorne, *Western Enterprise*, 270. The *oyatoi* are well documented. See also Edward R. Beauchamp and Akira Iriye, eds, *Foreign Employees in Nineteenth Century Japan* (Boulder, San Francisco and London: Westview Press, 1990); Jones, *Live Machines*. Exaggerating their role in Japan's modernization, *oyatoi*'s attitudes sometimes approximated the arrogance of merchants'. One observer noted that "There is nothing picturesque in the foreign employee. With his club, and his tennis ground, and his brick house, and his wife's piano, and the European entourage which he strives to create around him, he sometimes strikes a false note." Basil Hall Chamberlain, *Things Japanese*, 6th rev. ed., (London: Kegan Paul, Trench, Trubner and Co. Ltd., 1939), 184–5.

145 Wray, *Mitsubishi and the N.Y.K.*, 443–4.

146 JWM, January 28, 1882, March 28, 1891.

147 Ohara and Okata, *Japanese Trade and Industry*, 437, 505; Blum, *Yokohama in 1872*, 34.

148 Wray, *Mitsubishi and the N.Y.K.*, 483–5; 559, fn 49.

149 There is some question regarding the intent to defraud, as many Japanese merchants doubtless thought of the trademark as merely descriptive. Some Yokohama street signs included "Horseshoemaker imstracted by Frenchhorseleech," "Best Perfuming Water Anti-flea," "The Warm Belt for Belly," "Antemetic of Nausea Marina" and the inexplicable "Kippengelei." Dixon, *The Land of the Morning*, 208–9; Arthur H. Crow, *Highways and Byeways in Japan* (London: Sampson Low, Marston, Searle and Rivington, 1883), 93; KD, M135/20, McIvor to Uhl, No. 41, July 9, 1894; Ibid., 135/12, Van Buren to Blaine, No. 558, September 3, 1881; JWM, February 19, 1876.

150 This device was probably invented by Captain R.M. Varnum, an employee of Walsh, Hall and Company in Yokohama. U.S. consul Van Buren claimed that the new device, widely used, would render tea "cleaned and packaged any other way unsalable," and urged the State Department to take steps to protect it, claiming that Americans suffered from the "constant pillage of their property in Japan." See KD, M135/12, Van Buren to Davis, No. 615, March 20, 1882; Gribble, "The Preparation of Japan Tea," 18.

151 Holland, *Old and New Japan*, 272–5.

152 Notehelfer, *Japan Through American Eyes*, 37, note 130. Notehelfer points out that in 1872 Walsh, Hall and Company had, in conjunction with "other foreign investors," founded the Japan Paper Making Company in Kobe, and by 1877 had acquired sole control. In 1879, however, the Japanese Iwasaki Yanosuke "bought a half interest in these mills." In 1897, the death of John Greer Walsh caused his brother Thomas to give up the business and go back to the U.S. Based on Walsh, Hall's venture into paper making, Notehelfer observed that "by the early 1870s the firm was shifting its focus from being a trading and commission house to becoming a firm active in the industrialization of Japan." Though it is impossible to say how the firm allocated its capital, the frequency of its consular correspondence throughout the treaty port years on matters concerning imports and exports casts some doubt on this assertion.

153 Ohara and Okata, *Japanese Trade and Industry*, 186–8; Holland, Old and New Japan, 272, 276. Some other larger companies had begun to fail earlier. The British firm of Malcolm, Hudson and Company went bankrupt in 1876 with total liabilities of £85,000 and assets of only £6,000. JWM, April 8, 1876. The financial pressure on some Western merchants was evident earlier as well. By 1868, the American firm of Case and Company had fallen heavily into debt to the British firm of H. Fogg and Company, which traded largely on the China coast. The British company had imported substantial amounts of merchandise on Case and Company's behalf from New York. In order to continue in business, Case and Company voluntarily mortgaged

"all of their stock in trade, including all goods, wares and merchandise in their Nagasaki, Kobe and Osaka" branches to Fogg and Company. OHMC, Mortgage of Case and Company to Fogg and Company, October 2, 1868.

154 Holland, *Old and New Japan*, 276.

155 Lockwood, *Economic Development of Japan* (1968), 329–30. For a summary of Frazar and Company's career in Japan, 1867–1941, see "Yankee Traders," *Fortune* (November 1945): 132–6, 269–70, 272, 276, 279.

156 Allen and Donnithorne, *Western Enterprise*, 203.

157 Ibid., 124, 202–3.

158 KD, M135/18, Greathouse to St. Clair, unofficial despatch, July 16, 1890. See also ND, M660/131, Birch to Porter, No. 5, June 7, 1887; R. Hoffman, *The Anglo–German Trade Rivalry* (Philadelphia, 1933), 32–5.

159 Hoare, *Japan's Treaty Ports*, 137–9. For the increase in the percentage of German trade, see Hattori, *Foreign Commerce of Japan*, 72, fn 1.

160 Miyakawa, "Early New York Issei," 161.

161 In addition to those already discussed, a notable example of an American firm remaining in business over a long period is that of Frazar and Company, which traded continuously in Yokohama from 1867 to 1941. Lockwood, *Economic Development of Japan*, 329.

162 Jones, *Extraterritoriality in Japan*, 79–91, 99–100, 108–9.

CHAPTER TWO

1 George T. Murray, *The Land of the Tatami, Travels in Japan* (Shanghai: North China Herald, 1906), 51.

2 "Bishop of Homoco," *Exercises in the Yokohama Dialect*, 2nd ed., (Yokohama: Japan Gazette Office, 1879). "Chickshaw" is an untranslatable Japanese swearword.

3 Dixon, *Land of the Morning*, 171.

4 Quoted in Payson Treat, *Early Diplomatic Relations*, 131. Japanese preparation of the foreign concessions for merchant residence extended to the erection of godowns. See OHMC, S. Doi to Robinet, November 24, 1869.

5 Blum, *Yokohama in 1872*, 2; Heco, *Narrative of a Japanese*, 1: 203; Smith, *Ten Weeks in Japan*, 254–5.

6 Smith, *Ten Weeks in Japan*, 250.

7 Williams, *Foreigners in Mikadoland*, 93.

8 See Williams, *Foreigners in Mikadoland*, chapter entitled "Yokohama: The Wild West of the Far East," passim; Hugh Cortazzi, "Yokohama: Frontier Town, 1859–1866," *Royal Society of Asian Affairs Bulletin* 18 (February 1986): passim. As late as 1876 one newspaper noted that the west end of Main street "smelled overpoweringly bad" because of poor drainage, and later observed that "the most flagrantly immoral parts of Japan at present are the slums and neighborhood of the open ports." JWM, July 22, 1876; May 21, 1892.

9 Black, *Young Japan*, 2: 25–6; Williams, *Foreigners in Mikadoland*, 98; One observer estimated the damages at $2,800,000. See Satow, *A Diplomat in Japan*, 164.

10 "New Yorker," "A New Yorker in Japan" *Dublin University Magazine* 80 (December 1872): 658.

11 Isabella Bird, *Unbeaten Tracks in Japan* (1880; reprint, Rutland, Vt. and Tokyo: Charles E. Tuttle Co., 1973), 6–7.

12 Rudyard Kipling, *Letters from Japan*, ed. Donald Ritchie and Yoshimori Harashima (Tokyo: Kenkysha, 1962), 16; Crow, *Highways and Byeways in Japan*, 35; Dixon refers to the settlement as "a piece of a western American city." Dixon, *Land of the Morning*, 244.

13 Murray, *Land of the Tatami*, 51.

14 For one shopping trip for curios, see Samuel Pellman Boyer, *Naval Surgeon: Revolt in Japan, 1868–1869, The Diary of Samuel Pellman Boyer*, eds. Elinor Barnes and James A. Barnes (Bloomington: Indiana University Press, 1963), 59. Many recommended vigilance in detecting counterfeit goods. See JWM, October 6, 1888. One resident claimed that some "unceremoniously marched off with" shop goods for which Japanese merchants overcharged. M.L. Gordon, *An American Missionary in Japan* (Boston and New York: Houghton, Mifflin Co. 1895), 34. When haggling over prices in curio shops, travellers watched Japanese merchants calculate the cost on the soroban, or abacus, which merchants assumed Westerners did not understand, leaving them at a disadvantage in bargaining. Chamberlain, *Things Japanese*, 9.

15 "New Yorker in Japan," 659; Scidmore, *Jinrikisha Days in Japan*, 13–19; Finck, *Lotos Time in Japan*, 17–18.

16 Crow, *Highways and Byeways*, 204; Scidmore, *Jinrikisha Days in Japan*, 20; Clark, *Life and Adventure in Japan*, 15.

17 Finck, *Lotos Time in Japan*, 20. See also Clark, *Life and Adventure in Japan*, 2, 126–7. One observer, noting the pleasant chatter of Japanese women picking the tea leaves in the fields of Suruga and that of the women working over the fires in Yokohama, remarked that "the little leaf begins and ends in gossip." For this and other details of the tea harvest, see Clark, *Life and Adventure in Japan*, 123–7; Gribble, "The Preparation of Japan Tea," 1–33, an extensive report. One American set up a steam saw mill to provide tea chests to exporters for shipment. See Scidmore, *Jinrikisha Days in Japan*, 352–3.

18 E.G. Holtham, *Eight Years in Japan, 1873–1881, Work, Travel and Recreation* (London: Kegan Paul, Trench and Co., 1883), 16. One visitor claimed that the women worked as much as twelve to fifteen hours a day in the busy season. See Crow, *Highways and Byeways*, 29.

19 Gribble, "The Preparation of Japan Tea," 12. One piece of evidence suggests that Japanese convicts worked in the tea-firing godowns. In 1878, the prefectural office at Kobe sent the following message to the U.S. consul: "With regard to the prisoners sent from this Kencho to the tea factory kept by Messrs. Smith Baker and Company, U.S. Citizens, at number 3 concession ... will you kindly acquaint the company with my intention to despatch hereafter to the factory, police officers for the purpose of overseeing them in their labors." OHMC, Government Office to Benson, June 14, 1878. It is unclear whether the police supervision was to prevent escapes or abuse.

20 Harold S. Williams, *The Story of Holme Ringer and Company, Ltd. in Western Japan, 1868–1968* (Tokyo: Charles Tuttle and Co., 1968), 26.

21 OHMC, A.O. Gay to Paul Frank, June 30, 1871.

22 JWM, "The Ownership of Land in the Settlements," August 15, 1891. See also Gordon, *An American Missionary in Japan*, 86–7.

23 KD, M135/16, Greathouse to Porter, No. 5, August 20, 1886.

24 JWM, September 30, 1876.

25 KD, M135/16, Greathouse to Porter, No. 47, April 14, 1887.

26 KD, M135/16, Greathouse to Porter, No. 4, August 20, 1886. For other such men, see Ibid., No. 14, September 22, 1886; No. 20, October 30, 1886. For something of the flavor of life in Bloodtown, see "How the Other Half Lives," *Eastern World*, November 2, 1895.

27 Arrests for drunkenness and petty assaults were so common at Yokohama that Van Buren asked for more clerical help to handle the paperwork. KD, M135/12, Van Buren to Blaine, No. 613, March 6, 1882; JWM, November 11, 1876.

28 JWM, May 13, October 21, 1876.

29 KD, M135/22, McIvor to Rockhill, No. 217, September 8, 1896; Ibid., McIvor to

Rockhill, No. 275, March 29, 1897. The foreign community also contributed $2,800 to relief fund for some 870 Japanese victims of a fire in Tokyo in 1876. JWM, December 30, 1876.

30 "Invitations Issued by the Imperial Household Department," JWM, February 22, 1890.

31 Murray, *The Land of the Tatami*, 51.

32 Reischauer, "Alien Land Tenure in Japan," 29. One visitor wrote of the Bluff, "Everybody lives there who can afford it." JWM, October 6, 1888. For the "messes," see Hallett Edward Abend, *Treaty Ports* (Garden City, New York: Doubleday, Doran and Company, Inc., 1944), 184.

33 Poole, *The Death of Old Yokohama*, 24–7. A clever dramatic send-up entitled "The Leisure Hour at Home, A Bluff Idyll" poked gentle fun at the domestic routine of a busy merchant. See F. Schroeder, *Eastern World Back Numbers*, 1892–1907 (Yokohama: Eastern World Office, 1908), 395–9.

34 Dixon, *Land of the Morning*, 243; Finck, *Lotos Time in Japan*, 15; Poole, *The Death of Old Yokohama*, 22; Crow, *Highways and Byeways*, 201–2; Griffis, *The Mikado's Empire*, 339; Scidmore, *Jinrikisha Days in Japan,* 10–11. For the rental rates, see Abend, *Treaty Ports*, 184. Toward the end of the treaty port era, some well-off foreigners in the Kobe area moved from Kitano-cho even further out to the beautiful area of Suma, where they lived near the Shioya Country Club. Reg Clark, "Shioya Country Club," *Kansai Time Out*, No. 75 (May 1983): 35.

35 JWM, September 30, 1876.

36 OHD, M460/5, Smithers to William Wharton, enclosing inventory and appraisal of Carroll's estate, January 4, 1892.

37 Griffis, *The Mikado's Empire*, 406.

38 A "comical American" auctioneer from Yokohama presided humorously over one such affair, at one point playing a piano on which he was accepting bids. Dixon, *Land of the Morning*, 264–6.

39 Crow, *Highways and Byeways*, 30.

40 Griffis, *The Mikado's Empire*, 337, 342; Abend, *Treaty Ports*, 183. Griffis acknowledged American affinity for Britain: "the American," he wrote, "finds more to love, to honor and to admire in the Englishman" than in anyone else. The rivalry between Britain and America, "the two civilizing powers of the world," was bound to benefit Japan: "Like flint and steel before the dead cold mass of Asiatic despotism, superstition and narrowness, it must result in kindling many a good spark into flames of progress and knowledge." Griffis, *The Mikado's Empire*, 343.

41 AHC, HM-37-1, Farley in Yokohama to Heard, January 14, 1872.

42 Lafcadio Hearn, *The Japanese Letters of Lafcadio Hearn*, ed. Elizabeth Bisland (Boston and New York: Houghton Mifflin Co., 1910), 262. Some preferred even such society to the loneliness of the interior. Arthur Collins Maclay took a teaching post in Tokyo where he would be closer to other foreigners, concluding that the "loneliness of life in the interior is too sepulchral" and that its "monotony is extremely wearing." Arthur Collins Maclay, *A Budget of Letters From Japan* (New York: A.C. Armstrong and Son, 1886), 84.

43 Letter from J. Okada in *London and China Express*, January 25, 1884. William Elliot Griffis agreed with the Japanese assessment, disdaining "that numerous class in Japan, who, with pecuniary power and social influence far above that they could gain at home, ape the manners and succeed in copying the worst faults of the better class of their countrymen." This, though they lived among a people capable of "teaching them good manners." Griffis, *The Mikado's Empire*, 343.

44 Dixon, *Land of the Morning*, 259–60; Finck, *Lotos Time in Japan*, 10–11.

45 Isaac Dooman, *A Missionary's Life in the Land of the Gods* (Boston: The Gorham Press, 1914), 307. The following is a good example of the minutiae appearing in the

papers: "Alexander McLean, a seaman of the British ship *Eme* now undergoing imprisonment in the British Consular gaol, made an attempt to destroy himself yesterday morning. Fortunately, his suspenders, by which he attempted to hang himself to an iron window bar, gave way and he fell to the ground. He is now doing well." See JWM, May 13, 1879.

46 Clark, *Life and Adventure in Japan*, 147.

47 The *Deutsche Gesellschaft fur Natur und Volkerkunde Ostasians* dated from 1872 and Yokohama had its own German Club by the 1890s.

48 Crow, *Highways and Byeways*, 197–8; Rogers, "Life in the Foreign Settlements of Japan," 1234; Scidmore, *Jinrikisha Days in Japan, 25*.

49 One of the few exceptions to this was an attempt to form an "American Asiatic Society of Japan" in 1899. See KD, M136/1, J.F. Gowey to Hill, No. 142, June 27, 1899.

50 JWM, October 7, 14, 1876. Notably without controversy was the association's exclusion of Japanese bettos and grooms from races. JWM, October 28, 1876.

51 *Tokio* Times, May 4, 1878; *Japan Gazette*, December 1, 1890; Kimijima Ichiro, *Nihon yakyu soseki* (Tokyo, 1972), 13, cited in Roden, "Baseball and the Quest for National Dignity in Meiji Japan," 518, n30.

52 JWM, January 29, 1876.

53 Dixon, *Land of the Morning*, 262.

54 One Tokyo official was seen wearing "Japanese clogs, flannel drawers, swallow-tail coat, and opera hat." Dixon, *Land of the Morning*, 188–91; Finck, *Lotos Time in Japan*, 47–8; Crow, *Highways and Byeways*, 12. For the reaction of another Westerner to improperly worn Western clothes, see Clara A.N. Whitney, *Clara's Diary, An American Girl in Meiji Japan*, eds. M. William Steele and Tamiko Ichmata (Tokyo and New York: Kodansha International, Ltd., 1979), 240. Social contact between the two groups was equally difficult. Early in 1879, the Japanese planned a function sponsored at the Mitsui bank offices by Tokyo prefecture, the local assembly and the chamber of commerce. "A great many foreigners" including some merchants from Yokohama, attended, but one observer concluded that the gulf between the groups was impassable. Holtham, *Eight Years in Japan*, 251–3.

55 Harris, "All the World a Melting Pot?", 29–30.

56 JWM, January 11, 1873, December 23, 1876. In the event, the consulate did not compel Smith to register as an American. See OHD, M460/2, DeLong to Turner, No. 112, April 28, 1873.

57 JWM, January 25, 1873.

58 JWM, August 26, 1876.

59 One contemporary suggested that few Japanese of "good name and repute" responded to the inducement, and those who came were mostly "broken men, mere adventurers and speculators who had little to lose and possibly something to gain .... Respectable persons were afraid to come into contact with the foreign 'barbarians,' with their strange speech and uncouth, outlandish ways." Heco, *Narrative of a Japanese*, 1: 249. Other evidence corroborates the attraction to the ports. On the eve of Kobe's opening in 1868, one observer "found that the people were in high spirits at the prospect of the opening of the port. In Kobe, where the foreign settlement was to be, there had been seven days of feasting and merry-making, and there had been processions of people dressed in red crape with carts which were supposed to carry earth for the site of the new settlement .... The people obviously saw that foreign trade would spell prosperity for them." Redesdale, *Mitford's Japan*, 62.

60 "Servants' Associations," *Japan Times*, December 31, 1897.

61 Rogers, "Life in the Foreign Settlements," 1234; Edward H. House, *Japanese Episodes* (Boston: James R. Osgood and Co., 1881), 133; Scidmore, *Jinrikisha Days*

in Japan, 23–4. Scidmore mentions that many household servants came from the samurai class. Believing what they saw – the foreign display, if not the substance, of wealth – Japanese servants sometimes charged their employers according to their social position. See Dixon, *Land of the Morning,* 169, 229. Servants had a sliding scale, charging diplomatic and consular officials the highest rates. Merchants and bankers paid an intermediate scale, while "despised jobs with missionaries" paid the least. See Abend, *Treaty Ports,* 185.

62 Griffis, *The Mikado's Empire,* 353, 427, 512. Griffis referred to two bettos as "a pair of native ponies on which oats are never wasted." Ibid., 353. Francis Hall referred to the propensity of bettos to drink: "Betto was so drunk that he could not mount after getting into the fields." Bettos often ran or walked in front of the rider's horse, holding a tether. See Notehelfer, ed., *Japan Through American Eyes,* 216, 90. Hall noted "serious riots in the courtesan's quarter arising out of the arrest of some bettos by the police." When two bettos were arrested, "their comrades" attacked the police, killing or severely wounding two policeman. Ibid., 500. An illustration of a betto by Sadahide can be found in Albert Altman, "Eugene Van Reed, A Reading Man in Japan, 1859–1872," *Historical Review of Berks County* 30 (Winter 1964–5): 9.

63 *Minato-no-hana. Yokohama kidan* (Chinji Gokakoku: Yokohama Banashi, 1862), cited in Williams, *Foreigners in Mikadoland,* 108–9. Williams also describes a "'Bettos race' for Japanese ponies ridden by betto," a special event on a program otherwise restricted to 'Subscribers and Officers of the Navy.'" Williams, *Foreigners in Mikadoland,* 146–7.

64 Williams, *Foreigners in Mikadoland,* 172. Foreign firms employed numerous bettos – Francis Hall, an American partner in the firm of Walsh, Hall and Company, once referred to "our 20 bettos." Bettos sometimes accompanied their employers on trips; once, Hall's bettos, fearing their employer would be caught in a rainstorm during a long excursion, followed him with rain cloaks, returning "at 2 A.M. the following morning." See Notehelfer, *Japan Through American Eyes,* 331, 339, 429. At least one source called the reliability of bettos into question: *Murray's Handbook* cautioned the traveller in Japan against the hazard of "run-away grooms" in the interior. See Basil Hall Chamberlain and W.B. Mason, *A Handbook for Travellers in Japan,* 8th ed. (London: John Murray, 1907), 10. For bettos' cheap wages, see OHMC, Lyons to Frank, December 1, 1869. Bettos, like all Japanese servants working for foreigners, made more than the wages paid them. Being responsible for the care and feeding of their employers' horses, they took every opportunity to add their "squeeze" (see note 66) to the bill presented for hay, oats and exercise. For a description of the atoshi, see Abend, *Treaty Ports,* 184.

65 Hearn, *The Japanese Letters of Lafcadio Hearn,* 37.

66 Dixon, *Land of the Morning,* 248–50; Scidmore, *Jinrikisha Days in Japan,* 23. Resentment against "squeezes" – amounts of money added by servants for services rendered – sometimes took the form of striking back when and how one could. One American missionary related that residents sometimes walked away from jinrikisha drivers without paying, and that "these heroes afterward have recounted their triumphs with great glee." Gordon, *An American Missionary in Japan,* 34.

67 Rogers, "Life in the Foreign Settlements," 1234. See also House, *Japanese Episodes,* 165–6.

68 Griffis, *The Mikado's Empire,* 341.

69 Abend, *Treaty Ports,* 182–3.

70 *Hiogo News,* May 20, May 27, 1869.

71 Ibid., September 3, 1868.

72 Crow, *Highways and Byeways,* 38; Scidmore, *Jinrikisha Days in Japan,* 22.

73 JWM, August 10, 1872.

74 Rogers, "Life in the Foreign Settlements," 1234; JWM, June 24, 1876.

75 Williams, *Tales of the Foreign Settlements*, 130–1.

76 JWM, February 12, 1882.

77 JWM, February 8, 1873, May 20, 1876.

78 Chamberlain, *Things Japanese*, 55–56. Examination of the membership lists of the *Transactions of the Asiatic Society of Japan* yields the names of no American merchants.

79 Rogers, "Life in the Foreign Settlements," 1234.

80 Baroness Albert D'Anethan, *Fourteen Years of Diplomatic Life in Japan* (London: Stanley Paul and Co., 1912), 174–7.

81 Quoted in Jacobson, *Barbarian Virtues*, 105.

82 Quoted in Madelon Powers, *Faces Along the Bar, Lore and Order in the Workingman's Saloon, 1870–1920* (Chicago: University of Chicago Press, 1998), 47.

83 OHMC, Van Valkenburgh to Frank, April 18, 1868.

84 Robert Greenhalgh Albion, *The Rise of New York Port, 1815–1860* (1939. Newton: David and Charles, 1970), 255.

85 Howard P. Chudacoff, *The Age of the Bachelor, Creating an American Subculture* (Princeton: Princeton University Press, 1999), 41.

86 Chudacoff, *Age of the Bachelor*, 150.

87 Lord Ronald Gower, *Notes of a Tour From Brindisi to Yokohama, 1883–1884* (London: Kegan Paul, Trench and Co., 1885), 68–9. Crow, *Highways and Byeways in Japan*, 197–8; Rogers, "Life in the Foreign Settlements," 1234.

88 Holtham, *Eight Years in Japan*, 321–2. For a discussion of the proliferation of billiards in the U.S. during the same period, see Chudacoff, *Age of the Bachelor*, 115–21. Although the date is not precisely clear, eventually the Kobe Club became "overburdened with a bank overdraft, accumulating expenses, and repairs." The club managed to continue by issuing bonds which its members purchased to keep the club afloat. Later, members agreed to a reduction of the bond interest rate to reduce financial pressure. The club was unable to redeem some of the bonds, even when the bond-holders fell on hard times. Williams, *Tales of the Foreign Settlements*, 234–5.

89 Libraries also served the foreign communities at Foochow, Tientsin, Peking and "elsewhere in China and throughout Asia." Quoted in Harold M. Otness, "Expatriate Libraries of China's Treaty Ports," Paper delivered at the Conference of the International Association of Orientalist Librarians in Conjunction with the International Congress of Asian and North African Studies, Hong Kong, August 24, 1993, an extensive discussion of foreign libraries on the China coast.

90 The book was published under the pseudonym "Dietrich Knickerbocker." Boyer, *Naval Surgeon*, 45, 50. The Osaka/Hyogo chamber of commerce dealt with some concerns beyond the purely mercantile, appointing one committee in 1868 to form a library. See OHD, M460/1, Stewart to Fish, No. 22, October 12, 1869, enclosing "Minutes of the Ordinary Half-Yearly General Meeting of the Hyogo and Osaka General Chamber of Commerce, July 30, 1869," 7.

91 Powers, *Faces Along the Bar*, 64. The proliferation of bars toward the end of the century was staggering. "An 1895 survey of ninety-five American cities found an average of one licensed saloon for every 317 residents (including all people, minors as well as adults). Chudacoff, *Age of the Bachelor*, 108.

92 Abend, *Treaty Ports*, 183.

93 Boyer, *Naval Surgeon*, 36, 43.

94 Powers, *Faces Along the Bar*, 7–8.

95 Holtham, *Eight Years in Japan*, 321–2.

96 Chudacoff, *Age of the Bachelor*, 113.

97 Williams, *Tales of the Foreign Settlements*, 232–4; Abend, *Treaty Ports*, 182–3; *Eastern World*, February 4, 1899. Inland Sea pilots, crucial to foreign trade, ranked high. Abend, *Treaty Ports*, 183.

98 Powers, *Faces Along the Bar*, 21.

99 Ibid., 94–5.

100 Abend, *Treaty Ports*, 183, 185.

101 Quoted in Chudacoff, *Age of the Bachelor*, 43.

102 Crow, *Highways and Byeways*, 219; Rogers, "Life in the Foreign Settlements," 1234; Scidmore, *Jinrikisha Days in Japan*, 27, 42; F.D. Bridges, *Journal of a Lady's Travels Around the World* (London: John Murray, 1883), 279–81. Merchants in Kobe also vacationed in more pleasant areas outside the concessions. On one occasion, a British merchant and the American J.D. Carroll competed to rent an attractive cottage in Arima near Kyoto. See OHMC, copy of Fisher to Annesley, British Consul at Kobe, July 9, 1875.

103 House, *Japanese Episodes*, 150–1.

104 Jacobson, *Barbarian Virtues*, 110.

105 Abend, *Treaty Ports*, 185.

106 Finck, *Lotos Time in Japan*, 11; Scidmore, *Jinrikisha Days in Japan*, 27; JWM, December 13, 1879.

107 Clarence Ludlow Brownell, *Tales From Tokio* (New York: Warner and Brownell, 1900), 95–101.

108 E. Anthony Rotundo, *American Manhood, Transformations in Masculinity from the Revolution to the Modern Era* (New York: Basic Books, 1993), 240–2.

109 Chudacoff, *Age of the Bachelor*, 35.

110 Scidmore, *Jinrikisha Days in Japan*, 12.

111 For literature on Victorian expressions of "manliness" through sports, see Roden, "Baseball and the Quest for National Dignity in Meiji Japan," 511, note 1.

112 Holtham, *Eight Years in Japan*, 279.

113 JWM, April 1, May 6, 1876; Crow, *Highways and Byeways*, 248; Reg Clark, "The Kobe Regatta and Athletic Club," *Kansai Time Out*, 36. Residents took intersettlement competition seriously. Even tiny Tsukiji fielded a cricket team "in the hope of walloping Yokohama." Holtham, *Eight Years in Japan*, 309.

114 JWM, May 13, 1876. Another article compared the virtues of croquet and tennis in agonizing detail before concluding that tennis was superior. JWM, June 17, 1876.

115 Yokohama Country and Athletic Club, *125th Anniversary Commemorative Magazine*, 1993, 10–11.

116 "The Fate of the 'Popular Man' in the Far East," *Eastern World*, April 1, 1905. A spate of businessmen's suicides in Shanghai prompted the article.

117 Powers, *Faces Along the Bar*, 41.

118 For the discussion of credit, see Brownell, *Tales From Tokio*, 95–101. For the reference to working hours see Ibid., 96. Another source stated, "most offices closed from noon until two o'clock and closed again after tea at four." Abend, *Treaty Ports*, 183. The *Japan Weekly Mail* stated that the working day began at ten and ended at five, and that "between 12 and 1 you might as well look for an elephant as for a merchant, for they are all at tiffin." JWM, October 6, 1888. A third source claimed that the working hours of most foreign merchants were three hours in the morning, a two-hour lunch break spent at the club, then three hours in the afternoon. Poole, *Death of Old Yokohama*, 26.

119 Harold Williams, *The Story of Shioya, of the James Estate, of James Yama and of the Shioya Country Club* (Kobe: The International Committee of the Kansai, 1984), 4.

120 *Eastern World*, August 5, 1905.

121 Powers, *Faces Along the Bar*, 96–7.

122 Scidmore, *Jinrikisha Days in Japan,* 26. In the early 1890s, a traveler could leave New York with $1200, and spend three months in Japan if he lived economically. Finck, *Lotos Time in Japan,* 1–2. Globetrotters could be very dismissive of what they saw. One visitor claimed there was "little besides [the Hyogo Hotel] to detain one at Kobe," stayed a day and pushed on to Kyoto. Gower referred to Mitsubishi as *Midgi Bitchi.* See Gower, *Notes of a Tour from Brindisi to Yokohama,* 65, 68. One can easily imagine how Kobe residents, proud of their settlement as a garden spot in the East, reacted to this.

123 JWM, October 6, 13, 27, 1888, November 10, 1888. In the October 13 issue, "A British Merchant" thanked Hall for speaking so eloquently in defense of the mercantile community. Norman later published a book entitled *The Real Japan* (1908; reprint, Wilmington, Delaware: Scholarly Resources, Inc., 1973) in which he sought to offer a view of Japan that filled the gap between "large and elaborate treatises on history, geography, monuments, etc." and the "superficial narratives" of globetrotters.

124 *Japan Gazette,* May 10, 1884.

125 Dixon, *Land of the Morning,* 244, 272–3; Gordon, *An American Missionary in Japan,* 199.

126 Crow, *Highways and Byeways,* 298; Finck, *Lotos Time in Japan,* 280. A more reliable source suggests that the number of missionaries in 1890 was 175. Hillevi Toiviainen, "Search For Security: United States Citizens in the Far East, 1890–1906," Ph.D. diss., Jyvaskylan Yliopisto, Jyvaskyla, 1986, 353. One estimate of the American financial investment in Japanese missions from 1859 to the 1950s exceeded 100 million dollars. Schwantes, *Japanese and Americans, A Century of Cultural Relations,* 257. Often, Japanese were more interested in missionaries as sources of information than of religious enlightenment. One missionary related: "One man spent a whole forenoon with me talking about Christianity, his real purpose being to find out whether Christian funerals cost as much as Buddhist ones." Gordon, *An American Missionary in Japan,* 50.

127 William Elliot Griffis, *Verbeck of Japan* (New York: Fleming H. Revell, 1900), 100; Crow, *Highways and Byeways,* 203. One visitor speculated in 1880 that the impending construction of a tea-firing godown next to the Union church in Kobe would force the church to move because of the chatter of the coolies. See Bridges, *A Lady's Travels,* 302. While missionaries welcomed foreign residents of any nationality, their churches were intended for the Japanese; Reverend C.M. Williams' Yokohama church was a good example. Henry St. George Tucker, *The History of the Episcopal Church in Japan* (New York: Charles Scribner's Sons, 1938), 80.

128 Mary Pruyn, *Grandmamma's Letters from Japan* (Boston: James H. Earle, 1877), 79, 22–3; Scidmore, *Jinrikisha Days in Japan,* 26. Pruyn, observing the degraded condition of the Japanese lower classes, wrote, "The people are very wicked and have some very bad practices; and God punishes them by letting them be weak and sickly." Pruyn, *Grandmamma's Letters,* 85. Clark later felt compelled to praise the "TRUE GOD" by singing a religious hymn while sitting in the lap of the "great bronze idol" of the Daibutsu at Kamakura. Yet after many months in the interior away from Western civilization, Clark was overjoyed to see the "civilized and Christian community" of Yokohama once again. See Clark, *Life and Adventure in Japan,* 15, 19–20, 135.

129 Gordon, *An American Missionary in Japan,* 119; Griffis, *The Mikado's Empire,* 344–5; Finck, *Lotos Time in Japan,* 63; Crow, *Highways and Byeways,* 230, 40. Missionaries earned the wrath of others as well: Lafcadio Hearn once wrote, "Personally, of course, I think the missionaries ought to be put on a small ship, and the ship scuttled at a reasonable distance of one thousand miles from shore." Hearn, *The Japanese Letters of Lafcadio Hearn,* 190.

130 Scidmore, *Jinrikisha Days in Japan,* 11; Dixon, *Land of the Morning,* 243.

131 Sandra Taylor, "Abby M. Colby: The Christian Response to a Sexist Society," *The New England Quarterly* 52 (March 1979): 69; Gordon, *An American Missionary in Japan*, 4–13.

132 Gordon, *An American Missionary in Japan*, 11.

133 "The Same Old Humbug," *Eastern World*, October 3, 1896; "An Annual Humbug," Ibid., July 28, 1900.

134 Rotundo, *American Manhood*, 172–3.

135 Chudacoff, *Age of the Bachelor*, 174–80.

136 Travel outside the ports – for health purposes or scientific work only – was possible only by applying at the American consulate for a special passport that listed the intended route and all planned stops. Passports were valid for six months, and those stopped in the interior without them were subject to arrest. MD, M133/60, Swift to Blaine, No. 45, September 18, 1889; Ibid., M133/61, No. 124, June 2, 1890. Though the regulations remained in force, by the 1880s the Japanese had relaxed their enforcement somewhat, allowing missionaries to teach and do missionary work in the interior. Some missionaries believed that the proscription on travel was primarily to prevent trade in the interior, and took advantage of the chance to go inland. Gordon, *An American Missionary in Japan*, 88.

137 Two Canadian missionaries named Cochran and McDonald provide a good example of this, not being "content to live comfortably in the pleasant Western settlement on Yokohama Bluff. They had come more than 8,000 miles 'to preach to the heathen' and felt that it was 'poor policy to stay within twenty miles of them, instead of going right in amongst them where they were,' that is, in Tokyo." Letter from George Cochran, April 22, 1874, *Wesleyan Missionary Notices* 24 (August 1874): 377, quoted in A. Hamish Ion, *The Cross and the Rising Sun, The Canadian Protestant Missionary Movement in the Japanese Empire, 1872–1931* (Waterloo, Ontario: Wilfrid Laurier University Press, 1990), 39.

138 One prospective employee of the Japanese government refused to sign a contract containing a clause prohibiting him to teach the Christian religion. "It is impossible," he said, "for a Christian to dwell three years in the midst of a pagan people, and yet keep entire silence on the subject nearest his heart." In this case, the Japanese relented and struck out the clause. See Clark, *Life and Adventure in Japan*, 10–12. For a good summary of missionary attitudes, see Ibid., Chapter 11, "The Missionary Outlook," 215–30.

139 Neuman, *America Encounters Japan*, 68; Gordon, *An American Missionary in Japan*, 87–8; MD, M133/62, Swift to Blaine, No. 157, October 6, 1890; Ibid., No. 169, October 25, 1890. Missionaries supported treaty revision in the hope that it would mollify anti-foreign agitation and increase their safety. See MD, M133/63, Swift to Blaine, No. 206, February 7, 1891; Ibid., M133/62, No. 171, October 31, 1890; Ibid., October 25, 1890, enclosing, Newton to Swift, October 17, 1890.

140 MD, M133/62, Swift to Blaine, No. 171, October 31, 1890. J.C. Hepburn, a Presbyterian missionary of long experience in Japan, wrote that "the mercantile community are quite satisfied with the old order but it is a great obstacle to missionary work." Presbyterian Board of Foreign Missions, Presbyterian Historical Society, Hepburn to Gillespie, January 21, 1890, reel 110, cited in Hillevi Toiviainen, "Search For Security," 372.

141 A majority of missionaries to Japan in the late nineteenth century were women. For this and many other details concerning women missionaries in Japan, see Taylor, "Abby M. Colby: The Christian Response to a Sexist Society," 68–79. In October, 1860, the American consul gave a ball "in honor of the Commodore and the officers of the *Hartford*" – the first ever in Kanagawa – to which all Americans were invited. Joseph Heco noted that "very few ladies were present; only two Englishwomen and

three or four female American missionaries," but that the function was "a great success" nonetheless. Heco, *Narrative of a Japanese*, 1: 257.

142 Abend, *Treaty Ports*, 177. Abend mentions that the "International Banking Corporation ... did not permit its white employees to marry until they had reached the grade of accountants, which usually required a decade of service in the Orient." The American firm of Augustine Heard and Company had a similar policy.

143 According to the American Citizens' Registry for 1890, only three of twenty-nine merchants were married: Daniel Barton Taylor, a tea taster; F.H. Ziegfeld, a clerk; and Alfred J. McGlew, a tea buyer, who had three children. OHD, M460/4, Smithers to Wharton, No. 6, January 22, 1891, enclosing Register of American Residents at U.S. Consulate at Osaka and Hyogo, December 31, 1890. For a more detailed discussion of the implications of the gender imbalance, see Chapter 2.

144 Ronald Hyam, "Empire and Sexual Opportunity," *Journal of Imperialism and Commonwealth History* 14 (1986): 53. Hyam's article, dealing with British imperialism, emphasizes the relationship between the diminished opportunity for sexual expression at home after the 1880s and its flowering abroad. One visitor observed in 1871 that there were only thirty "socially acceptable women" in Yokohama. Blum, *Yokohama in 1872*, 27. Some female port residents were "not exactly refined." Once, a parson's wife "got drunk at a ball in 1865 and 'made a fearful exhibition of herself. She was sick and managed to make an awful mess over herself and others,'" Quoted in Cortazzi, "Yokohama: Frontier Town, 1859–1866," 14.

145 Rotundo, *American Manhood*, 121. See also Charles E. Rosenberg, "Sexuality, Class and Role in 19th-Century America" in Elizabeth H. and Joseph H. Pleck, eds., *The American Man* (Englewood Cliffs: Prentice-Hall, Inc., 1980), 219–54.

146 Griffis, *The Mikado's Empire*, 344.

147 Smith, *Ten Weeks in Japan*, 263. Lines from Rudyard Kipling's "MacAndrew's Hymn" suggest that Westerners sometimes acted without moral restraint in the eastern ports: "Judge not, O Lord, my steps aside at Gay Street in Hongkong .... Jane Harrigan's and Number Nine." See Williams, *Tales of the Foreign Settlements in Japan*, 41. One visitor to the Gankiro expressed surprise at the "systematic way in which the authorities conducted this establishment." Two Japanese officers pointed out the building's beauties "with as much pride as if they were exhibiting an ancient temple sacred to their dearest gods." Posted on the wall was a "tariff of charges," and "seated in rows on the verandah were the 'moosmes' themselves." De Fonblanque, *Niphon and Pe-che-li*, 45–6. Americans referred to the establishment as the "Grand Cairo"; the British as the "Crystal Palace." Blum, *Yokohama in 1872*, 43.

148 Rotundo, *American Manhood*, 124.

149 Abend, *Treaty Ports*, 177–80. The "China Coasters" were Americans from the barbary coast of San Francisco, and some Europeans, many of whom "amassed considerable fortunes by their tours." Ibid., 178. Some club events, such as the one held on the evening of May 25, 1868 at the Yokohama United Club, were held especially for bachelors. See Boyer, *Naval Surgeon*, 47. One American from Nevada, tired of petite Japanese women, remarked upon finally seeing a Western woman, "Well, now, I guess it's a fine thing to see a full-grown white woman again." Bridges, *A Lady's Travels*, 298.

150 Works dealing with the rise of leisure culture include Kathy Peiss, *Cheap Amusements: Working Women and Leisure in Turn-of-the-Century New York* (Philadelphia: Temple University Press, 1986); David Nasaw, *Going Out, The Rise and Fall of Public Amusements* (New York: Basic Books, 1993); Lewis A. Erenberg, *Steppin' Out: New York Nightlife and the Transformation of American Culture, 1890–1930* (Chicago: University of Chicago Press, 1981).

151 Boyer, *Naval Surgeon*, 31–2. One observer described foreigners who "attached [themselves] to one of the charming little girls which Japanese matrimonial agents are

always ready to produce, and whose services as housekeepers can be obtained upon easy terms for a definite or indefinite period." See Holland, *Old and New Japan*, 274.

152 For one of many examples of the missionary accusation, see Finck, *Lotos Time in Japan*, 63. For the use of prostitutes, see Eastern World, February 4, 1899. Those living in the interior, no doubt, made similar arrangements. Arthur Collins Maclay suggested that the boredom of living amidst the Japanese caused many to "leave an unfortunate progeny to drag out a degraded existence" after they returned home. Maclay, *A Budget of Letters*, 84. For the directory, see *Minato-no-hana, Yokohama kidan* (Chinji Gokakoku: Yokohama Banashi, 1862), cited in Williams, *Foreigners in Mikadoland*, 109–10.

153 Chudacoff, *Age of the Bachelor*, 135–9; Cressy quotation from Ibid., 139.

154 Abend, *Treaty Ports*, 179. Some evidence suggests that Japanese mistresses may have caused some embarrassment. Speculating on why foreigners moved away from Kitano-cho, Harold Williams stated that "Some of the élite in Kitano-cho, Kobe, were inclined to look down on those who went so far out to live ... Shioya [in Suma] was a place where foreigners with money sought to hide their thirsts or their domestic arrangements." Quoted in Clark, "Shioya Country Club," 35.

155 For the Americans marrying Japanese, see KD, M135/18, Greathouse to Wharton, No. 194, June 29, 1889; Ibid., No. 243, July 12, 1890; Ibid., Scidmore to Wharton, No. 298, January 12, 1891. A description of Edward Lake appears in Earns and Burke-Gaffney, *Across the Gulf of Time*, 128. Other Westerners, including James Williams, N. Gray and Michael Banks, either cohabited with or married Japanese women. see Ibid., 79, 85, 100.

156 OHMC, Yamada to Stahel, December 2, 1879; OHD, Stahel to Payson, November 18, 1879. There were, no doubt, many such children; an American missionary referred to an Englishman who forsook responsibility for several children he had by a Japanese woman; she took one of them in. See Pruyn, *Grandmamma's Letters from Japan*, 95–6.

157 "Hence Loathed Melancholy," JWM, February 16, 1879. This letter came in response to an earlier letter to the editor entitled "The Letter of an Exile." Missionaries saw the value of women differently, their main purpose being to illustrate the "Christian doctrine of the worth of a woman as the immortal child of God" to a nation without sufficient respect for its own women. Gordon, *An American Missionary in Japan*, 173–85.

158 Robert V. Hine, *Community on the American Frontier, Separate but Not Alone* (Norman: University of Oklahoma Press, 1980), 74.

159 Robert R. Dykstra, *The Cattle Towns* (Lincoln: University of Nebraska Press, 1968), 253.

160 Quoted in Chudacoff, *Age of the Bachelor*, 120.

161 Scidmore, *Jinrikisha Days in Japan*, 25.

162 Jeanne-Pierre Lehmann, *The Image of Japan, from Feudal Isolation to World Power, 1850–1905* (London and Boston: Allen and Unwin, 1978), 43.

CHAPTER THREE

1 Smith, *Ten Weeks in Japan*, 70.

2 Jacobson, *Barbarian Virtues*, 4.

3 Ralph W. Emerson, *The Conduct of Life and Other Essays* (London: Dent, 1908), 192.

4 Lester Frank Ward, *Dynamic Sociology, or Applied Social Science* (1883; reprint, New York: Greenwood Press, 1968), 35.

5 For one summary of such persistent mythology, see Trachtenberg, *The Incorporation of America*, 87. Other statements of it include Mansel G. Blackford and K. Austin Kerr, *Business Enterprise in American History* (Boston: Houghton Mifflin, 1990), 114–16.

6 Malloy, *Treaties, Conventions*, 2: 1002.

7 Representing this view are Charles S. Campbell, *The Transformation of American Foreign Relations, 1865–1900* (New York: Harper and Row, 1976), 107–21; and

David M. Pletcher, *The Awkward Years, American Foreign Relations Under Garfield and Arthur* (Columbia: University of Missouri Press, 1962), 195–218.

8 Charles Stuart Kennedy, *The American Consul, A History of the United States Consular Service, 1776–1914* (New York: Greenwood Press, 1990), 168–9.

9 The most notable example was Heard's use of Dorr to get currency exchanged into gold for export for profit from Japan in the autumn of 1859. See Chapter 1.

10 Henry Arthur Tilley, *Japan, the Amoor and the Pacific* (London: Smith, Elder and Company, 1861), 119–20.

11 Allen Nevins, *Hamilton Fish: The Inner History of the Grant Administration* (New York: Dodd, Mead and Co., 1936), 119.

12 William Barnes and John Heath Morgan, *The Foreign Service of the United States: Origins, Developments and Functions* (Washington D.C.: Government Printing Office, 1961), 134.

13 ARP, "Samuel S. Lyon," Pitney to William McKinley, June 14, 1897. One U.S. Consul recommended his son for the post of deputy consul, a recommendation that the State Department approved. See OHD, M460/4, Smithers to Wharton, No. 171, October 26, 1891; Ibid., No. 210, January 30, 1892.

14 ARP, "Thomas R. Jernigan," W.P. Roberts to Secretary of State, February 27, 1885; Ibid, W.N.H. Smith to M.W. Ransom, March 2, 1885; Ibid., R.H. Battle to Grover Cleveland, March 5, 1885; Ibid., O. Coke to M.W. Ransom, April 25, 1885.

15 ARP, "Julius Stahel," Julius Stahel to Carl Schurz, March 1, 1877.

16 De Benneville Randolph Keim, *A Report to the Hon. George S. Boutwell, Secretary of the Treasury, upon the Condition of the Consular Service* (Washington D.C.: Government Printing Office, 1872), 184. "It has always struck me," Keim wrote, "that a majority of the persons filling the consular offices, unable or unwilling to appreciate the importance of their positions in the eyes of the community in which they reside, as soon as they get beyond the restraints of public opinion at home, cut loose from all moral obligations, and act in a manner as astonishing to themselves, I should say, as it is to the calm judgement of those who are able to preserve their self-respect without the influence and assistance of home opinion."

17 Keim, *Report*, 174.

18 Dennett, *Americans in Eastern Asia*, 669, 670, 672.

19 See Eldon Griffin, *Clippers and Consuls, American Consular and Commercial Relations with Eastern Asia, 1845–1860* (Ann Arbor, Michigan: Edwards Brothers, Inc., 1938), 59–100.

20 OHD, M460/1, Turner to Assistant Secretary of State, No. 13, August 31, 1872; OHD, M460/3, Patton to Addee, No. 6, August 4, 1884. Three years later, the consulate lacked "blanks and envelopes of all kinds, a postal scale" and was "quite destitute of flags." OHD, M460/2, Newwitter to Cadwalader, No. 7, December 7, 1875. Often consuls were called upon to explain what seemed – to officials with no understanding of local conditions – outrageous expenses to the State Department. A good example was Julius Stahel's irritated response to a demand for information about the scope of the Kobe consulate's activity and the expenses it incurred. See OHD, M460/3, Stahel to Davis, No. 198, April 16, 1883.

21 OHD, M460/4, Smithers to Wharton, No. 8, December 19, 1889.

22 OHD, M460/4, Smithers to Wharton, No. 22, May 29, 1890.

23 Griffin, *Clippers and Consuls*, 110. In response to a request from Nathan Newwitter to translate an official document, the American missionary O.H. Gulick responded by stating that he was too busy, and added that he hoped Newwitter would "be successful in finding one more competent than myself [for] the work of translation." OHMC, Gulick to Newwitter, January 25, 1876.

24 OHMC, State Department to Stewart, September 15, 1868; Ibid., Comptroller's Office to Stewart, April 21, 1870; OHD, M460/2, Stahel to Seward, No. 3, August 23,

1877. American difficulties with interpreters contrast sharply with the British. Ernest Satow, for example, remained in Japan from 1862 until 1882, and by 1866 was speaking Japanese quite well. See Satow, *A Diplomat in Japan*, preface, 156–8.

25 KD, M135/14, Van Buren to Davis, No. 739, September 21, 1883. Earlier, the U.S. legation at Kanagawa suspended its interpreter A.L. Portman for incompetence. OHMC, DeLong to Frank, December 3, 1870.

26 OHD, M460/3, Stahel to Adee, No. 245, December 26, 1883. Even when competent interpreters were on hand, merchants were forced to deal with "Japanese officials through the medium of two interpreters," a task that quickly became "wearisome." De Fonblanque, *Niphon and Pe-che-li*, 90–1.

27 KD, M135/14, Van Buren to Davis, No. 836, September 18, 1884.

28 Ezra J. Warner, *Generals in Blue: Lives of the Union Commanders* (Baton Rouge: Louisiana State Press, 1964), 469–70; ARP, "Julius Stahel," clippings from *New York Times*, December 4, 1912; *Washington Post,* December 5, 1912. One letter of support to the State Department, without apparent hyperbole, described Stahel as "a gallant officer, learned in several languages and a gentleman of intelligence and integrity with excellent business qualifications." Ibid., W. MacVeagh to Frederick W. Seward, July 14, 1877.

29 ARP, "Julius Stahel," S.W. Pomeroy to W.M. Evarts, October 24, 1878; Ibid., H.B. Hyde to Henry C. Bowen, April 18, 1882.

30 OHD, M460/2, Stahel to Payson, No. 39, October 14, 1879. Stahel later requested copies of "Abbot's or Bouvier's Law Dictionary" to supplement consular holdings. OHD, M460/3, Stahel to Adee, No. 212, July 23, 1883. Concerning different matters, other consuls displayed as much integrity as Stahel. Thomas Jernigan, consul at Kobe in 1886, confronted an American sea-captain, Horace Staples, whom he probably suspected of "running out" his ship – a practice by which a captain would make life aboard ship unbearable, inducing some of the crew to desert, and saving the wages due them upon discharge. The captain then hired cheaper Asian crewmembers, saving the difference in wages. Determined to protect American seamen from abuses, Jernigan resolved to "promote justice all around." Jernigan fined Staples $25 for his "insolent behavior" in court. He also noted that Staples' struck a Japanese shoemaker over a disagreement about a bill. "Such conduct," he wrote, "is calculated to bring my government into disrepute among the working classes of this consular district … among whom it is now extremely popular." OHD, M460/3, Jernigan to Porter, No. 11, June 17, 1886. For the practice of running out, see De Benneville Randolph Keim, *A Report*, 174. Earlier, Thomas Van Buren had worked to eliminate running out in Shanghai, stating, "I have made up my mind to cure this evil." See OHMC, Van Buren to Stahel, February 20, February 13, 1879.

31 MD, M133/27, John Bingham to Hamilton Fish, No. 45, January 17, 1874; Ibid., No. 56, February 19, 1874; Ibid., No. 65, March 9, 1874; Ibid, M133/28, No. 114, August 31, 1874.

32 Dennett, *Americans in Eastern Asia*, 515.

33 MD, M133/31, Bingham to Fish, No. 328, January 19, 1876.

34 Bingham to Grant, undated, Bingham Papers, Ronsheim Collection, reel 4, No. 2075, cited in Philip Ned Dare, "John A. Bingham and Treaty Revision with Japan: 1873–1885," Ph.D. diss., University of Kentucky, 1975, 78.

35 MD, M133/36, Bingham to Fish, No. 356, March 9, 1876; Ibid., No. 636, September 27, 1877. Consistent with the spirit of Bingham's position, the U.S. government in 1883 returned the Shimonoseki indemnity, which Japan had paid as a result of an attack on an American ship twenty years earlier. Furthermore, in April 1879, the U.S. proclaimed a new commercial convention with Japan, which annulled the previous unequal treaties and returned a measure of tariff autonomy to the Japanese. The 1879

agreement would not, however, go into effect until the Japanese concluded similar conventions with all other treaty powers. Treat, *Diplomatic Relations*, 2: 167–181; Malloy, *Treaties, Conventions*, 1021–24. Clearly, the U.S. was unwilling to give up the commercial advantage it enjoyed until all other nations did so; the treaty suggests American sympathy for the Japanese position, if not an actual commitment to Japanese equality. For a complete treatment of Bingham's career in Japan, see Dare, "John A. Bingham and Treaty Revision with Japan."

36 For a detailed analysis of the role of these three men, see Deborah Claire Church, "The Role of the American Diplomatic Advisors to the Japanese Foreign Ministry, 1872–1887, Ph.D. diss., University of Hawaii, 1978. E.H. House, the American editor of the *Tokio Times*, was also an unabashed opponent of the unequal treaties. See E.H. House, "The Martyrdom of an Empire," *Atlantic Monthly* 47 (January–June 1881): 610–23.

37 ARP, "Thomas M. Patton," Kobe residents, including J. Walsh, C.P. Hall, M. Drummond, Colgate Baker, R.S. Walsh and F.H. Ziegfeld to Grover Cleveland, April 27, 1885.

38 ARP, "Julius Stahel," Stahel to Carl Schurz, March 17, 1877; *Hiogo News*, July 7, 1884.

39 OHD, M460/2, Stahel to Seward, (No despatch number) October 8, 1877.

40 *Hiogo News*, August 1, 1868.

41 Under the U.S. statutes after 1878, U.S. consuls could hear and decide "all cases where the maximum fine did not exceed $500, or the maximum term of imprisonment did not exceed ninety days." In all cases where the fine exceeded $100 or the imprisonment sixty days, the accused had the right to appeal to the U.S. Minister to Japan. Richard T. Chang, *The Justice of the Western Consular Courts in Nineteenth-Century Japan* (Westport, Conn. and London: Greenwood Press, 1984), 11.

42 JWM, October 7, 14, 21; December 9, 1876; E.G. Holtham, *Eight Years in Japan*, 218–19. The Japanese response to this case was predictable. They were concerned much less with the specifics of the case than with the principle involved when an "independent Government with sovereign rights" was forced to go before a consular court "in the same manner [as] ordinary commoners." See *Nichi Nichi Shimbun*, December 11, 1876, translated in JWM, December 16, 1876.

43 *Nichi Nichi Shimbun*, translated in JWM, February 12, 1876.

44 Chang, *Western Consular Courts*, 122, 131–2. Of all leading cases referred to by one authority on the U.S. consular courts, only one could be construed as unfair to a Japanese plaintiff. In 1868, the Japanese merchant "Wooyedaya Shosichi" sold Schultze, Reis and Company an amount of tea, and delivered it to the company's godown, where it was later destroyed by fire before inspection. The court decided that the American merchant was not liable for the loss, even though the goods "were in his trust and he became responsible for their safety" after his servant accepted delivery. See G.H. Scidmore, *Outline Lectures*, 239. Under the provisions of extraterritoriality, appeals were heard in the circuit court for the district of California. One of the few cases appealed in this jurisdiction – a dispute between the China and Japan Trading Company and Hashimoto Tozayemon over the terms of a lease – resulted in a favorable decision for the Japanese. See OHMC, Fobes to Turner, June 28, 1872; Gon Rei of Hiogo ken to Newwitter, December 21, 1876; China and Japan Trading Company to Newwitter, December 23, 1876; Decision of U.S. Circuit Court in the case of John Twombly vs. Hashimoto Tozayemon, November 26, 1877.

45 Chang, *Western Consular Courts*, 128–9.

46 Ibid., 53, note 45.

47 Chang, *Western Consular Courts*, 13; Keim, *A Report*, 3–11.

48 Griffin, *Clippers and Consuls*, 43.

49 Ibid., 103.

50 For consultation in solving the variety of merchants' problems, the consulate at Hyogo was stocked with the following volumes: Wheaton's *International Law*; Parsons on shipping, insurance, partnership, notes and bills and contracts; Sedgwick on damages; Greenleaf on evidence, Kent's *Commentaries*; Wharton's *Criminal Law*. OHMC, Inventory of Property of U.S. Consulate for Osaka/Hiogo, August 1, 1884.

51 Rotundo, *American Manhood*, 203.

52 Wiebe, *The Search For Order*, 27.

53 Rotundo, *American Manhood*, 195–6.

54 Ibid., 205.

55 OHMC, Staples to Frank, February 18, 1871.

56 OHMC, Statement of Benjamin Gall to Morioka, June 29, 1877; Ibid., Robinet to Saibansho, April 10, 1869.

57 OHMC, Jenkins to Benson, September 30, 1878; Wiggins to Benson, May 7, 1878; Government Office to Stahel, January 23, 1878; Government Office to Benson, June 7, 1878; Board to Stahel, October 28, 1878; Government Office to Stahel, January 20, 1878. Japanese guilty of such petty thievery would not, one assumes, have come to the ports for employment had they had been well off to begin with. These cases represent scores of similar reports from the Kobe archive. The Yokohama archive, destroyed by fire in 1923, doubtless contained such reports in proportion to its larger American merchant population.

58 For a detailed discussion of the treatment of Japanese lawbreakers in the ports, see Chapter 5.

59 OHMC, Walsh, Hall and Company to Frank, November 4, 1871. Sometimes the American consulate acted as rent collector for Japanese landlords. For one example involving the collection of $300 rent owed to a Japanese by the China and Japan Trading Company tendered through the consular office, see OHMC, Fobes to Turner, May 10, 1873.

60 OHMC, Simon to Frank, August 14, 1869. The foreign settlements in Japan, unlike those of China, were not segregated by nationality. Reischauer, "Alien Land Tenure in Japan," 26.

61 For two examples, see OHMC, H. Nethersole to British Consul, January 23, 1871, which discusses a British subject suing two American citizens, and OHD, M460/2, Stahel to Woolley, No. 1604, June 9, 1882, which deals with a dispute between Meyer and Company, an American firm, and a British firm.

62 OHMC, Statement of Assistant Surgeon of U.S.S. *Colorado* J. R. Tryon, July 24, 1872; OHMC, Statement of Johnson to A. Gower, British Consul, July 21, 1872; OHMC, Thornton Jenkins to Turner, July 24, 1872. The records do not reveal the resolution of the conflict.

63 E. Sydney Crawcour, "The Tokugawa Heritage," in William W. Lockwood, ed., *The State and Economic Enterprise in Japan*, 42–4.

64 E. Sydney Crawcour, "Economic Change in the Nineteenth Century" in Marius Jansen, ed., *The Cambridge History of Japan* (Cambridge: Cambridge University Press, 1989), 5: 573, 577.

65 Alcock, *Capitol of the Tycoon*, 1: xvi.

66 Beasley, *Select Documents*, 50–1. For evidence that the Japanese government continued to withhold currency from foreign traders, see OHMC, Warren Tillson and Company to Paul Frank, February 28, 1868. Tillson related that he "went down to the Custom House with $500 to exchange into Boos" and was informed that he could get "only 291 Boos [ichibus] for $100." Tillson protested against "such a rate of exchange as being most unjust."

67 Smith, *Ten Weeks in Japan*, 247, 261–2.

68 Smith, *Ten Weeks in Japan*, 70–1. Japanese boatmen, or sendoes, occasionally exercised control over their Western employees. When Tillson and Company discharged its head sendo over a dispute, his crew refused to work until the man was reinstated. OHMC, Tillson and Company to Newwitter, July 28, 1877.

69 OHMC, Government Office to Paul Frank, January 24, 1868.

70 OHMC, Gon Chiji of Osaka to Newwitter, December 12, 1876; Ibid., Government Office to Newwitter, May 28, 1877. One foreign merchant, passing by a dog in a rickshaw, killed it with his fowling piece, causing local Japanese to complain about foreigners firing guns in crowded areas. Ibid., Government Office to Stahel, November 21, 1877. On one occasion, the government office complained that a Japanese policeman patrolling the Bund was bitten by a dog owned by Warren Tillson. Ibid., Government Office to Stahel, October 10, 1878. One visitor remembered that "Those who come into Tus'kiji [the foreign quarter in Tokyo] have little blocks of wood with Chinese characters upon them hanging from their belts" as cards of admission to the foreign settlement. "No native can enter ... without such blocks, which are given them by some official of the government." Julia D. Carrothers, *The Sunrise Kingdom, or Life and Scenes in Japan, and Woman's Work for Woman There* (Philadelphia: Presbyterian Board of Publication, 1879), 55.

71 OHMC, Government Office to Stahel, February 18, 1879; Ibid., Ito to Frank, April 8, 1868. Such control extended to restrictions on the importation of pigs and cattle after 1871, when a disease known as Rinderpest infected many animals in Russia and central Europe. JWM, August 30, 1871. The Japanese also made clear their intention to restrict the activities of the occasional foreigner determined to do business outside the treaty limits. Eugene Van Reed, who opened a rice and oil exchange in the city of Yedo, found that the Japanese government forbade its citizens to transact business there, causing him to go out of business. MD, M133/20, Shepard to Fish, No. 36, enclosing Delong to Fish, April 29, 1872.

72 After an unsuccessful attempt at managing its own municipal affairs, the foreign community at Yokohama turned local administration over to the Japanese. See Chapter 1.

73 OHMC, A.O. Gay, Chairman of Hiogo and Osaka general Chamber of Commerce to Stewart, September 2, 1870; Ibid., Chamber of Commerce to Frank, January 20, 1871; Ibid., Nakayama to Frank, January 30, 1871.

74 OHMC, Carroll and Company to Newwitter, September 7, 1877; Ibid., Government Office to Newwitter, September 13, 1877.

75 OHMC, Charles Wiggins to Newwitter, March 9, 1876. Other matters of concern included "offensive water running through the concession drains" and Japanese workmen, who in spite of all entreaties would not finish work according to specifications or on time. See Ibid., Osaka Municipal Council to Newwitter, January 15, 1877; John Keetch to Newwitter, August 14, 1877. On another occasion, an American merchant complained about the removal of a portion of the roadway to his house. Through his attorney, he threatened to "hold the local authorities responsible for any depreciation in value" resulting from the action. OHMC, Arthur Groom, Attorney for J.J. Staples to Newwitter, June 1, 1877. Japanese construction on Westerners' homes also went forward slowly. For a good example of merchant frustration, see *Eastern World*, March 7, 1896.

76 OHD, M460/3, Patton to Adee, No. 21, November 24, 1884; *Hiogo News*, November 18, 1884.

77 Malloy, *Treaties, Conventions*, 1007.

78 John Baxter Will, *Trading Under Sail Off Japan, 1860–99, The Recollections of Captain John Baxter Will, Sailing Master and Pilot*, ed. George Alexander Lenson (Tokyo: Sophia University Press, 1968), 23–4.

79 OHMC, Captain William J. Jones to Paul Frank, April 14, 16, 1868; R.B. Van

Valkenburgh to Paul Frank, May 5, 1868. The Japanese officials in question were instructed to apologize personally and unofficially, assuring Frank that "strict order has been given to them so that a similar occurrence will be avoided in the future." See Ito Shunske to Frank, April 29, 1868. The Japanese, ever sensitive to the illegal importation of opium, rigidly enforced the restrictions stating that the seals of cargo holds must be unbroken upon inspection. On one occasion, the captain of the American barque *J.H. Bowers* stated that his men, who "were intoxicated," accidentally broke the seal. Ibid, Japanese Customs to Stahel, April 9, 1879.

80 OHMC, Paul Frank to Moriyama, January 6, 1868; Ibid., Ito Shunske, vice governor of Hiogo to Paul Frank, February 26, 1868.

81 OHMC, Directive from U.S. Legation to Paul Frank, January 2, 1868; Ito Shunske to Frank, April 13, 1868. Restrictions tended to accumulate as time wore on. In 1873, the customshouse informed the U.S. consuls that they could no longer send ships stores or cargo by their own houseboats or cargoboats without a license and first registering their boats at the Saibansho. See OHMC, Carroll and Company to Turner, August 28, 1873; China and Japan Trading Company to Turner, August 28, 1873.

82 Bird, *Unbeaten Tracks in Japan*, 4.

83 OHMC, Ito to Stewart, February 27, 1869; Walsh, Hall and Company to Stewart, February 13, 1869; DeLong to Stewart, December 14, 1869. Walsh, Hall and Company paid such duties under protest and insisted that the monies be returned. Later, improvements in ships and improved strains of coal meant that coal export became possible on steamships, but American merchants insisted that the exemption from the export duty should continue. See *Tokio Times*, December 29, 1877, December 7, 1878; Japan Daily Herald, November 29, 1878.

84 OHMC, Walsh, Hall and Company to Stewart, April 13, 1869.

85 OHMC, Urin to Turner, June 11, 1873; Legation to Turner, May 27, 1873; Walsh, Hall and Company to Turner, June 30, 1873; Urin to Turner, July 3, 1873; Urin to Turner, December 19, 1873; Walsh, Hall and Company to Urin, December 29, 1873; Walsh, Hall and Company to Urin, February 12, 1874; Walsh, Hall and Company to Customshouse, February 26, 1874.

86 OHMC, Walsh, Hall and Company to Turner, May 27, 1873; Urin, Superintendent of Customs, to Turner, June 2, 1873.

87 Bridges, *Journal of a Lady's Travels*, 300. Aware of the danger of such fires, the Japanese proposed appropriate safety regulations in the form of a more stringent "flash test." See Treat, *Diplomatic Relations*, 2: 170.

88 KD, M135/12, Van Buren to Hitt, No. 549, July 26, 1881; Treat, *Diplomatic Relations*, 2: 106. The American consul, Thomas Van Buren, argued that government regulation would "deprive some of [the merchants] of rights clearly guaranteed by the treaties." Article III of the proposed regulations provided that owners would be responsible for defraying the cost of discrepancies between "weights and dimensions of goods presented for storage and those specified in the application" for storage. To American merchants this represented an unwarranted intrusion into the internal affairs of their companies; it was tantamount to keeping the Japanese government informed of their inventories. See Ibid., "Regulations," March 6, 1877. As early as 1873, an American merchant in Kobe named Flood had complained that the "local authorities of Hiogo have entirely omitted to provide for storage accommodation of inflammable goods." OHMC, Focke, German Consul to Turner, October 17, 1873. It seems clear that Americans wanted to enjoy the benefits of subsidized storage without submitting to the supervision accompanying such privileges.

89 Treat, *Diplomatic Relations*, 2: 130.

90 OHD, M460/5 Connolly to Uhl, No. 27, October 29, 1895, enclosing merchants' letters, esp. Walsh, Hall to Connelly, September 13, 1895.

91 OHMC, Committee of foreign merchants to Stewart, September 25, 1868. Earlier, the same committee complained specifically of the "obstructions imposed on traffic between Osaka and Kobe ... Osaka authorities are requiring a tax to be paid on produce – tea for example – and native merchants are unwilling to pay that as well as the customshouse tax required in Kobe. We the undersigned want Japanese merchants free of restrictions in disposing of their produce." Ibid., Committee of foreign merchants to Stewart, September 11, 1868.

92 MD, M133/20, Shepard to Fish, No. 36, enclosing Delong to Fish, April 29, 1872.

93 OHMC, J.D. Carroll and Company to Turner, March 1, 1873. Another example of alleged interference in trade was the Japanese government's complaint that the China and Japan Trading Company had stored 15,000 cases of kerosene oil in an unsafe godown, and wanted the oil moved. Fobes, the agent for the firm, replied that his company had enjoyed the privilege for "many years and could not justify the expense" of moving the oil, and stated that "any future request would be cheerfully complied with." Kanda to Newwitter, March 17, 1876; China and Japan Trading Company to Newwitter, March 18, 1876.

94 Dixon, *Land of the Morning*, 166–7; Tilley, *Japan, the Amoor and the Pacific*, 140; "Fantasies and Faces," JWM, August 26, 1876. Foreigners also complained of Japanese "literal mindedness." Once, a foreign resident who broke his glasses soon after arriving in Tokyo sent them out to be repaired. After waiting two weeks, he was told that the artisan could not reproduce the word "Philadelphia," on the frame, through which the crack ran. D.B. Simmons, "Five Years in Japan," *Galaxy* 5 (May 1868): 614.

95 Hoare, *Japan's Treaty Ports*, 129–30. More than once, the foreign merchant community demanded a foreign customs service such as the one in place in China. Foreigners handling goods for import and export, they believed, was one way to circumvent Japanese efforts to curtail smuggling. See, for example, *Nagasaki Express*, January 22, 1870. That the Japanese had no intention of allowing the mechanics of their trade to be supervised by foreigners only exacerbated the tension. One American, Richard Risley, undertook to import ice to Yokohama from Tientsin. At the customshouse, the inspector affixed his chop, and the ice was reloaded for delivery. By the time it reached its final destination however, the chop "had disappeared with the drippings, and the official at the dock refused to allow it to be landed." Blum, *Yokohama in 1872*, 23–4.

96 House, *Japanese Episodes*, 177–9.

97 Malloy, *Treaties and Conventions*, 1007.

98 OHMC, Smith, Baker and Company to Frank, January 12, 1871; Nakayama to Frank, January 12, 1871; Okamura to Frank, February 12, 1871; DeLong to Frank, July 2, 1871; Nakayama to Frank, September 27, 1871.

99 OHMC, A. Center to Paul Frank, September 6, 1871.

100 "Customs Notification," *Hiogo News*, May 27, 1873. Walsh, Hall and Company once complained that they were refused permission to ship goods from the jetty in front of their office. "The conduct of the customshouse officials," the company observed, "has been vexatious and much loss of time has been the consequence." OHMC, Walsh and Hall to Turner, July 18, 1872.

101 OHMC, Nakamura to Frank, September 27, 1871; Henry Wilson to Turner, March 6, 1874. For protests regarding night-loading permits, see Blanchard, agent of PMSSC, to Turner, August 8, October 31, 1874; Nagaoka Yoshiyuki to Turner, October 27, 1874. I have found no evidence of any successful appeals. Some of the appeals were based on the uneven application of the regulations – the Pacific Mail Steamship Company claimed that such fees were not assessed at Yokohama and Nagasaki.

102 OHMC, J. Gorham to Nathan Newwitter, August 20, 1877; Charles Wiggins to Benson, April 8, 1878; Customshouse to Daniel Turner, January 5, 1874.

103 OHMC, Nakazuira Sakutaro to Paul Frank, February 14, 1868; Earl English to J.B. Creighton, March 27, 1868.

104 JWM, February 12, 1887.

105 Paying bribes to customshouse officials was not unusual. For example, Albert Farley, the agent in Kobe for Augustine Heard and Company, remarked in 1868 that "living for the foreigners is dear, they having to submit to great squeezes from the custom house officials." See AHC, HM-37-1, Farley to A.F. Heard, January 19, 1868. One early visitor to Yokohama observed that "merchants, for their personal benefit, frequently obtain, by means of presents, what otherwise they might apply for in vain ... they have long since discovered the secret of softening the rigor of trade regulations of consular laws." De Fonblanque, *Niphon and Pe-che-li*, 58. Morimura Ichizaemon, a Japanese merchant doing business in Yokohama in the 1860s importing arms for the government forces, "gave up this lucrative business when he was requested – as a privileged merchant – to pay bribes to an official." Yasuzo Horie, "Entrepreneurship in Meiji Japan," in William Lockwood, ed., *The State and Economic Enterprise in Japan*, 192.

106 Smith, *Ten Weeks in Japan*, 403; 401–2.

107 Will, *Trading Under Sail*, 29.

108 OHMC, Nakayama to Frank, October 1, 1871. For additional examples of smuggling, see OHMC, Ito to Stewart, April 21, 1869; Government Office to Newwitter, March 10, 1875; Government Office to Stahel, September 24, 1881. That the Japanese were intent on enforcing the regulations against smuggling is clear from the case of the American vessel *Shimoda*, which Japanese customshouse officials boarded in May, 1870. The Japanese officer found that "the seals put on the hatches in the twilight of the day before were cut off" and that the cargo was partially out of the hatches. The officer informed an English subject named Lucas, the consignee of the vessel, that he would be assessed with a $60 penalty for the infraction. The customshouse held up unloading of another ship whose cargo was consigned to Smith, Baker and Company because the seal on the hatch was broken. See OHMC, Nakayama to Stewart, March 25, 1870; T.S. Kotaki, Superintendent of customshouse in Kobe to Frank, June 25, 1868.

109 KD, M135/18, Greathouse to Wharton, No. 236, June 11, 1890; Ibid., No. 258, September 2, 1890.

110 KD, M135/20, Tillotson to Quincy, No. 148, April 27, 1893. Ibid., 135/16, Greathouse to Porter, No. 26, December 21, 1886. The American merchant Eugene Gill once made application to export 124 packages of tea which he claimed were of Chinese origin to avoid the export duty. When the tea was found to be Japanese, Gill was required to pay the proper duty on the tea. The superintendent of the customs reported that Gill's original applications were made with intent to "defraud the revenue of Japan." OHMC, Superintendent of Customs in Kobe and Osaka to Lewis, September 8, 1875.

111 "Municipal Administration," JWM, February 16, 1879.

112 "The Appropriation of the Foreign Land Rent," JWM, February 23, 1879. Some Yokohama residents were reluctant to pay for gas obtained from a Japanese gas company to keep 100 lights burning in Yokohama. See "Street Lighting," JWM, February 26, 1876. Walsh, Hall and Company refused on principle to pay "certain back taxes" to the Municipal Council. Treat, *Diplomatic Relations*, 1: 468. Walsh, Hall and Company, sometime before 1875, loaned $474,000 to "Japanese contractors who engaged in filling up a swamp and building a canal at Yokohama." Ibid., 1: 578.

113 The paper pointed to a variety of projects as evidence of Japanese fiscal responsibility: a new wharf, jetties, breakwaters, bonded warehouses and roads, swamp reclamation and improvements to the Bund. JWM, July 29, 1882.

114 "The Arteries of Wealth," JWM, April 8, 1872.

115 OHMC, Hiogo Government Office to James Harris, July 17, 1872; Nakamura to Paul Frank, August 9, 1871. The Japanese habit of enforcing regulations on even the smallest amount of goods no doubt greatly irritated Americans. The China and Japan Trading Company complained once that it was forced to pay a duty on "three flowers" it shipped from Osaka to Kobe. See OHMC, China and Japan Trading Company to Turner, July 12, 1873.

116 JWM, May 6, 1876.

117 OHMC, Van Buren to Stahel, July 11, 1879.

CHAPTER FOUR

1 JWM,, October 6, 1888

2 Bird, *Unbeaten Tracks in Japan*, 16–18.

3 See Heco, *Narrative of a Japanese*, 1: 235. Heco's fluency in English made him naturally appealing as a business partner. With the exception of the multi-national China and Japan Trading Company, which in 1874 had two English, one Dutch and two American partners, (See OHMC, China and Japan Trading Company to Turner, November 4, 1873) Americans alone owned and operated all the other American firms, so far as the records I have consulted indicate.

4 For a fairly detailed discussion of some kinds of correspondence, see Pat Barr, *The Deer Cry Pavilion, A Story of Westerners in Japan, 1868–1905* (New York: Harcourt, Brace and World, Inc., 1968), 102–3. One resident recorded that "ship arrivals and departures meant red-letter days .... For a day or two before sailing, every business office in Yokohama was feverishly busy, sometimes the entire night through, with the preparation and hand-copying of letters and documents. Then followed days, even weeks, of leisurely routine until the next mail packet was ready to sail." Blum, *Yokohama in 1872*, 22.

5 AHC, HM-37-1, Farley in Yokohama to Heard, January 14, 1872; HM-55-1, Cunningham to Heard, January 27, 1873.

6 AHC, HM-55-1, J.K. Cunningham to Farley, January 8, 1873.

7 AHC, HM-55-1, J.K. Cunningham to Heard, February 19, 1873.

8 OHMC, China and Japan Trading Company to Benson, June 25, 1878.

9 OHMC, Van Buren to Stahel, February 13, 1879.

10 OHMC, Rice to Stahel, March 27, 1879. Van Buren acknowledged on one occasion the receipt of "an order upon Messrs Walsh and Hall in my favor" for U.S. gold $109.72. See OHMC, Van Buren to Stahel, May 22, 1879; Van Buren to Stahel, February 20, 1879. Apparently the practice was widespread. Warren Tillson and Company also agreed to employ a "young man named Shaw, now on the American ship Mount Washington" in his firm. Tillson promised that "he will not in any way become a charge on the government of the U.S.... should it be necessary to discharge him, we will undertake to pay his passage to any port on the coast or ship him in some homeward bound vessel." OHMC, D.H.Tillson and Company to Benson. May 29, 1878. It remains unclear whether such transactions amounted to a form of graft. The great Kanto earthquake and subsequent fire of 1923 destroyed practically all of the internal records of the Yokohama consulate, and no official record of how such money was applied to government accounts exists.

11 Williams, *Tales of the Foreign Settlements in Japan*, 337; Barr, *Deer Cry Pavilion*, 189. M.L. Gordon used the term "foreman" to describe a Christian banto in the service of an English merchant. Gordon, *An American Missionary in Japan*, 120.

12 Williams, *Tales of the Foreign Settlements*, 178.

13 "Japanese Character," JWM, April 12, 1884. Another contemporary wrote that "a trade was cultivated with the interior through native agents or *bantos*." J. Morris,

Advance Japan: A Nation Thoroughly in Earnest (London: W.H. Allen and Co., Ltd, 1895), 220.

14 KD, M135/16, Greathouse to Porter, No. 26, December 21, 1886, Enclosures A, B and C. Limited evidence suggests that other merchants ventured out of the ports in violation of the treaties to do business. In 1875, for example, Eugene Gill requested a pass from the Kobe consulate for the "purpose of studying the productions of tea of the following Ken: Hiroshima, Yamaguchi, Hamada, Shimane, Totori, Toiyooka and Tsuruga." OHMC, Eugene Gill to Turner, February 27, May 6, 1875. F.C. Jones observed that "Some Italian merchants in Japan for the purpose of buying silkworm eggs were much hampered by the restrictions on travel imposed on foreigners." This caused the Italian government to "negotiate a revised treaty which would have given partial judicial autonomy to Japan in return for freedom of movement for Italians within Japan." The objections of the other treaty powers killed the proposed agreement. Jones, *Extraterritoriality in Japan*, 86.

15 JWM, February 9, 1884. The missionary M.L. Gordon noted that passports were granted only for "health or scientific purposes," and stated that some believed this was a "technical phrase whose real object is to prevent trade in the interior. The ready granting of these passports to 'globetrotters,' circus companies, and so on, g[ave] color to this view." Gordon, *An American Missionary*, 88. Shifts in Japanese trade policy compounded the risk involved in exporting goods. In 1868, for example, the Japanese government suddenly decided to prohibit the shipment of rice from the port of Hyogo. OHMC, Stewart to Smith, Baker and Company; Walsh, Hall and Company; J.D. Carroll and Company; and Case and Company, August 15, 1868.

16 JWM, May 27, 1876. One globetrotter noted that the Hachioji Inn – just inside the treaty limits from Yokohama – was frequented by foreign merchants in the silk trade. Dixon, *Land of the Morning*, 131. He added that the charges there were outrageous. Ibid. Some limited evidence suggests that foreigners could go outside the treaty limits to conduct trade with passports meant only for travel. One American applied for a passport to visit Kyoto, and the U.S. consul, Burge Lewis, observed that "as the rose with any other name smells as sweet, and as the Japanese would not know the difference, you could just as well use my passport if I did not want it." OHMC, S.R. Moniz to Dr Adams, October 19, 1876.

17 JWM, October 27, 1888. There are numerous cases of bantos routinely transacting business for Western merchants. One representative example was "Matsugoochi," a banto employed by the American firm of Case and Company, who arranged for the sale of 570 red blankets to a Japanese merchant. OHMC, Henderson Grant to Scott Stewart, December 16, 1868.

18 Beasley, *Rise of Modern Japan*, 64. An even more lurid possibility was that of the Japanese government using peasant blood to dye the cheap woolen blankets of foreign manufacture. See Barr, *Deer Cry Pavilion*, 42.

19 OHMC, A.O. Gay to Turner, December 21, 1874.

20 OHMC, Kanda to Newwitter, January 11, 1876; J.D. Carroll and Company to Newwitter February 18, 1876; Kanda to Newwitter, May 30, 1876.

21 OHMC, Stewart to Robinet, Vice consul at Osaka, January 30, 1869.

22 OHMC, Schultz, Reis and Company to Stewart, May 29, 1869. See also OHMC, Saibansho to Turner, March 3, 1874, in which the Saibansho notified the China and Japan Trading Company that one of its servants had been arrested for gambling and was in the hands of the municipal police. This produced a similar letter of complaint. Merchants also feared Japanese control over other employees. Most Western visitors and residents were outraged by Japanese nudity. When foreigners declared Japan uncivilized because of such practices, the Governor of Kanagawa issued a formal notice instructing boatmen, carters, porters, laborers and coolies in what proper dress

was, and giving "coolie masters liberal assistance" to enforce the new guidelines. Finck, *Lotos Time in Japan*, 287. On one occasion, two Japanese policemen attacked two sendoes (Japanese boatmen necessary for unloading cargo) employed by Tillson and Company for wearing only their loincloths in defiance of the Japanese law forbidding public nudity. The police "severely clubbed" both men and inflicted two sword cuts on one. Tillson was outraged that the incident had occurred on his property and complained, "I do not think any policeman, foreign or native has a right to enter foreign dwellings without [a] warrant." OHMC, Tillson to Newwitter, May 29, 1877.

23 See, for example, OHMC, Daisangi of Hiogo to Stewart, October 19, 1870; Saisho Chozo to Frank, January 3, 1871. The Japanese government also reminded the American consuls that, until China negotiated a formal treaty with Japan, Chinese employees of American citizens need not be registered with the Japanese government, but that their American employers were "responsible for their conduct." Ibid., Saisho Chozo to Stewart, January 29, 1870. After 1868, the Chinese, whose status in Japan had been unclear, were required to register with the Japanese government. In 1878 those in the treaty ports became subject to Japanese authority.

24 *Hiogo News*, May 6, 1869. On one occasion, a merchant named Edward Kuhnhardt bought a number of kerosene bottles from a Japanese through his banto. When Kuhnhardt demanded to inspect the bottles before making payment, the Japanese became enraged; Kuhnhardt later wrote that the man used "abusive language, such as 'Mucha' and other words which I, although not understanding them, thought to be insulting and impertinent, the much more so, as they were accompanied by very wild, fierce and defying gestures." OHMC, Kuhnhardt to Newwitter, September 17, 1877.

25 OHMC, Fobes to Turner, July 13, 1874; Walsh, Hall and Company to Benson, May 27, 1878.

26 See, for example, OHMC, Government Office to Newwitter, September 19, 1877.

27 OHMC, Saibansho to Turner, August 29, 1874. Numerous other examples of such notification include the case of Goshibe Tarokichi, a China and Japan Trading Company employee, arrested and held for questioning concerning stolen goods. OHMC, Gon Rei of Hiogo ken to Newwitter, October 10, 1876.

28 His punishment was sixty blows. OHMC, Saibansho to Turner September 24, 1873. For other examples see OHMC, Saibansho to Lewis, August 15, 1875; Saibansho to Newwitter, September 19, 1879; Saibansho to Stahel, August 2, 1880.

29 OHMC, Saibansho to Turner August 26, 1874; Hiogo Saibansho to Newwitter January 24, 1876; Saibansho to Turner, June 10, 1874. Punishment varied in severity; the Japanese Yamazo was accused of stealing some inexpensive goods from Bush and Company, and was sentenced to "15 days circumspection over self." OHMC, Saibansho to Stewart, February 14, 1870.

30 OHMC, Chief officer of the Japanese Police to Robinet, September 10, 1869.

31 OHMC, Saibansho to Turner, December 21, 1869.

32 OHMC, Fobes to Turner, June 29, 1874.

33 One example is the claim of A. Watts against his servant Nakagawa. The Saibansho obtained ¥601 from Nakagawa's estate and remitted the money to Watts. OHMC, Osaka Saibansho to Newwitter December 18, 1876. On one occasion, a Japanese merchant died and the Saibansho liquidated his entire estate to pay his debts, leaving his widow, still indebted to an American merchant named Morse, pleading for more time to pay. See OHMC, Kobe Saibansho to Newwitter, April 25, 1877.

34 OHMC, China and Japan Trading Company to Stahel, July 12, 1879.

35 See OHMC, Ito to Stewart, May 26, 1868.

36 *Hiogo News*, May 6, 1869. This paper was the official organ of the American consulate in Kobe.

37 OHMC, Walsh, Hall and Company to Stahel, February 16, 1879.

38 OHMC, R.S. Walsh of Walsh Hall and Company to Stahel, March 12, 1879.

39 See, for example, Heco, *Narrative of a Japanese*, 1: 207.

40 James Edward Hoare, "The Chinese in the Japanese Treaty Ports, 1858–1899: The Unknown Majority," *British Association for Japanese Studies* 2 (1977): 20.

41 *Chronicle and Directory for China, Japan and the Philippines*, 1894.

42 Section IV of the regulations for land renters at Nagasaki stipulated that "No claimants who have hitherto conducted the business of Compradors ... shall be entitled to a selection of Water Frontage Lots, on the ground that it is their intention to carry on a wholesale business in future, as the nature of their previous occupation shall be considered evidence to the contrary." See National Archives, RG 84, Nagasaki Land Records, American Land Renters, Nagasaki, 1867. The land regulations issued by the foreign consuls at Kanagawa specified that only "bona-fide residents" could make application for land rental through the consuls. This excluded the Chinese because China lacked a formal treaty with Japan at the time. Heco, *Narrative of a Japanese*, 1: 251–2.

43 AHC, HM-37-1, Farley in Yokohama to Heard, January 14, 1872. One source claimed that in many households the Chinese butler, or head boy, "rule[d] the establishment." Scidmore, *Jinrikisha Days in Japan*, 20–1.

44 AHC, HM-58-1, Van Reed to Heard, May 4, 1864. The Chinese presence extended beyond commercial firms. In 1881, for example, the Grand Hotel in Yokohama employed a compradore named Long Ah Pow. See *Chronicle and Directory*, 1881.

45 John K. Fairbank and Merle Goldman, *Trade and Diplomacy on the China Coast, the Opening of the Treaty Ports, 1842–1854* (Cambridge: Harvard University Press, 1953), 13. Fairbank states that "the compradore, after 1842, enlarged his functions to supplant the hong merchant as the native Chinese collaborator of the foreign trader." Ibid., 466. See also Hao Yen-p'ing, *The Compradore in Nineteenth Century China: Bridge Between East and West* (Cambridge: Cambridge University Press, 1970).

46 Charles Drage, *Taikoo* (London: Constable and Co., 1970), Appendix III, 285–7. The term compradore is of Portuguese origin; the Chinese word, mai-pan, meant "selling manager."

47 Redesdale, *Mitford's Japan*, 29.

48 Smith, *Ten Weeks in Japan*, 71–2. One resident noted that "The Chinaman stands high in the estimation of the foreign merchant. His spoken word is taken without question even where tens of thousands of dollars are involved, when the most explicit contract in writing, signed and stamped with the Japanese merchant's seal, would be valueless, except as a memorandum." Brownell, *Tales From Tokio*, 72.

49 Quoted in Jacobson, *Barbarian Virtues*, 71.

50 Higham, *Strangers in the Land*, 25. See also Lucy Salyer, *Laws Harsh as Tigers: Chinese Immigrants and the Shaping of Modern Immigration Law* (Chapel Hill: University of North Carolina Press, 1995).

51 Jacobson, *Barbarian Virtues*, 75–6.

52 Jacob A. Riis, *How the Other Half Lives: Studies Among the Tenements of New York* (1890. Reprint. New York: Hill and Wang, 1967), 68. See also Michael Kimmel, *Manhood in America, A Cultural History* (New York: The Free Press, 1997), 93; Iriye, *Across the Pacific*, 30–1.

53 AHC, HM-55-1, A.O. Gay at Yokohama to Albert Heard in Canton, December 17, 1864.

54 AHC, HM-55-1, Cunningham to Heard, January 27, 1873.

55 Williams, *Tales of the Foreign Settlements*, 179–80.

56 Gribble, "The Preparation of Japan Tea," 12; Brownell, *Tales From Tokio*, 72.

57 Ohara and Okata, *Japanese Trade and Industry*, 155; Scidmore, *Jinrikisha Days in Japan*, 355. One one occasion, the Yokohama representative of Augustine Heard and

Company noted that some goods shipped from Japan weighed less upon their arrival in China. The Heard employee could not "account for it in any other way than that there has been a collusion to defraud between the Japanese merchants and the Chinese in charge of the godowns, and great care will be taken to prevent this in future." AHC, LV-1A, Letters from Franklin Field to Albert Heard, June 23, 1860.

58 MD, M133/20, Shepard to Fish, No. 49, June 20, 1872.

59 Tsuneo Tamba, *Yokohama ukiyoe* (Reflections of the Culture of Yokohama in the Days of the Port Opening), (Tokyo: Asahi shimbun sha, 1962), print numbers 10, 77, 80, 84, 85, 129, 293 and 353 illustrate many of these themes. I am indebted to James Edward Hoare, whose article, "The Chinese in the Japanese Treaty Ports, 1858–1899: The Unknown Majority," suggested the use of the ukiyo-e as a source.

60 Crow, *Highways and Byeways in Japan*, 13–4; Scidmore, *Jinrikisha Days in Japan*, 20–1. The *pidjin* phrase is from "Bishop of Homoco," *Exercises in the Yokohama Dialect*.

61 Griffis, *The Mikado's Empire*, 337–9. See also Dixon, *Land of the Morning*, 245.

62 Bird, *Unbeaten Tracks*, 15–16. See also Henry Knollys, *Sketches of Life in Japan* (London: Chapman and Hall, 1887), 226–7. Another visitor remarked that the Yokohama's numerous Chinese were "fat and well-to-do." Greey, *Young Americans in Japan*, 175. As late as the mid-1890s, one visitor noted that "Chinese compradores continue to walk unsmilingly through the streets in quiet majesty." Mabel Loomis Todd, *Corona and Coronet* (Boston and New York: Houghton, Mifflin and Company, 1898), 153.

63 Pruyn, *Grandmamma's Letters from Japan*, 73–4.

64 Greey, *Young Americans in Japan*, 176.

65 See, for example, AHC, HM-55-1, A.O. Gay at Yokohama to Albert Heard in Canton, September 29, 1865.

66 Barr, *Deer Cry Pavilion*, 101.

67 Crow, *Highways and Byeways*, 28; Black, *Young Japan*, 2: 24.

68 Tamba, *Yokohama ukiyoe*, print numbers 10, 81.

69 JWM, May 19, 1883.

70 OHMC, Government Office to Newwitter, August 29, September 1, September 10, 1877; Eugene Gill to Newwitter, August 31, September 3, September 5, September 10, September 25, 1877. Another typical example was the request of Thomas McGrath of the China and Japan Trading Company for American official help in securing the release of McGrath's Chinese "boy." See OHMC, China and Japan Trading Company to Nathan Newwitter, April 9, 1877. On September 1, 1896, Japanese authorities in Kobe seized a Chinese named Sae Fi Nam for entering the country with opium and smoking paraphernalia concealed in a pillow. Though he pleaded ignorance of Japanese laws, he remained in Japanese custody for some seven weeks before sentencing, much to the consternation of the foreign community. Cases like this were disturbing because they illustrated the local authorities' power to arrest Chinese and potentially disrupt foreign business. OHD, M460/5, Connelly to Rockhill, No. 84, October 27, 1896, enclosure 1, *The Kobe Herald*, October 23, 1896.

71 *Eastern World*, December 5, 1906.

72 See Homoco, *Yokohama Dialect*, 17.

73 AHC, Case 9, Memoranda of agreement between A. Heard and Chun Min Chee, dated July 6, 1864.

74 For an example of a Japanese request to register Chinese citizens in American employ, see OHMC, Nakayama to Frank, January 16, 1871. For British reluctance to subject the Chinese to Japanese control. see F.O. 262/149, Lowder at Yokohama to Parkes, No. 60, August 4, 1868; F.O. 262/173, M. Flowers at Nagasaki to Parkes, No. 5,

February 22, 1869, cited in Hoare," The Chinese in the Japanese Treaty Ports, 1858–99: The Unknown Majority," 23.

75 See JWM, 18 August, 1894. Laws against gambling and opium use were strongly enforced in Japan, but the Chinese did both and were usually not prosecuted in the ports. McIvor arranged with the Chinese consul to deport all Chinese known to engage in such abuses to protect the law-abiding segment of the Chinese community. Chinese leaders feared that untoward behavior by any Chinese would cause anti-Chinese incidents because of the animus of the Japanese common classes. The Chinese consul rounded up 500 shady characters on August 4, 1894, and escorted them to the Yokohama docks under strong police escort, along with 222 who went voluntarily. KD, M135/20, Consul General McIvor to Undersecretary Uhl, No. 50, August 13, 1894.

76 JWM, January 25, 1873.

77 Ibid.

78 Ibid.

79 JWM, February 1, 1873.

80 JWM, October 6, 1888.

81 JWM, November 10, 1888.

82 Ion, *The Cross and the Rising Sun*, 39, 39n16.

83 Lehmann, *The Image of Japan*, 50.

84 Todd, *Corona and Coronet*, 149, 153.

85 "Grenon," *Verdant Simple's Views of Japan*, (Yokohama: Kelly and Walsh, 1890), 8–9.

86 Holland, *Old and New Japan*, 268–9. The occasional Westerner in Japan was able to move from prejudice to acceptance. Clara Whitney, an American who married a Japanese, wrote a diary that traces the gradual transformation from revulsion at "heathen Japan" to genuine appreciation of Japan's sophistication. See Clara A.N. Whitney, Clara's Diary, *An American Girl in Meiji Japan*, eds. M. William Steele and Tamiko Ichimata, (Tokyo, New York: Kodansha International, Ltd, 1979).

87 Lears, *No Place of Grace*, 107–17.

88 Donald J. Mrozek, *Sport and American Mentality*, 1880–1910 (Knoxville: University of Tennessee Press, 1983), 3, Chapter 1.

89 OHMC, Upton to Newwitter, including "Translation of the Directions Printed in Japanese on Back of Passport," May 10, 1875.

90 Holtham, *Eight Years in Japan*, 62.

91 OHMC, H. Upton to Newwitter, November 6, 1876; Government Office to Newwitter, November 16, 1876.

92 JWM, October 7, 1876. For Japanese attempts at regulation, see OHMC, Van Buren to Newwitter, enclosing regulations, licensing requirements and fines, January 17, 1877.

93 Holtham, *Eight Years in Japan*, 63–4. One blatant case of foreigners ignoring the treaty regulations involved the shooting of 500 pheasants in Sendai to fulfill an order from London. See JWM, February 11, 1882.

94 JWM, October 6, 1888

CHAPTER FIVE

1 JWM, October 27, 1888.

2 Peter Dobkin Hall, "What Merchants Did with Their Money: Charitable and Testamentary Trusts in Massachusetts, 1780–1880" in Conrad Edick Wright and Katheryn P. Viens, eds, *Entrepreneurs, The Boston Business Community, 1700–1850* (Boston: Massachusetts Historical Society, 1997), 365.

3 Edward Chase Kirkland, *Dream and Thought in the Business Community, 1860–1900* (1956; reprint, Chicago: Ivan R. Dee, 1990), 7.

4 Ibid., 8–9. "The rate of failure in the post-bellum business world suggests how exceptional were the robber barons and their lesser cousins." Trachtenberg, *The Incorporation of America*, 86.

5 Quoted in Ibid., 22–3.

6 Ibid., 26. See also Thomas V. Dibacco, *Made in the U.S.A., The History of American Business* (New York: Harper and Row, 1987). Because of increasing productivity and the resulting deflation, Dibacco states that the "period after the Civil War until the turn of the century saw enormous business difficulties." Ibid., 140.

7 Jacobson, *Barbarian Virtues*, 14.

8 Kirkland, *Dream and Thought in the Business Community*, 26–7.

9 Ibid., 10.

10 Rotundo, *American Manhood*, 168.

11 Ibid.

12 For some of some of the details of Van Reed's career I have relied on Altman, "Eugene Van Reed, a Reading Man in Japan, 1859–1872". My interpretation of Van Reed's activities in Japan in association with Augustine Heard, however, is based on my own reading of his correspondence with the company.

13 AHC, HM-58-1, Van Reed to Albert Heard, September 20, 1863.

14 At Shimonoseki, Van Reed immediately applied for 100 tsubos of land – one parcel for Heard and Company, one for himself. "Should the town be opened to foreign intercourse," he stipulated, "this application was to remain valid as first applicants." AHC, HM-58-1, Van Reed to Albert Heard, September 9, October 3, 1864.

15 AHC, HM-58-1, Van Reed to Albert Heard, September 20, 1863. Later, he wrote, "Were it possible to procure the Russian Consulate, you would find it worth your while ... Official position is of great service with Jap. ideas." Ibid., Van Reed to Albert Heard, May 4, 1864.

16 AHC, HM-58-1, Van Reed to Heard, June 6, 1864.

17 In December Van Reed wrote that "Mr. Gay [another Heard representative] seemed to hang back" during the negotiations, and "did not relish at all the contract" but added that he would "be happy to assume their [Satsuma's] risk." Realizing Heard was in competition with Glover, he wrote, "We will yet drive Glover's from the field." AHC, HM-58-1, Van Reed to Heard, May 27, June 14, December 22, 1864.

18 At Van Reed's request, Heard had a "sample cannon" sent to him to show to the daimyo of Satsuma. AHC, HM-58-1, Van Reed to Albert Heard, July 27, August 20, September 11, 1864.

19 As early as August, 1864 – at Van Reed's request – three San Francisco merchants had written letters of support to the U.S. Legation for his application for the post of consul for the Sandwich Islands, vouching for his "capacity and integrity." See AHC, HM-58, letter of "committee of merchants," August 27, 1864. The fullest treatment of Van Reed's activities relating to contract labor in Hawaii are Hilary Conroy, *The Japanese Expansion into Hawaii, 1868–1898* (San Francisco: R and E Associates, 1973), 23–37, and Masaji Marumoto, "'First Year' Immigrants to Hawaii & Eugene Van Reed" in Hilary Conroy and T. Scott Miyakawa, eds, *East Across the Pacific, Historical and Sociological Studies of Japanese Immigration and Assimilation* (Santa Barbara: Clio Press, 1972), 5–39.

20 AHC, HM-58-1, Van Reed to Albert Heard, April 3, 1865.

21 The agreement under which the Japanese emigrants came to Hawaii stated that some of the workmen's wages would be "paid through the Hawaiian Consul General in Yokohama." Whether Van Reed anticipated profits in this way is unclear. See Conroy, *Japanese Expansion Into Hawaii*, 205. Official Japanese emigration to Hawaii was first approved in 1884, and for the next ten years, the N.Y.K. transported the great majority of laborers under government sponsorship. By 1895, some 27,000 emigrants had gone to Hawaii. Wray, *Mitsubishi and the N.Y.K.*, 264.

22 Rotundo, *American Manhood*, 204–5.

23 Thomas C. Cochran, *200 Years of American Business* (New York: Basic Books, 1977), 28.

24 Glen Porter and Harold C. Livesay, *Merchants and Manufacturers, Studies in the Changing Structure of Nineteenth-Century Marketing* (Chicago: Ivan R. Dee, 1971), 16.

25 "Japanese Character," JWM, April 12, 1884. Japanese sometimes took advantage of foreigners' ignorance by borrowing money and never repaying the loans. The Yokohama Augustine Heard representative lamented in 1872 that "Our experience of loans to Japanese is a bitter one. We made these loans on what we supposed to be the security of lands, but we were taken in. The documents we got for mortgage have turned out to be nothing other than paper, and the Houses and lands had been mortgaged over and over again before we had a finger in the pie. Japanese who borrow money are rogues of the first rank." AHC, HM-37-1, Farley to Heard, January 27, 1872.

26 KD, M135/16, Greathouse to Porter, No. 26, December 21, 1886, Enclosure A.

27 JWM, July 25, 1885.

28 Ohara and Okata, *Japanese Trade and Industry*, 156. Many American companies were small and lacked the financial resources to easily absorb such losses.

29 Cochran, *200 Years of American Business*, 28.

30 Quoted in Lewis E. Atherton, *The Frontier Merchant in Mid-America* (Columbia: University of Missouri Press, 1971), 13.

31 Finck, *Lotos Time in Japan*, 283.

32 JWM, July 22, 1876.

33 Joseph H. Longford, "The Commercial Morality of the Japanese," *Contemporary Review* 87 (January–June, 1905), 710.

34 JWM, February 9, 1884.

35 "The Japanese Bankruptcy Law," JWM, June 24, 1876; Ibid., September 2, 1876. The new bankruptcy law sometimes protected Western merchants more than they admitted. One Japanese merchant owed the China and Japan Trading Company $1,133 Mexican when he went out of business, and the American firm received all but $335 when his property was disbursed. See OHMC, Statement concerning Tsukamoto estate, July 1, 1874.

36 JWM, October 27, 1888.

37 OHMC, Walsh, Hall and Company to Turner, July 1, 1874.

38 OHMC, Saibansho to Newwitter, August 10, 1875.

39 OHMC, Saibansho to Newwitter, September 27, 1876; Walsh, Hall to Newwitter, September 29, 1876.

40 Letter from "Merchant" in JWM, October 27, 1888.

41 Letter from "Daikokuten" in JWM, October 27, 1888. For additional evidence suggesting that Japanese reneged on business contracts when the "market went against them," see Finck, *Lotos Time in Japan,* 283. Sugiyama states that Japanese merchants required "a certain amount of capital and the market was inevitably closed to those unable to raise sufficient money for purchasing" to enter into transactions with foreign merchants. Sugiyama, *Japan's Industrialization*, 71–2. The frequency of merchants' complaints about the hazards of doing business with small and obviously undercapitalized Japanese merchants, however, suggests that this was not the case.

42 Brownell, *Tales From Tokio*, 67. See also Holland, *The Old and New Japan*, 271.

43 OHMC, China and Japan Trading Company to Newwitter, December 13, December 16, 1875.

44 OHMC, Schultz, Reis and Company to Frank, November 10, 1871.

45 OHMC, China and Japan Trading Company to Stahel, April 8, 1879; Ibid., Government Office to Stahel, April 30, 1879.

46 OHMC, China and Japan Trading Company to Turner, June 18, 1875. Another such case involved a transaction between the American merchant Andrew Watts and the

Japanese Okada Kinyamon. The Japanese, after presenting himself as a merchant of some means, promised to deliver 2,700 tons of rice to Watts for export within forty days. He paid Watts 3,000 rios as bargain money, but failed to follow through. See OHMC, Statement of Andrew Watts against Okada Kinyamon, June 20, 1874.

47 OHMC, Yoshi to Frank, March 25, 1871.

48 M. Paske-Smith, *Western Barbarians in Japan and Formosa in Tokugawa Days, 1603–1868*, 2nd ed. (1930; reprint, New York: Paragon Book Reprint Corp., 1968), 220–1. As this is the only reference to "office boys" I have found, it seems likely that Paske-Smith referred to bantos.

49 Quoted in Brownell, *Tales From Tokio*, 68. In spite of the difficulties associated with their dealings with the yamashi, Americans seldom inquired about alternate business opportunities. One rare example was that of C.L. Westwood, who in 1867 applied to the Bakufu for permission to build a railroad between Edo and Yokohama. Ohara and Okata, *Japanese Trade and Industry*, 524. Another was that of the merchant W.P. Lyons, who requested permission to establish a stage line to carry passengers and freight between Namba and Sakai. The local authorities stated that a Japanese had already inquired before Lyons, that there was an "insufficient amount" of passengers and freight, and refused permission. See OHMC, Japanese Government Office, Osaka, to Frank, December 2, 1870. The Japanese were not eager to have foreign money invested in their economy. The *Japan Weekly Mail* pointed out in 1876 that foreigners were prohibited from holding shares in Japanese mines or from lending money on the security of a mine, and that the mine of one Japanese who took a foreigner into partnership became subject to confiscation. JWM, January 15, 1876.

50 JWM, August 2, 1876.

51 JWM, July 14, 1883. For another such example, see Ibid., May 20, 1876. Importers of tea into the U.S. had to contend with uncertainty concerning the import tariff. When the duty question caused a rise in the New York market, merchants enjoyed the business of importers eager to place orders before the expense increased, but this led to corresponding troughs as the importers decided to withhold orders until the tariff question was settled. See JWM, August 12, 1876. Such fluctuations in prices and demand were, of course, beyond the control of Americans trading in Japan.

52 KD, M135/12, Van Buren to Davis, No. 617, March 28, 1882.

53 Mikiso Hane, *Modern Japan, A Historical Survey* (Boulder, Co., and London: Westview Press, 1986), 85–9. Many han engaged in trade directly with foreign firms, but their often poor financial condition forced them to buy on credit, using their export goods as security to buy arms and munitions. By 1872, twenty-eight han were indebted to forty-four foreign traders, for about ¥4,000,000. Portions of these debts were finally paid by the Meiji government in June, 1875. Ohara and Okata, *Japanese Trade and Industry*, 396–7.

54 OHMC, Fobes, China and Japan Trading Company to Turner, June 16, 1874.

55 OHMC, Behncke to Frank, December 14, 1871; Ibid., Frank to Assistant Secretary of State, December 16, 1871. See also Treat, *Diplomatic Relations*, 1: 465, 515n.

56 OHMC, Frank to Assistant Secretary of State, May 25, 1872.

57 OHMC, Statement of Japanese officials, included in Frank to Assistant Secretary of State, December 16, 1871.

58 OHMC, Saibansho to Frank, November 1, 1873.

59 JWM, April 22, 1876.

60 JWM, January 8, 1876.

61 Dixon, *Land of the Morning*, 230–1. The wide cultural chasm between East and West helped merchants on both sides to justify the urge to cheat. One visitor who had a wide range of contacts among Japanese readily labeled Japan "a land where all men are liars." De Fonblanque, *Niphon and Pe-che-li*, 5.

62 Judy Hilkey, *Character is Capital, Success Manuals and Manhood in Gilded Age America* (Chapel Hill: University of North Carolina Press, 1997), 132–3.

63 Wray, *Mitsubishi and the N.Y.K.*, 41; Black, *Young Japan*, 2: 451.

64 KD, M135/18, Scidmore to Wharton, No. 269, September 20, 1890; Will, *Trading Under Sail Off Japan*, 99.

65 OHMC, Ito Goi to Stewart, March 24, 1869.

66 Greathouse placed Howell and Company of Hakodate in touch with the shippers and insurers of the cargo of the American ship *Cheseborough*, which ran aground off northern Japan. The firm sold what was salvageable from the wreck for a commission. KD, M135/18, Greathouse to Wharton, No. 287, December 15, 1890.

67 OHMC, Smith, Baker and Company to Stewart, August 2, 1869.

68 Wray, *Mitsubishi and the N.Y.K.*, 45. Smith Baker and Company, until the company later appointed its own agent at Kobe, served as agents for the Pacific Mail Steamship Company, booking freight and passengers for a commission.

69 *Hiogo News*, September 3, 1868. Foreign hotels also profited by selling "night soil" to Japanese farmers. Abend, *Treaty Ports*, 184–5.

70 One representative sample was an auction held by the American firm of Scott and Company in June, 1869. A partial list of goods sold included hats, white shirts, socks, glassware, table cutlery, knives, cups and saucers, lamps, watches, clocks, assorted rifles and a small amount of stationery. *Hiogo News*, June 17, 1869. The high mortality rate among foreign companies in the ports ensured an on-going need for such services.

71 Will, *Trading Under Sail*, 61–2. American merchants sometimes purchased vessels to supply Westerners' needs in the treaty ports. Eugene Gill, for example, bought the steamer *Peiho* to ply Japanese coastal waters. See OHMC, Osaka and Hiogo Customshouse to Lewis, November 17, 1875. Occasionally, merchants took advantage of opportunities for short-term profits: when the Meiji government outlawed the wearing of swords by samurai, certain "speculative merchants in Yedo" made extensive purchases, planning to sell them abroad. JWM, April 15, 1876.

72 OHMC, W.H. Morse to Stewart, September 13, 1870.

73 OHMC, Wakita Ichiro of Kagoshima Han to Hiogo Consulate, October [no date] 1870.

74 For the two students who went to Reading, see Louis Richards, "The Earliest Japanese Visitors to Reading," *Transactions of the Historical Society of Berks County* 2 (1910): 304. One of the two boys who went to Van Reed's parents became Prime Minister of Japan, and later described his poor treatment while under their supervision. See Altman, "Eugene Van Reed," 11–12.

75 In the event that Vauley died, Frank was directed to "have him decently interred in the naval cemetery." OHMC, G.H. Cooper, Commander of U.S.S. *Colorado* to Frank, January 22, 1871. The doctor who cared for Vauley noted that Carroll and Company provided his food while he was ill. Ibid., Dr. Schokkenhummink to Frank, February 2, 1871.

76 OHD, M/460/5, Connelly to Rockhill, No. 89, December 16, 1896, Enclosure containing Theo. Search to Connelly, October 24, 1896; OHMC, Grange Sard, of the National Association of Stove Manufacturers, Albany, New York, to Stahel, October 21, 1878. Other typical requests included that of a woodworking machine company that allowed agents "a commission of 33 1/3%" on sales and that of Rumsey and Company, manufacturers of pump and fire engine works. OHMC, H.B. Smith Machine Company to Stahel, October 23, 1878; Ibid., Rumsey and Company to U.S. consul, Osaka, April 24, 1879. Often, overworked consuls asked the merchants themselves to gather information to answer such requests. See, for example, a note from an American stove manufacturer in 1879, thanking Thomas McGrath of the

China and Japan Trading Company for the information he had provided in response to the company's request for market information. OHMC, Rathbone and Sard to Stahel, March 14, 1879. Several English firms, including Charles Cammell and Company, a steel and iron works in Sheffield, England, advertised their wares in illustrated catalogs written in Japanese. The U.S. consul knew of "no such catalogs issued by firms in the United States." See KD, M135/20, McIvor to Uhl, No. 51, August 13, 1894, where a sample catalog is reproduced. The urgent tone of McIvor's despatch suggests that American merchants were doing little to increase imports.

77 Cochran, *200 Years of American Business*, 88.

78 Barbara Welter, "The Cult of True Womanhood, 1820–1860," *American Quarterly*, 18 (Summer 1966): 151.

79 Rotundo, *American Manhood*, 195.

80 See, among other examples, Maclay, *A Budget of Letters from Japan*, 39.

81 JWM, March 21, 1891.

82 JWM, September 13, 1890. Not all reputable Japanese houses avoided the foreign trade. Some of the local dealers shipping tea from Shizuoka ken to Yokohama were "of a long line of ancestors such as the Hagiwara-ya and Kaki-ya." Ohara and Okata, *Japanese Trade and Industry in the Meiji-Taisho Era*, 152.

83 Longford, "The Commercial Morality of the Japanese," 709.

84 "Some Notes on Pending Questions," JWM, May 6, 1882.

85 Longford, "The Commercial Morality of the Japanese," 705–11.

86 Richard Hofstadter, *Social Darwinism in American Thought* (Boston: The Beacon Press, 1955), 171, 170–200. Hofstadter points out that the idea of Social Darwinism gave further impetus to American expansionism rooted in existing convictions of superiority. See also Winthrop D. Jordan, *White Over Black, American Attitudes Toward the Negro, 1550–1812* (Balto.: Penguin Books, Inc., 1969); Rydell, *All the World's a Fair*; George M. Fredrickson, *The Arrogance of Race: Historical Perspectives on Slavery, Racism and Social Inequality* (Middletown, Conn.: Wesleyan University Press, 1988); George M. Fredrickson, *The Black Image in the White Mind* (Middletown, Conn.: Wesleyan University Press, 1971).

87 Eric Seizelet, "European Law and Tradition in Japan," in W.J. Mommsen and J.A. De Moor, eds, *European Expansion and Law, The Encounter of European and Indigenous Law in 19th and Twentieth Century Africa and Asia* (New York: Berg Publishers, 1992), 63.

88 W.J. Mommsen and J.A. De Moor, eds, *European Expansion and Law, The Encounter of European and Indigenous Law in 19th and Twentieth Century Africa and Asia*, (New York: Berg Publishers, 1992), 4–5.

89 Josiah Strong, *Our Country: Its Possible Future and Its Present Crisis* (New York: The American Home Missionary Society, 1885), 168. For the connection between expansion and racism, see also Albert K. Weinberg, *Manifest Destiny, A Study of Nationalist Expansion in American History* (Balto.: The Johns Hopkins Press, 1935) and Frederick Merk, *Manifest Destiny and Mission in American History* (New York: Alfred A. Knopf, 1963).

90 JWM, October 6, 1888.

91 Hattori, *Foreign Commerce of Japan*, 30.

92 Longford, "The Commercial Morality of the Japanese," 709. Some limited evidence questions the claim that Japanese merchants' low status allowed them to take advantage of foreigners. One source claimed that Japanese merchants' status grew, particularly after the Meiji Restoration, and that the previous disgrace associated with trade diminished to the extent that some "influential citizens of Tokyo" were merchants. See Dixon, *Land of the Morning*, 231.

93 Brownell, *Tales From Tokio*, 65–7. For a description of the difficulties encountered by the British firm of Jardine, Matheson and Company in making "country purchases" through the Japanese silk merchant Takasuya Seibei, who "defrauded Jardines of substantial sums," see Sugiyama, *Japan's Industrialization*, 55–64.

94 "Our Blood Tax," *Eastern World*, December 12, 1896; Ibid., August 5, 1905. There was considerable alcohol intake in the ports. In one spoof, "Old resident" offered to introduce "New Arrival" to the "agents for any whiskey in town," after which the newcomer would know "a couple of hundred as good fellows as you'll find." See "Local Fame," Ibid., April 30, 1898. On another occasion, the editor recalled four men talking at a table in a Yokohama hotel about the "symptoms of delirium tremens" exhibited by their friends. Of the four, one "drank himself to death, another became hopelessly insane, the third left Japan and subsequently committed suicide." Ibid., February 4, 1899. One notable example of "white collar" crime was that of Charles Edward Miller, the treasurer of the China and Japan Trading Company, who "absconded from Hiogo" in September, 1892 after embezzling $30,000 from the firm. OHD, M460/4, Smithers to Wharton, No. 150, January 7, 1893. For failure as "a sign of poor character" see Rotundo, *American Manhood*, 179.

95 JWM, October 6, 1888.

96 "The suicide of Mr. O. Keil," *Eastern World*, February 4, 1899. Norman A. Walter, an English Yokohama merchant of thirty-seven, committed suicide by cutting his throat in January, 1902, unable, according to his obituary, to sustain his "breathless chase after pleasure." See Ibid., "Suicide of a Foreign Broker in Yokohama," January 18, 1902.

97 Rotundo, *American Manhood*, 185–93; Elliott J. Gorn, *The Manly Art, Bare-Knuckle Prize Fighting in America* (Ithaca: Cornell University Press, 1986), 187.

98 Lears, *No Place of Grace*, 50–1. For discussions of the affliction, see Ibid., 47–58; Gail Benderman, *Manliness and Civilization, A Cultural History of Gender and Race in the United States, 1880–1917* (Chicago: University of Chicago Press, 1995), 84–92.

99 Murray, *Land of the Tatami*, 77. Murray gets at something of the heart of Westerners' failure to understand Japanese in his brief treatments of "The Japanese smile" and "The Japanese Grin." See Ibid., 76–8.

100 See, for example, Dixon, *Land of the Morning*, 280, which refers to a servant "beaten with a stick for the most trivial infractions."

101 OHMC, Government Office to Frank, May 3, 1871; OHMC, Government Office to Turner, July 4, 1872.

102 OHMC, Saibansho to Turner, enclosing statement of Seikichi, servant of Masaharu Onodera, June 6, 1873; Doi to Turner, June 14, 1873. The records do not tell us if Ferrier was ever punished, only that he was preparing to leave Kobe for Yokohama just after the incident. Many observers commented on such behavior. See, for example, Clive Holland, who wrote that "as employers, the foreigners were generally harsh, and frequently even brutal." Holland, *Old and New Japan*, 270. The Japanese response to such treatment could sometimes be violent. Willis Flood, an American merchant, reported in 1875 an attack by a Japanese who jumped from behind a wall, "caught hold of [his] coat and called [him] a 'Tojin' (foreigner)" while three other coolies joined in the fray. OHMC, Flood to Lewis, November 15, 1875.

103 For the Iwakura Embassy's experience in the U.S., see Marlene Mayo, "A Catechism of Western Diplomacy: The Japanese and Hamilton Fish," *Journal of Asian Studies* 26 (May 1967), 389–410. The Embassy began with the United States, and though it proved unwilling at that time to relinquish extraterritorial rights or grant Japan tariff autonomy, it did conclude a Postal Convention with Japan on August 6, 1873, the first treaty that recognized Japan as an equal partner. Edward H. House, "The Thraldom of Japan," *Atlantic Monthly* 60 (December 1887), 731–2. The U.S. government also

agreed that its citizens would be subject to Japanese law while travelling in the interior, though those who violated Japanese law would be tried in the U.S. consular courts. Payson Treat, *Japan and the United States, 1853–1921* (Stanford: Stanford University Press, 1928), 119 ff.

104 JWM, November 25, 1882.

105 Jacobson, *Barbarian Virtues*, 37.

106 "Japan's Direct Trade," JWM, September 22, 1883. Inevitably, some arguments were tied to the state of Japan's "civilization." Many agreed by 1882 that Japanese law was acceptable to foreigners, but their concern that Japan's civilization was still "new and untested" lingered; the possibility that the country might "slip back into barbarism" was reason enough to postpone treaty revision. "Some Notes on Pending Questions," JWM, May 6, 1882.

107 Smith, *Ten Weeks in Japan*, 263.

108 JWM, January 8, 1876.

109 An extensive discussion of the land tax appears in Beasley, *The Meiji Restoration*, 390–400.

110 JWM, July 12, 1879. See also Iriye, *Across the Pacific*, 60–3.

111 JWM, May 20, 1882.

112 Jacobson, *Barbarian Virtues*, 50.

113 *Jiji Shimpo*, quoted in JWM, April 17, 1886.

114 The participants elected a committee on the spot comprising fifteen British, five German, four French, four American, three Swiss, three Italian, three Dutch, one Portuguese and one Chinese. *Japan Gazette*, September 12, 1890. See also MD, M133/62, Swift to Blaine, No. 154, September 23, 1890.

115 MD, M133/62, Swift to Blaine, No. 180, December 2, 1890; "Kobe," JWM, September 13, 1890; "Rude Conduct of Japanese Toward Foreigners," JWM, June 12, 1897.

116 *London and China Express*, quoted in JWM, December 30, 1876.

117 Crow, *Highways and Byeways*, 93; JWM, September 9, 1876.

118 For a good example of this approach, see William Elliot Griffis, *A Maker of the New Orient, Samuel Robbins Brown* (London and New York: Fleming H. Revell Co., 1902).

119 Iriye, *Across the Pacific*, 17.

120 Letter from W.R. Lawson in *London and China Express*, July 9, 1897.

121 *Japan Gazette*, February 26, 1881.

122 *Eastern World*, April 14, 1900.

123 JWM, October 13, 1888.

124 Evarts Boutell Greene, *A New Englander in Japan, Daniel Crosby Greene* (Boston and New York: Houghton Mifflin Co., 1927), 115–16. Greene did not exaggerate his work habits: one visitor spent several hours at Greene's residence and remarked, "The time for active Christian labor had not yet come; but the language was being mastered, and his morning hours were golden in the study." Griffis, *The Mikado's Empire*, 406.

125 Gordon, *An American Missionary*, 14–15. Gordon describes in detail the difficulties of grasping the levels of politeness the language imposes on all speakers. Ibid., 17–18.

126 Gordon, *An American Missionary*, 25–6. The chapter entitled "Mastering the Language" (pp. 14–26) is instructive, and includes a commentary on the substantially more difficult task of learning the written language. See also Dooman, *A Missionary's Life in the Land of the Gods*, chapter entitled "A Short Study of the Japanese Language," 92–125.

127 Taylor, *Advocate of Understanding*, 28.

128 Though Van Reed knew Joseph Heco, a native Japanese, while still in the U.S., it is questionable how much Japanese Van Reed learned then and after coming to Japan. See Altman, "Eugene Van Reed," 7–9. Francis Hall's obituary claimed that he "mastered the language, so that he could speak, read and write it with as much fluency

as a native," almost certainly an enormous exaggeration. See *Elmira Semi-Weekly Advertiser*, August 29, 1902. For another view of the level of Hall's Japanese, see Notehelfer, *Japan Through American Eyes*, 30–1. For evidence of few Western merchants learning Japanese, see JWM, July 17, 1886.

129 Some tools for learning the rudiments of Japanese were at hand. Some examples include J.C. Hepburn, *A Japanese and English Dictionary* (Shanghai: American Presbyterian Mission Press, 1867, revised 1872); Johann J. Hoffman, *Japanese–English Dictionary*, 3 vols. (Leyden: Brill, 1881–92); William Imbrie, *Handbook of English–Japanese Etymology* (Tokyo, 1880); William G. Aston, *A Grammar of the Japanese Spoken Language*, 4th ed. (Yokohama: Lane, Crawford and Company, 1888).

130 Holtham, *Eight Years in Japan*, 249–50. English could sometimes be misunderstood as well as well – a resident of Nagasaki observed that a foreign merchant struck a Japanese interpreter named Kitamura "with the handle of his umbrella on the side of his head" because the Japanese, commenting on some goods he had entered in the customshouse, told him that the goods "were very cheap" which the merchant "mistook for cheat." Paske-Smith, *Western Barbarians*, 387.

131 "Bishop of Homoco," *Exercises in the Yokohama Dialect.* "Homoco" was the pseudonym adopted by a Yokohama resident named Hoffman Atkinson. Homoco was a seedy area of Yokohama noted for its cheap bars and prostitution. It seems clear that Atkinson was mocking the residents of Yokohama; nevertheless the work is one of the few sources dealing with this type of speech, and though it doubtless exaggerates somewhat, it illustrates some of the main characteristics of the dialect.

132 Chamberlain, *Things Japanese*, 399–400. Pidgin was common enough to appear in port newspapers – the *Japan Weekly Mail* printed this version of "Little Jack Horner": Littee Jack Horner, Makee sit inside corner, Chow-chow he Clismas pie, He put inside t'um, Hab catchee one plum, *Hai yah!* what one good chilo my! JWM, August 26, 1876.

133 MD, M133/20, Charles Shepard to Hamilton Fish, No. 28, April 10, 1872, enclosing clipping from *Hiogo News*. Admittance to the exhibition was free, foreigners were protected by guards and visitors were permitted to visit lake Biwa on excursions. For Japanese guards, see also OHMC, Watanabe to Frank, March 29, 1872.

134 OHMC, Shepard to Frank, March 15; April 10, 1872. The Japanese allowed foreigners to exhibit goods in Kyoto without attending in person (OHMC, Hiogo Government Office to Frank, April 1, 1872), but considering merchants' general satisfaction with their confinement to the treaty ports, it seems unlikely that many would have made such arrangements.

135 *The Far East*, June 17, July 16, August 1, 1872. It is unclear who the exhibition's promoters were. *The Far East* described foreign uncertainty over whether the Japanese government or Kyoto merchants funded the event. See Ibid., July 16, 1872.

136 *The Far East*, August 1, 1872. The earliest reference to the exhibition in the American consular records is March 15. OHMC, Shepard to Frank, March 15, 1872.

137 The *Japan Weekly Mail* and *The Far East* for the month following the exhibition in the years 1873–5 contain no more than brief passing references to the event. For the event's annual recurrence, see OHMC, DeLong to Turner, February 1, 1873; Government Office to Turner, February 27, 1874; Bingham to Turner, December 28, 1874; Bingham to Newwitter, February 3, 1876; Morioka to Newwitter, March 6, 1877.

138 "Why Not?," JWM, March 25, 1876.

139 "Sovereign Rights and Customs Duties," *Japan Daily Herald*, July 18, 1878.

140 Merchants made clear that expansion of trade was the least of their priorities. By 1880, merchants spurned the opening of new treaty ports, a development that would only diminish the trade of existing ones. "New Treaty Ports," *Japan Mail*, December 12, 1879.

141 JWM, September 13, 1890.

CONCLUSION

1 See Roden, "Baseball and the Quest for National Dignity," 521.
2 Ibid., 523–4, 529, 530.
3 JWM, May 30, June 13, 1896.
4 Jones, *Extraterritoriality in Japan*, 128–55; Treat, *Diplomatic Relations*, 3: 419–20. For a detailed treatment of Japanese legal reform, see Eric Seizelet, "European Law and Tradition in Japan during the Meiji Era, 1868–1912," in Mommsen and De Moor, eds., *European Expansion and Law*, 59–82.
5 Iriye, *Across the Pacific*, 73.
6 De Fonblanque, *Niphon and Pe-che-li*, 70.
7 MD, M133/37, Bingham to Evarts, N. 792, May 9, 1878; Ibid., M133/47, Bingham to Frelinghuysen, No. 155, August 28, 1882.
8 "Pending Questions," JWM, May 6, 1882.
9 JWM, October 6, 1888. This observation contrasts sharply with that of William Elliot Griffis, who twenty-five years earlier had stated that the competition between British and Americans in Japan "must be productive of immense good .... Like flint and steel before the dead cold mass of Asiatic despotism, superstition and narrowness, it must result in kindling many a good spark into flames of progress and knowledge." Griffis, The Mikado's Empire, 343.
10 J. Morris, *Advance Japan: A Nation Thoroughly in Earnest*, 239. Western merchants in China had access to the Chinese interior since 1860, but they continued their pattern of coastal residence and isolation in the Chinese treaty ports throughout the nineteenth century. A member of the British Board of Trade stated in 1863 that "The paramount difficulty and danger to be avoided in our dealings with China is all unnecessary contact between British traders and the natives." Quoted in Pelcovits, *Old China Hands and the Foreign Office*, 11.
11 "No Compulsion," JWM, April 12, 1884.
12 Daigoro Goh, "A Japanese View of New Japan," *Nineteenth Century* 29 (January–June 1891), 274–5.
13 *Kobe Herald*, March 25, 1902, quoted in Shyam Krishna Bhurtel, "Alfred Eliab Buck: Carpetbagger in Alabama and Georgia," Ph.D. diss., Auburn University, 1981, 226.
14 Jones, *International Business in the Nineteenth Century*, 72.
15 Ibid., 28.
16 W.J. Reader, "Businessmen and Their Motives" in D.C. Coleman and Peter Mathias, eds, *Enterprise and History, Essays in Honor of Charles Wilson* (Cambridge: Cambridge University Press, 1984), 44.
17 Vernon Parrington, *Main Currents in American Thought* (New York: Harcourt, Brace and World, 1930), 3: 326.
18 David Dary, *Entrepreneurs of the Old West* (New York: Knopf, 1986), ix.
19 Yonekawa and Yoshihara, eds, *Business History of General Trading Companies*, 112–3.
20 Scidmore, *Jinrikisha Days in Japan*, 25.
21 Hine, *Community on the American Frontier*, 176–7. For an excellent summary of the relevant historiography, see Carlton C. Qualey, "Ethnic Groups and the Frontier" in Roger L. Nichols, ed., *American Frontier and Western Issues, A Historiographical Review* (New York: Greenwood Press, 1986), 199–216.
22 Scidmore, *Jinrikisha Days in Japan*, 283–4.
23 Ibid., 292.
24 Francis Sutton, *et al.*, *The American Business Creed* (New York: Schocken Books, 1956), 11.
25 Ibid., 13.
26 Ibid., 276.

27 John Higham, "The Reorientation of American Culture in the 1890s" in John Weiss, ed., *The Origins of Modern Consciousness* (Detroit: Wayne State University Press, 1965), 27.

28 W. Somerset Maugham, *The Summing Up* (New York: The New American Library 1938), 84.

29 The argument that there was a broad "crisis of masculinity" at the turn of the century is questionable. Clyde Griffen suggests that the "crisis" interpretation tends to emphasize broad social trends like the end of the frontier and the declining opportunity for economic independence in an age of business bureaucratization. The impact of these trends on particular groups within the middle class is arguable ..." Clyde Griffen, "Reconstructing Masculinity from the Evangelical Revival to the Waning of Progressivism: A Speculative Synthesis" in Mark C. Carnes and Clyde Griffen, eds, *Meanings for Manhood, Constructions of Masculinity in Victorian America* (Chicago: University of Chicago Press, 1990), 183–4. Treaty port residents were immune from such a "crisis" because of the gender imbalance, so too might other groups of men have been unaffected. For another challenge to the "crisis" interpretation, see Benderman, *Manliness and Civilization*, Chapter 1, especially pages 11ff.

30 Margaret Marsh, "Suburban Men and Masculine Domesticity, 1870–1915" in Carnes and Griffen, eds, *Meanings for Manhood*, 111–12.

31 Jacobson, *Barbarian Virtues*, 125. On Westerners' generalizations about foreign peoples, see Edward Said, *Culture and Imperialism* (New York: Alfred A. Knopf, 1993); David Spurr, *The Rhetoric of Empire, Colonial Discourse in Journalism, Travel Writing and Imperial Administration* (Durham: Duke University Press, 1993); Mary Louise Pratt, *Imperial Eyes, Travel Writing and Transculturation* (New York: Routledge, 1992).

32 Alan M. Kraut, *The Huddled Masses, The Immigrant in American Society, 1880–1921* (Arlington Heights, Il: Harlan Davidson, Inc, 1986), 150. See also Knobel, "America for the Americans."

33 The contradiction was much less obvious to Americans observing Japan from a distance. The Oriental exhibits building at the Portland exposition in 1905 showed "the nations of the orient with their old ideas and customs, while above, looking over the whole, is America, extending to these countries her civilization through the medium of education." Quoted in Rydell, *All the World's a Fair*, 203.

34 Harris, "All the World a Melting Pot?", 31–4, 43.

35 Akira Iriye, ed., *Mutual Images, Essays in American–Japanese Relations*, 21.

36 Ibid.

37 Holland, *Old and New Japan*, 270–1.

38 Totman, *A History of Japan*, 306, 330.

39 A. Morgan Young, *Imperial Japan 1926–1938* (New York: William Morrow, 1938), 295, 320n.

40 *Kobe Chronicle*, January 3, 1900.

41 Hoare, *Treaty Ports*, 169.

42 Louis G. Perez, *Japan Comes of Age, Mutsu Munemitsu and the Revision of the Unequal Treaties* (London: Associated University Presses, 1999), 172.

43 Henry Adams, *Letters from Japan*, Donald Richie and Yoshimori Harashima, eds, (Tokyo: Kenkyusha, n.d.), xv.

44 Osman Edwards, *Residential Rhymes* (Tokyo: T. Hasegawa, n.d.). The date would almost certainly be 1894, when Britain agreed to treaty revision.

REFERENCES

NATIONAL ARCHIVES

RG 84, Nagasaki Land Records, American Land Renters, Nagasaki, 1867
RG 84, Miscellaneous Correspondence, (Letters received) Osaka/Hiogo
RG 84, Miscellaneous Correspondence, (Letters received) Nagasaki
RG 59, M133, Despatches from U.S. Ministers in Japan
RG 59, M135, Despatches from U.S. Consuls at Kanagawa
RG 59, M460, Despatches from U.S. Consuls at Osaka/Hiogo
RG 59, Letters of Application and Recommendation

MANUSCRIPT COLLECTIONS

Augustine Heard Collection, Baker Library, Harvard Business School
Appleton Collection, Baker Library, Harvard Business School

NEWSPAPERS

Eastern World
Elmira Semi-Weekly Advertiser
Hiogo News
Japan Daily Herald
Japan Gazette
Japan Weekly Mail
London and China Express
The Chrysanthemum
The Far East
Tokio Times

PUBLISHED WORKS

Abend, Hallett Edward. *Treaty Ports.* Garden City, New York: Doubleday, Doran and Company, Inc., 1944.
Adams, Henry. *Letters from Japan.* Edited by Donald Richie and Yoshimori Harashima. Tokyo: Kenkyusha, n.d.

Albion, Robert Greenhalgh. *The Rise of New York Port, 1815–1860.* 1939. Newton: David and Charles, 1970.

Alcock, Sir Rutherford. *The Capital of the Tycoon, A Narrative of a Three Years' Residence in Japan.* 2 vols. New York: Harper Brothers, 1863.

Allen, George C. and Donnithorne, Audrey G. *Western Enterprise in Far Eastern Development, China and Japan.* 1954. Reprint. New York: Augustus M. Kelley, 1968.

Altman, Albert. "Eugene Van Reed, a Reading Man in Japan, 1859–1872." *Historical Review of Berks County* 30 (Winter 1964–5): 6–12, 27–8, 30–1.

Aston, William G. *A Grammar of the Japanese Spoken Language.* 4th ed. Yokohama: Lane, Crawford and Company, 1888.

Atherton, Lewis E. *The Frontier Merchant in Mid-America.* Columbia: University of Missouri Press, 1971.

Bacon, Alice Mabel. *A Japanese Interior.* Boston: Houghton Mifflin, 1893.

Bailey, Thomas A. *A Diplomatic History of the American People.* 6th ed. New York: Appleton-Century-Crofts, Inc., 1958.

Barnes, William, and Morgan, John Heath. *The Foreign Service of the United States: Origins, Developments and Functions.* Washington D.C.: Government Printing Office, 1961.

Barr, Pat. *The Coming of the Barbarians, A Story of Western Settlement in Japan, 1853–1870.* London: Macmillan, 1967.

Barr, Pat. *The Deer Cry Pavilion, A Story of Westerners in Japan, 1868–1905.* New York: Harcourt, Brace and World, Inc., 1968.

Beasley, William G. *The Meiji Restoration.* Stanford: Stanford University Press, 1972.

Beasley, William G. *The Rise of Modern Japan.* New York: St. Martin's Press, 2000.

Beasley, William G., ed. and trans. *Select Documents on Japanese Foreign Policy, 1853–68.* London: Oxford University Press, 1955.

Benderman, Gail. *Manliness and Civilization, A Cultural History of Gender and Race in the United States, 1880–1917.* Chicago: University of Chicago Press, 1995.

Bhurtel, Shyam Krishna. "Alfred Eliab Buck: Carpetbagger in Alabama and Georgia." Ph.D. diss., Auburn Univeristy, 1981.

Bird, Isabella. *Unbeaten Tracks in Japan.* 1880. Reprint. Rutland Vt. and Tokyo: Charles Tuttle and Co., 1973.

Black, John R. *Young Japan, Yokohama and Yedo, 1858–1879.* 2 vols. Tokyo: Oxford University Press, 1968.

Blackford, Mansel G. and Kerr, Austin K. *Business Enterprise in American History.* Boston: Houghton Mifflin, 1990.

Blum, Paul C. *Yokohama in 1872.* Tokyo: The Asiatic Society of Japan, 1963.

Boyer, Samuel Pellman. *Naval Surgeon: Revolt in Japan, 1868–1869, The Diary of Samuel Pellman Boyer.* Edited by Elinor Barnes and James A. Barnes. Bloomington: Indiana University Press, 1963.

Boyle, John Hunter. *Modern Japan, The American Nexus.* Fort Worth: Harcourt Brace, 1993.

Bridges, F.D. *Journal of a Lady's Travels Around the World.* London: John Murray, 1883.

Brooks, George E., Jr. *Yankee Traders, Old Coasters and African Middlemen, A History of American Legitimate Trade with West Africa in the Nineteenth Century.* Boston: Boston University Press, 1970.

Brownell, Clarence Ludlow. *The Heart of Japan.* London: Metheun and Co., 1902.

Burks, Ardath, ed. *The Modernizers: Overseas Students, Foreign Employees and Meiji Japan.* Boulder, Col.: Westview Press, 1985.

Campbell, Charles S. *The Transformation of American Foreign Relations, 1865–1900.* New York: Harper and Row, 1976.

Carrothers, Julia D. *The Sunrise Kingdom, or Life and Scenes in Japan, and Woman's Work for Woman There.* Philadelphia: Presbyterian Board of Publication, 1879.

Cashman, Sean Dennis. *America in the Gilded Age, From the Death of Lincoln to the Rise of Theodore Roosevelt.* New York: New York University Press, 1993. Chamberlain, Basil Hall, and Mason, W.B. *A Handbook for Travellers in Japan.* 8th ed. London: John Murray, 1907.

Chamberlain, Basil Hall, and Mason, W.B. *Things Japanese.* 6th rev. ed. London: Kegan Paul, Trench, Trubner and Co. Ltd, 1939.

Chang, Richard T. *From Prejudice to Tolerance.* Tokyo: Sophia University Press, 1970.

Chang, Richard T. *The Justice of the Western Consular Courts in Nineteenth-Century Japan.* Westport, Conn. and London: Greenwood Press, 1984.

Chisolm, Lawrence W. *Fenollosa: The Far East and American Culture.* New Haven: Yale University Press, 1963.

Chronicle and Directory for China, Japan and the Philippines. 1869, 1870, 1881, 1891, 1893. Also published as *Hong Kong Directory* for 1891.

Chudacoff, Howard P. *The Age of the Bachelor, Creating an American Subculture.* Princeton: Princeton University Press, 1999.

Church, Deborah Claire. "The Role of the American Diplomatic Advisors to the Japanese Foreign Ministry, 1872–1887." Ph.D. diss., University of Hawaii, 1978.

Clark, E. Warren. *Life and Adventure in Japan.* New York: American Tract Society, 1878.

Clark, Reg. "Shioya Club." *Kansai Time Out* No. 75 (January 1983): 35.

Clark, Reg. "The Kobe Regatta and Athletic Club." *Kansai Time Out* No. 71 (January 1983): 36–7.

Cochran, Thomas C. *200 Years of American Business.* New York: Basic Books, 1977.

Conroy, Hilary. *The Japanese Expansion into Hawaii, 1868–1898.* San Francisco: R and E Associates, 1973.

Cortazzi, Hugh. "Yokohama: Frontier Town, 1859–1866." *Royal Society of Asian Affairs Bulletin* 18 (February 1986): 3–17.

Crawcour, E. Sydney. "The Tokugawa Heritage." In *The State and Economic Enterprise in Japan*, edited by William W. Lockwood. Princeton: Princeton University Press, 1965.

Crawcour, E. Sydney. "Economic Change in the Nineteenth Century." In *The Cambridge History of Japan*, edited by Marius Jansen. Cambridge: Cambridge University Press, 1989.

Crow, Arthur H. *Highways and Byeways in Japan.* London: Sampson Low, Marston, Searle and Rivington, 1883.

D'Anethan, Baroness Albert. *Fourteen Years of Diplomatic Life in Japan.* London: Stanley Paul and Co., 1912.

Dare, Philip Ned. "John A. Bingham and Treaty Revision with Japan: 1873–1885." Ph.D. diss., University of Kentucky, 1975.

Dary, David. *Entrepreneurs of the Old West.* New York: Alfred A. Knopf, 1986.

De Fonblanque, Edward Barrington. *Niphon and Pe-che-li; or, Two Years in Japan and Northern China.* 2d ed. London: Saunders, Otley and Company, 1863.

De Santis, Vincent P. *The Shaping of Modern America: 1877–1920.* Wheeling, IL: Harlan Davidson, 1989.

Dennett, Tyler. *Americans in Eastern Asia. A Critical Study of United States' Policy in the Far East in the Nineteenth Century.* 1922. Reprint. New York: Barnes and Noble, 1941.

Dibacco, Thomas V. *Made in the U.S.A., The History of American Business.* New York: Harper and Row, 1987.

Dickens, F.V. *The Life of Sir Harry Parkes.* 2 vols. 1894. Reprint. Wilmington, Delaware: Scholarly Resources, Inc., 1973.

Dixon, William Gray. *The Land of the Morning.* Edinburgh: James Gemmell, 1882.

Dooman, Isaac. *A Missionary's Life in the Land of the Gods.* Boston: The Gorham Press, 1914.

Drage, Charles. *Taikoo.* London: Constable and Co., 1970.

Dykstra, Robert R. *The Cattle Towns.* Lincoln: University of Nebraska Press, 1968.

Earns, Lane R. and Burke-Gaffney, Brian. *Across the Gulf of Time. The International Cemeteries of Nagasaki.* Nagasaki: Nagasaki Bunkensha, 1991.

Edwards, Osman. *Residential Rhymes.* Tokyo: T. Hasegawa, 1900.

Emerson, Ralph Waldo. *The Conduct of Life and Other Essays.* London: Dent, 1908.

Fairbank, John K. and Goldman, Merle. *Trade and Diplomacy on the China Coast, the Opening of the Treaty Ports, 1842–1854.* Cambridge: Harvard University Press, 1953.

Falt, Olavi K. *Clash of Interests: The Transformation of Japan in 1861–1881 in the Eyes of the Local Anglo-Saxon Press.* Rovaniemi: Historical Association of Northern Finland, 1990.

Finck, Henry T. *Lotos Time in Japan.* London: Lawrence and Bullen, 1895.

Fletcher, M.E. "The Suez Canal and World Shipping, 1869–1914." *Journal of Economic History* 18 (1958): 556–73.

Fredrickson, George M. *The Black Image in the White Mind.* Middletown, Conn.: Wesleyan University Press, 1971.

Fredrickson, George M. *The Arrogance of Race: Historical Perspectives on Slavery, Racism and Social Inequality.* Middletown, Conn.: Wesleyan University Press, 1988.

Garraty, John A. *The New Commonwealth, 1877–1890.* New York: Harper and Row, 1968.

Gibson, Arrell M. *Yankees in Paradise, the Pacific Basin Frontier.* Albuquerque: University of New Mexico Press, 1993.

Ginger, Ray. *The Age of Excess: The United States from 1877 to 1914.* New York: Macmillan, 1965.

Goh, Daigoro. "A Japanese View of New Japan." *Nineteenth Century* 29 (January–June 1891): 267–78.

Gordon, M.L. *An American Missionary in Japan*, Boston and New York: Houghton, Mifflin Co., 1895.

Gorn, Elliott J. *The Manly Art, Bare-Knuckle Prize Fighting in America.* Ithaca: Cornell University Press, 1986.

Gower, Lord Ronald. *Notes of a Tour From Brindisi to Yokohama, 1883–1884.* London: Kegan Paul, Trench and Co., 1885.

Greene, Evarts Boutell. *A New Englander in Japan, Daniel Crosby Greene.* Boston and New York: Houghton Mifflin Co., 1927.

Greey, Edward. *Young Americans in Japan, or the Further Adventures of the Jewett Family and Their Friend Oto Nambo.* New York: John R. Anderson, 1902.

"Grenon." *Verdant Simple's Views of Japan.* Yokohama: Kelly and Walsh, 1890.

Gribble, Henry. "The Preparation of Japan Tea." *Transactions of the Asiatic Society of Japan* 12 (1883–4): 1–33.

Griffen, Clyde. "Reconstructing Masculinity from the Evangelical Revival to the Waning of Progressivism: A Speculative Synthesis." In *Meanings for Manhood, Constructions of Masculinity in Victorian America*, edited by Mark C. Carnes and Clyde Griffen. Chicago: University of Chicago Press, 1990.

Griffin, Eldon. *Clippers and Consuls, American Consular and Commercial Relations with Eastern Asia, 1845–1860*. Ann Arbor, Michigan: Edwards Brothers, Inc., 1938.

Griffis, William Elliot. *The Mikado's Empire*. New York and London: Harper and Bros., 1899.

Griffis, William Elliot. *Verbeck of Japan*. New York: Fleming H. Revell, 1900.

Griffis, William Elliot. *A Maker of the New Orient, Samuel Robbins Brown*. London and New York: Fleming H. Revell Co., 1902.

Hall, Peter Dobkin. "What Merchants Did with Their Money: Charitable and Testamentary Trusts in Massachusetts, 1780–1880." In *Entrepreneurs, The Boston Business Community, 1700–1850*, edited by Conrad Edick Wright and Katheryn P. Viens. Boston: Massachusetts Historical Society, 1997.

Hane, Mikiso. *Modern Japan, A Historical Survey*. Boulder, Co., and London: Westview Press, 1986.

Harley, C.K. "The Shift from Sailing Ships to Steamships, 1850–1890." In *Essays on a Mature Economy: Britain After 1840*, edited by D.N. McCloskey. Princeton, N.J.: Princeton University Press, 1971.

Harris, Neil. "All the World a Melting Pot? Japan at American Fairs, 1876–1904." In *Mutual Images, Essays in American-Japanese Relations*, edited by Akira Iriye. Cambridge: Harvard University Press, 1975.

Hattori, Yukimasa. *The Foreign Commerce of Japan Since the Restoration, 1869–1900*. Baltimore: The Johns Hopkins Press, 1904.

Hearn, Lafcadio. *The Japanese Letters of Lafcadio Hearn*. Edited by Elizabeth Bisland. Boston and New York: Houghton Mifflin Co., 1910.

Heco, Joseph. *Narrative of a Japanese*. 2 vols. Edited by James Murdoch. Yokohama: Yokohama Printing and Publishing Co., n.d.

Hepburn, J.C. *A Japanese and English Dictionary*. Shanghai: American Presbyterian Mission Press, 1867, revised 1872.

Higham, John. "The Reorientation of American Culture in the 1890s." In *The Origins of Modern Consciousness*, edited by John Weiss. Detroit: Wayne State University Press, 1965.

Higham, John. *Strangers in the Land: Patterns of American Nativism, 1860–1925*. 1955. Reprint. New York: Artheneum, 1978.

Hine, Robert V. *Community on the American Frontier, Separate but Not Alone*. Norman: University of Oklahoma Press, 1980.

Hoare, James Edward. "The Chinese in the Japanese Treaty Ports, 1858–1899: The Unknown Majority." *Proceedings of the British Association for Japanese Studies* 2 (1977): 18–33.

Hoare, James Edward. *Japan's Treaty Ports and Foreign Settlements, The Uninvited Guests, 1858–1899*. Sandgate, Kent: Japan Library, 1994.

Hoffman, Johann J. *Japanese-English Dictionary*, 3 vols. Leyden: Brill, 1881–92.

Hoffman, R. *The Anglo-German Trade Rivalry*. Philadelphia, 1933.

Hofstadter, Richard. *Social Darwinism in American Thought*. Boston: The Beacon Press, 1955.

Holland, Clive. *Old and New Japan*. London: J.M. Dent, 1907.

Holtham, E.G. *Eight Years in Japan, 1873–1881. Work, Travel and Recreation*. London: Kegan Paul, Trench and Co., 1883.

"Homoco, Bishop of." [Hoffman Atkinson] *Exercises in the Yokohama Dialect.* 2d ed. Yokohama: Japan Gazette Office, 1879.

Horie, Yasuzo. "Modern Entrepreneurship in Meiji Japan." In William Lockwood, ed., *The State and Economic Enterprise in Japan.* Princeton, N.J.: Princeton University Press, 1965.

House, Edward H. *Japanese Episodes.* Boston: James R. Osgood and Co., 1881.

House, Edward H. "The Martyrdom of an Empire." *Atlantic Monthly* 47 (January – June 1881): 610–23.

House, Edward H. "The Thralldom of Japan." *Atlantic Monthly* 60 (December 1887): 721–34.

Hyam, Ronald. "Empire and Sexual Opportunity." *Journal of Imperialism and Commonwealth History* 14 (1986): 34–90.

Hyde, Francis E. *Far Eastern Trade,* 1860–1914. no location: Harper and Row, 1973.

Ion, A. Hamish. *The Cross and the Rising Sun, The Canadian Protestant Missionary Movement in the Japanese Empire, 1872–1931.* Waterloo, Ontario: Wilfrid Laurier University Press, 1990.

Imbrie, William. *Handbook of English–Japanese Etymology.* Tokyo, 1880.

Iriye, Akira. *Across the Pacific, An Inner History of American-East Asian Relations.* New York: Harcourt, Brace and World, Inc., 1967.

Iriye, Akira, ed. *Mutual Images, Essays in American-Japanese Relations.* Cambridge, Mass.: Harvard University Press, 1975.

Jacobson, Matthew Frye. *Barbarian Virtues, The United States Encounters Foreign Peoples at Home and Abroad, 1876–1917.* New York: Hill and Wang, 2000.

Jansen, Marius B. *Sakamoto Ryoma and the Meiji Restoration.* Stanford: Stanford University Press, 1971.

Jansen, Marius B. *The Cambridge History of Japan. Volume 5, The Nineteenth Century.* Cambridge: Cambridge University Press, 1989.

Japan Year Book, 1933.

Jones, Charles A. *International Business in the Nineteenth Century, The Rise and Fall of a Cosmopolitan Bourgeoisie.* New York: New York University Press, 1987.

Jones, Chester Lloyd. *The Consular Service of the United States, Its History and Activities.* Philadelphia: John C. Winston Co., 1906.

Jones, Francis C. *Extraterritoriality in Japan and the Diplomatic Relations Resulting in Its Abolition, 1853–1899.* 1931. Reprint. New York: AMS Press, 1970.

Jones, Hazel. *Live Machines: Hired Foreigners in Meiji Japan.* Vancouver: University of British Columbia Press, 1980.

Jordan, Winthrop D. *White Over Black, American Attitudes Toward the Negro, 1550–1812.* Balto.: Penguin Books, Inc., 1969.

Kaempfer, Engelbert. *History of Japan.* 2 vols. Tokyo: Yushodo Booksellers, 1979.

Kato, Yuzo. *Yokohama Past and Present.* Yokohama: Yokohama City University, 1990.

Keim, De Benneville Randolph. *A Report to the Hon. George S. Boutwell, Secretary of the Treasury, upon the Condition of the Consular Service.* Washington D.C.: Government Printing Office, 1872.

Kennedy, Charles Stuart. *The American Consul, A History of the United States Consular Service, 1776–1914.* New York: Greenwood Press, 1990.

Kiernan, V.G. *The Lords of Human Kind, European Attitudes to the Outside World in the Imperial Age.* Harmondsworth: Penguin, 1972.

Kimmel, Michael. *Manhood in America, A Cultural History.* New York: The Free Press, 1997.

Kipling, Rudyard. *Letters from Japan*. Edited by Donald Ritchie and Yoshimori Harashima. Tokyo: Kenkyusha, 1962.

Kirkland, Edward Chase. *Dream and Thought in the Business Community, 1860–1900*. 1956. Reprint. Chicago: Ivan R. Dee, 1990.

Knobel, Dale T. *"America for the Americans" The Nativist Movement in the United States*. New York: Twayne Publishers, 1996.

Knollys, Henry. *Sketches of Life in Japan*. London: Chapman and Hall, 1887.

Kraut, Alan M. *The Huddled Masses, The Immigrant in American Society, 1880–1921*. Arlington Heights, Il: Harlan Davidson, Inc., 1986.

LaFeber, Walter. *The New Empire, An Interpretation of American Expansion, 1860–1898*. Ithaca: Cornell University Press, 1963.

Lears, T.J. Jackson. *No Place of Grace, Antimodernism and the Transformation of American Culture, 1880–1920*. New York, Pantheon Books, 1981.

Lehmann, Jeanne-Pierre. *The Image of Japan, from Feudal Isolation to World Power, 1850–1905*. London and Boston: Allen and Unwin, 1978.

Li, Lillian M. "Silks by Sea: Trade, Technology, and Enterprise in China and Japan." *Business History Review* 56 (Summer 1982): 192–217.

Lockwood, William W. *The Economic Development of Japan, Growth and Structural Change*. Princeton: Princeton University Press, 1968.

Lockwood, William W., ed. *The State and Economic Enterprise in Japan. Essays in the Political Economy of Growth*. Princeton: Princeton University Press, 1965.

Longford, Joseph. "The Commercial Morality of the Japanese." *Contemporary Review* 87 (January–June 1905): 705–11.

Maclay, Arthur Collins. *A Budget of Letters From Japan*. New York: A.C. Armstrong and Son, 1886.

McMaster, John. "The Japanese Gold Rush of 1859." *Journal of Asian Studies* 19 (1960): 273–87.

Malloy, William M., comp. *Treaties, Conventions, International Acts, Protocols and Agreements between the United States of America and Other Powers, 1776-1909*. 2 vols. Washington: D.C.: Government Printing Office, 1910.

Marsh, Margaret. "Suburban Men and Masculine Domesticity, 1870–1915." In *Meanings For Manhood, Constructions of Masculinity in Victorian America*, edited by Mark C. Carnes and Clyde Griffen. Chicago: University of Chicago Press, 1990, 111–127.

Marumoto, Masaji. "'First Year' Immigrants to Hawaii and Eugene Van Reed." In *East Across the Pacific, Historical and Sociological Studies of Japanese Immigration and Assimilation*, edited by Hilary Conroy and T. Scott Miyakawa. Santa Barbara: Clio Press, 1972.

Maruyama, Masao. *Studies in the Intellectual History of Tokugawa Japan*. Translated by Mikiso Hane. Princeton: Princeton University Press, 1974.

Maugham, W. Somerset. *The Summing Up*. New York: The New American Library 1938.

Mayo, Marlene. "A Catechism of Western Diplomacy: The Japanese and Hamilton Fish." *Journal of Asian Studies* 26 (May 1967): 389–410.

Merk, Frederick. *Manifest Destiny and Mission in American History*. New York: Alfred A. Knopf, 1963.

Miyakawa, Scott T. "Early New York Issei: Founders of Japanese–American Trade." In *East Across the Pacific, Historical and Sociological Studies of Japanese Immigration and Assimilation*, edited by Hilary Conroy and Scott T. Miyakawa. Santa Barbara, Ca.: Clio Press, 1972.

Mommsen, W.J. and De Moor, J.A., eds. *European Expansion and Law, The Encounter of European and Indigenous Law in 19th and Twentieth Century Africa and Asia*. New York: Berg Publishers, 1992.

Morris, J. *Advance Japan: A Nation Thoroughly in Earnest*. London: W.H. Allen and Co., Ltd, 1895.

Mrozek, Donald J. *Sport and American Mentality, 1880-1910*. Knoxville: University of Tennessee Press, 1983.

Murphey, Rhoads. *The Outsiders, The Western Experience in India and China*. Ann Arbor: University of Michigan Press, 1977.

Murray, George T. *The Land of the Tatami, Travels in Japan*. Shanghai: North China Herald, 1906.

Neumann, William L. *America Encounters Japan, From Perry to MacArthur*. Baltimore and London: The Johns Hopkins Press, 1963.

Nevins, Allen. *Hamilton Fish: The Inner History of the Grant Administration*. New York: Dodd, Mead and Co., 1936.

"New Yorker." "A New Yorker in Japan." *Dublin University Magazine* 80 (December 1872): 658–64.

Norman, Henry. *The Real Japan*. 1908. Reprint. Wilmington, Delaware: Scholarly Resources, 1973.

Notehelfer, F.G. *American Samurai, Captain L.L. Janes and Japan*. Princeton: Princeton University Press, 1985.

Notehelfer, F.G., ed. *Japan Through American Eyes, The Journal of Francis Hall, Kanagawa and Yokohama, 1859–1866*. Princeton: Princeton University Press, 1992.

Ohara, Keishi and Okata, Tamotsu. *Japanese Trade and Industry in the Meiji-Taisho Era*. Tokyo: Obunsha, 1957.

Painter, Nell Irvin. *Standing at Armageddon: The United States, 1877–1919*. New York: Norton, 1987.

Parrington, Vernon. *Main Currents in American Thought*. Vol. 3. New York: Harcourt, Brace and World, 1930.

Paske-Smith, Montague. *Western Barbarians in Japan and Formosa in Tokugawa Days, 1603–1868*. 1930. Reprint. New York: Paragon Book Reprint Corp., 1968.

Pelcovits, Nathan A. *Old China Hands and the Foreign Office*. New York: King's Crown Press, 1948.

Perez, Louis G. *Japan Comes of Age: Mutsu Munemitsu and the Revision of the Unequal Treaties*. London: Associated University Presses, 1999.

Perry, John Curtis. *Facing West, Americans and the Opening of the Pacific*. Westport: Praeger, 1994.

Peterson, Richard H. *The Bonanza Kings, The Social Origins and Business Behavior of Western Mining Entrepreneurs, 1870–1900*. Lincoln: University of Nebraska Press, 1971.

Pletcher, David M. *The Awkward Years, American Foreign Relations Under Garfield and Arthur*. Columbia: University of Missouri Press, 1962.

Pletcher, David M. *The Diplomacy of Trade and Investment, American Economic Expansion in the Hemisphere, 1865–1900*. Columbia: University of Missouri Press, 1998.

Poole, Otis M. *The Death of Old Yokohama in the Great Japanese Earthquake of September 1, 1923*. London: George Allen and Unwin, Ltd, 1968.

Porter, Glen and Livesay, Harold C. *Merchants and Manufacturers, Studies in the Changing Structure of Nineteenth-Century Marketing*. Chicago: Ivan R. Dee, 1971.

Powers, Madelon. *Faces Along the Bar, Lore and Order in the Workingman's Saloon, 1870–1920*. Chicago: University of Chicago Press, 1999.

Pratt, Mary Louise. *Imperial Eyes, Travel Writing and Transculturation*. New York: Routledge, 1992.

Pruyn, Mary. *Grandmamma's Letters from Japan*. Boston: James H. Earle, 1877.

Qualey, Carlton C. "Ethnic Groups and the Frontier." In Nichols, Roger L. ed. *American Frontier and Western Issues, A Historiographical Review*. New York: Greenwood Press, 1986.

Reader, W.J. "Businessmen and Their Motives." In D.C. Coleman and Peter Mathias, eds, *Enterprise and History, Essays in Honor of Charles Wilson*. Cambridge: Cambridge University Press, 1984, 42–51.

Redesdale, Algernon Bertram Freeman-Mitford. *Mitford's Japan: The Memories and Recollections, 1866–1906, of Algernon Bertram Mitford*. London and Dover, N.H.: The Athlone Press, 1985.

Reischauer, Haru Matsukata. *Samurai and Silk, A Japanese and American Heritage*. Cambridge: Belknap Press, 1986.

Reischauer, Robert Karl. "Alien Land Tenure in Japan." *The Transactions of the Asiatic Society of Japan* 2d ser., 13 (July 1936): 1–33.

Richards, Louis. "The Earliest Japanese Visitors to Reading." *Transactions of the Historical Society of Berks County* 2 (1910): 294–305.

Riis, Jacob A. *How the Other Half Lives: Studies Among the Tenements of New York*. 1890. Reprint. New York: Hill and Wang, 1967.

Roden, Donald. "Baseball and the Quest for National Dignity in Meiji Japan." *American Historical Review* 85 (June 1980): 511–34.

Rogers, Eustace B. "Life in the Foreign Settlements of Japan." *Harper's Weekly* 38 (December 29 1894): 1234.

Rosenberg, Charles E. "Sexuality, Class and Role in 19th-Century America." In *The American Man*, edited by Elizabeth H. and Joseph H. Pleck. Englewood Cliffs: Prentice-Hall, 1980.

Rosenstone, Robert A. *Mirror in the Shrine: American Encounters with Meiji Japan*. Cambridge: Harvard University Press, 1988.

Rotundo, E. Anthony. *American Manhood, Transformations in Masculinity from the Revolution to the Modern Era*. New York: Basic Books, 1993.

Rydell, Robert W. *All the World's a Fair, Visions of Empire at American International Expositions, 1876–1916*. Chicago: University of Chicago Press, 1984.

Said, Edward W. *Culture and Imperialism*. New York: Alfred A. Knopf, 1993.

Salyer, Lucy. *Laws Harsh as Tigers: Chinese Immigrants and the Shaping of Modern Immigration Law*. Chapel Hill: University of North Carolina Press, 1995.

Satow, Ernest. *A Diplomat in Japan*. 1921. Reprint. Tokyo and New York: Oxford University Press, 1968.

Schroeder, F. *Eastern World Back Numbers, 1892–1907*. Yokohama: Eastern World Office, 1908.

Schwantes, Robert, *Japanese and Americans, A Century of Cultural Relations*. New York: Harper and Row, 1955.

Scidmore, Eliza R. *Jinrikisha Days in Japan*. New York: Harper Bros., 1891.

Scidmore, George H. *Outline Lectures on the History, Organization, Jurisdiction, and Practice of the Ministerial and Consular Courts of the United States of America in Japan*. Tokio: Igirisu Horitsu Gakko, 1887.

Seizelet, Eric."European Law and Tradition in Japan." In *European Expansion and Law, The Encounter of European and Indigenous Law in 19th and Twentieth Century Africa and Asia*, edited by W.J. Mommsen and J.A. De Moor. New York: Berg Publishers, 1992.

Simmons, D.B. "Five Years in Japan." Galaxy 5 (May 1868): 606–17.

Smith, D.W. *European Settlements in the Far East*. New York: Charles Scribner's Sons, 1900.

Smith, George. *Ten Weeks in Japan*. London: Longman, Green, Longman, Roberts, 1861.

Spurr, David. *The Rhetoric of Empire, Colonial Discourse in Journalism, Travel Writing, and Imperial Administration*. Durham: Duke University Press, 1993.

Strong, Josiah. *Our Country: Its Possible Future and Its Present Crisis*. New York: The American Home Missionary Society, 1885.

Sugiyama, Shinya. *Japan's Industrialization in the World Economy, 1859–1899*. London and Atlantic Highlands, N.J.: The Athlone Press, 1988.

Sugiyama, Shinya. "Thomas B. Glover: A British Merchant in Japan." *Business History* 26 (July 1984): 115–138.

Summers, Mark Wahlgren. *The Gilded Age or, The Hazard of New Functions*. Upper Saddle River, NJ: Prentice Hall, 1997.

Sutton, Francis X., *et. al*. *The American Business Creed*. New York: Schocken Books, 1956.

Taylor, Sandra. "Abby M. Colby: The Christian Response to a Sexist Society." *The New England Quarterly* 52 (March 1979): 68–79.

Taylor, Sandra. *Advocate of Understanding, Sidney Gulick and the Search for Peace with Japan*. Kent: Kent State University Press, 1984.

Tilley, Henry Arthur. *Japan, The Amoor, and the Pacific*. London: Smith, Elder and Company, 1861.

Todd, Mabel Loomis. *Corona and Coronet*. Boston and New York: Houghton, Mifflin and Company, 1898.

Toiviainen, Hillevi. "Search For Security: United States Citizens in the Far East, 1890–1906", Ph.D. diss., Jyvaskylan Yliopisto, Jyvaskyla, 1986.

Totman, Conrad. *A History of Japan*. Cambridge: Blackwell, 2000.

Trachtenberg, Alan. *The Incorporation of America, Culture and Society in the Gilded Age*. New York: Hill and Wang, 1982.

Treat, Payson. *Early Diplomatic Relations Between the United States and Japan, 1853–1865*. Baltimore: The Johns Hopkins Press, 1917.

Treat, Payson. *Japan and the United States, 1853–1921*. Stanford: Stanford University Press, 1928.

Treat, Payson. *Diplomatic Relations Between the United States and Japan*. 3 vols. Gloucester, Mass.: Peter Smith, 1963.

Tucker, Henry St. George. *The History of the Episcopal Church in Japan*. New York: Charles Scribner's Sons, 1938.

United States Tariff Commission, *The Foreign Trade of Japan*. Washington, D.C.: Government Printing Office, 1922.

Ward, Lester Frank. *Dynamic Sociology, or, Applied Social Science*. 1883. Reprint. New York: Greenwood Press, 1968.

Warner, Ezra J. *Generals in Blue: Lives of the Union Commanders*. Baton Rouge: Louisiana State Press, 1964.

Weinberg, Albert K. *Manifest Destiny, A Study of Nationalist Expansion in American History*. Balto.: The Johns Hopkins Press, 1935.

Welter, Barbara. "The Cult of True Womanhood, 1820–1860." *American Quarterly* 18 (Summer 1966): 151–74.

Whitney, Clara A.N. *Clara's Diary, An American Girl in Meiji Japan.* Edited by M. William Steele and Tamiko Ichimata. Tokyo, New York: Kodansha International, Ltd, 1979.

Wiebe, Robert. *The Search For Order, 1877–1920.* New York: Hill and Wang, 1967.

Wildes, Harry E. *Aliens in the East, A New History of Japan's Foreign Intercourse.* Philadelphia: University of Pennsylvania Press, 1937.

Will, John Baxter. *Trading Under Sail Off Japan, 1860–99. The Recollections of Captain John Baxter Will, Sailing Master and Pilot.* Edited by George Alexander Lenson. Tokyo: Sophia University Press, 1968.

Williams, Harold. *Shades of the Past, Indiscreet Tales of Japan.* Rutland, Vt. and Tokyo: Charles Tuttle and Co., 1958.

Williams, Harold. *Tales of the Foreign Settlements in Japan.* Rutland, Vt. and Tokyo: Charles Tuttle and Co., 1958.

Williams, Harold. *Foreigners in Mikadoland.* Rutland, Vt. and Tokyo: Charles Tuttle and Co., 1963.

Williams, Harold. *The Story of Holme Ringer and Company, Ltd in Western Japan, 1868–1968.* Tokyo: Charles Tuttle and Co., 1968.

Williams, Harold. *The Story of Shioya, of the James Estate, of James Yama and of the Shioya Country Club.* Kobe: International Committee of the Kansai, 1984.

Williams, William Appleman. *The Tragedy of American Diplomacy.* 1959; reprint, New York: Dell Publishing, 1972.

Wray, William D. *Mitsubishi and the N.Y.K., 1870–1914, Business Strategy in the Japanese Shipping Industry.* Cambridge: Harvard University Press, 1984.

"Yankee Traders." *Fortune* 32 (November 1945): 132–36, 269–76.

Yen-p'ing, Hao. *The Compradore in Nineteenth Century China: Bridge Between East and West.* Cambridge: Cambridge University Press, 1970.

Yokohama Country and Athletic Club, *125th Anniversary Commemorative Magazine,* 1993.

Yonekawa, Shin'ichi and Yoshihara, Hideki, eds, *Business History of General Trading Companies.* Tokyo: University of Tokyo Press, 1987.

Young, A. Morgan. *Imperial Japan 1926–1938.* New York: William Morrow, 1938.

INDEX

Lightning Source UK Ltd.
Milton Keynes UK
UKOW06f0324190216

268694UK00005B/27/P